WORLD ECONOMIC GROWTH

D1528379

WORLD ECONOMIC GROWTH

Edited by

ARNOLD C. HARBERGER

ICS PRESS

Institute for Contemporary Studies
San Francisco, California

Inquiries, book orders, and catalog requests should be addressed to ICS Press, Suite 750, 785 Market Street, San Francisco, CA 94103 (415) 543-6213.

Library of Congress Cataloging in Publication Data
Main entry under title:

World economic growth.

    Includes index.
    1. Economic development—Addresses, essays, lectures.
2. Economic policy—Addresses, essays, lectures.
I. Harberger, Arnold C. II. Institute for Contemporary
Studies.
HD87.W67 1984   338.9   84–19179
ISBN   0–917616–63–4
ISBN   0–917616–62–6 (pbk.)

CONTENTS

IV

Summary and Conclusion

PREFACE

In the past decade and a half, discussions of economic growth have assumed several interesting forms. By the early 1970s, the industrial countries had taken growth for granted for most of this century and longer, and many people assumed it would continue, almost independently of economic policy. At the same time (and perhaps related), inequality of wealth among nations was becoming the central concern in North-South relations, and demands were growing for redistribution of wealth to Third World countries. A major theme in these demands included the claim that growth was not so much produced as *extracted* from other people and countries—hence their right to share in the bounty.

Beginning in the early 1970s, another theme appeared, as important elements in the New Left began to question the very idea of economic growth and material progress. This concern became most explicit in certain extreme parts of the ecology and environmental movements; and although it has subsided since its apex in the mid-1970s, it is still evident in important parts of the opinion-making elites today.

By the end of the 1970s, which were a decade of economic stagnation in both the industrial and developing countries, the debate took a new turn. Policymakers became absorbed with understanding what factors underlay the economic "miracles" in the Pacific Basin—Japan, Korea, Taiwan, Indonesia, and other places—where explosive economic growth was experienced over most of the postwar period. They also sought to understand why countries such as Great Britain and many developing areas, particularly in Africa, experienced economic stagnation and even decline.

To explore the policy implications of economic growth, the Institute asked Arnold C. Harberger to assemble a group of economists to examine the growth experiences of both industrial and developing economies and try to evolve policy "lessons" widely shared by economic policy professionals. This ambitious undertaking was the subject of a major conference the Institute held in Mexico City in April 1983. In attendance in addition to the contributors to the study were an illustrious group of economists and economic policymakers from Europe, Asia, and especially South America.

This volume presents the papers prepared for the conference, together with some of the discussion. The result is a "handbook" on policies that encourage economic growth—a vital resource for policymakers, journalists, people in business and labor, and all others who are concerned about this important issue.

Glenn Dumke
President
Institute for Contemporary Studies

I

Introduction and Overview

1

ARNOLD C. HARBERGER

Introduction

This volume, and the conference whose proceedings it records, seeks to explore the connections between economic policy and economic growth. To the layman this may appear to be a simple task, but quite emphatically, it is not.

A good starting point for demonstrating that the task is not easy is to go back to the era of the immediate postwar period, when many people thought it was. This period marked the birth of the modern theory of economic growth. Its hallmark, the so-called Harrod-Domar model of economic growth, was built on the basis of two simplifying assumptions: (1) the national income of a country is proportional to its capital stock, and (2) increases in the capital stock come from the savings of the people, which is assumed to represent a given proportion of the national income. This was a simple world indeed, and the policy implication of the underlying analysis was clear: to increase growth, one should increase the national savings rate.

This approach gave rise to an extended period in which the discussion of economic growth focused almost exclusively on the stock of physical capital, and on the national savings rate as a means of increasing that stock. Within this framework it was easy

3

to identify the force that produced economic growth, and it was also reasonably easy to test whether a particular policy was likely to increase or impede that force. A simple theory, a straight-forward causal mechanism, and easy identification of growth-producing policies: an economist's paradise, it would seem, until it was realized that this paradise did not even come close to capturing the reality of the world in which we live.

Older analysts of economic growth, even as far back as Adam Smith (1776), did not start with a theoretical model but tried to build up their analyses on the basis of their observations of the real world. Their writings exude the complexity of the growth process as if from the pores.

Starting in the middle 1950s, the spirit of the older analysts was revived, as the approach taken in the Harrod-Domar model was broadened and extended so as to include a much more comprehensive list of the sources of economic growth. These sources would include:[1]

- increases in the active labor force through demographic growth, increased labor force participation, or absorption of the unemployed;

- improvement in the quality of the labor force through education, experience, and on-the-job training;

- improvements in efficiency through better allocation of the labor force, i.e., the shifting of labor force from lower-productivity to higher-productivity jobs;*

- increases in the capital stock through increased private-sector or public-sector savings (adjusted, of course, for the negative growth stemming from the depreciation or retirement of old components of the capital stock);

- improvements in the quality of components of the capital stock through improved design and technical innovation;

- improvements in efficiency through better allocation of the capital stock, i.e., the shifting of capital from lower-productivity to higher-productivity activities;*

---

*"Productivity" in these cases should be taken to refer to marginal productivity, gross of taxes, and similar distortions.

- improvements in efficiency through the expansion of activities subject to economies of scale;

- improvements in efficiency through the reduction of distorting elements such as (1) taxes that give differential treatment to the use of resources in some activities vis-à-vis others; (2) quotas and licensing schemes that prevent resources from flowing into certain activities, even though those resources would be highly productive there, and (3) monopoly elements and other private restraints that impede the efficient allocation of resources within the economy;

- improvements in efficiency through finding cheaper and better ways of producing existing products;

- improvements in efficiency through the improvement of existing products and the development of new ones.

Readers will quickly appreciate the common sense reflected in the above list. It would be hard to quarrel with or to amend. It appears truly to reflect the reality and complexity of our world. The only trouble is that now, faced with this more realistic interpretation of how the process of economic growth works, it becomes harder to identify how policy measures impinge on that process.[2] Thus even up to the present day, those who have tried to analyze actual growth rates by the modern theory of economic growth have found themselves limited (substantially) to giving empirical estimates of how much of the observed growth was due to the accumulation of capital, how much to the increment of the number of workers, the improvement of the quality of labor, the better allocation of resources, or to technical advances. Economists have not been able, then, to move forward and say what role government policies have played in the entire process.

Sometimes it is possible to study the effects of a single government policy on the rate of economic growth. This is relatively easy to do where the policy operates mainly on a single source of growth. Thus, an educational program works to improve the quality of the labor force; if the degree of improvement can be estimated (as indeed it often can), one can estimate the contribution of that particular policy to economic growth. It has also proved possible to estimate, for example, the contribution to economic

growth made by the research programs that developed (and subsequently improved) hybrid corn, and similar varietal improvement
programs. The task of linking a particular policy with its "contribution" to economic growth is also relatively easy when one is
dealing with, say, a tax incentive designed to expand investment.

But how does one build a link between a country's growth rate
and the entire package of laws, decrees, administrative measures,
judicial constraints, etc., that constitute that country's economic
policy at any given moment? This is a question that, though they
are building on the very solid advances we have seen in the past
thirty years, economists have not been able to answer.

This volume attempts, using a much more holistic approach, to
get around the difficulty—indeed the virtual impossibility—
of building a direct link of modern theory between the observed
growth rate of a country and its overall economic policy. The underlying idea is to identify episodes of successful growth, stagnation, and even retrogression in economic activity, and then to try
to see whether different types or styles of economic policy characteristically prevailed in these different episodes. In particular
there is the question of whether what economic science would call
"good" economic policy seems to be associated with "good" results,
and similarly whether "bad" policy tends to be associated with
"bad" results.

Many of the countries covered in this volume provide an excellent opportunity for comparisons among episodes of different
types. This is especially true of the less-developed countries
(LDCs), because in those instances the possibility of episodic comparison was actually one of the criteria applied in compiling the
list of countries to be studied.

Jamaica and Ghana are dramatic examples. In the former country, gross domestic product (GDP) rose about 3.8 percent per year
from 1960 to 1966, then rose over 6 percent per year from 1966 to
1972, and finally fell, between 1973 and 1980, by a total of about
18 percent. In Ghana, income was growing at about 5 percent per
year around the turn of the decade of the 1960s; then, from 1962
to 1968, the rate fell to 1.7 percent per year. This was followed by a
sharp spurt from 1968 to 1971, again at about 6 percent, after

which growth slowed to about 3 percent before turning sharply negative after 1974.

Uruguay's GDP grew a total of 9 percent from 1955 to 1973, while population grew about 17 percent. Thus GDP per capita gradually eroded over this period. GDP then grew by 46 percent (or 5.6 percent per year) from 1973 to 1980, while population rose by only 6 percent.

Tanzania's economy grew at an average annual rate of 5.4 percent per year during the period 1965 to 1977, while population grew at 3 percent. Thereafter, output virtually stagnated, while population expanded by 9 percent in the four years between 1977 and 1981.

The dramatic changes in the Mexican economy were not in the GDP growth rate, but in other variables. Between 1953 and 1973, domestic inflation averaged less than 5 percent per year; during the next seven years the average rate was 22 percent; from 1980 to 1982 the average was 42 percent. Another way of seeing Mexico's situation is to note that from 1953 to 1973 the average growth rate of GDP was 7 percent, while from 1973 to 1982 it was less than 6 percent. This apparently innocuous difference takes on new meaning once one realizes that the earlier period predated Mexico's major oil discoveries, while the later witnessed their full exploitation.

Indonesia and Taiwan are the big success stories among the less-developed countries represented in this volume. But even in their cases one can find a basis for contrasting good episodes with bad. As is characteristic of success stories, in these two cases the bad episodes came at the beginning, and were relatively brief. Indonesia's economy was declining in per capita terms in the early 1960s. Her 1967 GDP was 14 percent higher than her 1960 GDP, while population was 19 percent higher. Moreover, inflation burgeoned to over 300 percent per year during this episode. In contrast, from 1968 to 1980 GDP grew at an average rate of 8 percent and the average rate of inflation was 23 percent per year.

In Taiwan the comparison is perhaps best described as being between outstanding episodes on the one hand and a merely "good" initial performance on the other. From 1955 to 1960, income per capita rose by a mere 15 percent (over the five-year period). Successive subsequent quinquennia, in contrast, generated growth

rates of 37 percent, 43 percent, 31 percent, and 43 percent. The
Taiwan story, then, concerns how the country passed from a more
or less ordinary situation to being labeled the "Taiwan miracle."

The economically advanced countries represented in this
volume were chosen mainly for their importance in the world
economy. The United States, Japan, West Germany, and England
are four of the five largest national economies in the non-
Communist world. In addition there are interesting differences
among them as to institutional arrangements, styles of economic
policy, and above all, growth performance. Sweden was added to
the group as a particularly good representative of the democratic
socialist approach to economic policy. Table 1 gives certain key
items of information concerning both the industrial countries and
the LDCs covered in this volume.

In addition to the twelve studies of individual countries, this
volume also contains a paper specifically oriented to the topic of
trade liberalization. The reason for this will become apparent to
readers as they digest the material in the studies of individual
countries, particularly those referring to the LDCs. The degree of
openness of an economy is one of the strategic variables on which
its policymakers must decide, and much evidence suggests that a
relatively high degree of openness is a key factor in permitting a
small economy to enjoy rapid growth over an extended period.
Thus the process of trade liberalization is often an important component of programs designed to modify a country's economic
policy so as to promote economic growth. It is surely of sufficient
importance to warrant its inclusion as a special topic in a series of
studies on the relationship between economic policy and economic
growth.

One final note: though a serious effort was made, in advance of
the conference recorded in this volume, to ensure a certain degree
of compatibility among the separate studies, they remain the independent works of their respective authors. The relation of economic policy to economic growth is the unifying theme, and I
believe that a substantial degree of unity has been achieved. But
in the end this book should be recognized for what it is: a collection
of the intellectual output of thirteen authors, each exercising full
independence of judgment and initiative in determining the content, organization, and tone of his or her contribution.

TABLE 1

Basic Indicators of Economic Performance

	GDP growth rate		Population growth rate		Average inflation rate	
	1960–70	1970–81	1960–70	1970–81	1960–70	1970–81
Industrial countries						
West Germany	4.4	2.6	0.9	0.0	3.2	5.0
Japan	10.4	4.5	1.0	1.1	5.1	7.4
Sweden	4.4	1.8	0.7	0.3	4.3	10.0
United Kingdom	2.9	1.8	0.6	0.1	4.1	14.4
United States	4.3	2.9	1.3	1.0	2.9	7.2
Less developed countries						
Ghana	2.1	–0.2	2.3	3.0	7.6	36.4
Indonesia	3.9	7.8	2.1	2.3	4.9	20.5
Jamaica	4.4	–1.2	1.4	1.5	4.0	16.8
Mexico	7.6	6.5	3.3	3.1	3.5	19.1
Tanzania	6.0	5.1	2.7	3.4	1.8	11.9
Taiwan	9.8	8.2	3.1	1.9	3.4	10.7
Uruguay	1.2	3.1	1.0	0.4	51.1	60.2

Sources: World Bank, *World Development Report 1983*, Tables 1, 2, 19; for Taiwan, *Statistical Yearbook of the Republic of China*, various issues.

II

Developed Countries

2

WILFRED BECKERMAN

Economic Policy and Performance in Britain since World War II

Introduction and Summary

Any attempt to establish connections between the economic policies followed by governments and subsequent economic performance is fraught with enormous difficulties, of which the following are only a selection:

- The success or failure of policies can be evaluated only in relation to specified objectives. But governments rarely spell out their objectives precisely, and there are few if any objectives that would find universal agreement among commentators.

- Most people would want to evaluate economic performance in terms of some long-run growth record, but most policies may affect only "static" inefficiency rather than growth; i.e., the *level* of output rather than its *growth rate*. Of course, some

policies may directly affect growth rates, such as those affecting investment in education, and others may affect growth indirectly.

- Performance is often, indeed usually, influenced by outside
  events that are beyond the control of policymakers (such as the
  oil shocks). True, some policies may make it more difficult to
  adjust to external disturbances, but it is still difficult to distinguish precisely how far poor performance is the result of the
  bad policies and how far the result of the external shocks.

- With the benefit of hindsight, it is always easier to see how
  policies went astray, but this does not mean one could have
  seen at the time that they would not have worked.

- Economists cannot carry out controlled experiments, and so
  can never confidently deduce how events might have differed in
  the counterfactual situations in which different policies might
  have been adopted.

In spite of all this, it may still be possible to extract some guidance from the past concerning the type of approach to economic
policy analysis that is most likely to be harmful. The experience of
the British economy is of some use in this connection, though not
as much as might have been expected. It is argued below that the
reasons for this include the following:

- Throughout the postwar period most governments in Britain
  followed very similar policies, so there is little scope for seeing
  how far, in the British situation, different policies affected the
  outcome.

- There is strong support for the view that the relatively poor
  performance of the British economy can legitimately be blamed
  largely on certain deeply ingrained institutional features of the
  British scene, rather than on exceptionally inept economic
  management.

- A major characteristic of British economic policy throughout
  the postwar period has been a reluctance (a very understandable one) to tackle these institutional obstacles and a retreat,
  instead, into simple panaceas, none of which ever looked like
  being very effective.

Background

In principle, examining British postwar economic performance ought to lead to conclusions concerning the extent to which different economic policies lead to differences in economic performance. During the last thirty years, government has alternated between two political parties, Conservative and Labour. These have been able to govern, when it was their "turn," with all the advantages that the British two-party system and constitutional system confer on the ability of the governing party to implement its policies without any great need to dilute them in order to placate dissenting members of its own or coalition parties. Furthermore, both parties have had periods in power that were long enough to ensure that the fruits of their policies would ripen during their period of office.

Unfortunately these almost ideal laboratory conditions for observing how far major differences in policy objectives can affect economic performance failed to provide any guidance. The reason was that, relative to other advanced industrialized countries, performance was just as bad with either party in power.

Britain's growth rate was the slowest in Western [and Eastern] Europe over the three decades following World War II, its inflation rate among the highest, and its balance of payments difficulties almost endemic. . . . In 1950 the economy was relatively favourably placed both to take advantage of beneficial developments in world trade and in technological innovation and to cope with any external disruptions. . . .Yet, during the next thirty years, growth was consistently and significantly lower than that of apparently less favourably placed economies.[1]

By 1982, Britain also had the highest unemployment rate of any advanced industrialized country.

This does not mean, however, that different policies can have no effect on the outcome. For there was a considerable element of truth in the 1950 "Butskellism" charge that the two main parties did not differ much with respect to various policies anyway.* In fact, until the recent advent of Mrs. Thatcher, the two parties differed more in their rhetoric than in their implementation of

---

The term "Butskellism" was intended to represent the mixture of policies that might have been attributed to the then-dominant influence of R. A. Butler and Hugh Gaitskell on the economic policies of the Conservative and Labour parties.

policies. For example, apart from the steel industry, none of the major nationalizations carried out by the Labour governments of 1945 through 1952 was undone by the Conservative governments of 1952 through 1964; nor did the Conservative government try to dismantle the apparatus of the "welfare state" that had been set up in the immediate postwar years.

Most of the policy debate in the 1950s was about the precise timing and magnitude of short-term management of demand and the different distributional implications of alternative demand management policies. And although the two parties naturally differed considerably in their income distribution objectives, the distribution of incomes remained remarkably stable.[2]

Only towards the end of the 1950s was there much emphasis on the supply side of the economy, notably on the possible scope for raising long-run supply growth by means of economic planning. Even in this respect the two parties did not differ totally; it was a Conservative administration in 1961 that set up the National Economic Development Council (NEDC), which was to provide a pale imitation of the then much-admired French Planning Commission. This was the main response to the growing awareness of the poor performance of the British economy during the 1950s, which continued during the 1960s and 1970s.

The magnitude of the decline in Britain's economic performance can best be seen by comparing the relative levels of "real" national product per head in 1950 and 1981, adjusted for international differences in relative internal price levels, as in table 1.

If differences in governments were not reflected in differences in economic performance in Britain, perhaps another way of testing whether or not different policies lead to different results is to consider how far its poor performance relative to the other advanced countries can be explained by Britain's having followed inferior economic policies. Naturally, this possibility was studied to some extent during the first ten to fifteen years after the war, but it is doubtful if any clear answer can be given. Various hypotheses were advanced to explain Britain's relatively slow rate of economic growth:

• Other countries, notably France, Germany, and Italy, had to "catch up" more than Britain because they suffered more wartime devastation.

Table 1

Indices of Gross Domestic Product per Head (at U.S. prices)
(U.K. = 100 in each year)

Country	1950	1981
Austria	55	112
Belgium	93	114
Denmark	93	120
France	85	120
Germany	65	124
Italy	48	95
Japan	30	115
Netherlands	90	113
United Kingdom	*100*	*100*
U.S.A.	156	156

Source: 1950 from Gilbert M. and Associates, *Comparative National Product and Price Levels* (Paris: OEEC, 1958), except for Japan which is from A. Maddison, "Phases in Capitalist Development," in *Banca Nazionale del Lavoro Quarterly Review,* No. 121, June 1977, Table A-36; 1981 estimates are from OECD *National Accounts, 1952–81* (Paris: OECD, 1983).

- Britain had an exceptionally "mature" economy in the sense that it had a far lower proportion of its labor force in agriculture and so could not obtain the overall productivity gains that other countries reaped by transferring labor out of agriculture into the expanding industrial activities, where the economies of scale were to be achieved, and where technical progress, embodied in new capital equipment to match the expanding labor force, could be fastest.

- Britain was hampered by sociological factors, such as the attitudes of labor in general, or of British trade unions in particular—notably a Luddite resistance to innovation and technical progress—or the stodgy amateurishness of British management, too long cossetted by the privileges and disregard for professional merit characteristic of the "old boy network" and too long shielded by protected markets in what had once been the British Empire. Class distinctions and class antagonism in Britain are also often culpable in sociological explanations of Britain's relatively poor economic performance.

- Export-led growth models, in which the emphasis was placed on the importance of optimistic demand expectations for investment, innovation, and output per unit of total factor input. In very open economies, a precarious foreign balance resulting from an uncompetitive exchange rate would both reduce the rate of profit (and the liquidity available for investment finance) and dampen the prospects of sustained expansion of demand.

It would be out of place here to consider the evidence for and against the alternative explanations of Britain's comparatively poor economic performance.[3] One can ask what would have been the implications for policy of these alternative explanations and how far the policy debates of the time—and the policies adopted—bore any relation to them. As regards the "catching-up" hypothesis, clearly there would not be much that Britain could do about it short of becoming involved in a new major war that she might lose. In any case, by the late 1950s it was clear that this factor could no longer play an important role in explaining the continued rapid growth of the other European countries.

Nor was there very much that could be done to speed up Britain's growth if the cause of slow growth was the relative maturity of the economy and the absence of any source of extra manpower for manufacturing. Nevertheless, this was one of the explanations that did, in fact, have an influence on policy—though not until the mid-1960s. In 1966 the Labour government introduced a "Selective Employment Tax," a payroll tax that discriminated against labor in service and distributive trades in favor of manufacturing (which even received a slight subsidy).

As regards the sociological and institutional factors, naturally one cannot expect much detailed agreement about which of them mattered. But there was a widespread impression, shared by foreign commentators and observers such as the teams that twice reported on the British economy,[4] that these included an unusual degree of class consciousness and mistrust between the classes, as well as a powerful trade union movement that generally opposed technical progress and did not share any desire to improve the competitiveness of the firms in which their members were employed. To varying degrees this may also be the fault of weak management, isolated by barriers of class and educational background from the aspirations of their employees, and professionally ill-equipped to handle the industrial relations problems of the British economy under conditions of full employment.[5]

In education, the segregation of children at the age of eleven into three different kinds of schools was abolished by the 1964–70 Labour administration, but nothing was done to tackle the other—and probably predominant—sociological obstacle to innovation and growth, namely the trade union movement. The political reasons for this are obvious. In Britain the trade union movement is closely linked to the Labour party; it has a loud and direct voice in the organization of the party, its annual congresses, and the election of its leaders, and it is also a major source of the party finance. Hence, it is almost inconceivable that the Labour party would ever embark on policies that ran counter to what union leaders saw as their vital vested interests. This did not preclude various forms of "income policy" from being tried out after 1962, when the National Incomes Commission (NIC) was set up; but none of these had much teeth, except for short-period wage freezes or wage norms during the 1960s and again in 1976, when the trade union leaders were clearly frightened by the very rapid acceleration of inflation in the mid-1970s. The Labour government did seriously consider a basic reform of industrial relations towards the end of the 1960s, but it had to be abandoned finally in the face of trade union hostility and political calculations by certain leaders of the Labour party who did not want to weaken their personal support in the trade union movement.

The proposition that British trade unions have been a major obstacle to technical progress and innovation is by no means confined to "union-bashing," pro-capitalist propagandists. For example, a recent, self-styled Marxist interpretation of economic growth and crisis in the contemporary world repeatedly drew attention to the fact that

in the United Kingdom, the restrictive practices of the unions acted as an effective brake on the accumulation process, via, for instance, closed shop agreements, resistance to new methods of production (particularly to shift-work), or the persistence of very decentralized wage negotiations. . . . The United Kingdom's low productivity growth was linked to the difficulties encountered by British firms in introducing labor-saving investment. . . . In the United Kingdom, . . . the restrictive practices of the unions acted after the beginning of the 1960s as an effective brake to the installation of new methods of production.[6]

That British unions, or other unions for that matter, should behave in this manner is not a phenomenon that has to be left entirely to the sociologists, of course. Mancur Olson, for example, has set out in detail an economic analysis of the growth of special-interest groups, notably trade unions, and of their harmful effect on growth rates.[7] Alternatively, the behavior of British unions could be explained in terms of various models of union behavior that are firmly grounded in microeconomic theory. For example, a type of model familiar in that part of the recent literature of labor economics that is concerned chiefly with explaining sluggish wages attributes to unions an objective function in which two arguments are wage rates and employment, and which is maximized subject to a constraint that corresponds to the firm's demand curve for labor. If the firm puts up only feeble resistance to wage demands and simply tries to pass them on in higher prices, and if governmental monetary policy (and/or exchange rate policy) allows this to happen, then the chief effect will be that in those industries where unions are strongest and push up wages most, prices will rise most. In such industries, therefore, there is likely to be the biggest threat to employment from competing supplies (notably imports) or from attempts by firms to replace increasingly expensive labor by labor-saving innovations. However, unions will then have to adapt by trying to resist such innovations and redundancies. The stronger the unions are, the more effectively they will be able to do this, although in the end the result has often been the gradual elimination of the industrial sectors in question (as in British ship-building, docks, steel, railways, and newspaper printing by conventional labor-intensive methods). In this process, of course, weak management also plays a role, along with strong unions and accommodating governments.

The fourth explanation of Britain's poor performance listed above is Britain's poor export performance as a result mainly of the postulated overvaluation of the exchange rate during most of the 1950s and the early 1960s. This was the subject of much discussion in the early 1960s. However, one of the first decisions taken by the new incoming Labour administration under Harold

Wilson and his Chancellor of the Exchequer Mr. Callaghan in October 1964 was to maintain the exchange rate. In addition, any overt official discussion of this exchange-rate policy option was virtually banned in government departments until the pound was, in effect, forced off its exchange rate in November 1967. The 1964 decision not to devalue was never defended on grounds that bore any recognizable relation to economic analysis. Such grounds would have been that the elasticities happened to be such that no change in the exchange rate would affect the foreign balance; or that the decision was justifiable on global monetarist lines (global monetarism had not really been invented at that time); or that the inflationary consequences would be undesirable and would eventually wipe out the competitive advantage anyway (a sort of primitive global monetarism without the stable demand for money entering into the story). The defense of the exchange rate, when ministers dared mention the topic, was invariably in terms of semimystical references to the need to keep faith with our creditors.[8] The exchange rate was, in fact, treated as an objective of economic policy rather than an instrument of policy.

In addition to political constraints and wishful thinking, economic policies and policy debates during the 1950s and 1960s were also characterized by two major analytical weaknesses. First, instead of seeing a need to find the optimum combination of different policy objectives, governments tended to swing dramatically from obsession with one objective at any cost to obsession with another. More particularly, they swung from concern with the balance of payments (to protect the exchange rate) to concern with unemployment (very low, of course, by historical or contemporary standards). Hence, the usual sequence, known as "stop-go" policy, would be sharp deflation to bring the balance of payments back into equilibrium at the old exchange rate, followed sooner or later (depending on the proximity of the next election) by rapid expansion designed to eliminate the unemployment caused by the preceding policy stance. This would eventually lead to a new balance-of-payments crisis (they became more and more acute each time), and so on. The second characteristic weakness of policy was the belief in simple panaceas such as planning (1964 to 1966), entry into the Common Market, or (1979 to the present) monetarism.

The planning solution became popular when it became increasingly obvious towards the end of the 1950s that Britain's relatively slow growth rate could no longer be attributed to transient phenomena, such as the "catching-up" hypothesis mentioned above. Since, at the same time, the French economy seemed to be doing rather well, quite a wide range of interests in Britain began to espouse the claims of economic planning. (The German economy was doing even better, of course, which might have indicated the virtues of a freer market, but fashions in economic policy preferences are rarely based on scientific evidence.) Hence the notion that planning would provide a means of overcoming the supply-side constraints on British economic growth was accepted not merely by the Labour party (hardly surprising) but also by influential sections of the business community.

The NEDC created by the Conservative government in 1961 did not, however, have any actual powers. Even as a vehicle for indicative planning, its scope was never intended to be significant. But when the Labour government took office in October 1964, economic planning became the center of the strategy. The whole operation of drawing up Britain's first National Economic Plan by autumn 1965 was carried out energetically and on a large scale.

Outside the public sector, there was no means for ensuring any acceleration of investment or technical progress. Furthermore, the overriding limitation on the Plan—and one that was apparent to almost everybody involved in its preparation—was that it was based on wishful thinking about an absence of any supply and foreign balance constraints that was completely inconsistent with the accompanying assumption of no change in the exchange rate. It was not altogether surprising, therefore, that within barely a year of the Plan's publication steps had to be taken to restrain internal demand in the interests of the foreign balance. These steps involved abandonment of the Plan's targets, and in 1967, when a devaluation became unavoidable, the planning panacea was quietly dropped.

By that time, however, a new panacea had appeared on the horizon: joining the Common Market. However, Britain became a member only on January 1, 1973, a few years after the resignation of President de Gaulle, and at the end of long and arduous negotiations. The tenth anniversary of Britain's formal entry into the

Community is now being celebrated—or mourned, as the case may be. While some observers still maintain that, on balance, British membership has been beneficial, most commentators would probably agree with *The Financial Times'* verdict that

perhaps it was inevitable at the point when British politicians were mesmerized by years of economic decline, that exaggerated claims should have been made for Community membership during "the great debate." Yet the sheer irrelevance of membership for Britain's subsequent economic performance is what strikes one 10 years on.[9]

The reasons why the early faith that many people had placed in the impact of the Common Market on British economic growth was disappointed are very complex and quite outside the scope of this paper. It can be stated here only that the economic pros and cons weighed far less heavily in the decision-making process than did political considerations. These included the desire by a highly influential section of the Labour party to inflict an internal Labour party defeat on the very left-wing Labour leader, Mr. Benn, who happened also to be a vociferous opponent of British entry.

The 1970s and the Advent of "Thatcherism"

It was unfortunate that Britain's formal entry into the Common Market on January 1, 1973, should just precede the most disastrous economic decade that the world has witnessed since before World War II. Whatever the handicaps that appear to doom Britain to slower growth, when the whole world embarked on a period of slow growth these handicaps ensured that Britain would begin to suffer not just relatively, but absolutely. On the average, during 1980 and 1981 Britain was the only major industrialized country in which industrial production was lower than in 1973–74. Unemployment had risen sixfold and, at about 13 percent of the active labor force, it was equaled only in Belgium and Canada. For manufacturing alone, Britain had by far the worst record: the trend rate of fall in manufacturing employment amounted to 22 percent between 1973 and 1981, which did not prevent output-per-man-hour from also showing a smaller rise over the same period than in any other industrialized country except the United States.

Of course, the whole advanced world suffered a sharp slowdown in economic growth during the 1970s, and there is little prospect of any return to earlier growth rates. Many factors may contribute to this general slowdown—including, probably, the accumulation of capital and a consequent decline in its rate of return; a gradual rise in the risk premium required for investment once it became apparent, during the 1970s, that governments could no longer be relied upon to pursue full employment policies at any cost; the effects of inflation on company tax burdens and nominal interest rates and hence liquidity; the delayed effects of the two oil shocks of 1973–74 and 1979; accumulated changes in the relative bargaining strengths of labor and management, which may have contributed to an excessive rise in the real wage in some countries; growing competition from the NICs; the fragility of certain developing economies that had become overstretched financially; and various other factors, all overlaid by increased determination by governments to give priority to fighting inflation as against full employment objectives.[10] Britain has not been spared any of these.

Until Mrs. Thatcher's election victory in 1979, there was no major difference in policy between the two main parties that held office in the 1970s. For example, after the failure of the Heath (Conservative) administration's dash for growth in the early 1970s and its disastrous confrontation with the unions in the winter of 1973–74, a new Labour government was returned to power later in 1974. But towards the end of 1976 it was this government that officially announced that the old notion that countries could spend their way out of recessions was in error and needed to be buried. It was also this government that signed the "Letter of Intent" to the International Monetary Fund (IMF) at the end of 1976, in which it committed itself to ultraorthodox policies of restraining the public-sector borrowing requirement (PSBR) in the interest of controlling the growth of the money supply. For a while the policies seemed to be succeeding, although much of the credit has to be given to the acceptance by the unions of a severe pay restraint. However, the maintenance of this policy would have required a degree of farsightedness and cooperation that was too much for the traditional rhetoric and archaic, fragmented structure of the British union movement: the policy broke up in the "winter of discontent" of 1978–79, which paved the way for the election of a Conservative government under Mrs. Thatcher in 1979.

This meant that Britain embarked on a period of economic experimentation of a kind that has probably not been seen for decades in any advanced industrialized country. As James Tobin remarked recently, "The Thatcher program is as close as we are likely to come to an experiment testing the Fellner strategy of the credible threat. . . . As a social scientist he would not like to interrupt this experiment now before its efficacy and cost have been tested."[11] This comment was made in September 1981, and since then unemployment has risen much further from what were already tragically high levels, and very few economists—let alone Professor Tobin—even in their most detached spirit of scientific inquiry, would want to persist further in testing the British economy to destruction.

An official statement of the policy of the new Thatcher government was contained in a letter from the Chancellor of the Exchequer, Sir Geoffrey Howe, to a Parliamentary committee. In it he said that "the main objectives of the Government's economic strategy are to reduce inflation and to create conditions in which sustainable economic growth can be achieved," and that, in contrast to previous Labour *and* Conservative administrations, it did not believe that income policy was the appropriate way to achieve price stability. The key to price stability was slower growth of the money supply, which required a cut in the PSBR. This, in turn, meant a cut in public expenditure, for increases in taxes were not in accordance with the supply side of the strategy. This strategy consisted of restoring incentives to enterprise by cutting taxes; shifting the weight of taxation from taxes on income to taxes on spending (although, in the first budget of June 1979, the doubling of the value-added tax rate added a few points to the inflation rate); and restoring "a broad balance of power in the framework of collective bargaining" by changing the laws related to picketing and closed shops, and taking other measures aimed at enabling market forces to work freely and flexibly.

A concomitant of this policy was that the exchange rate would be allowed to rise in response to the tight money policy. The tighter monetary policy was not reflected in a slower growth of the money supply (particularly in 1980 and 1981) largely due to the effect of deepening depression on the automatic stabilizers. But it was reflected in the official policy with respect to interest rates. In other words, the government was following a more old-fashioned "monetary" policy rather than a "monetarist" policy. If the exchange rate had not been allowed to rise, the money target would have been threatened even further by an even greater influx of foreign exchange reserves. Furthermore, as Buiter and Miller argue persuasively (in line with recent work by Dornbusch), the foreign exchange market was probably relatively efficient, and if it was convinced that Mrs. Thatcher's tight monetary stance would lead to a rise in interest rates given the sluggishness of domestic prices, the exchange rate would appreciate, in the short run, above its longer-run expected equilibrium value (in order to preserve international interest rate parity).[12]

At the same time, there was an initial sharp rise in domestic prices and costs. This was the result of various factors. First, there was the follow-through of the wage "explosion" following the winter of discontent referred to above. Also, there was the fact that the new administration carried out its election pledge of honoring large pay awards (around 25 percent) in the public sector made by the outgoing administration (which, of course, set a standard for private-sector pay claims), the large increase in value-added tax, and, of course, the 1979 oil price rise. The combination of fast-rising domestic wages and a sharp appreciation of the exchange rate meant that British competitiveness collapsed between 1979 and 1981. This was obviously not the only factor contributing to the sharp rise in unemployment in recent years, but it probably helps to explain why Britain's unemployment rate is well above the average of the advanced industrialized countries.

However, the way in which these developments increased unemployment is not straightforward. It is often argued that much of the unemployment is the result of workers' having "priced themselves out of the market." For unlike earlier periods, the rising exchange rate and the generally restrictive monetary and fiscal stance made it impossible for firms to pass on the higher wages in higher prices. Real wages—to the employees—rose slightly in manufacturing, but the warranted real wage (i.e., allowing for changes in productivity and in the terms of the trade) fell slightly.

Indeed, the experience of the last two or three years may seem to provide a striking demonstration of Milton Friedman's view

that labor unions cannot be responsible for inflation, only governments can, insofar as they follow an accommodating policy; all
that unions can do is to cause unemployment. Throughout the
1950s, 1960s, and early 1970s, British governments had more or
less followed accommodating policies in response to wage push,
thereby leading to inflation with relatively little unemployment.
Since nonaccommodating policies were introduced—at first
mildly by the Labour administration of the late 1970s and then
much more fiercely by the present Conservative administration—
inflation has been brought down and unemployment has dramatically increased. But what the nonaccommodating policy has
not done has been to prevent an unwarranted rise in real wages.[13]
Indeed, it has had the opposite result, inducing a rise in the exchange rate and a further slowdown, at least at first, in the growth
of productivity. However, the fact that real wages appear to have
risen more than would be justified by changes in productivity and
the terms of trade by no means proves that unemployment has
been caused by excessive upward pressure on wages as distinct
from other factors—including government policy—that depressed demand.[14]

Of course, the appreciation of the sterling exchange rate cannot
be attributed entirely to a tight monetary policy. The 1979 sharp
rise in oil prices, and the achievement by 1982 of oil self-sufficiency
and then surplus, meant that Britain did not suffer the same
balance-of-payments constraint or automatic deflationary impact
as did countries that were major oil importers. The counterpart of
this was that the higher oil surplus in the British balance of payments, or the higher relative reward to oil exports, meant that
resources had to be moved out of other occupations, notably
manufacturing exports, and the higher exchange rate would be
the means by which this transfer would be assisted. But in the
medium run this can be a very painful process, accompanied by
rising unemployment in manufacturing, which may persist into
the long run given the low labor intensity of the oil industry.[15]

The two tests of this policy are (1) how far price stability can be
maintained if unemployment is ever to be significantly reduced,
and (2) how far longer-run growth prospects are damaged by a
prolonged period of mass unemployment. That is, has the patient
been killed by the medicine administered? The prospects under

either heading are not promising. As regards the latter, revival of investment now probably would require that profit rates be brought back not merely to their 1960 levels but even higher, in order to allow for a probable rise in the risk premium. Given the present exceptionally high capital-output ratio and share of wages in value added, there is little chance that the labor share will fall sufficiently to restore minimum profit rates in the absence of a substantial expansion of output. Furthermore, such investment as is likely to take place with current real wages relative to productivity is likely to be concentrated on labor-saving investment and hence still make very little contribution to reducing unemployment. And as for the former test, the prospects of a high level of output and employment in Britain being maintained without at least a limited—and possibly a more unlimited—return to excessive wage pressures are not very good. Nothing has been done to reform the workings of the labor market in a way that can ensure that full employment is compatible with price stability (or, in terms of a more neoclassical view, that the natural rate of unemployment can be reduced).

In addition to its emphasis on the PSBR and the money supply, a further distinguishing feature of the current administration's professed economic policy is its emphasis on stimulating an expansion of supply, which, it is alleged, will help create "real jobs." These are presumably distinct from the "imaginary jobs" that people used to have and that, perhaps not surprisingly, over three million of them have now lost. A major plank in the Conservative party's program in 1979 had been its intention of reducing taxes in order to increase incentives for work, innovation, enterprise, and all the alleged Victorian virtues for which Mrs. Thatcher expresses such admiration. During the course of the election campaign of May–June 1983, one heard far less about this objective, presumably for fear that the leader of the Labour party, Michael Foot, might have riposted by pointing out that the share of taxation in national income had in fact risen since Mrs. Thatcher took office (a rather groundless fear, since it soon became obvious during the campaign that Mr. Foot probably knew nothing about the burden of taxation, and even if he did, he would have thought "the higher the better" and have found it less likely to dazzle the electorate than pursuit of unpopular Labour party policies such as unilateral disarmament).

Of course, the belief that high taxation in Britain has been a major obstacle to the growth rate of the British economy has been widely held and by no means confined to British Conservative politicians. Since the U.K. until recently had the highest starting rate of taxation and the highest final rate in the world (except for Algeria and Egypt), it is not surprising that this belief is shared by many commentators. Of course, there are great difficulties in comparing tax burdens across countries, but there is little doubt that the U.K. is well above others in the starting rate of tax; it is also the country in which the highest percentage of taxpayers are paying the same standard rate.[16]

On the other hand, there is little convincing evidence that the high marginal (personal income) tax rates faced by a large proportion of the working population in Britain significantly dampen work incentives or initiative, and corporate taxation in Britain raises hardly any revenue anyway. In any case, the pre-tax corporate rate of return in Britain has been much lower than in most other similar countries for a very long time, and Britain's growth rate and technological performance have lagged behind those of her main competitors since the latter part of the nineteenth century—long before tax rates were significant.[17] Finally, although the particular pattern of taxation in Britain may lead to the characteristics pointed out above, the overall tax burden has been hardly above the average of major industrialized countries. The personal income tax has been higher, but corporate taxes and other taxes have been lower.

It may well be that the unbalanced structure of taxation does inhibit growth, as well as produce static resource misallocation. But the picture is confused. It is true that there were very high rates of tax on investment income, but at the same time there were generous investment subsidies. The unbalanced tax structure may distort choices in the labor and capital markets. Also, as Pechman points out, it may produce inequitable results for people in essentially the same economic circumstances, as well as provide strong incentives to find means of legal tax evasion.[18] But there is still no firm evidence that the tax burden has been a significant factor in explaining the slow growth and productivity performance of the British economy that goes back about a century now.

Furthermore, the present Thatcher government has done little to reduce it; indeed, the overall tax take has risen in the last three years. According to some very authoritative estimates, the marginal tax rate for most family types also rose by about 2.5 percent over the same period.[19]

Thus the tight monetary policy seems only to have exacerbated the fall in British competitiveness, and it is far from certain how much it has changed basic attitudes in a way that will permit price stability to be maintained when—and if—employment recovers. The attempt to improve the supply side by changes in taxation has not yet been carried very far, although the reduction in the marginal rate at the top of the income scale may have some effect on the small proportion of the population affected by it.

The notion that there has been a new breath of realism blowing through British industry that will show up in much better productivity performance in the future has yet to be tested. So far slack demand seems to have been associated with poor productivity performance and vice versa,[20] which is the reverse of the correlation that one would predict if improved productivity were the result of the shakeout and shake-up associated with a much tougher economic climate.

That the present government should not only have adopted its current policy but also have been able to do so without suffering any noticeable decline in its popularity is partly the result of other political factors, notably the disarray in the Labour party. But it probably also partly reflects the fact that, although 13 percent of the labor force may now be unemployed, a large proportion of the remaining 87 percent may prefer price stability to full employment. Mrs. Thatcher may well be able to say, in effect, that it is not her fault if the institutions are such that the level of unemployment at which prices are stable is extremely high, and that since price stability is what the majority want, she has no alternative but to inflict high unemployment on the economy.[21] But if that is indeed the choice facing the British economy—high and accelerating inflation versus mass unemployment—then it is rather like being faced with a choice between two alternative ways of committing suicide—shooting oneself or jumping off the tenth floor balcony. In such a situation, one might well search around desperately for some other way out. In Britain, and perhaps in many other countries, this would appear to involve some basic reform of labor-management relations. However, this would be a very difficult and daunting process; it promises no simple panaceas like controlling the money supply, and it means not so much following a clearly charted course as hacking one's way through a jungle without seeing clearly where one has to go, and being prepared to make slow progress by trial and error. This is obviously not the sort of policy that appeals to policymakers or to electorates—or to most economists, for that matter.

It could well be that the automatic corrective forces of the market mechanism would enable the British economy to recover eventually; continued high unemployment and price stability might gradually lead to some deep-seated shake-up of British management and thence to durable changes in work practices and labor-management relations, as well as to a change in the size and composition of the capital stock that would permit higher employment. This might lead to a sufficient increase in British competitiveness and industrial flexibility, given the exchange rate, to enable labor to move out of more traditional manufacturing industries into expanding new areas and some nontraded goods and services (for there is little prospect of much labor being absorbed in the oil industry!). The basic changes must take place within the next few years, because by the end of this decade even oil will not protect Britain from a growing balance-of-payments constraint. If by the time the oil balance has moved back into deficit there is not much left of British manufacturing to fall back on, it is difficult to see what could save the British economy from a very serious long-run decline.

A Persuasive Explanation for Slow Growth

Britain has suffered from the usual collection of interferences in the economy that can be found, to varying degrees, in almost every other advanced economy, such as various price controls, subsidies, inconsistencies and unnecessary complications in the tax system, and unwarranted protective devices. There are two reasons why these are barely touched upon in this paper, or in most other studies of Britain's poor postwar growth record. First, they are just as bad—and are often much worse—in many other similar economies that have had impressive growth rates over the same period. Secondly, most of them explain, at best, only why the *level* of output would be lower, not why the *growth rate* would be slower. And the evidence suggests that even such features of the scene that might have more dynamic effects on the rate of growth of output, such as certain characteristics of the tax system, do not go far toward explaining the low post-tax rates of return on investment in the private sector or other determinants of the growth rate. One must turn elsewhere for explanations of Britain's slow growth rate.

One of the most persuasive explanations presented is in terms of the gradual evolution, over a century or more, of a complex interaction of economic and sociological factors that produced institutional structures and patterns of behavior that slowed down technical progress—notably trade union resistance to innovation and management impotence. Insofar as any blame may be attached to economic policy, it would be to sins of omission rather than commission. Little or no serious effort has ever been made to weaken the resistance of unions to technical progress, or to reduce class antagonisms, or to raise the professionalism of management. Instead, attempts have been made to find relatively simple and painless panaceas, such as economic planning, entry into the Common Market, and more recently, monetarism (simple but not so painless).

Of course, the political and social obstacles to any reform of long-established institutional prerogatives and patterns of behavior should not be underestimated. Nor is it easy to find any degree of agreement about where to start, or about what is really wrong with our institutions, as it is with narrower economic explanations. In a sense, therefore, it may well be that Britain has chosen slow growth rather than the gamble with the social upheaval and the loss of certain attractive features of the British way of life that might be necessary to accelerate growth. The current Thatcher experiment is still not completed. The prospects for any fundamental change in the institutions that exert a grip on Britain's economic dynamism, or lack of it, do not seem to be bright. But our ignorance of the interaction between sharp economic changes and subsequent social behavior is even greater than in the more narrow area of economic cause and effect. In the unlikely event that current policies will have beneficial long-run effects on attitudes toward work and innovation, it is still doubtful whether the lessons that could be learned will have much relevance for other economies with very different historical backgrounds.

COMMENTS

David Laidler

There is very little in Wilfred Beckerman's paper with which I disagree; on the whole I found it stimulating and instructive. And such differences as I do find I have with him are matters of emphasis rather than principle. Thus, I shall limit my comments to supplementing what he has said rather than to disputing it.

First of all, it is worth commenting briefly on the question of whether Britain's growth performance has, after all, been that bad. Beckerman's own data suggest that Britain has performed no worse than the United States and only a little worse than Switzerland during the postwar years. Moreover, Britain's growth in that period seems to have been more rapid than it was during that alleged heyday of Victorian and Edwardian prosperity, the four decades preceding World War I. If British growth has been unsatisfactorily slow—and perhaps on balance it has been—this problem is neither new to Britain nor unique among the developed countries.

I share Beckerman's skepticism about the "mature economy" explanation of the problem, and about the explanation based on the theory that Britain suffered relatively little physical damage in World War II. The idea that a developed and productive economy, well-endowed with capital equipment, should somehow find it more, rather than less, difficult to expand its productive capacity seems to me preposterous. Moreover, I share his concern with the way in which British policymakers have run from one ineffective panacea to another over the years. There is a ready market for economic snake oil in Britain, and Mr. Beckerman is unfortunately correct in arguing that recent enthusiasm for "monetarism" as a cure-all for Britain's ills is in large measure another manifestation of that market at work.

Britain's poor economic performance surely has a multiplicity of roots. In addition to the factors that Beckerman has mentioned, I would draw attention here to the so-called regional and housing policies. Under the best of motives, the regional policy has in part been geared to driving new industry away from areas judged to be already prosperous, with the result that such areas, notably the West Midlands, suddenly find themselves moribund, having been starved of new investment for decades. Regional policy also has involved a systematic practice of subsidizing capital-intensive development in areas of labor surplus (the short-lived regional employment premium of the late 1960s is an exception) the consequences of which are too obvious to spell out in detail here.

Housing policy grounded in rent controls first introduced as a temporary measure in 1915, but that did not really bite hard until the late 1940s; the widespread provision of housing by *local* (rather than federal) government; and heavy subsidies to owner-occupiers by way of the income tax system, are tailor-made to inhibit the geographic mobility of labor. Even more important, I think, is its effect on social mobility. The normal life-cycle progression from private rental housing to owner occupation that characterizes such a wide band of the North American social spectrum cannot occur in Britain. Tenure "choice" is much more likely to be for a lifetime, and given the tendency for public- and owner-occupied housing to be geographically segregated, particularly in the large industrial cities, this choice also involves location in what Beckerman correctly notes to be a remarkably well-defined social class system.

Though I have no doubt that it was the class system that first gave rise to housing policy in Britain, it is now housing policy (more than education policy) that perpetuates the class structure. It is a chicken and egg problem, certainly, but one cure for a plague of chickens might be to break a few eggs. Policymakers who are concerned about the baleful effects of class division on Britain's economic (not to mention social) performance could do worse than to consider radical reform in the field of housing as an indirect way of coming to grips with the problem. I might note in passing that if Britain's poor postwar performance relative to the rest of Western Europe is a result of her having been on the winning side, I believe it is equally important that this outcome preserved the class structure of the country—more so than that its capital equipment was also preserved.

Let me now turn to an issue that Beckerman deals with implicitly, but which deserves explicit attention: namely the influence of deeply ingrained "bad" economic theory on British policy discussion and practice. In particular I would single out two influences.

The first of these is the Smith-Marx labor theory of value, and in particular the distinction that theory makes between productive and unproductive labor. This distinction underlies what is almost an obsession with the industrial sector as opposed to the service sector as the source of economic well-being, an obsession that fuels much policy debate. It manifests itself in the following ways. There is a longstanding and widely-held suspicion that the "city" is failing to channel sufficient investment funds to "industry." Closely related to this is the idea that an overvalued exchange rate kept in place by "city interests" has systematically strangled British industry for most of this century. Then there is the current concern about the "de-industrialization" of Britain as a result of North Sea oil; more concretely, the imposition of a "Selective Employment Tax" in 1968 designed to shift labor from "less productive" service-sector jobs to "more productive" ones in industry; and, lest anyone think that I am cataloging sins of the Labour Party, let me suggest that the current government's oft-stated belief in the unproductiveness of government economic activity is yet another manifestation of the same fallacious theory of value.

My second example of "bad" economics is a deeply ingrained belief that the economy may be characterized by something approximating a simple Keynesian model in which there is no supply-side resource constraint, so that output is demand determined, and in which wages and prices are exogenously determined. In such a model, there is no meaningful distinction between short-term real expansion and long-term growth, and output can always be made to increase by expanding aggregate demand. The attempt to attain demand-led "growth" has been a recurring theme in British policy since the 1960s, and I believe it has had much to do with the deterioration of Britain's growth performance over the last fifteen years.

The Maudling "dash for growth" of 1963–64, which led to a balance-of-payments crisis, economic stagnation, and ultimately to the 1967 devaluation, is one example of this theme. Unfortunately, the lesson learned from this experience was not that there were supply-side constraints after all, so that demand expansion carried with it a danger of inflation; rather it was that the balance of payments could be seen as placing an extra "financial" constraint on fixed exchange-rate economy, and that the removal of this constraint by the adoption of a flexible exchange rate would have permitted the Maudling experiment to succeed. The Heath-Barber "Go for Growth" policy was in large measure, as the similarity of its slogan suggests, a repeat of the Maudling experiment, but with the addition of a flexible exchange rate. As we know, it broke down not from a balance-of-payments crisis, but from an upsurge in inflation that, if hardly galloping by Latin American standards, nevertheless set off at a trot brisk enough and comfortable enough to deeply unsettle inexperienced British riders.

One might have thought that this experience would have disabused the British political psyche of the economic fallacies that generated it, but what has happened is that they have found adherents on the other end of the political spectrum. Maudling, Heath, and Barber were Conservatives in the 1960s and 1970s when Labour was the sound money party. Now the Labour Party claims that Britain's economic malaise can be cured by fiscal expansion accompanied by a large-scale devaluation, repeated as necessary in order to maintain a "competitive advantage" for British industry.

Is there any hope, then, for an improvement in Britain's economic performance? Beckerman is pessimistic. Inflation is down, and productivity is up: the conditions for economic growth have been put in place, but only the economic conditions. Class antagonisms still exist and may be even worse than they were—as Beckerman suggests, ready to break out again as soon as the economy begins to expand. And yet there are others who claim to discern a "new attitude" among the working class. Perhaps, having got macropolicy painfully back on track, a reelected Thatcher government will prove pragmatic enough to install microeconomic (not to mention social) policies conducive to growth; there are some grounds for optimism. Even so, I agree with Mr. Beckerman to this extent: we are still a long way from having in place the preconditions for a British economic miracle.

3

YUTAKA KOSAI

Japan's Growth Problem

After maintaining growth rates exceeding 10 percent per year from 1955 to 1970, the Japanese economy experienced declining growth in the 1970s (to less than 5 percent), and further declines in three consecutive years in the 1980s (to about 3 percent). The period of rapid growth featured a combination of a relatively skilled labor force with large-scale technological innovation, rapidly increasing saving rates (both personal and corporate), extensive use of relatively cheap imported energy, and a growing labor force (growing about 2 percent per year).

The high growth period was encouraged by economic policies that encouraged allocation of resources to activities in which Japan had a comparative advantage, and by moderate fiscal policies, which stimulated saving and investment by generating frequent government budget surpluses as well as opportunities for tax reduction.

Apart from direct policy influences, Japan's high growth was also encouraged by certain structural influences, and their decline became important in explaining the decline in growth. One of the most important has been the decline in opportunities to "catch up" technologically with other industrial nations. Energy prices have also risen substantially, and saving rates have fallen.

41

Although it seems that Japan's high growth period is over, its future economic performance will still depend very much on the economic policies it pursues. Here a major problem exists in the continued growth of government spending and of associated public deficits, which are crowding out private investment.

This paper will consider the circumstances that led to the end of Japan's high economic growth and the policy issues raised by its slower growth over the past decade and a half.

Japan's Recent Growth Experience

The Japanese economy, after maintaining a high growth rate for fifteen years, moved into a new phase of slower growth in 1970. The rate of economic growth dropped sharply from 11.6 percent between 1965 and 1970, to 4.7 percent between 1970 and 1975, and to 4.9 percent between 1975 and 1980 (table 1). There are some signs of further deceleration. The gross national product (GNP) expanded by only around 3 percent in the years from 1980 to 1982.

Official and business forecasts of future growth are not much brighter. The government forecasts 3.4 percent growth for 1983. The Economic Council, an advisory organ to the Cabinet, is reported to have made a temporary growth projection of 3 to 4 percent for the period 1983 to 1987. According to a survey recently collected by the Economic Planning Agency, businessmen anticipated a 3.8 percent average rate of growth for the first half of the 1980s. Opinions about this differ only slightly. One side of the debate on Japan's growth potential foresees 5 percent growth; the other side, 3 percent. No one seems to believe a return to 10 percent is possible.[1]

The conclusion of Japan's high growth era created some difficult problems. Some have been resolved, but others remain and affect opportunities for growth in the 1980s. To understand these, we must recall the conditions and policies that made Japan's explosive growth possible. Four factors stand out in particular:

• *Rapid technological progress.* Japan was a latecomer to the industrial world. In the mid-1950s, with a relatively educated workforce, opportunities to implement industrial modernization existed along a wide technical frontier. Technological modernization had to be rapid if Japan were to catch up with the advanced industrial countries.

- *Rise in saving rates.* Saving rates rose very rapidly during the high growth period. The personal saving rate (personal savings divided by household disposable income) increased sharply between 1955 and 1960, and then, after a temporary pause, rose again, reaching 18.6 percent in 1970. The ratio of gross fixed business capital formation to GNP showed the same trend, rising from about 11 percent in 1955 to about 15 percent in 1965, and to 20 percent in 1970. The strength of the trend is even more evident when the ratio is expressed in current prices, with the prices of investment goods remaining relatively stable compared to those of consumer goods: the investment ratio rose about 5 percent a year in real terms from 1955 to 1970 (see table 2).

- *Extensive use of energy and other resources.* In the period of low energy prices before 1973, Japan imported most of its energy and resources inputs, with minimum concern about costs and improving terms of trade.

- *Increases in the labor force.* The labor force increased about 2 percent per year during the high growth period.

Table 1
Annual Growth Rates by Five-Year Periods
(percent)

Fiscal year	Real GNP	Gross fixed business capital stock	Population employed
1955–60	8.9	7.9	2.2
1960–65	9.7	11.0	1.7
1965–70	11.6	13.0	1.8
1970–75	4.7	10.3	0.4
1975–80	4.9	6.3	0.9

Source: Real GNP and gross fixed business capital stock for 1955–70 are taken from the old series (former SNA) at constant 1970 prices, while those for 1970–80 are from the new series (present SNA) at constant 1975 prices. They are not comparable due to definitional changes and revisions made in the estimation method. Population figures are from the Census.

Changes in Conditions for Growth

Among the influences accounting for the reduced growth rate, the retardation of capital accumulation accounted for about 2.5 percent of the slowdown; more than 3 percent was accounted for by a slower increase in final inputs; and 0.6 percent by the reduced increases in the labor force.

The saving rate could not rise indefinitely. Personal saving continued to rise until 1974 when it reached a record high of 23.1 percent, and declined somewhat thereafter. In nominal terms the ratio of gross fixed business capital formation to GNP fell from 20.9 percent in 1970 to 15.7 percent in 1980. At constant prices, however, the decline was much more limited: The same proportion of GNP was allocated to fixed business capital formation in 1980 at constant prices as in 1968, a typical year of the high growth era (table 2). One important question is why such a high proportion of GNP was allocated for building plant and equipment when economic growth decelerated remarkably. We will return to this question in a moment.

An economy with a rising saving ratio grows faster than the "natural rate of growth" (i.e., the rate determined by population increase and technical progress), and per capita output rises. When saving rates stabilize, the economy will return to its natural growth path. The saving rate at the end of the 1960s was so high that it could not have risen much further. In this sense, the high growth period could not last indefinitely.

Because of the sharp rises of crude oil prices in 1973 and again in 1979, Japan's terms of trade deteriorated by 45 percent in 1980 compared to 1970, in spite of the remarkable appreciation of the yen exchange rate in the meantime. The limited supply of labor, energy, and other resources certainly exerted a strong pressure on profit margins. The ratio of gross corporate income to gross fixed corporate capital declined from 28 percent in 1970 to about 13 percent in 1980 (table 2). This decline might have been responsible for the decline of growth in the capital stock, which fell from 13 percent growth in the 1965–70 period to 6.3 percent from 1975 to 1980 (table 1).

When the saving rate is rising, the gross fixed capital stock becomes younger and younger, so that new technologies that are

Table 2
Saving and Investment
(percent)

Fiscal year	Personal saving Personal disposable income	Gross fixed business capital formation GNP (nominal terms)	(real terms)	Gross corpo- rate income Gross fixed corporate capital stock (real terms)
1955	13.9	10.8	7.7	16.4
1960	17.4	19.6	14.0	24.0
1965	16.8	15.3	13.3	19.0
1970	20.3	19.8	20.0	22.0
1970	18.6	20.9	19.5	28.0
1975	22.2	16.0	16.1	15.4
1980	19.5	15.7	16.8	12.9

Source: National Income Statistics. Remarks from table 1 also apply.

"embodied" in newly built plants and equipment are more easily and widely put into use. But when saving reaches its limit, and capital accumulation drops, a beneficial growth cycle will turn into a vicious one.

The slower increase of inputs does not explain the entire decline in the growth rate after 1970. Overall technological progress itself appears to have slowed after that date for several reasons: Japanese industries had closed technological gaps; the population had moved almost entirely out of agriculture and into industry, and a higher proportion of workers were now in the service sector, where technical progress is less easy to utilize than it is in manufacturing industries. In fact per capita output in the service sector grew 2.9 percent per year in the 1970s, compared to 6.7 percent productivity gains in the industrial sector.

High energy prices have also reduced growth rates. Higher energy prices retard capital accumulation. One reason for this is that changes in the input and output price mixes will cause profit rates to fall. Another is that in a country like Japan, where energy resources are largely imported from abroad, worsened terms of trade will shift more resources into exports to finance the increased bill for imported energy. This reduces the resources available for domestic capital formation.

The decline in growth from the 5 percent levels achieved in the 1970s to 3 percent in three consecutive years in the 1980s raises the question of whether this further deceleration is a temporary phenomenon resulting from the recent recession or a second, permanent shift in Japan's long-term growth path. The answer will depend, at least in part, on the resolution of certain major policy issues, which have important growth implications.

Stagflation—A Passing Phase

Reduced economic growth implied smaller productivity gains and a comparatively bigger wage push, which tend to bring about inflation as well as unemployment. Fears of increased inflation were accentuated by the explosive revision of wages in the spring of 1974, when the base wage rate was raised an average of 32.9 percent for the members of big trade unions. Meanwhile, the wholesale price index and the consumer price index rose more than 20 percent, forcing the government to take stringent monetary and fiscal measures (table 3). The Japanese feared that stagflation would result from the clash between austere total demand management and deeply-rooted inflationary expectations.

Fortunately, that nightmare was only partially realized. In the two or three years immediately after the 1973 oil crisis, Japan suffered from rising prices and unemployment; however, inflation was rapidly subdued thereafter. In the mid-1970s and early 1980s, after a short-lived reemergence of inflationary pressures resulting from the second oil crisis of 1979, Japan was faced with slower growth, unemployment of more than 2 percent (high by the high growth period standard), and price stability instead of inflation. In 1982, consumer prices rose by less than 3 percent over the previous year, below the average rate of consumer price inflation of about 5 percent during the high growth era.

Two factors contributed to the price stability—stringent monetary policy and flexible wage determination. Monetary policy was reoriented twice in the 1970s. In the high growth era, monetary policy was redesigned to maximize economic growth under the constraint of a fixed exchange rate of 360 yen/dollar. On the one hand, the money supply was expanded as long as the balance-of-international-payments situation allowed it, and foreign reserves were kept thin, rarely exceeding $2 billion until 1970. On the other hand, whenever the balance of payments turned into deficits, the authorities never hesitated to impose rather severe measures. In 1954, 1957, 1961, and 1964, the Bank of Japan effectively suppressed aggregate demand and quickly restored the international balance to equilibrium. Japan at that time was under the strict regimen of the fixed exchange rate, which is not unlike that of the gold standard. The result was virtual stability of wholesale prices (particularly of export prices), which strengthened the international competitiveness of Japanese industries, while domestic consumer prices were allowed to rise as long as they did not endanger the price stability of tradeable goods.

Inflation abroad changed the situation in the early 1970s. The mounting surplus in Japan's current account was regarded as a cause of international financial instability. Instead of revaluating the yen to decrease the surplus, the Japanese government tried to expand fiscal expenditures and the money supply. Money supply was increased more than 20 percent annually over the previous year when the first oil crisis broke out in the fall of 1973 (table 3).

Table 3
Development of Unemployment and Prices
(percent)

Fiscal Year	Unemployment	Spring wage revision[a]	Inflation[b] Consumer price index	Wholesale price index	Increase in money supply[c]
1970	1.2	18.5	7.3	2.3	18.0
1972	1.3	20.1	5.3	3.2	25.1
1974	1.5	32.9	21.8	23.5	11.3
1976	2.0	8.8	9.4	5.5	12.8
1978	2.2	5.9	3.3	2.3	12.9
1980	2.1	6.7	7.9	3.3	6.9
1982 (Nov.)	2.4	7.0	2.3	1.7	9.2

[a]Rate is rounded.
[b]Rate over previous year.
[c]M_2 + CD
Sources: Statistical Bureau, Prime Minister's Office, and the Bank of Japan.

The Bank of Japan learned from this failure. It tried to get the money supply under control and keep it there. It declared price stability as its supreme concern. By the mid-1970s the new monetary policy succeeded in containing inflation and bringing about a business recovery with price stability in 1977–78. Facing another oil crisis in 1979, monetary authorities moved quickly to suppress inflationary development in early 1980 and successfully avoided double-digit inflation.

In the 1960s, the principal elements affecting money policy were wholesale prices, unemployment, and the balance of payments, but not consumer prices. However, in the 1970s, the principal elements were wholesale as well as consumer prices, but not so much balance of payments or unemployment. More recently, monetary policy has tended to be influenced—not by constant rates of inflation (measured in relation to the consumer price index), but by accelerating inflation rates.

Flexible wage determination was another element that brought the Japanese economy price stability rather than stagflation. Several institutional factors were involved. Enterprise-based trade unions, the common policy of guaranteed lifelong employment, and a one-year renegotiation of wage rates all served to make trade unions responsive to current business conditions[2]. The development of labor-saving technologies as well as the increase in the number of part-time job-seekers tended to limit the wage claims of the unions to the minimum.

Steady monetary policy combined with flexible wage determination brought about satisfactory price stability without aggravated unemployment. Two problems remain, however. If economic growth decelerates further, unemployment may increase, thus causing some social unrest. Unemployment still remains comparatively high in Japan today, and finding new jobs for high school graduates and female workers has become more difficult than in the past.

A second problem concerns the effects of stringent monetary policy in one country on other countries. Japan was able to expand its exports substantially in the mid-1970s to pay its increased bill for imported energy only because U.S. monetary policy at the time was fairly loose. In 1981 and 1982, however, U.S. monetary policy became extremely tight; interest rates rose; and its imports fell because of reduced demand. Stringent Japanese monetary policy thus yielded a prolonged recession at home, reduced exports, and a faltering yen. The experience of this period shows that successfully avoiding stagflation is not simply a matter of domestic policy.

Saving-Investment Adjustment

As we have seen, despite the decline in growth rates, which began around 1970, capital investment rates remained high into the early 1980s. The ratio of gross fixed business capital formation in 1980, for instance, was 15.7 percent in nominal terms and 16.8 percent at constant prices, compared to 18.9 percent and 16.4 percent respectively in 1968, a year in the high growth era. Several hypotheses have been proposed to explain these continued high investment rates at a time of declining economic growth. In considering various explanations, several data stand out. First, the ratio of new investment to total investment declined between 1970 and 1980 from 73 to 61 percent. The ratio of replacement investment, however (defined as equivalent to the investment levels of thirteen years ago—which is the average life of plant and equipment), increased from 27 to 39 percent (table 4). Although total capital formation and GNP are growing less rapidly today than before, replacement investment is increasing as rapidly as it did during the high growth period because plant and equipment installed then are reaching the end of their average thirteen-year life spans. Thus, an increasing share of replacement investment is reflected in the statistics of total capital formation and gross national product. Growth in replacement investment explains why Japan's ratio of capital formation to GNP remains high in spite of its reduced growth rate, and at the same time why the growth of the capital stock is lower while business capital formation remains high.

In the first half of the 1970s, when the ratio of gross fixed capital formation fell, the ratio of personal saving to personal disposable income increased. This sharp rise in personal saving created several problems as Japan adjusted to slower economic growth in the mid-1970s. Increased household saving (and reduced consumption) in the face of declining capital formation

Table 4

Shares of New and Replacement Investment

(percent)

	New investment	Replacement investment	Total
1970	72.9	27.1	100.0
1975	63.0	37.0	100.0
1980	60.7	39.0	100.0

Source: Economic Planning Agency, Estimate of Gross Fixed Business Capital Stock and National Income Statistics.

brought about deficits in the government and corporate sectors, which further restrained their investment activities. Businessmen reacted to the frustration by reducing inventories, restricting new employment, and refraining from venturing into new enterprises. This process might have continued indefinitely without the "floor" of replacement investment that was created and without the price and wage adjustments already mentioned.

The rise of personal saving in the mid-1970s can be seen as the household sector's reaction to the slowing of long-run expected growth and to increased uncertainties. The "permanent" portion of income declined as a result of lowered expectations of future income. The "observed" propensity to consume was thus reduced.

The relation between corporate and household saving may deserve special attention here. The decline in corporate saving (or the increase in business losses) can be regarded as both an effect and a cause of increased personal saving.

The personal saving rate once exceeded 20 percent in the mid-1970s, declining toward the end of the decade; but it remained at 19.5 percent in 1980, higher than the late 1960s average of 16.5 percent (table 2). In contrast with these increased personal saving rates, the ratio of corporate saving to GNP declined from 16.6 percent in 1970, bottomed in the mid-1970s, and reached only 8.9 percent in 1980.

More remarkably, deficits in the public sector increased. During the high growth era, tax revenues increased so rapidly that the government was able to reduce tax rates every year, keeping the ratio of taxes to national income at the same level, while still leaving room to expand government expenditure rather generously and to maintain surpluses. This situation changed after the first oil crisis. Annual increases in tax revenue became smaller. The tax cut in the fall of 1973 by the Tanaka Cabinet was unusually large. Concurrently, because of the generous social security reforms launched in 1973 by the same Cabinet, public transfers grew at a much higher pace. Public works projects were increased to overcome the recession after the first oil crisis. The deficit of the general government reached 5.5 percent of GNP in 1978 (table 5), and that of the general account of the central government reached 6.1 percent in 1979.

The government's program of fiscal austerity aimed at reducing the government deficit without increasing taxes. Public works expenditures were cut back in real terms and tax reduction was postponed. Even so, the budget deficit remained high because of smaller-than-expected increases in tax revenues during the recession of 1981−82. As a result, new austerity measures, including a freeze on public employee wages, were introduced in the 1983 budget.

Politically, the Cabinet was committed to the restoration of fiscal balances without introducing large-scale new taxes. From the

Table 5
Budget Deficits
(percent)

Fiscal Year	Deficit GNP		Fixed capital formation GNP
	General government	General account of central government	General government
1974	0.4	−0.2	5.4
1976	−3.7	−4.2	5.2
1978	−5.5	−5.2	6.5
1980	−4.2	−5.9	5.9
1982	—	−5.4	—

Sources: National Income Statistics and Ministry of Finance. See also Marumo Akinori "Zaisei Akaji to Chochiku" (Budget Deficit and Saving), *Chochiku to Keizai,* Bank of Japan, December 1982.

budget-balancer's viewpoint, the current situation is self-destructive, as the rate of growth of national income as well as that of tax revenue is considerably lower than the rate of interest on national bonds (8 percent currently; one-third of the general account expenditure is financed by issue of national bonds). Financial circles fear the crowding-out effects of the large amounts of national bonds issued. Economic accountants tend to regard the budget deficit as the natural consequence of high personal savings and of the high proportion of government fixed capital formation to gross national product. Rational expectation theorists argue that the deficits are irrelevant, as government spending is compensated by savings in the private sector.

Reducing the budget deficit sharply within a short time may exert deflationary pressures on the overall economy. While the pressures may be offset by a fall in private saving ratio, the experiences of the 1970s suggest that this offset is not complete. Private saving was inversely related to public saving in the 1970s—a change from the 1960s—but not by much.

Still, politically and administratively, the mounting budget deficits impose severe restrictions on governmental actions. It is safe to assume that Japan will be faced with stringent budgets and increasing tax burden in years to come, in spite of their possible unfavorable effects on economic growth and on internal and external economic balances.

Income Distribution

The high growth period featured considerable equality in income distribution. Slower growth since 1970, however, may have ended and even reversed that trend. This conclusion about overall patterns of income distribution emerges from complicated changes in relative positions of specific groups throughout the period.

Employee compensation rose as a share of national income in the 1960s, and that rise accelerated in the 70s (see table 6). Corporate income, which had remained at the same level relative to national income in the beginning and the end of the 1960s, declined remarkably in the mid-1970s and did not recover fully in 1980. Income from property continued to rise in its share relative to national income through the 1960s and the 1970s. The increase

Table 6

Changes in Shares of Income to National Income

(percent)

Fiscal year	Employee compensation (a)	Corporate income	Income of self-employed (b)	Income from property	$\frac{b}{a}$ per head
1960	50.0	14.6	26.3	9.9	61.2
1965	56.3	10.3	23.3	11.8	65.4
1970	54.5	15.4	19.6	11.7	67.8
1970	53.6	17.4	17.3	7.8	61.1
1975	66.5	7.6	15.0	10.1	52.7
1980	67.4	9.7	11.7	11.6	44.5

Source: National Income Statistics. Remarks from table 1 also apply.

in labor's share relative to capital was to be expected. This increase reduced aggregate saving, thus helping to balance saving and investment as economic growth slowed.

Income of the self-employed as a share of national income continued to fall through the 1960s and 1970s, reflecting the changing industrial structure. However, the per capita income of the self-employed moved toward parity with that of employees in the 1960s, then declined relatively in the 1970s. Meanwhile, wage differentials between employees of large and smaller business firms increased in the 1970s, reversing a trend toward narrower differentials in the 1960s, when labor markets were growing tighter (table 7).

These latter effects imply that income becomes less equally distributed as economic growth slackens and as unemployment increases. Enlarged wage differentials can be interpreted as a form of "disguised" unemployment and of a reemergence of the dual structure in the labor market. It is not clear, however, how far we can go with this interpretation. The disparities of rewards between employees and the self-employed, or between employees of different-sized firms, for example, may reflect the increased number of part-time workers (particularly housewives who seek jobs) in the small and medium-sized firms. Moreover, the extensions of retirement age in the large corporations (from 55 to 60 years of age) may raise the average wages of the employees of larger firms

Table 7
Wage Differential and Gini Coefficient

	Wage differential by firm size Number of employees				Gini coefficients			
					Wages and salaries		Other income	
	500+	100–499	30–99	5–29	Before tax	After tax	Before tax	After tax
1960	100.0	70.7	58.9	46.3	0.411	0.396	0.404	0.380
1965	100.0	80.9	71.0	63.2	0.344	0.325	0.439	0.414
1970	100.0	81.4	69.6	61.3	0.317	0.303	0.524	0.503
1975	100.0	82.9	68.7	60.2	0.301	0.292	0.537	0.509
1980	100.0	80.5	65.3	58.0	0.317	0.303	0.524	0.470

Sources: Wage differential, statistics from the Ministry of Labour's "Monthly Labour Statistics". Gini coefficients are calculated from National Tax Board, "Statistical Yearbook of National Taxation". Figures from 1960–75 are quoted from Ishi Hiromitsu, *Sozei Seisaku No Koka* (Effects of Tax Policy), Toyo Keizai Shimposha, 1979. Figures for 1980 are the author's calculation.

because of the "seniority" wage system in Japan. Moreover, despite the recent trend away from equality in wages and salaries, personal income differentials continue to be very small in Japan (table 7).

Impacts on International Economic Relations

Toward the end of the 1960s and in the early 1970s, the Japanese balance of payments ran a surplus from year to year (table 8). In response, the Sato and Tanaka governments tried to expand domestic demand by lowering interest rates and increasing the money supply and public expenditure, instead of by revaluing the yen. This policy imposed an unbearable burden on an economy already at full employment and growing 12 percent per year in real terms. The hyperinflation of 1973–74 was the result.

It was believed that the 1973 shift to a new system of floating exchange rates would bring relief, since the new system would allow authorities to execute policies without regard for international balances. Although the floating exchange rate regime survived the repeated oil crises, the high hopes for free and independent economic management that concentrated on domestic stability were not fully realized. Even under the floating exchange rates, slower economic growth and relative price stability in Japan brought about current surpluses in external balances, except during a short period of large deficits immediately after the oil crises. The success of Japanese policy aroused much criticism from abroad against the "export of unemployment from Japan." Under the floating-rate system, the yen took much longer than expected to appreciate and restore the current balance, and the restorations of equilibrium were of irregular duration, particularly between 1975 and 1978. Exchange rate fluctuations were also greater than expected.

In 1981 and 1982, the yen depreciated in spite of the current surpluses and domestic price stability, due to disparities in interest rates at home and abroad. Cries against the Japanese export of unemployment were repeated, while Japan was suffering from recession at home caused partly by a drop in exports. Monetary authorities maintained the high discount rate in order to avoid further depreciation of the yen and allowed the domestic

Table 8
External Balances

Fiscal year	Current balance / GNP — Nominal terms (%)	Current balance / GNP — Real terms (%)	Terms of trade	Exchange rate dollar/yen (end of year)
1955	1.0	1.4	136.3	360.0
1960	0.1	0.3	151.7	360.0
1965	1.3	1.4	146.7	360.0
1970	1.3	1.2	150.4	360.0
1970	1.2	−2.5	150.4	360.0
1975	0.1	0.3	97.2	299.7
1980	−0.5	4.4	68.0	211.0

Sources: Figures for current balance come from National Income Statistics. Remarks from table 1 also apply. Terms of trade are from Bank of Japan Export and Import Price Indexes (1975 = 100).

economy to slip further into recession. Imports declined as a result, and again the expected "insulation effect" of floating exchange rates was not as great as hoped.

More trade liberalization at this juncture is clearly desirable for Japan. At the same time, its potential contribution to improved trade balances will almost certainly be more psychological than substantive. Notwithstanding all its short-term defects, however, there seems to be no substitute for a floating exchange rate system. In the long run, the Japanese current account has balanced on average under the system, while the surplus in the real terms reflects deteriorated terms of trade. If the extraordinarily high interest rates in the United States declined to more normal levels, the floating exchange rate system should produce more balanced trade flows.

Another international impact of Japan's slower economic growth is its effect on the exports of other countries. Today, Japan's imports amount to 7.2 percent of free world imports. The growth of the Japanese economy and of its imports thus significantly affects the growth of world trade.

The newly industrialized and rapidly developing countries in the East and South Asia have a particularly deep trade connection with Japan. The slower growth of imports into Japan, resulting from slower growth of the Japanese economy and/or worsened terms of trade, should adversely affect the exports of these developing countries. During the 1970s, South Korea's exports to Japan grew by 29 percent annually in dollar terms, Taiwan's by 24.7 percent, Hong Kong's by 20 percent, Thailand's by 19.4 percent, Singapore's by 33 percent, Malaysia's by 23.5 percent, and the Philippines' by 13.9 percent, according to Japanese statistics.

Recent further deceleration of Japanese economic growth produced a decline in Japanese imports. The decline was remarkable in nominal terms rather than in real terms. Nonetheless, the failure of Japan to expand its import market rapidly may stifle (however temporarily) the growth of other Asian countries.

Perspectives for Growth in the 1980s

Japan successfully avoided the stagflation that could have resulted from the sharp decline of economic growth in the 1970s. A steady monetary policy and flexible wage determination made it possible to achieve relative price stability without excessive unemployment. Nevertheless, Japan today faces severe budget deficits at home and imbalances in external payments.

If Japanese growth continues to decline, a new adjustment process will be necessary. Declining growth would compel a reduction in the growth of capital investment (currently 6 percent per year). A decline in business investment would probably cause trouble for the capital goods industries, which were already hit by high energy costs. Under these circumstances, Japan's high personal saving rates—a past source of its ability to adapt and respond to changing economic conditions—instead may become a source of difficulty, even if only temporarily. With declining growth, another round of adjustments in saving and investment would have to begin. External imbalances may retard the industrialization process of neighboring countries, as will the reduced growth of Japanese imports.

If the current growth rates of saving and investment are maintained, one could expect Japan to grow by 4 to 5 percent in real terms for the rest of this decade. The current 3 percent growth in gross fixed capital formation should yield a 5 percent annual rate of capital accumulation (table 9). That 5 percent growth will con-

58   YUTAKA KOSAI

Table 9
Hypothetical Growth Rates of Capital Formation and Capital Stock
(percent)

Rate of increase in gross fixed business capital formation	Growth rate of gross fixed business capital stock Growth rate of replacement investment		
	13%	15%	18%
0 %	4.7	4.5	4.7
2.5	5.3	5.1	4.8
5	5.9	5.6	5.4
7.5	6.5	6.3	6.1

Source: Starting from the gross capital stock, gross capital formation and replacement investment at 1980, the rates of growth of gross capital stock under several assumptions are calculated.

tribute 1.5 to 2 percent to economic growth. The remaining growth should result from technical progress (2 percent) and the effect of 1 percent annual increases in the labor force. Four percent growth thus seems attainable. On the other hand, if demand fails to grow adequately, capital formation must decline further.

Confidence in the future encourages business investment and thus is important for sustaining economic growth. In particular, uncertainty resulting from continued budget deficits at home and depressed economic conditions abroad are a real problem for confidence, which will only disappear when those problems are overcome. To increase confidence, the government must initiate bold measures to reduce the budget deficits—but without resort to the shortsighted policy of freezing all government spending. The most important such measure would be a serious effort to control government spending. Besides the deficit, however, important structural reforms are also necessary—including reduction in unproductively high tax rates, reform of the social security system, and reform of federal grant programs to regional governments.

A program that included these elements would go a long way toward restoring public confidence and encouraging renewed economic growth.

4

ULF JAKOBSSON

Economic Growth in Sweden

The Swedish economy in the 1970s and early 1980s experienced slow growth and increasing structural imbalances.[1] During the same period, other industrial countries have exhibited similar problems, but the Swedish performance is in fact distinctively worse in industrial and overall growth (GDP) than the OECD average.

In one area, employment, Sweden has done better than average. But the reason is in reality related to the causes of decline in overall performance: Sweden's unemployment was reduced by an explosion in public spending, undertaken to mitigate the effects of the international recession. The result has been an enormous growth of public-sector expenditures and deficits, a large balance-of-payments deficit, and declining investment.

Despite these macroeconomic problems, the most important cause of Sweden's reduced productivity growth has been economic policies that have increased structural rigidities and reduced the economy's ability to adapt to a changing economic environment.

The first area of rigidity concerns issues of wage formation and flexibility in the labor market. In Sweden's centralized wage-bargaining process, the solidaristic wage policy has been a very important principle among labor unions. This policy aims at equal pay for equal jobs regardless of firm, branch, or region. The policy has the effect of introducing serious rigidities in wage determination and narrowing wage differentials. In the 1950s and especially the 1960s, this rigidity on the price side was accompanied by a very flexible labor-market policy, allowing parallel development of the wage structure and the real structure of the economy. In the 1970s Sweden experienced an increasing rigidity also in the labor market, so the wage structure tended to be adapted less and less to the real structure of the economy.

For most countries in the 1970s, the need for adjustment was most acute in relation to the dramatic increases in oil prices during the decade. For Sweden, however, the new competitive conditions in the shipbuilding and steel industries (for example) were also very important. While these changes prompted the need for microeconomic adjustments, most adjustment in the Swedish economy went in the wrong direction because of government subsidies and transfers to ailing sectors.

A third problem area concerns the explosion in public-sector spending and financing. In 1970 public-sector expenditure equaled 45 percent of GDP; in 1982 the same figure had risen to close to 70 percent. This rapid increase has been financed by increasing taxes and by rapid growth of public borrowing. Recent studies suggest that further increases in Swedish tax rates will not increase revenues and may even cause revenues to fall. Increased public-sector borrowing has not produced the dramatic increases in real interest rates that are evident in other countries with similar conditions, partly because of heavy regulation of the credit markets. But such regulation inevitably implies credit rationing, often by noneconomic criteria (especially political influence). And in Sweden, it should not be surprising that credit rationing has worked in the same direction as direct subsidies — supporting less efficient import-competing industries and thus retarding growth of more efficient export industries.

In all three areas, changes in policy between the 1960s and 1970s have worked generally toward slower growth and poorer functioning of the economy. While it is not easy to quantify the effects of these changes on overall economic performance, the evidence is strong that they explain much of the deterioration of Sweden's economic performance in the 1970s.

To get out of the present disequilibrium it is therefore probably necessary to change economic policies in all the areas mentioned. In the most recent years policies have changed considerably on some points. The competitive position of Swedish industry has been improved considerably in the last few years. This improvement has, however, been achieved by devaluations and not by internal adjustment. After 1980 there has been a slow-down of the growth of public-sector expenditure. This year zero-growth is forecasted.

Most notable is that a large portion of the industrial subsidies has been phased out. In the end of the paper there is a discussion on whether those changes are sufficient to get back to the non-inflationary growth path.

Some Indicators of Overall Economic Performance

Output and employment. In the 1970s there was a dramatic decline in economic growth in Sweden. In the 1950s the average yearly growth rate of GDP was 3.5 percent, and in the 1960s this rate increased to 4.5 percent; but in the 1970s it fell back to 1.75 percent. A more detailed picture of this turnaround is given in table 1.

The actual turning point occurred during the period 1973–74. The decline in production and productivity was most significant in the industrial sector, which experienced after 1974 an actual decline in production in conjunction with a very modest productivity performance. There was also some decline in production and productivity growth in other private business sectors, although the change was considerably less dramatic than in the industrial sector. In the public sector, growth and employment continued to increase by about 3.5 percent per year, which represented a decline in growth from the extreme high rate of 6.1 percent in the last half of the 1960s.

An interesting question is to what extent the decline in growth and productivity can be explained by the decline in capital forma-

Table 1

Production, Employment, and Productivity

(annual change in volume, percent)

	Production	Employment[a]	Productivity
Industry			
1965–70	5.1	−1.8	6.9
1970–74	3.5	−1.8	5.3
1974–81	−1.0	−2.6	1.6
1980–83	−0.1	−3.1	3.0
Other private business sectors			
1965–70	2.5	−1.4	3.9
1970–74	2.7	−2.1	4.8
1974–81	1.6	−0.4	2.0
1980–83	−0.8	−1.0	1.8
Public sector			
1965–70	6.1	6.1	0.0
1970–74	3.5	3.5	0.0
1974–81	3.7	3.4	0.3
1980–83	1.8	1.6	0.2
Total economy			
1965–70	3.8	−0.5	4.3
1970–74	3.1	−1.0	4.1
1974–81	1.1	−0.4	1.5
1980–83	0.7	0.3	0.4

[a]In hours.

Source: Central Bureau of Statistics, *National Accounts,* Stockholm, 1983.

tion. A recent study indicates that the decline in industrial productivity has to be explained by factors *other* than a decline in quantitative capital formation.[2] This is highlighted by table 2, which summarizes the results of the study on this point.

Use of resources. The weak growth of production in the 1970s was not accompanied by a parallel adjustment in domestic consumption. In the government's attempt to bridge over the international recession of the 1970s, consumption growth continued. This was especially true for public consumption, which grew by 3.5 percent per year during the whole decade, while private consumption stagnated in the latter part of that period. A gap rose between the

Table 2
Contribution of Capital Intensity to Productivity
in Swedish Industry
(average yearly percentage changes)

	1953–65	1965–73	1973–80
Productivity, explained by:	5.1	6.0	1.9
Capital intensity	1.3	2.1	2.0
Other factors	3.8	3.9	−0.1

Source: Y. Aberg, "Producktivitetsutvecklingen i industrin olika OECD=lander 1953–1980," unpublished manuscript, 1982.

growth of total consumption and national income, and this gap is still not closed. Figure 1 shows the development of total consumption compared with that of gross national income (GNI) in the 1970s through 1983. This gap, which represents a fundamental lack of balance in the Swedish economy, has arisen in conjunction with decreased investments and a growing deficit on current account.

Competitive position and export performance. Because Sweden is a small open economy, the competitive position of her industry and export performance is of great importance for the whole economy.

In the middle of the 1970s the competitive position of Swedish industry declined dramatically because of high increases in wage costs accompanied by an effective appreciation of the Swedish crown. The cost position was later on normalized by a combination of successive devaluations and a more modest development of wage costs.

The development of cost-competitiveness during the 1970s is given in figure 2. This figure also shows the development of Sweden's share of the OECD market for manufactured products. While the increase in Sweden's relative cost position in the middle of the decade caused a sharp fall in market shares, the normalization of cost position later on did not bring about a symmetrical increase in these shares. Instead Swedish shares on export markets seemed to show a downward trend. In figure 2 this decline is 15

Figure 1

GNI, Total Consumption, and Investments (1975 prices); Balance on Current Account (current prices)

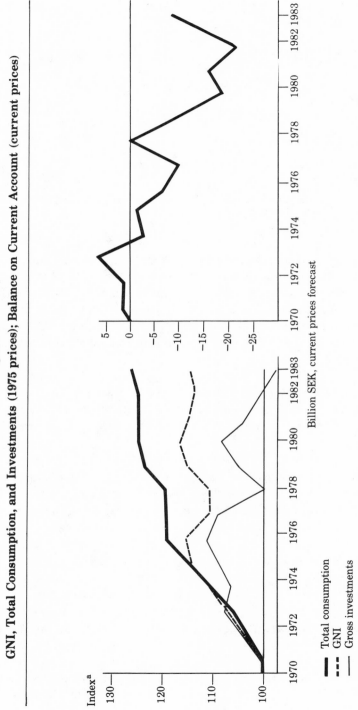

a1970=100.

Source: Central Bureau of Statistics, *National Accounts*, Stockholm, 1983.

Figure 2

**Relative Unit Labor Costs, Swedish Manufactured Exports'
Market Share, and Relative Price for the OECD Area**

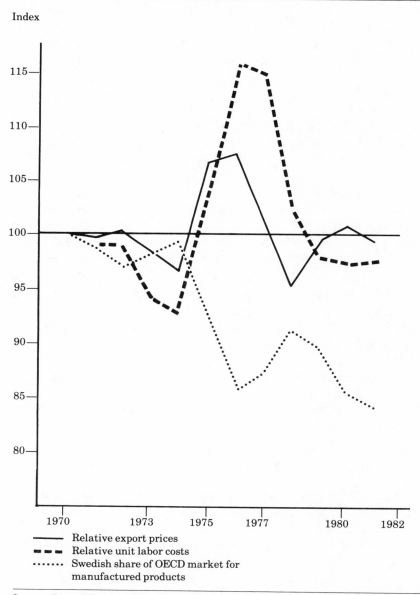

Source: Central Bureau of Statistics, *Statistisha Meddelanden,* Stockholm, 1982.

percent from 1970 to 1981; if the whole world market is included, the total fall amounts instead to 20 percent.

This development coincides with a markedly poorer performance for Swedish industry than the OECD average. This is illustrated by figure 3, which gives an index for Swedish industrial production during the period 1970–82 compared with an index of average OECD industrial production for the same time.

Inflation and unemployment. As in most countries, the inflation trend in Sweden moved upwards during the 1970s. However, there has been a strong cyclical pattern in inflation performance, with each peak and bottom respectively higher than its predecessor. The last inflationary peak in 1980 was 14 percent. Swedish inflation during the 1970s moved fairly close to the OECD average, although at present there is a discrepancy: while the OECD inflation average is moving downwards, inflation in Sweden is increasing.

Employment has been following a similar pattern of deterioration during the 1970s. In this case, however, Swedish performance is far better than the OECD average. While the OECD average is around 10 percent, the Swedish figure on open unemployment is about 3.5 percent, although it should be noted that the number of persons in relief work and other kinds of labor-market measures is quite high. At present they account for another 4 percent of the labor force.

To put the Swedish development into an international perspective, some summary measures on economic performance after 1970 for Sweden and some selected OECD countries are given in table 3.

Decline of the Swedish Model

In hindsight economic development in Sweden in the 1950s and 1960s was very favorable, backed up by a strong growth of investments and very rapid structural changes. Sweden took great advantage of these decades' opportunities for international specialization. Other important components in this development were the elimination of obsolete and/or ineffective capital and the rationalization and increased capacity of existing production.

Table 3

Economic Indicators for Selected OECD Countries

(Percent)

	Year	Sweden	United Kingdom	Denmark	Netherlands	Austria	Finland	Germany	Japan
Real GDP change 1970–79		20.8	17.8	24.7	30.7	44.0	42.0	31.5	65.5
Output per hour, manufacturing, change 1970–79		39.6	41.4	77.6	85.4	75.6	44.1	65.4	110.7
Output in manufacturing, volume, change 1970–79		8.3	–9.3	31.9	27.6	42.7	41.1	22.2	104.0
Exports of manufactured goods, volume, change 1970–1979		46.9	48.1	91.2	78.9	108.0	74.3	78.4	183.2
Industrial employment, share of total employment	1970	38.4	44.1	28.9	37.7	40.3	33.9	47.5	35.7
	1981	31.3	36.3	23.5	31.3	40.1	34.8	44.1	35.3
Public-sector employment, share of total employment	1970	20.6	18.0	16.9	12.1	14.1	12.0	11.2	5.8
	1979	29.8	21.5	24.5	14.7	18.5	18.0	14.7	6.5
Public consumption, share of GDP	1970	21.7	17.7	20.0	16.3	14.7	14.7	15.9	7.4
	1981	29.3	22.3	27.7	17.9	18.4	19.1	20.7	10.2
Private consumption, share of GDP	1970	53.5	61.9	57.4	57.2	54.7	57.6	54.2	52.5
	1981	52.1	60.9	56.1	60.8	56.3	54.5	56.6	57.6
Business investment, share of GDP	1970	10.3	10.7	—	13.6	—	14.2	13.9	23.7
	1979	8.9	10.5	—	10.4	—	11.8	12.4	16.8

Table 3 (cont'd)
Economic Indicators for Selected OECD Countries
(Percent)

	Year	Sweden	United Kingdom	Denmark	Nether-lands	Austria	Finland	Germany	Japan
General government, net lending, share of GDP	1970	4.1	2.5	3.0	-0.8	1.0	4.4	0.3	1.8
	1979	-2.7	-3.3	-3.3	-3.1	-3.4	0.7	-2.9	-4.7
	1981	-5.3	-2.0	-6.9	-4.8	-1.8	n.a.	-4.0	-3.9
Current external balance, share of GDP	1970	-0.8	1.5	-3.4	-1.6	-0.1	-2.2	0.5	1.0
	1979	-2.4	-0.9	-4.4	-1.6	-2.8	-0.5	-0.7	-0.9
	1981	-2.6	2.4	-3.2	2.2	-2.1	-0.6	-1.1	0.4
GDP deflator, change 1970–81		153.1	273.9	150.6	109.7	79.5	206.7	73.7	92.6
Rate of unemployment (national definitions)	1970	1.5	2.6	1.3	1.0	2.4	1.9	0.7	1.2
	1979	2.1	5.4	6.0	4.3	2.0	6.2	3.8	2.1
	1980	2.0	6.8	6.9	5.1	1.9	4.9	3.8	2.0
	1981	2.5	10.6	9.2	7.5	2.5	5.2	4.8	2.2
	1982	3.2	12.2		10.2	3.5		7.0	2.2
		-5.9	-2.0	-9.4	-5.7	-2.2	n.a.	-4.1	-3.3

Source: OECD, *Economic Surveys, 1982–83* (Paris: OECD, 1983).

Figure 3
Industrial Production in Sweden and in OECD, 1970–82

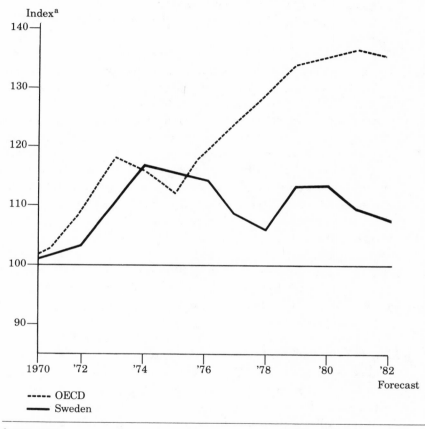

[a]1970=100.

Source: OEDC, *Indicators of Industrial Activity,* Paris, 1983.

An important explanation for the rapid rise of productivity was that Sweden was in an excellent situation due to structural adjustments after the war.[3] Another important explanation lay in economic and labor-market policy at that time. There was also a considerable degree of consensus among unions, employers, and government on basic strategy. Thus the latter 1950s and most of the 1960s can be described as the "golden age of the Swedish model."

The union contributions to this strategy were a recognition of the importance of international cost-competitiveness and a positive attitude (in principle) to mobility and change. A very important principle of labor-union wage policy, however, was the beforementioned strongly egalitarian solidaristic wage program,[4] the aim of which was equal pay for equal jobs regardless of firm, branch, or region. The contribution from the government was the labor-market policy with strong emphasis on mobility and flexibility. Other components were an active stabilization policy for full employment, strong growth in the public sector and in residential construction, and a liberal industrial policy that permitted good profitability.

An important explanation for the rapid structural transformation of the exposed sector lay in the tension between international prices and domestic costs. With a firm dollar and fixed exchange rates, the prices of manufactured goods in international trade were relatively constant. As this was accompanied by relatively rapid wage increases, unchanged margins presupposed that productivity was stepped up by means of investments, rationalization, and economies of scale. Enterprises whose productivity could not keep pace with wages saw their profit margins shrink and were ultimately eliminated.

Wage policy aimed at general wage increases on a scale that would permit unchanged profit margins in the expansive part of industry. These wage increases were also to be imposed on the weak parts of industry, where the resultant contraction and shutdowns would wrinkle out a supply of labor that through an active labor-market policy could then be transferred to the more profitable parts of industry. This would facilitate industrial expansion where Sweden had comparative advantages over producers abroad and where productivity could be increased via economies of scale. Wage formation accordingly helped to boost the rise of productivity and this in turn made it possible to combine good wage agreements with a relatively stable price level and unimpaired competitiveness in the expansive part of industry. At the same time it was possible to achieve an economically viable equalization of the wage structure. The labor discharged from the weak sectors was moved, as a rule, to new enterprises with higher productivity and a stronger wage potential. The equalization of wages accordingly went hand in hand with an equalization of the differences in productivity.

The Swedish wage formation process is closely associated with the so-called "Scandinavian inflation model" that served as a benchmark in the wage negotiations.[5] Wage increases—or the room for wage increases—in the exposed sectors are allocated by productivity growth and internationally determined price increases. Wages in the sheltered sectors are related to wages in the wage-leading exposed part of the economy and prices are determined as a markup on unit labor costs. This implies under certain assumptions an unchanged functional income distribution. Among a number of specific assumptions underlying the model, a level of profits sufficient to generate a high level of investment is perhaps the most crucial. Moreover, in order to preserve full employment and a balanced external position, the model in conjunction with the solidaric wage policy assumes a high degree of mobility of both capital and labor and a high rate of expansion in the high-productivity exposed sectors.[6]

A number of events in the beginning of the 1970s had made this framework less suitable. As we already have seen, wage developments in 1974—76 deviated very importantly from the wage paths given by the model, since the settlement did not anticipate the turnaround in international prices and the public sector tended to become a wage leader. Reduced labor mobility and rigidities reinforced by defensive industrial policies suggest that the model has become obsolete as a guideline for wage policy. Finally, the international recession and subsequent slow growth brought an end to the rapid expansion of output and productivity gains in the exposed sectors, thus limiting the ability of the private sector quickly to absorb employees released from competitive firms.

Even if the model has indeed become obsolete, the solidaric

wage policy has been pursued through the 1970s. This process has
made the wage structure less and less adapted to the structure of
the rest of the economy.

There are many visible effects of this problem. One is the
difficulty that firms now have in recruiting skilled workers even
in conditions of excessive slack in the economy. Another is the increasing amount of subsidies going to weak parts of Swedish industry. When the wage structure is rigid and there is effective
resistance to closing down firms, subsidies tend to become a political necessity.

Even if this process seems obvious enough, it is difficult to pin-
point empirically. Some evidence of the unbalanced development
of the wage structure with the rest of the economy is provided by a
study of the OECD secretariat presented in the 1981 OECD report
on the Swedish economy.[7] The main result of the study is summarized in figure 4, which shows sectoral wage and productivity
differentials from 1963 to 1979. The figure shows that while the
wage differential is decreasing steadily, except for a stop around
1972–73, productivity differentials stop decreasing at 1970. Turning to productivity differential at current prices, which is the more
relevant concept in this connection, one finds a dramatic increase
after 1974. The costs of sustaining this structure of narrowing
wage differential could be expected to be high in terms of inflationary bias and a furthering of the inflexibilities in the labor
market.

There is plentiful evidence of a continuous decrease of flexibility
in the labor market. One clear indication that is relatively independent of economic activity is given in figure 5, where the number of persons who are unemployed or covered by measures of
labor-market policy is related to the total number of vacancies in
the labor market. This shows that a given number of vacancies
has come to be associated with a larger number of persons who are
available for work but do not have a job. This imbalance is an indication that the labor market has become less able to match labor
supply with demand regardless of the demand situation.

Adjustment to a Changing Environment

Many Swedish economic problems during the recession of the
1970s have certainly been common to all industrialized countries.

Figure 4

Sectoral Wage and Productivity Differentials

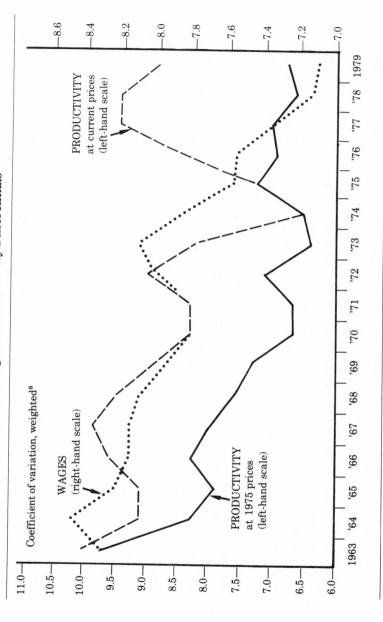

[a]Weighted by number of hours worked in each sector.

Source: OECD, *Economic Surveys; Sweden, June 1981*, Paris, 1981.

Figure 5
Registered Unemployment and Persons covered by Labor-Market Policy (U) in Relation to No. of Vacancies (V), Both as a Percentage of the Labor Force
(annual average)

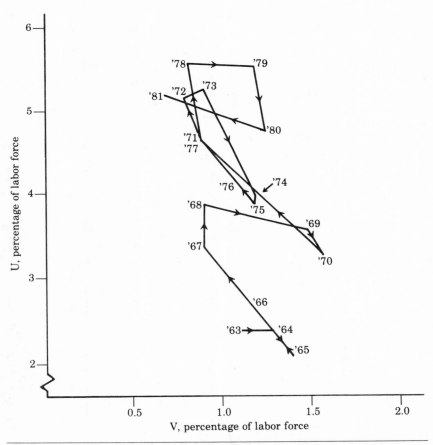

Source: Government Medium-Term Survey 1982, *Growth or Stagnation*
(Stockholm: Ministry of Economic Affairs, 1982).

From Sweden's viewpoint the problems have naturally been heightened by the weak, irregular development in other industrial countries. The new competitive conditions in mining, the steel industry, and shipbuilding were also of particular importance.

The price increases for oil did create a dilemma for stabilization policy in industrial countries because of the sharply impaired terms of trade. However, together with other changes in the world economy the price shifts also necessitated a structural adjustment among the industrial economies. It is becoming clear that an inability to make this adjustment goes far toward explaining the persistence of the problems in these countries, and this aspect of Swedish development warrants a brief recapitulation of the changes of the 1970s. Some of the important respects in which international development in the 1970s has called for structural adjustment in industrial countries, Sweden included, are as follows[8]

- The deterioration in terms of trade necessitates a relative downward adjustment of real earnings and total domestic consumption.

- A return of external balance in the longer run requires a shift in production from sheltered to exposed sectors.

- Achieving this shift in a market economy presupposes a shift in relative earnings and relative profitability in favor of the exposed sector; in other words, profits and earnings in industry must rise relative to other sectors.

- The changes in relative prices also make it necessary to restructure industry; the impaired conditions for shipbuilding and the basic metal industry have already been noted, but the need for structural change is not confined to these branches.

- The new relative prices mean that a considerable part of the existing capital stock is economically obsolete; extensive new investments are therefore needed to maintain the capacity for growth.

- With the higher prices for oil and energy, the irrelative utilization must be reduced.

The points listed above refer to changes that are needed chiefly as a consequence of increased prices for oil and energy together with new conditions for competition. It should not be forgotten, however, that structural change is part and parcel of economic development, not least via the introduction of new technology. With the additional factors listed above, there are many indications that development in the 1970s involved an accentuated need for economic flexibility.

Taking the 1970s as a whole, it can be said that the Swedish economy was not particularly successful in meeting these demands for structural change. There was in fact only one respect in which development moved in the right direction: the relative input of energy in general and oil in particular has decreased. In all other respects, adjustment on the whole has been contrary to what was desired.

The Real Wage Gap

After OPEC I real earnings Sweden, instead of falling, rose very strongly and then leveled off on a high plateau relative to productivity. This is illustrated in figure 6, which shows the "real wage gap" in the Swedish economy.

The same lack of adjustment is evident from figure 1, where total consumption is related to GNI. Both charts reflect the combined effects of the excessive wage-cost increases and the very expansionary bridging policy pursued in the middle of the 1970s. The effect was that the terms-of-trade loss from the oil price increase fell on profits and on the balance of payments.[9]

This contributed to an extremely depressed profit situation for Swedish industry in the latter part of the decade. Figure 7 illustrates this. As can be seen, the average rate of return on real capital in industry has after 1975 been far below the bond yield. The relevant comparison is of course between long-term bond yield and the anticipated rate of return on investment. However, the existence of a wide negative gap for a long time between historical averages of the two variables has most probably been creating the expectation that this situation will persist. Therefore there has not since the middle of the 1970s been any great incentive to invest in net new real capital in Swedish industry. From this perspective the stagnation and decline of capacity in Swedish industry after 1975 seems quite natural.

Real Wage Gap

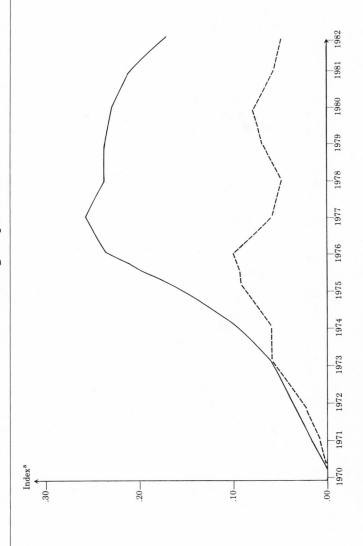

Index[a]

.30

.20

.10

.00

1970 1971 1972 1973 1974 1975 1976 1977 1978 1979 1980 1981 1982

—— Total real labor cost per person employed

--- Real GNI per person employed

[a]1970=100.

Source: Central Bureau of Statistics, *National Accounts, 1983*, Stockholm, 1983.

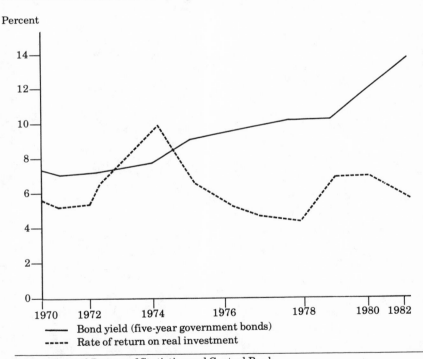

Figure 7
Rate of Return in Industry and Bond Yield

Percent

Bond yield (five-year government bonds)
Rate of return on real investment

Source: Central Bureau of Statistics and Central Bank.

Subsidies and Sectoral Adjustment

While economic policy on the macro level initially worked against the desirable adjustment, the same is true when it comes to sectoral adjustment. During the 1970s, as will be shown, subsidies to the business sector increased dramatically.

There exists a recent literature on the theory of effective protection.[10] This theory underlines the effects of a tariff for one sector on other sectors; in a general equilibrium setting one finds that a considerable part of an import duty is shifted on to the export sector in the form of a tax. This explains the observed fact that protection does not increase total employment. It also shows that there can be no protection for the economy at large: protection that enables some industries to maintain a larger scale of operations than would otherwise be possible is paid for by unintended and undesired shrinkage of other industries.

Unfortunately there does not seem to exist a similarly well-developed general equilibrium theory for subsidies. Intuitively, one could expect similar results as accompany the theory of effective protection. Since a subsidy generally introduces an inefficiency into the economy, the introduction of a subsidy could be expected to decrease or at least not to increase the total productive capacity. Therefore the resulting activity increase in a subsidized sector has to take place at the expense of the activity in unsubsidized sectors. The crowding out of the unsubsidized sectors will take place partly via the financing requirement introduced by the subsidies and partly via the wage increases them induced by them.

During the 1970s there has been in the Swedish economy an increasing subsidization of certain parts of the sheltered sector. Subsidies also rose strongly to the industrial sector, for the most part to the branches that should be contracted—e.g., shipbuilding, basic metal industries, and textiles.

Figure 8 summarizes the development between 1970 and 1980 of the direct transfers that have gone in one form or another to the various branches.[11] Agriculture and the food sector received 1.7 billion kronor in transfers in 1970; in 1980 the figure had risen to 5.3 billion or around 1 percent of GDP. The housing sector received the equivalent of not quite 1 percent of GDP in 1970, while in 1980 the amount was equivalent to almost 4 percent of

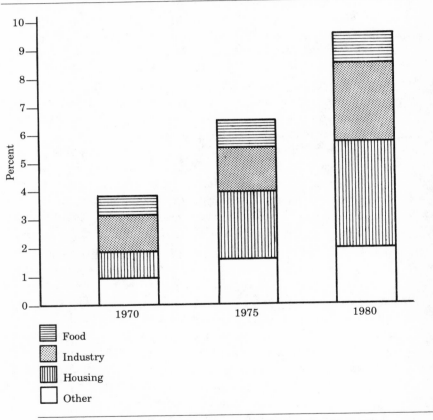

Figure 8

Public Subsidies to the Business Sector as a Percentage of GDP

Source: Government Medium-Term Survey, 1982, *Growth or Stagnation*
(Stockholm: Ministry of Economic Affairs, 1982).

GDP. In industry, subsidies and support in 1980 totaled 2.8 percent of GDP, while the figure in 1970 had been 1.3 percent.

In addition, several activities that belonged to the sheltered part of the market sector in the early 1970s and were subsidized to a certain extent have been incorporated in the public sector and are accordingly subsidized in full.[12] Furthermore it is estimated that at the end of the 1970s, border protection for the agricultural sector cost the Swedish economy 8.4 billion kronor,[13] i.e., 1.6 percent of GDP in 1980, though it is difficult to tell whether this represents an increase from 1970. For the textile industry corresponding calculations put the cost at the end of the 1970s at 1.6 percent of GDP.

On top of this there is the relative discrimination against industry that is inherent in the organization of the Swedish money and capital market. The ongoing rise in the general interest level has accentuated the capital market's discrimination against the non-priority sectors, of which industry is one.

Viewed in the short run, it is easier to see these subsidies' relative advantage for the sectors receiving them than the relative disadvantage for the other sectors. In the longer run, however, it is clear that other activities must suffer from this transfer of resources—one can hardly argue that the policy of subsidies has helped to enlarge the Swedish economy's total resources.

The burden on other sectors, including industry, can be illustrated with the aid of figure 8. Subsidies totaled 3.7 percent of GDP in 1970 and 9.6 percent in 1980, a difference that in 1980 is equivalent to over 30 billion kronor. This is more than half of the revenue from payroll charges or almost 90 percent of the revenue from value-added tax (VAT).

If the level of subsidies in 1980 had been the same as in 1970, there would have been financial scope to cut, for example, the payroll taxes by approximately 15 percent. This would probably have increased wages paid out and it would also have reduced total wage costs. The first effect would have given the unsubsidized sectors an increased share of consumption and the second would have led to an improvement in their relative competitiveness. A similar line of reasoning can be applied, of course, to the rapid expansion of public activities in the 1970s.

It may be less apparent that the regulation of money and capital markets has put industry at a disadvantage because it can be argued that, with this regulation, interest has been below the market rate even for nonpriority loans.

It is clear, however, that the system has shifted the relative profitability of investments to the detriment of the nonpriority sectors. Furthermore, the low interest rate in the priority sectors has been achieved via investment obligations on, for example, the National Pension Insurance Fund, other pension funds, and insurance companies. As a result, these institutions have had to levy higher charges than would have been necessary with a market rate for their investments. This in turn tends to raise the level of costs in the economy as a whole.

The effects of the relative discrimination of industry are visible enough (see, e.g., figure 3). Considering the order of magnitude of the subsidies to other sectors, this must be counted as an important explanatory factor behind the very poor performance of Swedish industry during the 1970s.

As mentioned earlier, it is only in the energy sector that adjustment during the 1970s has gone in the desired direction. The relative consumption of energy in general and oil in particular have both been reduced during the decade. This development is bound up with a policy of allowing external price increases for oil to work through to consumption. This price policy has been implemented, moreover, with an active policy for regulating energy-saving investments in various fields.

With respect to the need for greater flexibility in the economy, the policy of subsidies has had a contrary effect: it frequently shields individuals and firms from adjustments that are necessary from an economic point of view. There have also been other sources for decreased flexibility. We have already pointed to developments in the labor market. As we shall see in the next section, developments on the public-sector side seem also to have worked in the direction of decreased flexibility.

The remarks made in this section indicate that the oil shock per se might have been less of a disturbance to the Swedish economy than the negative internal adjustment process brought about by the economic policy response and the wage response to that shock. The cumulative effect of OPEC I and OPEC II on Swedish terms of trade has been estimated as a loss amounting to 3 percent of GDP. This is a significant amount. However, in a time span of ten years a strong and flexible economy should have the capacity to adjust to a disturbance of this order of magnitude. All of the needs for adjustment listed above are in conformity with a market response to the oil shocks.

A government policy of nonintervention and nonaccommodation would therefore probably have brought about the necessary adjustment at much lower costs than those inflicted by the policies actually pursued.

Growth of Public Expenditure

The Swedish economy has failed to adjust to the demands imposed by international developments. The resultant difficulties have underscored the problems that were created by the rapid growth of public consumption and public expenditure in Sweden in the 1970s. There is reason to stress that the growth of public expenditure is part and parcel of a fundamental structural change in the Swedish economy, whereby the public sector has come to play an increasing part in every sector of the economy.

This circumstance has been illustrated earlier in the figures on the rapid growth of subsidies to various sectors of the economy. Another illustration, presented in table 4, is provided by the marked increase since 1965 in the number of persons who are directly dependent on the public sector in one way or another. The table shows, by kind of transfer, the number of persons who are provided for annually mainly by the public sector via transfers (categories 2–7), as well as the labor input in man-years in the public sector (category 1). The total number of man-years in the private sector is also given for comparison (category 9). In relation to the total number of man-years, the number of persons provided for by the public sector almost doubled between 1965 and 1980.

On top of this, since 1965 there has been a continuous improvement in the relative standard accorded to those covered by public-sector insurance. Quantitatively, the most substantial improvement concerns pensions, with a marked increase in the real value of basic pensions and a growing number of persons who qualify for a national supplementary pension.

In 1981 there were 750,000 persons receiving national supple-

Table 4
Number of Persons in Public Production and Public Insurance and Number of Man-Years Worked
(in thousands)

	1965	1970	1975	1980
1 Employed in public sector[a]	572	854	893	1042
2 Old-age pensioners	827	947	1062	1362
3 Unemployed	44	59	68	84
4 Labor market measures	30	66	86	122
5 Disablement pensioners	161	188	289	281
6 Registered sick[b]	203	262	288	274
7 Parental leave[c]	26	28	46	75
8 Total in employment	4206	4189	3919	3856
9. Employed in business sector[a]	3634	3335	3056	2814
Total 1 through 7	1863	2404	2732	3240
Total 1 through 7÷8	0.44	0.57	0.70	0.84
Total 1 through 7÷9	0.51	0.72	0.89	1.15

[a]Workdays in hours converted into man-years.

[b]Average number per day receiving sick benefit.

[c]Average number receiving parental benefit (for 1965 and 1970, number of gainfully employed women receiving maternity benefit).

Source: Government Medium-Term Survey, 1982, *Growth or Stagnation* (Stockholm: Ministry of Economic Affairs).

mentary pensions. When this system is fully operative (around 1990) there will be more than 1.3 million.

Table 4 covers development in the market and public sectors. To catch the structural change behind these figures, one should also include production in the household sector and in the unregistered (black market) sector.

A key factor behind economic development in the twentieth century has been the greatly increased element of specialization in all parts of the economy. One consequence of this has been the diminishing part that households play as production units. Just as industrialization and the elimination of a peasant society primarily involved transferring the production of goods to the market sector, so in general has postwar development chiefly involved transferring the production of services to the market and public sectors. Notable examples are public health care, care of the aged, child care, and child-minding. In the home, these tasks were undertaken chiefly by women. The transfer of these services has accordingly been accompanied on the labor side by a sharp increase in participation rates for women.

The vigorous buildup of social insurance in the 1960s and 1970s has appreciably strengthened the economic security of those who become unemployed, ill, or old. At the same time, this too represents a transfer of activities from the household and market sectors to the public sector. Private savings, private insurance, and intrafamily transfers have been replaced by corresponding public activities financed from tax revenue.

Demographic development has gone in the same direction as other factors behind the public sector's rapid growth. The buildup of the pension system and public responsibility for care of the sick and aged have been accompanied by a large increase in the number of pensioners as a share of the total population as well as in absolute terms.

The process described here is common to all industrialized countries. What is unique for Sweden, however, is that such a large part of the growing service sector has also become part of the public sector. The resulting expenditure and tax pattern during the 1970s is given in figure 9. Public expenditure as a share of GDP has increased from 45 percent in 1970 to 70 percent in 1982.

During most of the 1970s the trend in public expenditure was to increase by about 6 percent a year in real terms. Since 1979 this growth rate has slowed down significantly. This is a result of a virtual stop in new spending programs, and to some extent of an effort to cut down on existing programs. Still, the expenditure growth after 1979 has been around 3 to 4 percent a year. It turns out that a growth rate of this magnitude is what emerges purely automatically in public spending. The driving forces here are the development of the national pension funds system, local government spending patterns, and interest payments on the fast-growing government debt.

At the same time, the tax ratio has increased from 40 percent in 1970 to a little above 50 percent in 1982. There has been a significant increase in the tax rate; but this has not been sufficient to finance the dramatic increase in public expenditure. Instead, the public-sector deficit has been growing at a fast rate. This certainly

Figure 9
Public-Sector Share of GDP

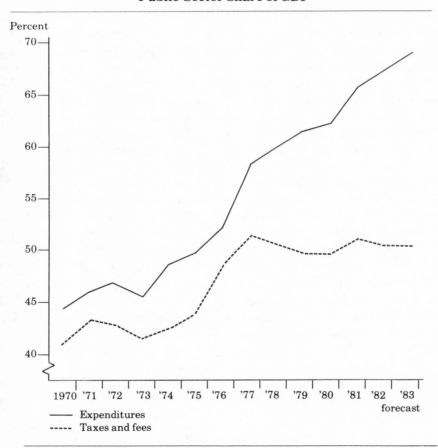

Percent

——— Expenditures
----- Taxes and fees

Source: National Institute of Economic Research, *The Swedish Economy 1983, 1984,* Stockholm, 1983, 1984.

reflects the fact that fiscal policy in certain years was unduly expansive in the sense that it generated an inflationary degree of capacity utilization. Above all, however, it reflects the economy's lack of structural adjustment. Fiscal policy no longer acts as a regulator of activity; instead, it has been used in a persistent attempt to keep demand and employment up in an economy that is not adapted to prevailing relative prices and demand conditions.

The rest of this section will be devoted to the question of the extent to which tax increases and deficit increases per se have been detrimental to economic growth and economic activity.

Starting with taxation, one has to consider marginal tax rates as well as the average ratio. During the 1970s the progressivity of the Swedish tax system in conjunction with the transfer system was increased considerably; therefore marginal tax rates in general have grown faster than average tax rates. The development of marginal tax rates for ordinary income earners since 1950 is given in table 5. The figures indicate the total marginal effect, so they include all taxes plus the marginal effect of income-dependent transfers. The table shows that the average total marginal effect for an average industrial worker has increased from about 67 percent in 1970 to nearly 82 percent in 1982. The same figures for an average white collar worker are 68 percent in 1970 and 88 percent in 1982.

Marginal effects of this magnitude could certainly be expected to have a significant influence on economic behavior. Recently various attempts have been made to estimate the relation between total tax rates and production in the Swedish economy. Stuart[14] and Feige[15] both reach the conclusion that Sweden is on the downward-sloping part of the Laffer curve. Stuart in his study finds that 75 percent of the decline in Swedish growth rates in the 1970s could be explained by increased taxes. Hansson and Stuart in their 1982 study based on average tax rates conclude that while Sweden is still on the upward portion of the Laffer curve, it is on a segment where tax increases have become sharply detrimental to output.[16] In a 1981 study focused solely on income taxation, Jakobsson and Normann reached a similar conclusion.[17]

Considering the height of Swedish tax rates, the conclusions reported seem rather plausible. If they are correct, the policy implications certainly are very strong. So far the results must be

Table 5

Total Marginal Effect at Different Incomes; Average Wages

(1980 prices, Swedish crowns)

| | Income level | | | | | Average wages | |
| | | | | | | Full-time blue | Full-time white |
Year	30,000	60,000	90,000	120,000		collar worker	collar worker
1955	37.9	45.3	49.4	52.0		~42,000	~56,000
1960	47.2	55.0	58.4	59.5		44,510	62,064
1970	64.0	68.3	67.0	68.1		59,725	86,952
1975	59.2	69.1	73.6	74.8		65,109	100,884
1980	61.8	70.2	80.8	85.5		61,100	93,192
1982	61.7	72.8	81.8	88.3		59,650	86,520

Sources: For marginal effects, Hansson (1983). See note 18. For average wages, SAF, *Wage Statistics* (Stockholm: SAF, 1983).

treated with caution because the studies are based upon very simplified models that rely necessarily on arbitrary assumptions. Feige shows that even if an extreme degree of flexibility is assumed in the behavioral equations, his results still hold— although further studies have to be made on the behavioral equations before firm conclusions will be possible. Thus far it is possible to affirm only that present Swedish tax rates at best severely restrict growth.

Turning to the effects of deficit financing, one might usefully begin by indicating how the development of the general budget deficit fit into the overall picture of savings and investment in Sweden during the 1970s and the beginning of the 1980s. In table 6 it is shown that public-sector financial savings moved from a surplus in 1970 of 4.5 percent to a deficit in 1982 of 6.6 percent as a share of GDP. Public-sector investments have increased somewhat as a share of GDP, thereby limiting the total fall in gross public saving to 10 percentage units of GDP. During the same period gross private savings were virtually unchanged, so total savings in the economy have fallen roughly the same amount as gross public savings.

The counterpart to the fall in public savings is given by a fall in gross fixed private investment by 4 percentage units of GDP, by a decrease in inventory investments by another 4 percent of GDP, and a decline of the current account position by 3.2 percent of GDP. (It is difficult to interpret the inventory figures. The excessive inventory buildup in 1970 actually hides a more favorable underlying external position at that time, while the reverse might be true in 1982.)

These figures seem to indicate a strong crowding-out process during the 1970s. There have, however, been few signs of such a process in credit and capital markets. Indeed, real interest rates in Sweden have been kept at a remarkably low level. This is illustrated in table 7, which compares Sweden with three other deficit champions and the total European community with respect to real interest rates, inflation, and monetary growth. The table gives averages for 1980–82. With mildly more inflationary financing than the average of the European community, Swedish real interest rates have been kept at the remarkably low level of 1.3 percent while the community average has been 2.3 percent.

Table 6
Change in Public-Sector Saving and Capital Formation

	1970	1982	Difference
Gross fixed private investment	17.0	13.0	−4.0
Gross public investment	4.9	6.0	1.1
Inventory investment	3.3	−1.0	−4.3
Current account	−0.5	−3.7	−3.2
Total saving	24.9	14.3	−10.6
Gross private saving	15.5	14.9	−0.6
Gross public saving	9.4	−0.6	−10.0
Public-sector surplus	4.5	−6.6	−11.1

Source: National Institute of Economic Research, *The Swedish Economy, 1971, 1983,* Stockholm, 1971, 1983.

Table 7
Deficit, Real Interest Rate, and Inflation, 1980−82
(percent per annum)

	Real interest rate	Inflation		Monetary growth	Public deficit as a share of GDP
		GDP deflator	Consumer price index		
Belgium	5.1	5.6	8.1	5.2	11.9
Denmark	7.5	9.5	10.7	9.6	7.5
Italy	1.2	18.5	18.5	17.3	10.6
EEC average	2.3	10.6	11.1	10.8	4.4
Sweden	1.3	10.2	11.4	12.5	5.0

Sources: EEC-Commission, *European Economy, No. 14, 1982,* Luxembourg, 1982; National Institute of Economic Research, *The Swedish Economy,* Stockholm, 1983.

Both Denmark and Belgium, where the shifts in use of savings from financing investment to financing deficit have been of a magnitude comparable to Sweden's, have had far higher interest rates than Sweden. One reason for the smoothness of this process in Sweden might be regulations in credit and capital markets that were designed in part precisely to keep interest rates down.

Part of the rationing system in the Swedish capital market has been that institutions—pension funds, insurance companies— have been obliged to buy bonds at lower-than-market rates, especially to finance housing investment. With falling housing investment in the 1970s the obligation to buy housing bonds has been shifted over to an obligation to buy government bonds for deficit financing.

Another reason for the apparent smoothness of the shifting process is the low rates of return investment in the business sector, meaning that there has been little need for high interest rates to hold back credit demand for business investment. This point is illustrated by figure 7, which shows the development from 1970 of the rate of return on real investment and the rate of return on long-term government bonds.

It has been shown how excessive increases in wage costs and public policies of subsidizing ailing sectors have created a crowding out of production and investment in the private sector. In particular this process has undermined the competitive position of Swedish industry. It has also contributed to the balance-of-payments problem in the Swedish economy. The fast growth of the budget deficit seems to be a result of this process rather than a cause of it.

An increase in investment activity and capital formation must, however, be an integral part of a return to equilibrium for the Swedish economy. If this process is ever to get started, one has to expect increasing difficulties in financing the deficit. As soon as the recovery process is under way, crowding out in the credit market will certainly become a major problem.

Present Policies and Prospects

During the last few years there has understandably been a growing awareness in Swedish society that the Swedish economy is running into a severe disequilibrium. Attempts have accordingly been made to change the general trends described in this paper. As already noted, the devaluation in 1977 in combination with a rather modest wage development have worked toward restoring the competitive position of Swedish industry.

In 1981 the former nonsocialist government embarked on a new policy toward public spending. By cutting in public programs it would be possible to counteract the automatic increases in public expenditure. During 1981 and 1982 a couple of "savings plans" for the public sector were implemented.

The present social-democratic government, which came into office in October 1982, to an extent has reversed this policy. However, this government also has a cautious approach to public spending. Consequently, growth of public spending this year will approach zero.

The most important area of reorientation is industrial subsidies. Very few new undertakings are made which means that the net result has been a rather fast phasing out of industrial subsidies.

The devaluations in combination with a cyclical upswing the last couple of years have created a climate where there is very little demand for new subsidies. Therefore the new restrictive policy on industrial subsidies has so far not been put to a severe test.

Apart from the area of industrial subsidies, the general principles for public sector spending have not been changed. Therefore cuts in public expenditure have to take place within the framework of the existing structure. Moreover, the dependence on the automaticity in the present programs is still very strong.

In 1982, two of the nonsocialist parties together with the social democrats decided upon a planned decrease of marginal tax rates in the income tax. Under favorable assumptions about developments of other taxes this reform would, according to a 1983 study by Hansson,[18] take total marginal tax rates as reported in table 5 back to the level of 1975. Even this modest change, however, will be diminished by some changes in the tax schedule that have been implemented recently.

In 1981 there was a devaluation of the Swedish Crown by 10 percent. The new social-democratic government made another devaluation, by 16 percent in 1982. These devaluations have improved the competitive position in Swedish industry as well as the profit situation considerably. The devaluations, of course, also work towards closing the real wage gap in the Swedish economy.

These improvements have made Swedish industry relatively well placed to take advantage of the international recovery. Swedish industry is now regaining shares of export markets and industrial growth in the upswing is markedly faster than the European average. In order to return to an equilibrium position with low inflation and full employment, it is necessary that the present improvement in capacity utilization is followed by capacity growth and a restructuring of the economy in the direction that is indicated by the price-signals of the devaluation.

In order for this process to take place the following two conditions will have to be met: (1) the supply side should be flexible enough to avoid inflationary bottlenecks; and (2) the relative cost and profit situation achieved should be maintained for a considerable time.

Concerning the first condition, most of the problems connected with a high public-sector expenditure remain. On the positive side, however, there has been a phasing out of industrial subsidies. The inflexibilities in the economy that are inflicted by the extremely high marginal tax rates will remain a restriction for growth and adjustment.

The growth of the public sector deficit has been halted; however, the deficit is still large enough to cause problems of financing. These problems will become acute when or if the broad-based growth of investment, which is an integral part of a self-sustained growth path, takes place.

In regard to the wage structure, the devaluation could be expected to further widen the gap between market shadow wages on the one hand and actual wages on the other. In the export-led upswing that is aimed at, this condition highly increases the risks of the inflation that always goes with a devaluation.

Many problems in the Swedish economy are the direct result of government economic policies. But despite a rather gloomy picture, there are areas of strength. One is the industrial base, which, despite stagnation in recent years, is still very strong. Another is the human capital base, with a skilled and well-educated labor force.

The future of the Swedish economy will depend on the broad

course of economic policy. If current policies remain basically unchanged, the economy will in all probability continue to deteriorate. On the other hand, major policy reforms could lay the basis for a buoyant economic future.

Whether such reforms will occur is an open question. While awareness of Sweden's economic problems is growing, most measures needed to restore economic growth run counter to the postwar political culture in Sweden. Policy reforms, by and large, have thus been limited to using devaluations to reduce real wages. The need for internal reform is still very great. It remains to be seen whether Swedish policymakers will have the courage to act.

5

FRANK WOLTER

From Economic Miracle to Stagnation: On the German Disease

Over the last three decades or so, the West German economy has exhibited impressive growth by international as well as historical comparison. Between 1950 and 1982, real gross domestic product (GDP) expanded at an average annual rate of 4.7 percent—which compares with 3.9 percent for the OECD countries as a whole over the same period, and 2.7 percent for Germany over the last 130 years.[1]

Despite strong average growth, Germany's growth rate was uneven during the post–World War II period. In fact, GDP growth declined from business cycle to business cycle. In the 1950s, historically unprecedented growth was accompanied by decreasing unemployment and low inflation. In the 1960s, lower but still rapid growth was accompanied by full employment and moderate

95

inflation. In the 1970s, a further slowdown of growth was accompanied by rapidly accelerating inflation and, after 1973, by a quadrupling of the unemployment rate. The 1980s began with stagnation combined with an even higher unemployment rate and persistent inflation (table 1).

Many factors contributed to this situation in which, within a generation, the German economy turned from a celebrated "miracle" into a serious problem—an economy suffering from serious malaise, much like many other industrial countries. To explain these developments, increasing numbers of people in Germany are concluding that the fault lies in the gradual, postwar erosion of market forces and the increasing institutional command over resources and relative prices—long lags of price responses to changes in the economic environment, weak feedbacks in case of overshooting, and an erosion of incentives to work, save, and invest.

The Economic Miracle

West Germany emerged from World War II as an occupied, segmented territory administered by the Allied Forces. The institutional and economic structure was largely destroyed; malnutrition prevailed; serious unemployment concomitant with the devastated capital stock was significantly aggravated by the inflow of millions of refugees and expellees from the eastern parts of the former Reich. Economic activity was strictly regulated under a system of rationing. Yet the country possessed important advantages for rapid economic growth: an inherited know-how for material production; an ample supply of entrepreneurial talents; and a highly motivated, skilled labor force (though mainly composed of old and young workers). As today, the key question was how to mobilize this potential.

The foundation of what often, in hindsight, was called an "economic miracle" was set by the decision to base the country's reconstruction on a liberal system. This meant private control over productive resources and competition as the engine of economic development.[2] Despite its emphasis on the market mechanism—including the conception of an open economy in Germany as the basic tool for resource allocation and the basic weapon

Table 1

Economic Growth, Unemployment, and Inflation in the Federal Republic of Germany, 1950–83[a]

(percent)

	Cycle[a]						
	1950–55	1955–60	1960–65	1965–70	1970–73	1973–79	1979–83
Economic growth[b,f]	9.5	6.3	5.0	4.2	3.9	2.4	0.2
Per capita[c,f]	8.4	5.0	3.7	3.5	3.2	2.6	0.1
Unemployment[d,f]	7.5	3.0	0.8	1.2	1.0	4.1	6.7
Inflation[e,f]	1.9	1.8	2.8	2.3	5.8	4.5	4.9

[a] Peak to peak.

[b] Average annual rate of change of real gross domestic product (1950 to 1960: prices of 1954; 1960 to 1983: prices of 1976).

[c] Average annual rate of change of real gross domestic product per inhabitant (1950 to 1960: prices of 1954; 1960 to 1983: prices of 1976).

[d] Average share of unemployed in total labor force excluding self-employed.

[e] Average annual rate of change of consumer prices.

[f] 1950 to 1960 excluding Saarland and Berlin (West).

Source: Statistiches Bundesamt, *Statistisches Jahrbuch*, various issues—estimates of the Institut für Weltwirtschaft.

against monopoly—the new economic order foresaw an active role
for the government. The public sector was to set and continuously
monitor the conditions for a smooth functioning of the market
("Ordnungspolitik"), to provide for a social infrastructure (a comprehensive social security system, education, care for war victims,
etc.), and to intervene in case of market failure. Moreover, it was
established that direct intervention should be consistent with the
maintenance of a competitive order ("marktkonform").[3] In fact,
throughout the 1950s, the government interfered extensively in
the allocation of resources to help overcome structural bottlenecks. Key sectors of the economy (basic foodstuffs, coal, steel,
transportation, communication, housing) remained under strict
government control, some of them up to the present.[4] Fiscal policy
was shaped to lower the fiscal burden and to favor investment at
the expense of consumption. The measures included a lowering of
tax rates (from a previously high level), numerous tax exemptions
for savings, accelerated depreciation allowances, reduced tax
rates for reinvested profits, an ample supply of soft loans,[5] and a
variety of export promotion measures.

Control of inflation was the second cornerstone of Germany's
growth policy. Price-level stability was regarded as an important
precondition for economic prosperity because confidence in the
value of money had been shaken by two large inflationary shocks
within the preceding thirty years. The newly established independent central bank pursued tight monetary policies throughout the
1950s. As a welcome side effect, high interest rates induced private savings that could be channeled into investment.

A third basic ingredient to the German recovery was the weakness of special-interest groups.[6] Many of these organizations had
been deprived of their power already under Nazi rule or, later, by
decree of the Allied Forces. They were embedded in a quasi-
anarchic economic environment, built on a weak financial basis,
and they enjoyed loose links to the new political leadership at best.
Hence they had only limited leverage throughout the 1950s. This
was in particular true for the unions, which in the second half of
the 1940s had reorganized themselves on the basis of in-
dustrywide associations. In view of the high unemployment and
the elastic labor supply, their bargaining power was severely circumscribed.[7] Pleas for an aggressive wage policy on the part of the

unions—allegedly designed to, among other things, force business into rationalization of its investment—found little support, not least because it was argued that a wage push would readily translate itself into inflation. The trade unions' position was also undermined by a worker mentality that could be labeled the "new modesty." Given this institutional framework, the virtuous cycle that the German economy was to enter rested on a number of catalysts, in particular:

- an elastic supply of venture capital due to foreign aid (Marshall Plan) and a high rate of domestic savings;[8]

- high international competitiveness at the going (fixed) exchange rate due to low real wages and negligible inflation relative to Germany's major trading partners;[9]

- bright demand prospects due to the stimuli for investment, suppressed consumer demand, and the liberalization of world markets in the framework of the General Agreement on Tariffs and Trade (GATT) and the Organization of European Economic Cooperation (OEEC);

- rapid productivity advances due to static economies of scale, learning by doing, restructuring from agriculture toward the relatively productive manufacturing sector, reallocations within sectors and firms, and positive vintage effects that came along with the reconstruction of the capital stock.

At the end of the 1950s, five million new jobs—corresponding to 24 percent of the 1950 labor force—had been created in addition to massive changes in the employment structure across and within sectors of the economy; full employment was attained; and the living standard of the population exceeded historical records.

Economic growth was disproportional with regard to sectors, regions, firms, institutions, and social groups: manufacturing expanded relative to other sectors, the coal and steel center of Nordrhein-Westfalen (Ruhr area) and the relatively industrialized state of Baden-Württemberg developed ahead of other German regions, large firms grew more rapidly than small- and medium-sized establishments, governmental growth lagged behind the private sector, and capital owners gained relative to labor (table 2). These disproportionalities were only partly the

Table 2

Economic Growth, Employment, Production Structure, and Income Distribution in the Federal Republic of Germany[a]

	1950	1955	1960
Real gross domestic product per capita (1950=100)[b]	100	149.9	191.5
Employment (thousands)	19,997	22,830	24,792
Gross fixed capital formation in percent of GNP[c]	22.6	26.3	26.8
Share of wages in GNP[d] (percent)	65.5	61.6	60.4
Real wages (1950=100)[e]	100	136.6	176.8
Labor productivity (1950=100)[f]	100	142.8	183.6
Terms of trade[g] (1950=100)	100	123	141
Share of government consumption in GNP[c] (percent)	14.5	13.4	13.4
Share of employment in large firms[h] (percent)	34.6[i]	36.8	40.1
Share of manufacturing in GNP[c]	38.3	41.4	42.4
Share of Nordrhein-Westfalen and Baden-Württemberg in GNP[c] (percent)	46.1	48.1	48.3

[a]Excluding Saarland and Berlin (West).

[b]In 1954 prices.

[c]In current prices.

[d]Adjusted for changes in the share of self-employed.

[e]Gross wages and salaries per employee deflated by prices for private consumption.

[f]Gross domestic product in 1954 prices per employee.

[g]Unit value of exports deflated by unit value of imports.

[h]Establishments with 1000 and more employees; manufacturing only.

[i]1953.

Source: Statistisches Bundesamt, *Statistisches Jahrbuch,* various issues.

result of market forces; they also reflected the specific policy mix adopted. The emphasis was on growth and employment stimulation via a strengthening of the supply side, even if it was to be achieved only at the expense of a deterioration of the income distribution. De facto, labor was prepared to support this conception because it produced a rapid rise of real wages.

Despite its undisputed successes, the new economic policy also had its drawbacks beyond the distributional issue. The various interventions in the capital market are likely to have led to a certain amount of capital waste and have biased Germany's economy toward capital-intensive production. The fixed exchange rate implied sooner or later an undervaluation of the currency or imported inflation, and presumably both.[10] Finally, further rigidities were introduced into the economy when social objectives were pursued partly via price policies rather than via direct transfers (mining, housing, transportation).

The Age of Capital

Germany entered the 1960s as a full-employment economy exhibiting high international competitiveness due to low input prices and a modern capital stock by international comparison. Throughout the 1960s economic growth remained well above the historical trend, although the economy grew less rapidly than in the 1950s.

The outstanding performance of the German economy with regard to historical standards was based on a high propensity to invest. On average, the share of domestic product devoted to investment surpassed the long-term average by a significant margin[11] and was even higher than in the 1950s.[12] This lively investment activity rested in turn on longer-term profit expectations that were optimistic for the following reasons: First, the new economic order had proved to be efficient in bringing about high economic growth and full employment. By then, this order was accepted by all major economic agents,[13] and hence formed the basis of a strong social consensus. Second, German investors benefited from being latecomers because forecasting future consumption patterns was significantly helped by looking at the experience of forerunners abroad. Also, at the development stage there was ample scope for imitating products and production processes developed in the leading nations of the world economy, in particular in the United States. Third, in the framework of GATT, barriers to entry to the world market were removed.[14] Germany could take particular advantage of this development because (1) as a country poor in natural resources, her economic development would have been seriously constrained were it not for the elastic supply of cheap raw materials and energy in world markets; (2) her supply structure was biased toward the income-elastic segment of the world market, notably capital goods and other manufactures; (3) given the rigid exchange system and Germany's relative price-level stability, German suppliers benefited from a high price competitiveness, on top of their reputation for product quality, service reliability, and delivery punctuality. Fourth, given all these factors and in view of a rapidly developing world economy, the level of uncertainty and hence the risk premiums demanded by investors were moderate.

In spite of the prosperous investment climate the growth rates of the 1950s could not be maintained, mainly because of emerging supply constraints. Scarcity of skilled labor and, not independently, a decline in capital productivity were among the major factors behind the slowdown in economic growth (table 3).[15]

Throughout the 1960s, the indigenous labor force shrank because the new cohorts entering the labor market were relatively small due to the low birth rates and the losses among the civilian population during and immediately after the war. At the same time, the influx of labor from the eastern parts of Germany had

Table 3
Economic Growth, Factor Input, and Factor Productivity
in the Federal Republic of Germany
(average annual rate of change in percent)

	Real gross domestic product[a]	Factor input			Factor productivity		
		Labor[b]	Capital[c]	Total[d]	Labor[b]	Capital[c]	Total[d]
1950–55	9.5	2.7	4.1	3.1	6.6	5.1	6.4
1955–60	6.3	0.6	6.0	1.8	5.7	0.3	4.5
1960–65	5.0	−0.1	5.9	0.6	5.1	−0.9	4.4
1965–70	4.2	−1.2	5.7	−0.1	5.4	−1.4	4.3

[a]In prices of 1976.

[b]Hours worked.

[c]Capital stock used.

[d]Labor and capital input weighted together with respective shares in factor income; weight for labor includes imputed remuneration for self-employed.

Source: Author's calculations.

dried up as a source of qualified manpower after the Berlin wall was erected in 1961. Moreover, after full employment was achieved in the late 1950s, trade unions used their enhanced bargaining power to successfully press for fewer annual working hours (shortening of the workweek, extended vacations).[16] Labor would have been an even more severe constraint for economic growth had it not been for the supply of workers from the Mediterranean periphery who were attracted by the relatively high wages prevailing in Germany and who were allowed to enter the German labor market under a relatively liberal immigration regime.[17] The foreign workers contributed to keeping the German labor market more elastic and flexible[18] than otherwise; the potential supply of labor from abroad served as a kind of industrial reserve army and helped to keep wage claims in check up to the late 1960s.

The decline of capital productivity was partly due to a base effect. In the 1950s, the incremental capital-output ratio had been low by international and intertemporal comparison as substantial pieces of the inherited capital stock were only partly destroyed and could be brought back from idle to productive uses with relatively small amounts of repair investment.[19] These stimuli for the development of capital productivity vanished when a high degree of capacity utilization was regained. Second, in view of the tightening labor market and gradually rising wage pressure, an increasing part of investment was geared toward substituting labor for capital and, hence, toward increasing labor rather than capital productivity.

Economic growth was pushed by the advance of factor productivity. Increasing capital input and decreasing labor input largely canceled one another out so that, in contrast to the 1950s, quantitative factor input contributed little or, later, nothing to the expansion of the economy. However, the slowdown in economic growth between the first and the second half of the 1960s was almost exclusively due to a reduction of labor input.

While the rate of growth of total factor productivity hardly changed over the 1960s, the driving forces of productivity advance altered significantly. An inspection of the proximate sources of productivity change warrants a couple of conclusions (table 4).

To begin with, in the first half of the 1960s, the advance of labor productivity fell short of the standards set in the 1950s but ex-

Table 4
Proximate Sources of Productivity Change
in the Federal Republic of Germany
(average annual rate of change in percent)

	Total economy		Nonresidential private business	
	1960–65	1965–70	1960–65	1965–70
Real gross domestic product per hour worked	5.1	5.4	6.0	5.8
Capital-labor substitution	0.7	1.1	1.1	1.4
Total factor productivity	4.4	4.3	4.9	4.4
Change in labor quality:	1.2	0.6	1.1	0.4
Education	0.3	0.3	0.3	0.3
Sex	0.1	0.1	0	0
Age	0.8	0.2	0.8	0.1
Reallocation of labor[a]	0.8	0.7	0.7	0.7
Reallocation of capital[b]	2.0	0.8	2.6	0.8
Volume changes:	0.4	0.6	0.4	0.6
Economies of scale	0.5	0.4	0.5	0.4
Capacity utilization	−0.1	0.2	0.1	0.2
Advances in knowledge, n.e.c.:	0	1.6	0.1	1.9
Domestic technical diffusion	0.6	0.1	n.a.	n.a.
Residual	−0.6	1.5	n.a.	n.a.

[a]Ten sectors.

[b]Eleven sectors.

Source: Author's calculations.

ceeded the growth of total factor productivity because of the wage-induced capital-labor substitution mentioned above. Among the various factors behind productivity growth, the reallocation of capital to more productive uses turned out to be the most important single component; economic growth was strongly promoted by structural change from agriculture and mining to manufacturing, and within manufacturing from labor-intensive consumer goods to skill- or capital-intensive industries, in particular chemicals and engineering.[20] Equally important for productivity growth were the combined effects of the reallocations of labor and the improvements in the quality of labor. As to the latter, the main impact came less from higher educational standards and a reduction of female participation rates than from learning-by-doing effects as the employed labor force aged on average. Given the strong investment activity and the fast expansion of domestic and international markets, productivity growth in Germany was also fueled by best-practice technologies incorporated in new investment, and by static economies of scale. Apart from the physical and technological rejuvenation of the capital stock, advances in knowledge had no measurable positive impact on productivity growth.[21]

In the second half of the 1960s, a slight decline in the advance of total factor productivity went along with enforced capital-labor substitution. The ranking of the proximate sources of productivity growth changed distinctly, and for at least three reasons advances in knowledge took the leading role in pushing ahead productivity growth. First, the domestic research and development activities initiated in the late 1950s and early 1960s bore fruit. Second, with rising income the supply of risk capital became increasingly elastic and, hence, the economy's propensity to engage in research and development increased.[22] The productivity of these investments can be considered to have been high because parts of the expenditures were used to adapt or imitate best-practice technologies and new products developed abroad. Third, Germany proved capable of attracting modern technology on a massive scale via foreign direct investment as the establishment of the Common Market induced a substitution of transatlantic trade for transatlantic factor flows; Germany was an obvious candidate for location because she constituted a growth pole within the Community and, presumably more important, because relatively low rates of inflation had brought about a substantial undervaluation of the deutsche mark vis-à-vis the U.S. dollar (and other currencies).

Because of all these factors, the German economy was able to maintain the rate of productivity growth of the late 1950s throughout the 1960s[23] and caught up nearly to the productivity level of the U.S. economy.[24]

The increasing scarcity of labor that constrained economic growth in the early 1960s, and even more so in the late 1960s, was in part man-made in that it was to some extent caused by distortions brought about by the exchange-rate policy. The federal government was under continuous pressure from the business community to maintain the fixed parity. This produced a dilemma:

given the high preference of Germans for price-level stability, there was always the danger of imported inflation.[25] In late 1961, an attempt to insulate the economy from the inflationary environment by way of a 5 percent revaluation of the deutsche mark vis-à-vis the U.S. dollar could not but mitigate the inflationary push from abroad that ebbed only later in the downswing.[26] When in the export-led recovery of 1964—65 the deutsche mark became again undervalued and inflation started again to accelerate, the business community convinced the federal government to reject proposals to revalue the deutsche mark because of an alleged failure of the 1961 revaluation: it was not recognized that this revaluation had come far too late and had been too modest to stem the effect of inflation.[27] Instead an austerity policy was adopted, including restrictive monetary policy and moral suasion, which in 1966—67—by producing Germany's first major postwar recession—interrupted the import of inflation and ushered in a strong undervaluation of the currency.

The federal government is widely credited with having overcome the recession by a demand management program. However, while the government undisputedly contributed to the ignition, the strong and long boom between 1967 and 1970 was mainly based on a high international price competitiveness of domestic suppliers due to the grossly undervalued currency. As in earlier cases, the export-led recovery ended up in a wage and price explosion, mitigated only by the introduction of an export tax and an import subsidy in the fall of 1968 ("Ersatz" revaluation) and a 10 percent revaluation of the deutsche mark vis-à-vis the U.S. dollar in 1969, which again was too little too late.

The recurring undervaluation of the deutsche mark brought about by the rigid exchange-rate policy amounted to taxing the nontradeables sector and subsidizing the tradeables sector, in particular manufacturing. In fact, throughout the 1960s Germany's share of manufacturing in gross domestic product was not only high by international comparison, but remained so after Germany had surpassed a stage of development from which the manufacturing sector's contribution to gross domestic product could have been expected to decline (appendix, table A-1).[28] Economic growth was impaired because, as compared to an equilibrium exchange rate, there was less competition and because there was an artificial obstacle to structural change. Labor-intensive industries that would have been displaced under the impact of competitive imports could survive at their German location; economic growth was more labor-intensive than otherwise.[29] Finally, there was a qualitative change in the role of government as it took direct responsibility for the achievement of adequate economic growth, price-level stability, full employment, and external equilibrium.[30] Active demand management was regarded as the principal and appropriate tool to achieve these targets. Yet by revaluing the deutsche mark in spite of prior oaths to defend the going exchange rate "to eternity," and by (nevertheless) allowing for a big catchup inflation in the late 1960s, the government began to destroy the very basis on which the new conception was founded: exchange-rate illusion, tax illusion, and money illusion.

The Age of Labor

In the 1970s the performance of the German economy further deteriorated to the point of stagnation since the last peak in 1976.[31] In contrast to the 1960s, the slowdown of economic growth in the 1970s was mainly associated with a (relative) decline of capital input and labor productivity (table 5). At a finer level of

Table 5

Real Gross Domestic Product, Factor Inputs, and Factor Productivities in the Federal Republic of Germany

(average annual rate of change in percent)

	Real gross domestic product[a]	Factor inputs			Factor productivities		
		Labor[b]	Capital[c]	Total[d]	Labor[b]	Capital[c]	Total[d]
1970–73	3.9	−1.2	4.5	−0.1	5.2	−0.5	4.0
1973–79	2.4	−1.7	3.6	−0.5	4.2	−1.1	2.9
1979–81	0.9	−0.4	2.8	0.3	1.6	−1.8	0.6

[a]In prices of 1976.

[b]Hours worked.

[c]Capital stock used.

[d]Labor and capital input weighted together with respective shares in factor income; weight for labor includes imputed remuneration for self-employed.

Source: Author's calculations.

disaggregation, it appears that the stimuli for productivity advance stemming from learning by doing (age-sex composition of the labor force), from the reallocations of capital and labor to more productive uses, from static economies of scale, and from domestic technical diffusion became weaker or even turned negative; catalytic processes of mutual causation that had been positive in the 1950s and 1960s lost their power when economic growth dwindled. Had it not been for a significant increase in the advance of knowledge, which corresponds to a substantial increase in the ratio of R&D expenditures to gross domestic product in the 1970s relative to the 1960s,[32] economic growth might have stagnated already beginning in 1973 (appendix, table A-2).

This malaise was mainly conditioned by changes in the economic environment that took place between the late 1960s and mid-1970s, consisting of drastic and unexpected changes in (relative) prices that met with increasing rigidities of the economic system. The resulting combination of low growth, high inflation, and high unemployment can be seen as the price the society had to pay for a reinforced, multidimensional struggle over distribution —capital versus labor; employed versus unemployed; young and old versus middle-aged; public sector versus private sector; national economy versus international economy; etc.

At the beginning of the period that finally ended in present stagnation, there was a significant change in the behavior of trade unions and government (appendix, table A-3). First, the labor shortage of the 1960s substantially strengthened the bargaining power of the unions. As a lagged response to the tight labor market, in the period 1969 to 1974 the unions successfully pressed for wage increases that exceeded the increases in labor productivity by a large margin. Until 1973, the wage push was accommodated by fiscal and monetary policy so that the level of employment was hardly affected.[33] However, inflation accelerated and, as this acceleration was not sufficiently anticipated in the capital market, the real rate of interest decreased significantly as compared to the level prevailing during the 1960s.

In addition to becoming more aggressive, trade unions pressed for a more even income distribution. In wage contracts, higher rates of growth were settled for low-skilled than for high-skilled labor; also, the variation of wage increases across industries became smaller. To paralyze counteracting forces from abroad, trade unions pleaded for an immigration stop for foreign labor (enacted in 1974) and later, supported by capital, for protection for labor-intensive industries.

The cost of labor was further increased by new labor legislation. This included, among other things, continued wage payments in case of illness (for six weeks), employers' contributions to employees' health insurance, and enhanced protection against firing. In particular the latter regulation made labor tend to become a fixed cost and hence induced the reduction of jobs in the course of natural fluctuation—via capital-labor substitution (rationalization), labor-saving technological progress (industrial robots), and extended overtime work instead of additions to the stock of the permanently employed. These processes were supported by low real rates of interest.

Finally, as economic growth was taken for granted, the federal government embarked upon an ambitious program of income redistribution and protection for the young, the old, the disabled, the unemployed, and the workers at large. Subsidies and benefits for education, retraining, child care, housing, and savings were substantially increased, pensions were raised, unemployment compensation became more generous, and subsidies for weak firms, weak industries (including infant industries), and weak regions were piled up. In addition, the public sector increased its supply of services and engaged in large-scale promotion of civil servants. As a result there was a massive expansion of public expenditures relative to gross national product and a shift from public investment to public consumption.

The explosion of wages, transfers, and regulations coincided with the need for high flexibility and adaptability due to massive pressure for structural change. The gradual erosion and final breakdown of the Bretton Woods system removed the undervaluation of the deutsche mark and, hence, the implicit subsidy for Germany's international sector at the expense of her domestic sector. The real rate of exchange appreciated considerably, in terms of unit labor costs even more than in terms of export prices due to the wage push. In consequence, German suppliers of tradeable goods suffered from a deterioration in their international competitiveness in addition to a wage-induced profit squeeze.

Further pressure on the manufacturing sector resulted from newcomers located in newly industrializing countries. German suppliers of labor-intensive and/or standardized manufactures were confronted with strong price competition and lost shares in domestic and international markets.[34]

A further need for change arose when the oil price shock of 1973 rendered economically obsolete parts of the existing capital stock and technological knowledge. The new price structure induced a time- and resource-consuming process of searching, learning, and restructuring. The price jump also raised the level of uncertainty—it was widely disputed whether or not the new prices would stay for long and what future shifts in relative prices should be expected. The existing knowledge about adjustment behavior —i.e., income, price, and substitution elasticities—had become meaningless. Similar adjustment needs and adjustment difficulties were evoked by the boom of raw material prices that occurred during the same time.

Lastly, new legislation put a positive price on the use of the environment and, hence, raised the input costs for polluting industries. Firms producing environment-intensive commodities or their complements suffered from decreasing competitiveness vis-à-vis those foreign suppliers that were burdened with lower charges for the use of the environment and vis-à-vis producers of substitutes. The costs of internalizing the externalities are likely to have been excessive because of direct regulation.[35]

On the whole, the German economy of the early 1970s exhibited features strikingly different from those of the 1950s and early 1960s: little scope for technological catch-up; expensive energy and raw materials; extensive regulations in the labor market and direct environmental control; large government (in a quantitative, but in particular, in a qualitative sense), including an extensive transfer system;[36] excessive real wages relative to productivity; depressed real interest rates; a high level of uncertainty due to accelerating inflation,[37] stop-and-go policies (in particular in 1973–74), and rising protectionism at home and abroad. Under the impact of these forces, profit margins declined and profit expectations were impaired at a time when both actual profits and profit expectations should have been high because of the premiums necessary to cover the cost of increased uncertainty. In turn there was massive pressure for structural change; capital formation was discouraged; the capital stock aged; and, not independently of all these factors, the growth of labor productivity fell (tables 5 and A-3).[38]

The structural weakness that had gradually developed in the German economy became evident in the severe recession of 1974–75. Economic coordination, especially economic policy coordination, practically collapsed when restrictive monetary policy designed to curb inflationary expectations coincided with a strong wage push that was in part provoked by a full-employment guarantee of the government and designed to defend the income position of labor in spite of the deterioration of the terms of trade brought about by rising raw material and energy prices. Later, the recession was reinforced by the worldwide downswing.

The manufacturing sector that had been subsidized for a long time under the fixed-exchange-rate regime had to bear the brunt of the adjustment burden. From 1970 to 1975, roughly one million jobs or 10 percent of manufacturing employment were lost in this sector (and have not been refilled since); production decreased relative to gross domestic product; and the contribution of manufacturing to gross domestic product (in current prices), which had been stable throughout the 1960s, declined (table A-1). Smooth adjustment through an expansion of the tertiary sector foundered, in part, on inelastic output supply because major segments of this sector—transport, communication, health, banking, insurance—are highly regulated, and in part because of excessive real wages.[39]

Expansionary fiscal policies eventually helped to overcome the recession, but at the price of rapidly increasing public debt and persistent, if declining, inflation. And while the recession had been deeper than that of 1967 and the fiscal stimulus much stronger, the recovery (1976 to 1979) was less steep than that of 1968 through 1970: demand management had become a weak weapon because economic agents had lost fiscal illusions. It appeared that at the going level of wage costs, including fringe benefits and the implicit costs of labor legislation, the economic capital stock was too small to allow for full employment (table A-3).[40] Nevertheless, in the period from 1976 to 1979, growth was resumed, inflation gradually declined, and the rate of unemployment decreased. These developments reflect the fact that the usual feedbacks of the recession, in particular lower cost pressure (labor, energy, raw materials), were still working in the German economy. But they also must be seen in the context of a new policy approach that amounted to substituting German-style supply-side policy for traditional demand management.[41]

As constitutive elements, monetary and fiscal policy were to become more predictable and steadier (oriented toward the medium run) in order to reduce one source of uncertainty. Government was to withdraw her full-employment guarantee; instead, wage-setting was to render possible the desired level of employment. The growth rates of public expenditures and public debts were to be reduced while government abstained from further increasing the tax burden. Public expenditures—including "tax expenditures"—and general government activity were to give (stronger) priority to:

- increasing the supply of venture capital by stimulating the reinvestment of profits, by promoting profit-sharing of workers as a (partial) substitute for wage increases, and by more strongly participating in entrepreneurial risk through the tax system;

- promoting research and development, and the regional, sectoral, and occupational mobility of labor;

- removing obstacles for economic activity—e.g., by giving clear guidance in energy policy or by allowing for more competition in the field of telecommunications (federal post office, public broadcasting);

- providing for strong competition by lowering barriers to entry for new enterprises (provision of venture capital, consulting, removal of bureaucratic obstacles, etc.), by promoting the development of small and medium-sized enterprises, by removing protection for senile industries, and by lowering barriers to international trade.

This concept resumed the tradition of a successful German economic policy—that of the early 1950s—adapted, however, to the needs of a country that in the meantime had developed from a follower to one of the leaders of development in the world economy.

The new policy conception was implemented too imperfectly and too gradually to put the German economy back on a firm footing. In effect, economic coordination and economic policy coordination never completely recovered from the failures of 1974–75. While an anticyclical monetary policy was not part of the supply-side concept, the Bundesbank took the initiative in supporting the recovery to the extent that an expansionary monetary policy was pursued beginning in 1977, as the cyclical upswing lost its momentum. The consequences became visible in a reacceleration of inflation in 1979 when capacity utilization had regained a high level.

A new slowdown of economic activity was induced by reverting to tight monetary policy, and was exacerbated by the second oil price shock. On the other hand, fiscal policy became even more expansionary, and in 1980 the budget seemed out of control; the deficit on current account, which had already emerged in 1979, increased dramatically. The ensuing loss of confidence in the deutsche mark produced a depreciation that led the Bundesbank to continue its restrictive course. Hence, the massive fiscal stimuli of 1980 and 1981 were largely lost. All the while, wage-setting repeated its mistake of 1974 by not taking into account the deterioration in the terms of trade. As a result, unemployment increased sharply in 1981.

Since then, the economic situation in Germany has further deteriorated. At the beginning of 1984, unemployment had attained a rate of 10.2 percent—the highest annual rate since 1950—while inflation is still substantial (consumer prices are 3.0 percent up over last year). The current number of bankruptcies exceeds that of any period in West Germany's postwar history.

Structural Rigidities

Within thirty years, the Federal Republic of Germany turned from a rapidly growing into a stagnating economy. This would not be a matter of serious concern if there were reason to believe that the metamorphosis mirrored a gradual change in preferences. However, the emergence of persistent mass unemployment makes this a highly questionable proposition. Instead, there is more reason to diagnose a serious disease.

Throughout the last thirty years economic growth has tended to decline, and a number of noteworthy trends went along with that decline (tables 2 and A-3):

- Economic growth was positively related to the rate of capital formation, and capital formation declined when profit margins (and hence, presumably, profit expectations) were impaired.

- Economic growth was rapid when government was small, and economic growth was slow when government became large. Moreover, the government itself was strong when it was small, but became weak after it grew larger (credibility gap).

- More fundamentally, during the phase of rapid economic development the government largely confined itself to working on the supply side, mainly by setting and monitoring the rules of the game and by supporting incentives to save and to invest. At the same time, the government deregulated the economy—including the removal of barriers to international trade and factor movements—and hence provided for intense competition. The phase of weak economic growth set in after a prolonged period of demand management, after a gradual rise in sectoral and regional subsidies, and when, because of growth-induced structural changes, the relatively regulated tertiary sector was to take the leading role in economic development.

- Economic growth was high when wage policies were moderate and when the income distribution shifted in favor of capital; at the same time, real wages increased rapidly and full employment was achieved. Economic growth became low after a phase of aggressive wage policies that pushed up the wage share in gross national product; soon thereafter, real wages increased slowly and mass unemployment emerged.

- Likewise, economic growth was rapid when public transfers were moderate, but sharply declined after a phase of prolonged emphasis on redistribution.

- Finally, economic growth was high when the price level was stable and relative prices were flexible, but dwindled when inflation accelerated under the impact of an intensifying struggle over distribution.

From these observations it can be inferred that the slowdown of economic growth was caused by fundamental changes in the German economy that developed gradually as the economy matured. Singular events, in particular the oil price shocks, contributed to the decline to the extent that they hit an aging economy; but these shocks only accelerated and accentuated a development that for other reasons would have taken place anyway.

Massive increases in investment will be necessary to restore sustained economic growth. But the stimulus to investment must come from brighter medium-term profit expectations, not from wage pressure (capital-labor substitution). Wage pressure would only render obsolete more of Germany's capital stock, crowd out marginal firms and employment, and inhibit creation of new jobs that otherwise would have been profitable.

A systematic program of reform should include the following elements:

- Reinstitute a stable monetary environment;

- Allow a lag of real wages behind productivity increases, which would also permit more differentiation in the wage structure, until satisfactory employment levels could be reestablished;

- Allow increases in public spending to lag behind growth of GNP, until the structural budget deficit has been eliminated;

- Restructure public expenditures by reducing public consumption and increasing public investment, as well as incentives for private investment and innovation;

- Reform the system of transfers to individuals in order to improve systems of control;

- Shift the tax burden from saving and investment to consumption; and

- Mount strong efforts to reduce international and intranational barriers to entry in commodity and factor markets in order to restore flexible price structures.

The present stagnation and unemployment undoubtedly contain significant cyclical elements. But structural rigidities have continued to harden over the course of past and present trade cycles. First, trade unions only hesitantly and temporarily accepted the responsibility for full employment. Second, the government had little room in which to maneuver in restructuring the budget because of statutory commitments to individual transfers, the dynamism built into civil service pay, and rapidly increasing debt service. These, in turn, mirrored the longer-term effects of pressures on the government from a large variety of interest groups, including the public bureaucracy. The crucial question is whether this institutional framework, as it has grown, is capable of translating meaningful reforms into policy rapidly and forcefully enough to put Germany on the road to prosperity again without incurring a severe economic crisis.

Appendix

Table A-1

Production Structure and Sectoral Growth in the
Federal Republic of Germany, 1960–81

(percent)

	Contribution to GDP in current prices			Average annual rate of gross value added in 1976 prices					
	1960	1970	1981	1960–65	1965–70	1970–73	1973–79	1979–81
Total economy	100	100	100	5.0	4.2	3.9	2.4	0.9
Agriculture, etc.	5.8	3.4	2.2	-1.3	4.0	0.9	0.5	2.8
Mining	2.8	1.3	0.9[a]	-1.5	-0.6	-5.3	-2.0	0.0
Electricity, gas, water	2.4	2.2	2.7[a]	6.3	8.6	9.3	6.0	—
Manufacturing	40.3	40.2	33.1	6.2	5.3	3.5	1.8	-0.5
Construction	7.7	8.0	6.7	5.9	0.9	4.3	-0.4	-0.9
Wholesale and retail trade	12.0	10.1	9.8	5.8	4.1	3.8	2.8	-2.1
Transport and communication	6.5	5.9	5.8	4.2	5.3	3.1	4.5	3.3
Finance, insurance	2.4	3.3	4.7[a]	9.1	9.1	7.2	5.0	—
Real estate	4.0	5.3	5.8	3.9	3.4	5.1	3.4	2.4
Other private services	7.2	9.1	13.1	3.7	3.0	4.4	4.1	4.1
Public services[b]	8.8	11.2	14.2	4.9	4.0	4.6	2.7	2.4

[a]1980.

[b]Including private households and private nonprofit organizations.

Source: Statistisches Bundesamt Wiesbaden "Volkswirtschaftliche Gesamtrechnungen," *Fachserie 18, Reihe 5.5* (Stuttgart and Mainz: Kohlhammer, 1982), results from 1960 to 1981.

Table A-2

Proximate Sources of Productivity Change in the Federal Republic of Germany, 1970–81

(average annual rate of change in percent)

	Total economy			Nonresidential private business		
	1970–73	1973–79	1979–81	1970–73	1973–79	1979–81
Real gross domestic product per hour worked	5.2	4.2	1.6	5.3	4.5	1.8
Capital-labor substitution	1.2	1.3	1.0	1.6	1.7	1.4
Total factor productivity	4.0	2.9	0.6	3.7	2.8	0.4
Change in labor quality:	0.2	0.3	n.a.	0.3	0.3	n.a.
Education	0.7	0.4	0.1	0.7	0.4	0.1
Sex	-0.1	-0.1	n.a.	0	0	n.a.
Age	-0.4	0	n.a.	-0.4	-0.1	n.a.
Reallocation of labor	0.3	0.4	n.a.	0.4	0.4	n.a.
Reallocation of capital	0.8	-0.1	n.a.	1.0	-0.1	n.a.
Volume changes:	0.1	0.1	-0.3	0.1	0.1	-0.3
Economies of scale	0.4	0.2	0.1	0.4	0.2	0.1
Capacity utilization	-0.3	-0.1	-0.4	-0.3	-0.1	-0.4
Advances in knowledge, n.e.c.:	2.6	2.2	n.a.	1.9	2.1	n.a.
Domestic technical diffusion	-0.2	-0.5	n.a.	n.a.	n.a.	n.a.
Residual	2.8	2.7	n.a.	1.9	2.1	n.a.

Source: Author's calculations.

Table A-3

Basic Economic Indicators for the Federal Republic of Germany

	Real gross domestic product in 1976 prices (rate of change in percent)	Real GNP per capita in 1976 prices (rate of change in percent)	Utilization of potential output (percent)	Unemployment ratio (percent)	Consumer prices (rate of change in percent)	Share of investment in GNP current prices (percent)	Profit margin[a] (percent)	Share of wages in GNP[b] (percent)	Real wage position[c] (rate of change in percent)	Real wages[d] gross (rate of change in percent)	net of taxes and social insurance (rate of change in percent)	Real rate of exchange based on unit values of export prices 1971=100	unit labor costs[e] 1971=100
1960	—	—	99.4	1.2	1.4	27.3	—	60.1	—	—	—	—	—
1961	5.1	3.4	98.9	0.9	2.3	27.2	—	61.8	—	7.9	7.0	—	—
1962	4.4	3.2	97.9	0.7	3.0	25.8	—	62.5	—	6.2	5.6	91.9	88.7
1963	3.1	2.1	96.1	0.9	2.9	26.3	—	63.0	-0.9	3.2	2.8	91.5	88.3
1964	6.7	5.6	97.8	0.8	2.3	28.1	—	62.0	-1.1	6.7	6.1	89.7	87.0
1965	5.5	4.3	98.3	0.7	3.3	28.5	8.8	62.3	0.3	5.8	6.7	89.8	86.7
1966	2.6	1.7	96.6	0.7	3.5	26.6	8.3	63.1	0.9	3.8	2.4	88.9	86.7
1967	-0.1	-0.3	93.3	2.1	1.7	23.0	8.4	62.9	-0.7	1.6	1.2	86.5	83.7
1968	5.9	5.8	95.9	1.5	1.7	24.5	7.3	61.2	-2.3	4.5	3.1	86.2	82.8
1969	7.5	6.5	99.6	0.8	1.9	26.1	7.3	61.4	3.0	7.3	5.6	85.9	84.1
1970	5.1	4.0	100.0	0.7	3.3	27.6	6.6	62.9	3.4	12.0	9.7	96.2	95.2
1971	3.1	2.1	98.3	0.8	5.2	26.7	6.3	63.7	1.2	6.1	4.2	100.0	100.0
1972	4.2	3.5	97.8	1.1	5.6	25.9	6.4	63.6	-1.0	3.6	3.9	103.8	103.1
1973	4.6	4.0	98.4	1.2	7.0	25.2	5.7	64.2	0.0	5.2	1.7	109.3	114.7
1974	0.5	0.3	96.0	2.6	7.0	22.1	5.0	66.0	2.4	3.9	2.4	104.4	113.4
1975	-1.7	-1.2	92.1	4.8	6.0	19.7	5.1	66.1	-1.8	0.4	0.7	106.2	107.4
1976	5.5	6.1	95.2	4.7	4.3	21.2	5.7	64.6	-1.6	2.7	0.1	107.5	104.6
1977	3.1	3.0	96.1	4.6	3.7	21.1	5.4	64.6	-0.2	3.1	2.0	109.4	109.0
1978	3.1	3.6	97.1	4.4	2.7	21.3	5.6	63.6	-0.9	2.7	3.7	111.7	110.8
1979	4.2	3.9	99.2	3.8	4.1	23.8	5.5	63.4	0.4	1.5	2.0	110.1	113.1
1980	1.8	1.5	98.8	3.8	5.5	24.0	4.8	64.7	1.7	1.1	-0.6	104.4	108.7
1981	0.1	-0.4	96.7	5.5	5.9	21.9	4.1	65.5	-0.4	-1.1	-1.5	94.4	93.6

Table A–3 (cont'd)

Basic Economic Indicators for the Federal Republic of Germany

	Productivity[f] (rate of change in percent)	Real rate of interest[g] (percent)	Variation of wage contracts[h]	Share of government consumption in GNP current prices (percent)	Ratio of public transfers to private enterprises and households to GNP (percent)	Expenditures of the public sector in percent of potential output	Taxes and social security contributions in percent of GNP	Interest on public debt in percent of tax receipts	Public gross fixed capital formation in percent of public expenditures
1960	—	5.2	17.0	13.3	14.1	32.8	33.3	3.1	9.8
1961	4.1	4.6	17.8	13.8	14.1	33.9	34.5	2.8	10.1
1962	4.3	4.9	15.0	14.7	14.2	35.2	35.0	2.7	11.0
1963	3.2	5.6	28.4	15.5	14.3	35.3	35.2	2.6	12.2
1964	7.6	5.1	19.8	14.8	14.3	35.7	34.7	2.6	13.6
1965	5.4	4.3	11.7	15.2	15.0	36.5	34.1	2.7	12.3
1966	3.2	6.1	29.7	15.5	15.1	35.9	34.6	2.8	11.7
1967	4.0	7.9	27.7	16.2	16.5	36.6	35.2	3.5	9.7
1968	6.9	7.3	21.5	15.5	17.7	38.0	36.0	4.0	9.8
1969	6.7	5.2	11.4	15.6	16.7	38.9	37.4	3.8	10.2
1970	3.8	3.3	13.5	15.8	15.9	39.1	36.5	4.0	11.8
1971	2.4	3.8	11.9	16.9	16.0	39.9	37.5	4.0	11.1
1972	5.3	5.6	23.4	17.1	17.0	40.5	38.0	4.2	9.9
1973	4.6	2.8	12.4	17.8	17.3	41.4	40.3	4.3	9.1
1974	2.7	-2.7	9.7	19.3	18.3	43.4	40.9	4.8	9.0
1975	1.2	4.0	5.9	20.5	21.5	45.7	40.9	5.6	7.8
1976	7.8	4.3	8.6	19.8	21.2	46.4	42.1	6.1	7.2
1977	4.0	3.7	—	19.6	21.5	46.7	43.2	6.4	6.8
1978	3.1	4.9	—	19.6	21.3	46.9	42.4	6.4	7.0
1979	3.5	2.8	—	19.6	20.9	47.7	42.1	6.7	7.4
1980	1.0	1.1	—	20.1	20.7	48.2	42.3	7.5	7.7
1981	1.0	2.8	—	20.7	21.3	48.1	42.4	9.1	6.9

[a]Profits in percent of sales before taxes of a sample of German companies collected by the Deutsche Bundesbank. For details see source.

[b]Adjusted for change of the share of self-employed in the total labor force.

[c]Changes in nominal wages per employee in the private business sector adjusted for changes in wage cost effect of employers' contributions to social insurances, in labor productivity, in capital costs, in the terms of trade, in cost effects of indirect taxes and subsidies, and in prices of private consumption and purchases from government. For details see Sachverständigenrat zur Begutachtung der gesamtwirtschaftlichen Entwicklung, *Jahresgutachten 1981/82* (Stuttgart and Mainz: Kohlhammer, 1982), pp. 222–25.

[d]Wages and salaries per employee deflated by consumer prices.

[e]Weighted unit values of export prices (unit labor costs) relative to 16 major trading partners, adjusted for changes in bilateral exchange rates (weight: share of trade volume of respective country in Germany's total trade volume with the 16 countries).

[f]Gross domestic product in 1976 prices per employee in the private business sector.

[g]Bond yields deflated by prices for industrial commodities.

[h]Coefficient of variation of wage contracts in industry (excluding electricity, gas, and parts of construction), 17 sectors.

Sources: Statistiches Bundesamt Wiesbaden, "Volkswirtschaftliche Gesamtrechnungen," *Fachserie 18, Reihe S.5* (Stuttgart and Mainz: Kohlhammer, 1982); Deutsche Bundesbank, "Jahresubschlüsse der Unternehmen in der Bundesrepublik Deutschland 1965 to 1976," *Sonderdrucke der Deutschen Bundesbank* (Frankfurt: Deutsche Bundesbank, 1977); Deutsche Bundesbank, *Monatsberichte* (Frankfurt: Deutsche Bundesbank, various issues); Sachverständigenrat zur Begutachtung der gesamtwirtschaftlichen Entwicklung, *Jahresgutachten* (Stuttgart and Mainz: Kohlhammer, various issues); calculations of the Institut für Weltwirtschaft.

6

ROBERT J. GORDON

U.S. Stabilization Policy: Lessons from the Past Decade

From a foreign perspective, the discussion of macroeconomics and stabilization policy in the United States may appear to be incurably insular. In the U.S., such issues are typically treated without reference to the outside world. Recommendations for changes in policy are established by reference to the institutional framework at the current moment, often within a context that takes problems related to particular domestic institutions to be universal rather than unique. Within the last few years, the discussion of stabilization policy within the United States has become more oriented to the rest of the world in only two respects—the attention now given to the impact of the flexible exchange-rate system, and concerns over possible defaults by nations heavily in debt to American banks.[1]

This research is supported by the National Science Foundation. Any opinions expressed are those of the author and not those of the National Bureau of Economic Research.

This chapter is an introduction to the U.S. policy discussion in the early 1980s. It is unapologetically insular, reflecting interactions with other nations only to the extent that such open-economy concerns actually arise in typical domestic policy discussions. Its main concern is the domestic business cycle. Why have business cycles recurred with increasing severity in the past decade, in the face of a massive effort by the best economists to understand and prevent such cycles? Can we achieve a sufficient understanding of the characteristics of an economy uncontrolled by policymakers, and of the flaws of past interventions, to establish a set of guidelines for future policies?

Since numerous foreign nations have been passively dragged into recession, high unemployment, and the risk of credit default by the impact of U.S. interest and exchange rates in the 1980s, the purely domestic orientation of this review of the policy debates may appear to foreign policymakers more analogous to a lesson on how to watch a spectator sport on television than to a training session for actual participants. The subject is, however, extraordinarily relevant to a wide array of problems in world economic growth, for there is no greater cause of slow worldwide economic growth in the past two years than restrictive monetary policy in the U.S. All participants have an interest in understanding why this policy was implemented and what should be done to replace it.

Conflicting Interpretations of U.S. Macroeconomic Behavior

In late 1982 the American economy experienced the most serious business slump since the Great Depression of the 1930s — a setback that lends urgency to the search for a new approach to achieve more stable economic growth. This current concern with economic instability stands in marked contrast to the heady optimism of the late 1960s, when courses labeled "Business Cycles" were being expunged from the economics curriculum and when conferences were being organized to debate the topic "Is the Business Cycle Obsolete?"

In retrospect the nine-year business expansion between early 1961 and late 1969 appears to have been the exception that deluded economists into organizing such ephemeral conferences.

In other decades of this century recurrent expansions and contractions have been the rule. Between late 1949 and early 1961 there were three complete business cycles, with an average duration of 3.7 years. Between late 1970 and late 1982 again there were three complete business cycles, with an average duration of 4.0 years. Worse yet, by almost any measure, economic performance during the 1970–82 period was inferior to that between 1949 and 1961. Some U.S. economists have felt a serious professional guilt—they need to explain why macroeconomic performance should have deteriorated while the tools of their trade have advanced in sophistication.

The adverse turn of events in the 1970s had not been predicted by the reigning orthodox wisdom of the 1960s, which combined a textbook Keynesian approach to aggregate demand behavior with a Phillips curve approach to aggregate supply behavior. Not surprisingly, this consistent set of surprises and forecast errors unleashed an intellectual counterrevolution. Milton Friedman and Robert Lucas have often been viewed as the Copernicus and Galileo of a new business cycle theory, overthrowing the previous Aristotelian orthodoxy of postwar Keynesianism. In fact Lucas and his colleague Thomas Sargent consciously adopted a revolutionary rhetoric, and in a famous polemic described themselves as "sorting through the wreckage" of the Keynesian revolution.[2]

Friedman and Lucas built models of the economy that differed in important respects. Friedman's version showed that policymakers had no *long-run* influence on unemployment, which would gravitate automatically toward its "natural rate." The Lucas Sargent version showed that systematic attempts by policymakers to influence unemployment would be ineffective even in the *short run*. Despite this difference over the applicable time horizon, both versions concurred that only a single government policy action could dampen the business cycle, and this was maintenance of a constant growth rate of the money supply.

Among the babble of labels that commentators have put forward for the Friedman and Lucas doctrines, James Tobin's suggestion of "Monetarism Mark I" and "Monetarism Mark II" has the important advantage of identifying the common thread— the joint recommendation of a constant-growth monetary rule (CGMR) for policymakers. The CGMR was a simple and comprehensible approach to policymaking, advocated as a replacement for the "fine-tuning" or "activist" monetary and fiscal intervention favored by mainstream Keynesians. And it seemed superficially appealing, since the poor performance of the economy after 1969 appeared to condemn activism as at best ineffective and more likely as downright perverse. In fact, many commentators have interpreted the October 1979 shift by the Federal Reserve toward greater emphasis on targets for monetary growth aggregates as representing the official demise of activism and the offical adoption of monetarism.

This paper distinguishes four central characteristics of the U.S. economy's response to policy actions. These characteristics help us to understand just where the mainstream Keynesian approach went wrong; but they also help us to understand why the monetarist CGMR panacea fails to provide a solution within the U.S. context to the flaws in the 1960s Keynesian remedy.

The first characteristic concerns the nature of the economy's fluctuations in nominal aggregate demand, and the other three relate to the response of real output, i.e., aggregate supply:

1. Over postwar U.S. business cycles the growth rate of nominal GNP has been highly variable, averaging almost 8 percentage points faster at an annual rate over expansion phases of the business cycle than over recession phases. Procyclical fluctuations in the growth rate of the money supply, however, account for only a trivial fraction of fluctuations in nominal GNP growth — 14 percent on average over seven postwar business cycles. This first characteristic, the small amplitude of fluctuations in money contrasted with the large amplitude of fluctuations in nominal GNP, casts doubt on the potential of a CGMR policy to achieve a substantial dampening of the cycle within the U.S. setting.

2. Changes in real GNP occur by definition when changes in nominal GNP differ from the rate of inflation. Real GNP could remain stable in the face of wide swings in nominal GNP growth only if the inflation rate duplicated those wide swings with little or no lag. But a fundamental characteristic of the U.S. inflation process is the sluggish adjustment or "inertia" of inflation in response to fluctuations in the growth rate of

nominal GNP. Thus the dampening of business cycles requires that nominal GNP fluctuations be moderated, unless a way can be found to increase substantially the speed of inflation's response to those fluctuations.

3. The U.S. evidence now seems compelling in support of Milton Friedman's proposition that the economy has a natural rate of unemployment. Any attempt to maintain unemployment for a long period below the natural rate generates a continuously accelerating inflation rate, as we learned from the late 1960s experience in the United States. An unemployment rate substantially above the natural rate generates downward pressure on the inflation rate, as we have seen in 1981–83. These opinions are based on the author's recent evidence that the natural unemployment rate was at least 5.1 percent in the 1950s and in the 1970s climbed (for demographic reasons) to 6.0 percent.

4. A counterpart of inflation inertia is that "supply shocks," sudden changes in the prices of important raw materials like oil, have consequences for the aggregate inflation rate, simply because prices in the rest of the economy (i.e., non-oil prices) are not capable of dropping quickly enough when oil prices rise, nor of rising quickly enough when oil prices fall. Adverse supply shocks pose a fundamental dilemma for policymakers, since the previous rate of inflation cannot be maintained without a significant loss of non-oil output, whereas maintenance of the previous level of output will cause a marked and perhaps permanent acceleration in the rate of inflation.

Behavior of the U.S. Economy in Postwar Business Cycles

The central actors in any macroeconomic drama are output, unemployment, inflation, and money. While there are numerous theories about the connections among these variables, one undeniable fact is the definition that links output, inflation, and money. This is the growth-rate version of the famous "quantity equation," which states that:

monetary growth + velocity growth = inflation + real growth.

Data for seven postwar business cycles are exhibited in the appendix in the same arrangement as the quantity equation. The timing of each cycle is dictated by the choices of the National Bureau of Economic Research (NBER), which has established a chronology of U.S. business cycles extending back to 1837. The appendix shows each business cycle in a grouping of three lines, labeled "expansion," "plateau," and "recession." The "expansion" begins in the calendar quarter designated by the NBER as the official cycle "trough." The "recession" begins in the quarter designated as the official NBER "peak." The period between trough and peak is divided into two intervals at the quarter when real GNP reaches its highest level relative to its secular trend. During the plateau phase, the economy exhibits continued real GNP growth at a rate slower than the secular trend.

The five growth rates in columns (3) through (7) of the appendix do not by themselves tell us much about extreme highs and lows experienced by the unemployment rate or real GNP. Column (9) exhibits the official unemployment rate observed in the first quarter of each of the three cyclical phases. Column (8) exhibits a detrended concept called the "output ratio" that purges real GNP of its secular growth trend and shows its underlying cyclical movements. The output ratio is constructed by a two-step procedure, in which a detailed econometric study of the postwar inflation process is used to derive the "natural" unemployment rate consistent with a constant rate of inflation. Then a "natural" real GNP series is constructed to indicate how much the economy could have produced each quarter if, hypothetically, it had been operating at its natural rate of employment. The output ratio is then the ratio of actual to natural real GNP.[3]

The data displayed in the appendix provide evidence to support our interpretation of the four central macroeconomic characteristics of the postwar economy. Common features of the seven cycles are summarized in the bottom section of the table, which provides averages of the variables for each phase over all seven cycles, with each phase weighted by its length. Columns (3) through (5) show that nominal GNP growth was highly volatile, with a 10.2 percent average growth rate during expansion phases and a 2.6 percent rate during recession phases, for a difference of 7.6 percent. In contrast, M_1 growth was much less volatile, with growth in expansion phases only 1.1 percent faster on average than in recession phases. As a result, fluctuations in monetary growth accounted on average for only 14 percent (1.1/7.6) of fluctuations in nominal GNP growth. The remaining 86 percent is accounted for by fluctuations in the growth rate of velocity.

This fact implies that a hypothetical policy that maintained rigid growth of the money supply over business cycle phases would not stabilize nominal GNP growth. Nevertheless, monetary mischief was partially responsible for the poor macroeconomic outcome of the past fifteen years. First, we notice a consistent tendency for monetary growth to be lower in recessions during the three business cycles between 1949 and 1961. This destabilizing behavior may be viewed, along with the procyclical movements of money during the Great Depression, as the catalyst for Friedman's CGMR proposal. The proposal might not achieve complete stabilization of the growth of nominal GNP, Friedman reasoned in 1960, but it was likely to result in more stability than had been achieved by the actual monetary policies observed up to that time.[4]

Another prominent feature in the appendix is the steady acceleration of monetary growth in successive business cycles beginning in 1961. The weighted average growth rates of money, velocity, and nominal GNP in successive cycles were (in percent):

	Money	Velocity	Nominal GNP
1958–61	1.9	3.3	5.2
1961–70	4.4	2.7	7.1
1970–75	6.2	3.1	9.3
1975–80	7.5	3.3	10.8
1980–82	6.1	1.5	7.6

Since velocity growth exhibited no significant change over these cycles, except for 1980–82, the behavior of money can be blamed for the long-term increase in nominal GNP growth and in the rate of inflation in the 1970s as compared to the 1950s and early 1960s. Thus a careful distinction must be made between the *small* role of money growth in contributing to the short-run timing of in-

dividual cycles, and its *large* role in contributing to overheating in
the 1964—74 decade taken as a whole.[5]

The behavior of the inflation rate in column (6) averaged over
all cycles shows a striking countercyclical pattern, with an
average growth rate of 5.2 percent in recessions. An examination
of the individual cycles, however, suggests that the seven-cycle
average mixes up three quite different types of experience. The
recessions between 1949 and 1961, as well as the most recent
1980—82 episode, display the expected procyclical movement. The
middle three cycles between 1961 and 1980, however, exhibit a
strong countercyclical pattern that helps to demonstrate the
effect of two of our central characteristics.

Recall that characteristic (3) refers to the continuous upward
adjustment of the inflation rate that occurs when unemployment
remains below its natural rate. This gradual adjustment of inflation was most obvious in the long 1961—70 cycle. Because inflation
adapted with substantial inertia to rapid nominal GNP growth
(characteristic 2), the economy experienced a period between
1964 and 1969 when the output ratio substantially exceeded 100
percent and the actual unemployment rate fell substantially below
the natural rate of unemployment. The gradual upward adjustment of inflation continued into the 1969—70 recession, which witnessed faster inflation than previous phases despite slower
nominal GNP growth. A complementary explanation is that the
slowdown in nominal GNP growth in 1969—70 was the mildest of
any of the postwar cycles, further inhibiting any deceleration of
inflation.

Finally, characteristic (4) refers to the impact of supply shocks
on the aggregate inflation rate. If the growth rate of nominal GNP
were to remain constant, then a spontaneous upsurge of the inflation rate following a supply shock would cause a reduction in real
GNP growth, and, in severe cases, a recession. The 1970—75 and
1979—80 business cycles both ended with recessions that were
triggered by supply shocks and amplified by a slowdown in
nominal GNP growth. Between late 1972 and 1975 the relative
price of oil increased by 25 percent, and again by more than 40
percent between late 1978 and late 1981. The relative price of food
increased by about 10 percent between 1972 and 1974. Finally, the
recession of 1973—75 was aggravated by the extra inflation that

occurred after the termination in May 1974 of the Nixon-era price control program.[6]

As a result the inflation rate observed in the recession phase of these two cycles was substantially higher than in the expansion phase. The marked difference between the countercyclical behavior of inflation in the 1973–75 and 1980 recessions, and its procyclical behavior in the 1981–82 recession, provides a strong confirmation of the view that supply shocks matter (characteristic 4) and refutation of those who focus narrowly on prior fluctuations in the growth rate of the money supply in explaining the inflation rate.

There was an additional consequence of supply shocks. Partly as a result of cost-of-living escalators in wage contracts, supply shocks had the effect of permanently raising the rate of inflation at any given unemployment rate. This forced policymakers to choose between prolonged recession and an acceleration in monetary growth to ratify the upward ratchet of inflation caused by the supply shock. During the 1975–78 expansion the choice was made to ratify the inflation rate. In this sense the postwar peak in the growth rates of money and nominal GNP during the 1975–80 cycle was not simply a perverse action by misinformed policymakers, but rather an indirect consequence of the supply shocks themselves.

Interpretation of Macroeconomic Events in the Past Decade

My own research on the U.S. inflation process yields an estimate of the natural rate of unemployment compatible with steady inflation. Associated with that is an estimate of the level of natural real GNP that the economy can produce at that unemployment rate. A comparison between actual and natural real GNP is shown in the top frame of figure 1. The vertical striped bars outline the GNP gap, the difference between natural and actual real GNP. The GNP gap in late 1982, roughly 10 percent, seemed to be maintaining its historical relationship with the difference between the actual and natural rates of unemployment.

The lower frame in figure 1 shows the four-quarter rate of change of the GNP deflator. From early 1973 to early 1975 the

Figure 1
Real GNP and Inflation, 1973–82

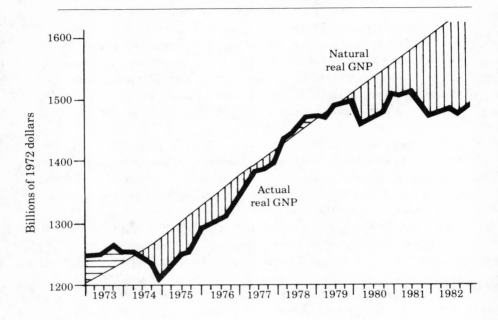

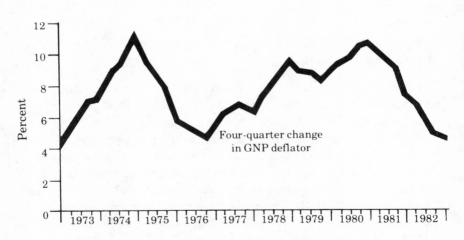

Source: Natural real GNP is from Robert J. Gordon, "Inflation, Flexible Exchange Rates, and the Natural Rate of Unemployment," in *Workers, Jobs and Inflation,* ed. M. N. Baily (Washington, D.C.: Brookings, 1982), pp. 88–157; other series are from U.S. Department of Commerce.

behavior of both real GNP and the inflation rate was dominated by the first oil shock, augmented by the depreciation of the dollar in 1972–73, by a doubling of farm prices, and by a uniquely American phenomenon—the price rebound following the May 1974 termination of the Nixon-era price control program. My econometric interpretation explains the sharpness of inflation's upsurge and output's slump in 1973–74 by the coincidence of these four events, as compared to 1978–80 when there was no post-controls rebound and when the other inflationary stimuli were more spread out in timing.

The rate of growth of inflation and that of real GNP will be negatively correlated in response to a supply shock unless the monetary authority acts to cancel out the impact on either inflation or real output (it cannot cancel both impacts). An important virtue of this interpretation is that it salvages the negative Phillips curve trade-off between inflation and unemployment, which had been abandoned in the early 1970s by casual observers who noticed the positive relation between inflation and unemployment in 1973–76. The negative trade-off remains intact when variables are included to represent the impact of supply shocks.

The early stages of the recovery from the 1973–75 recession primarily reflected the unwinding of the first round of supply shocks. The relative price of oil stabilized and even declined a bit, as did the effective exchange rate of the dollar. The rebound after the price controls also had only a temporary impact on the rate of change of prices.

The economy's rapid expansion in 1977 and 1978 brought the real GNP above its "natural" level, as shown in figure 1. At the same time the inflation rate accelerated. In 1977 the inflation rate appeared to have settled down to a "no shock" rate of about 6 percent, and the speedup of the inflation rate during 1978 was an unpleasant surprise to policymakers in the Carter administration. Their policy had been based on the idea that the unemployment rate could be pushed to 5 percent or below without another acceleration of inflation, and the evidence of 1978 introduced a shift in policy emphasis. In retrospect the acceleration of inflation in 1978 was due partly to the speed of the economy's expansion and partly to the 13 percent depreciation in the effective exchange rate between 1977:Q1 and 1978:Q4. The latter event in turn reflected the much-discussed conflict in economic policy between the United States and other industrial nations, with the U.S. promoting expansionist measures and Germany and Japan resisting them.

Figure 1 shows that real GNP experienced a long period of zero growth, lasting from early 1979 to early 1983. The level of real GNP in the first quarter of 1983 was $1,488 billion, the same as in 1979's third quarter. As natural real GNP continued to grow, the economy fell further and further below the level of production that would maintain unemployment at the natural rate. Unemployment correspondingly rose. This occurred in two stages, first in early 1980 when the unemployment rate rose from 6 to 7.5 percent, and then between mid-1981 and late 1982, with a further increase to 10.7 percent.

In the official chronology of the National Bureau of Economic Research (NBER), there were two recessions. The first occurred for only two quarters, between 1980:Q1 and 1980:Q3. The second began one year later in 1981:Q3 and ended in 1982:Q4. The NBER chose to distinguish two recessions, instead of one longer episode lasting from 1979 to 1982, because it has traditionally used as its criterion the level of real GNP rather than the size of the gap between actual real GNP and a trend-like variable such as natural real GNP. (Figure 1 reveals that the real GNP in early 1981 rose slightly above the previous peak.)

The bottom frame of figure 1 shows that inflation accelerated during the 1980 recession and decelerated continously during the 1981−82 recession. This would appear to brand the 1980 recession as due to supply shocks and the 1981−82 episode as reflecting a deflation in the growth of nominal aggregate demand. While this interpretation of the 1981−82 recession is accurate and reflects the sharp decline in velocity growth highlighted in the appendix, it oversimplifies the story of the short and peculiar 1980 recession. Superimposed on the effect of the 1979 oil shock was a sharp and short-lived reduction in the demand for durable goods in response to credit controls imposed by the Carter administration and the Federal Reserve. This disruptive and ill-advised intervention was a reaction of panic to an inflation rate of 16 percent registered by the Consumer Price Index (CPI) in 1980:Q1. Arcane measurement procedures used in the CPI exaggerated the inflation problem, which barely exceeded 10 percent in the GNP deflator, and thus indirectly caused the credit controls.[7] Without the latter, the 1980 recession might have been gradual and prolonged instead of short and sharp.

The appendix singles out velocity growth as the main source of the deep 1981–82 recession. This velocity behavior requires explanation. It is helpful to divide the episode into two intervals, the first extending from about April 1981 to June 1982, and the second from June 1982 to the winter of 1982–83. The proximate cause of the late 1981 business slump was the sharp deceleration of monetary growth instituted by the Federal Reserve in the spring of 1981. There was virtually no growth in M_1 between April and November, 1981; the growth rate dropped from 10 percent in the year ending in 1981:Q2 to 0.2 percent at an annual rate in 1981:Q3. Short-term interest rates soared to their postwar peaks in May and June. Most of the appreciation of the dollar occurred in this period. The effective exchange rate increased 26 percent in the first three quarters of 1981, and then only another 11 percent in the remaining five quarters through the end of 1982. This double onslaught of high interest rates and an appreciation of the dollar back to the level of 1971 was more than the economy could take, and spending gradually began to decline. The importance of the exchange rate is evident in the observation that fully *three-quarters* of the decline in real GNP between 1981:Q1 and 1982:Q4 is accounted for by a decline in real net exports.

The factor dividing the first and second stages of the recession was a shift in monetary policy. After dropping from 10 percent in the year ending 1981:Q2 to 4.7 percent in the year ending 1982:Q2, monetary growth began to pick up in the summer of 1982, and short-term interest rates dropped quite quickly to single-digit levels. As the autumn proceeded, a trickle of M_1 growth became a torrent, and the annual growth rate in the six months ending in March 1983 reached 15 percent. While many monetarists of the Mark I variety predicted an imminent resurgence of inflation, it was more common for this episode to be viewed as a result of portfolio shifts caused by financial deregulation and the accompanying invention of new types of interest-bearing checkable bank accounts.

Current Policy Issues

The rest of the world has an essential stake in the current policy debate in the United States. How rapidly will the U.S. economic recovery proceed? Will the recovery lead to a resurgence of inflation? The future course of world interest rates and of the dollar's exchange rate depend at least in part on the outlook for U.S. inflation and output growth. It is also necessary to take account of another prominent problem facing policymakers: large and growing fiscal budget deficits.

Designing a glide path for a soft landing. In previous research cited in footnote 3 above, this author has developed an econometric relationship explaining postwar U.S. inflation. If the parameters of this inflation equation can be assumed to remain stable over the next few years, as they have in the past few years, then that device can be used to predict the division between inflation and output growth that would accompany various alternative paths of nominal GNP growth. If the economy were starting out at the natural level of real GNP, then the choice of a nominal GNP path would be easy—we would set nominal GNP growth equal to the sum of inherited inflation plus the growth rate of natural real GNP. Then in the absence of supply shocks the economy could enjoy steady growth. But the control problem is much more difficult when the economy starts out as far from natural output as it did in early 1983. A constant growth rate for nominal GNP inevitably leads to overshooting the feasible level of real GNP, since inflation steadily decelerates in response to economic slack and causes real GNP growth to accelerate just as the economy approaches the natural rate.

The difficulties of managing the economy when the initial unemployment rate is far away from the natural rate can be likened to the problem of a pilot in bringing an airplane in for a smooth landing on a runway. Here altitude corresponds to the unemployment rate, and the runway corresponds to the natural unemployment rate. The problem is to avoid crashing into the runway. The worst thing the Fed can do is choose a constant growth rate of nominal GNP and stick to it, for that would guarantee a crash.

Figure 2

**Alternative Simulations of Inflation and Unemployment Rates
with Steady Nominal GNP Growth of 8 Percent**

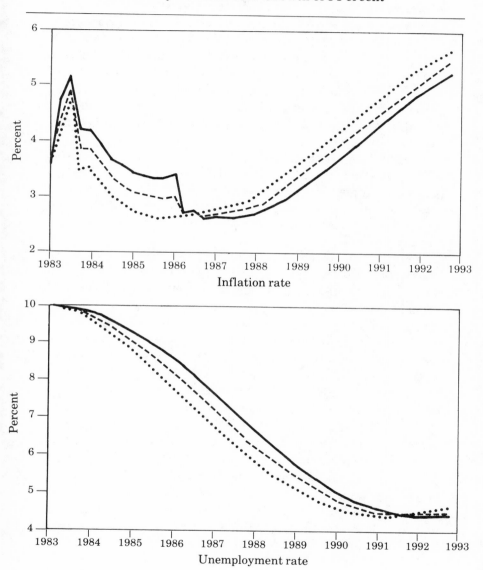

This point is illustrated in figure 2, which shows what happens in a simulation with my econometric inflation equation when the growth rate of nominal GNP is set at 8 percent forever. The economy's recovery is slow, inflation continues to decelerate in response to economic slack, and by definition real GNP growth speeds up. It is as if the pilot had pointed the plane's nose toward the runway and then had turned on the engines full throttle. The lower frame of figure 2 shows how the economy crashes through the assumed 6 percent natural rate of unemployment in the period 1987–88, and the upper frame shows how a companion airplane, the inflation rate, takes off at the same time.

The Fed's task is tougher than the pilot's, because there is no chart that shows the exact altitude of the runway. The band of possible outcomes in figure 2 exhibits only one of the possible sources of uncertainty—the likely future behavior of the main supply shock variables (the relative prices of imports, food, and energy, as well as the exchange rate). The pessimistic path assumes a "full rebound," that all of those variables return to what their values were at the end of 1980 (i.e., that the value of the dollar falls by about one-third in 1983–85 and that the nominal price of oil rises to about $40 per barrel). The optimistic path assumes "no rebound" in these variables, and that they remain at their values as of late 1982. An even more optimistic outcome, not shown, would occur if the real price of oil were to decline further from its late 1982 value.

The maneuver necessary for the pilot to make a soft landing is illustrated in figure 3. Here the growth rate of nominal GNP starts out at 10.5 percent, but in late 1985 is slowed suddenly to 8 percent. With either the optimistic or pessimistic assumptions about supply shocks, the unemployment rate glides smoothly in to the assumed 6 percent natural rate of unemployment. And, as shown in the top frame, the inflation rate (p) smoothly adjusts to the long-run 5 percent rate that is compatible with an 8 percent nominal GNP growth rate (y) and a 3 percent growth rate of natural real GNP (q^N), since in the long run $p = y - q^N$.[8]

The Fed must decelerate the growth rate of nominal GNP when the economy nears its natural rate of unemployment. That is the prerequisite for a soft landing. But a likely side effect of any attempt to achieve a sudden slowing of nominal GNP growth is a

Figure 3

**Alternative Simulations of Inflation and Unemployment Rates
with Nominal GNP Growth of 10.5 Percent in 1983–85 and
8 Percent Thereafter**

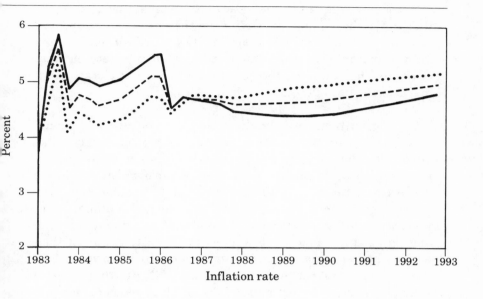

Inflation rate

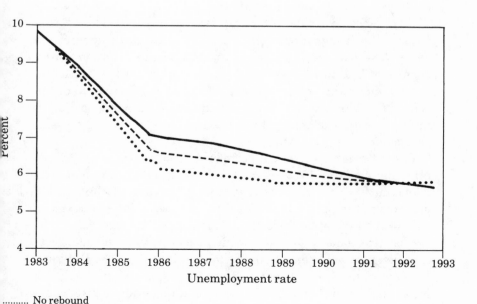

Unemployment rate

.... No rebound
– – – Half rebound
——— Full rebound

sharp increase in interest rates, and perhaps a recession during the transition period. To minimize the danger of inducing this type of instability, the Fed should plan to induce a rapid recovery when the economy is far from the natural rate and gradually to taper the growth rate of nominal GNP from then on. There is no compelling alternative. Rapid nominal GNP growth maintained forever guarantees a crash landing. But even moderate nominal GNP growth maintained forever eventually leads to a crash landing, as shown in figure 2.

Coping with supply shocks. The problems raised by supply shocks can again be separated into two subproblems: those that arise when the economy was previously operating at the natural rate, and those that arise when the unemployment rate is far above the natural rate. When the Fed stabilizes nominal GNP growth and an adverse supply shock introduces spontaneous upward pressure on the inflation rate, real GNP growth must decline and the unemployment rate is likely to rise. The Fed must then decide whether to maintain constant nominal GNP growth, to "accommodate" the shock by raising nominal GNP growth to insulate unemployment, or to "extinguish" the shock by reducing nominal GNP growth to insulate the inflation rate.

If the shock is truly temporary, e.g., a freeze in Florida that reduces the orange crop, then accommodation is the appropriate policy. The lost crop will soon return, and the inflation consequences will soon be reversed. The temporary bulge of inflation has no important welfare consequences, since it is soon to disappear. Maintenance of stable unemployment avoids potential future problems of readjusting after a recession caused by non-accommodation.

The optimal response to a permanent shock, e.g., the OPEC oil price increases of 1973–74 and 1979–80, poses a more serious dilemma. If there is a one-time upward ratchet of the relative price of oil, then there is a temporary positive bulge in the *rate of change* of the relative price of oil. If the nominal wage rate in the rest of the economy were to remain constant, then the aggregate inflation rate would exhibit only a temporary bulge. The Fed could accommodate without fearing a permanent increase in the rate of inflation. But, unfortunately, the nominal wage rate in most countries is implicitly or explicitly escalated in response to changes in the consumer price index. Thus a permanent oil shock causes inflation to ratchet upward permanently to a new higher rate. The Fed must choose between ratifying permanently higher inflation or causing lost output and higher unemployment if it chooses a nonaccommodative policy.

If all tax rules, regulations, and institutions had been inflation-neutralized, there would be no problem. It would be optimal to ratify the faster inflation. Critics could claim rightly that the process of inflation-adjusting the institutions had actually *caused* the faster inflation, but defenders of the Fed's accommodation would point out that this criticism was now irrelevant because the inflation rate no longer mattered, at least within limits.[9] And defenders of accommodation would point out that the extra unemployment caused by failure to accommodate has not just been a short-run cost, but also has created a long-run cost by causing future economic instability and making a soft landing more difficult to achieve.

There is an additional aspect of the accommodation debate that reflects the benefit of hindsight. Oil conservation is a gradual process. This creates a natural "overshooting" phenomenon, since a jump in the relative price of oil, like that achieved by OPEC in 1979–80, breeds a lagged adjustment process by hundreds of millions of consumers around the world. Eventually after a few months or years the demand for oil relative to real GNP begins to fall, and downward pressure is exerted on the relative price. In this sense an oil shock that appears at the time to be permanent is not permanent, and with sufficient patience the Fed can avoid making the difficult choice among accommodative, constant nominal GNP growth, and extinguishing policies. Patience, however, is eminently lacking from the policy process and from the political oratory that surrounds it.

A novel decision problem was created by the decline in the relative price of oil that occurred in 1982 and 1983, when the economy was away from the natural rate of unemployment. This "beneficial supply shock" may appear to be an unalloyed blessing, in that it would allow a more rapid growth rate of real GNP for any path of nominal GNP growth. And the example of figure 3 suggests that real GNP growth should be as rapid as possible at the beginning of the recovery in order to minimize the cost of high unemployment while allowing for a slowdown later on.

The main argument for resisting rather than enjoying the decline in the relative price of oil was not monetary but fiscal. The interval of declining relative oil prices provided an ideal environment for introducing a substantial excise tax on imported oil. This policy, endorsed by many economists as early as 1974, took on an added appeal in light of large projected structural fiscal deficits. In view of the estimates of figures 2 and 3, any such excise tax was unlikely to cause an acceleration of inflation, particularly if it was introduced in stages.

Coping with federal budget deficits. In the United States it is common to distinguish between cyclical budget deficits caused by a shortfall of actual below-natural real GNP, and the structural budget deficit, sometimes called the "high employment deficit." After remaining in the range of 0 to 2 percent of GNP in the period between 1965 and 1980, the structural deficit is scheduled under present policies to grow to roughly 5 percent of GNP by the mid-1980s. This new deficit problem results from two of the central policy components of the Reagan administration's economic program: a "supply-side" reduction of 25 percent in the personal income tax rate (adopted by Congress in 1981 and implemented in three stages between 1981 and 1983), and rapid growth in real defense spending, offset to only a partial extent by reductions in nondefense spending.

Casual journalistic commentaries on the U.S. economic situation express concern that large budget deficits could "abort" the economic recovery in 1984 and later years. But this fear stands economic analysis on its head. For any given growth rate of the money supply, the growth of nominal spending will be greater with a growing structural deficit than with a shrinking one. Policymakers should set the speed of the economic recovery by examining the consequences of alternative growth paths for nominal GNP; if the recovery appears to falter below the chosen path, the Fed can reduce interest rates and cause the exchange rate to depreciate with a suitable set of open-market operations accompanied by clear explanations of what it is intending to achieve (without the explanation, markets may fear that the Fed has made a mistake and will soon reverse itself).

When the economy returns to its natural level of real GNP, there can be no doubt that large structural deficits will "crowd out" private investment. A deficit of 5 percent of GNP could reduce net fixed investment to half of its historical level. Many commentators rightly fear that the economic recovery will consist of too large a share of consumption in real GNP, and too small a share of private investment and of the foreign trade surplus.

The prospect of large structural deficits and the failure, at least so far, for the "supply-side" income tax reductions to unleash any noticeable increase in work effort or saving, have led to a flurry of creative new proposals for drastic revamping of the U.S. tax system. Some urge adoption of a progressive consumption tax by gradually lifting the taxation of saving, while others support adoption of a "flat"—i.e., proportional—income tax with a much broader tax base. The prime motivation behind the two proposals is different, with devotees of the consumption tax mainly interested in stimulating national saving in order to promote more private investment and, hopefully, economic growth; whereas supporters of the flat income tax are primarily interested in tax simplification and in improving the economic efficiency of the society by reducing the energy devoted to tax avoidance and by shifting portions of the underground economy out into the daylight.

Economic Thinking in America

The American policy debate in 1983 reminds one of a three-ring circus, with all the important and interesting action taking place inside a central tent and with most of the audience confused by false directions to remain outside, wandering from sideshow to sideshow. A peek inside the central tent would reveal four rings containing the real issues in the struggle for sustainable economic growth.

1. *Government vs. private investment.* Many discussions of fiscal policy treat achievement of a government surplus as the main prerequisite for a revival in the growth of output and productivity. Yet Japan and Italy, among others, grew faster than the United States during the past decade with much larger structural fiscal deficits. Other analyses—particularly the 1983

Economic Report of the President—treat boosting private net fixed capital formation as the main prerequisite. Yet legions of econometricians have failed to find more than a minor role for capital formation in explaining the slowdown of productivity growth in the U.S. since the mid-1960s. We have heard too often that private investment is good and government spending bad, and too infrequently that there is a trade-off between private investment, government investment, and government consumption. More government investment and less private investment could conceivably make the economy better off in the long run. The large amounts being spent by American corporations in remedial training for high school graduates who are deficient in reading, writing, and math suggest that education has been shortchanged. I suspect that we need a mixture of "throwing money at the problem," particularly in focused activities like providing minicomputers for inner-city schools, and the use of scarce but inexpensive leadership at the national level to pressure and cajole local school districts into upgrading requirements for basic courses and changing teacher and student attitudes. There is similar room for a mixture of money and leadership in the areas of retraining, relocation, industrial policy, and labor-management relations.

2. *Nominal GNP targeting and the choice of a growth path.* In 1983 the financial press carried a blizzard of words about Federal Reserve operating procedures, financial deregulation, and the accusations by some monetarists that double-digit growth of M_1 was irresponsibly inflationary. Yet the 1981–82 recession demonstrated that it was nominal GNP growth, not the growth of some arbitrary monetary aggregate, that mattered for inflation. Monetarists talked and wrote as though money growth mattered only for inflation and velocity growth mattered only for output; but inflation continued to decelerate as velocity collapsed and M_1 growth exploded, suggesting that nominal GNP is what matters. If so, that should be the main control variable of the Federal Reserve. And this new focus on what actually matters would allow the Fed to concentrate on central issues, like the choice of a glide path as in figures 2 and 3 above.

3. *Protectionism, industrial policy, and regulation.* While the main

orientation of this paper has been toward business cycles and macroeconomics, there are interesting areas of overlap with present microeconomic concerns, particularly those relating to protectionism and "industrial policy." The new wave of sentiment for greater trade protection in the United States followed promptly in response to the 1981–82 depression in the U.S. durable goods industries, which led some observers to describe the industrial Middle West as the "Rust Bowl" (a play of words on the mid-1930s drought-ridden "Dust Bowl" immortalized in John Steinbeck's *Grapes of Wrath*).

Most descriptions of the plight of U.S. heavy industry attributed the problem to only one cause, "low-cost competition" from underpaid foreign workers, often aided by unfair government subsidies and "dumping" by foreign producers. There was little comment on the obvious macroeconomic component of the price advantage enjoyed by foreign producers, the 1981–82 appreciation of the American dollar that accompanied the unprecedented increase in U.S. real interest rates. In this sense the lower wage rates of Japanese workers measured in dollars is a phenomenon made in Washington, not in Tokyo. Accordingly, I found enthusiastic agreement in a recent conversation with a senior vice-president of the Ford Motor Company with the observation that "the best cure for the 'rust bowl' disease is a dollar worth 175 yen, rather than either protection or industrial policy."

The surge of sentiment in the U.S. for a "new industrial policy" emerges from a confluence of causes. Some proponents are genuinely distressed by the plight of workers whose lives and communities are harmed by plant closings, and they feel with some justification that U.S. corporations should be forced to adopt the set of prenotification rules now common in some Northern European countries. Other proponents are less thoughtful and are playing the popular new American game called "copy the Japanese," citing the role of the Japanese Ministry of Industry and Technology (MITI) in steering investment into specific areas that in some cases have had a high-tech component. Skeptics in the U.S. doubt that the MITI strategy would work in our setting, in light of the vigor of the U.S. venture capital market that scans Silicon Valley in California with the intensity of an electron microscope and almost instantly endows any promising high-tech company with start-up money and later with a high price-earnings ratio on its initial stock offering. In my view the real problems in U.S. industrial structure have to do not with the need to stimulate new industries but with the macroeconomic environment, particularly the large prospective structural deficits that cause the dollar to be overvalued (thus aggravating the adjustment problem of the Rust Bowl) and that "crowd out" job-creating private investment by soaking up an excessive proportion of the pitiful amount of household saving that Americans manage to do.

The current microeconomic policy issue that seems furthest removed from macroeconomic concerns is the recent U.S. push for deregulation, after fifteen years of increasing government regulation (particularly in the areas of environmental quality and occupational safety and health). In the macroeconomic context I would point to regulation as a direct source of the worldwide productivity slowdown and an indirect source of the upsurge of inflation in the 1970s. But careful work by Edward Denison and others attributes only a small part of the U.S. productivity slowdown to the regulation phenomenon, even *before* taking account of the fact that the benefits of such regulation (cleaner air and water, less death and illness from black and brown lungs) are not included in GNP or productivity statistics. Macroeconomists can say little about this topic except to repeat one of the most important lines from any good undergraduate principles textbook, namely that there is no pregiven right amount of pollution to eliminate, neither 0 nor 100 percent. The right amount depends on marginal costs and benefits of eliminating pollution, and the right way to influence private firms to eliminate the optimal amount is to levy "smoke taxes" rather than engage in quantitative regulation.

4. *Loosening institutional constraints.* It is now a commonplace to recognize that monetary policy is not made in isolation, and that other decision-makers, particularly politicians who declare wars and create structural fiscal deficits, force central banks to make difficult choices. It is less generally recognized that a wide range of society's institutions constrain monetary

policy. Instead of allocating to monetary and fiscal policy the dominant role in discussions of unemployment, inflation, and growth, increased attention should be given to shifts in institutions to improve macroeconomic efficiency and place less of a burden on traditional policy tools.

The list of institutions that matter for macroeconomic policy is a long one. Three-year union wage contracts in the United States contribute significantly to wage and price inertia and raise the output cost of disinflation (albeit while reducing the short-run inflation cost of an output boom that pushes unemployment beneath the natural rate). Deposit rate ceilings and usury laws prevent the adjustment of interest rates to inflation, contribute to inflation's redistribution of wealth from creditors to debtors, and thus raise the welfare cost of inflation. Financial deregulation has reduced those welfare costs and has shifted the balance of argument in favor of a rapid rather than slow recovery, while at the same time making traditional monetary aggregates increasingly irrelevant as intermediate targets for monetary policy. Although indexation of tax brackets has been proposed for 1985, the continuing failure to set tax rules of interest deductability and capital gains taxation in real terms, and the failure of the government to offer an indexed bond, add to inflation's welfare cost. Our constitutional system and its associated legislative lags inhibit adoption of well-timed countercyclical fiscal policies, like the Swedish investment fund and the Japanese practice of variable timing for public works. The absence of a national value-added or sales tax prevents policies, recommended by Arthur Okun and myself in 1974–75, to insulate the price level from adverse supply shocks by taxing the shocked product and reducing the sales tax on the unshocked sector. Improved labor market institutions and government attention to retraining and mobility could lower the natural unemployment rate itself, which should not be viewed as truly natural, optimal, or immutable.

Unfortunately, however, institutional reform is a slow process, and economists have not advanced very far in understanding why apparently counterproductive institutions exist.

Appendix

Basic Characteristics of U.S. Business Cycles

1949–1982

Phase	Date phase begins	Length of phase in years	Four-quarter growth rates Money supply (m)	+ Velocity of M_1 (v)	= Nominal GNP (y)	= GNP deflator (p)	+ Real GNP (q)	Value at start of phase Output ratio	Unemployment rate
	(1)	(2)	(3)	(4)	(5)	(6)	(7)	(8)	(9)
Expansion	1949:Q4	3.50	4.3	6.5	10.8	3.3	7.5	93.5	7.0
Plateau	—	—	—	—	—	—	—	—	—
Recession	1953:Q2	1.00	0.8	−2.7	−1.9	1.4	−3.3	104.5	2.6
Expansion	1954:Q2	1.50	2.9	5.6	8.5	2.0	6.5	98.3	5.8
Plateau	1955:Q4	1.75	0.8	6.1	6.9	3.6	3.3	103.5	4.2
Recession	1957:Q4	0.75	0.6	−3.2	−2.6	1.0	−3.6	100.5	4.2
Expansion	1958:Q2	1.00	4.5	6.3	10.8	2.7	8.1	95.6	7.4
Plateau	1959:Q2	1.00	−0.6	3.8	3.2	1.5	1.7	100.6	5.1
Recession	1960:Q2	0.75	1.9	−1.4	0.5	0.6	−0.1	98.8	5.2
Expansion	1961:Q1	5.00	3.8	3.9	7.7	1.9	5.8	96.1	6.8
Plateau	1966:Q1	3.75	5.0	2.3	7.3	4.3	3.0	105.7	3.9
Recession	1969:Q4	1.00	5.0	−0.1	4.9	5.0	−0.1	102.3	3.6
Expansion	1970:Q4	2.25	7.7	3.5	11.2	4.6	6.6	98.1	5.9
Plateau	1973:Q1	0.75	4.8	4.7	9.5	7.3	2.2	103.7	4.9

Recession	1973:Q4	1.25	4.4	1.4	5.8	10.1	-4.3	102.6	4.8
Expansion	1975:Q1	3.75	7.1	4.7	11.8	6.5	5.3	94.3	8.2
Plateau	1978:Q4	1.25	7.4	2.7	10.1	8.5	1.6	100.9	5.8
Recession	1980:Q1	0.50	10.8	-5.5	5.3	9.5	-4.2	99.0	6.2
Expansion	1980:Q3	0.50	7.9	8.5	16.4	10.2	6.2	95.5	7.5
Plateau	1981:Q1	0.50	4.5	3.6	8.1	7.7	0.4	97.0	7.3
Recession	1981:Q3	1.50	6.1	-1.6	4.5	5.9	-1.4	95.5	7.4
Average all cycles (weighted by length)									
Expansion		2.53	5.1	5.1	10.2	3.8	6.4	95.9	6.9
Plateau		1.28	3.9	3.5	7.4	4.9	2.5	101.9	5.2
Recession		0.98	4.0	-1.4	2.6	5.2	-2.6	100.5	4.9

Sources: Column (1) Federal Reserve System; (4) derived as residual; (5–7) Department of Commerce; (8) Robert J. Gordon, "Inflation, Flexible Exchange Rates, and the Natural Rate of Unemployment," in *Workers, Jobs and Inflation*, ed. M. N. Baily (Washington, D.C.: Brookings, 1982), pp. 88–157; (9) Bureau of Labor Statistics.

COMMENTS

Michael J. Boskin

As usual, I have found Bob Gordon's paper interesting, informative, and enjoyable reading. Unfortunately, it has little to do with the primary focus of the conference, economic growth, except in a very short-term sense. Clearly, there is at least a temporary relationship between economic fluctuations and long-term economic growth, and one can even develop various models in which the interaction is permanent. But Gordon does not even dwell on these sorts of issues, a point to which I will return in a moment.

We are presented with an interesting analysis of the recent performance of the U.S. economy with respect to inflation, output, unemployment, and money growth. Gordon is somewhat convincing in claiming that his strawman opponent, a constant-growth monetary rule (CGMR), would not completely dampen economic fluctuations in the United States. Of course he, as most of us, oversimplifies the "monetarist" position. The monetarist proposition would have been more accurately presented if it stated that a CGMR would have been preferable to the active demand management, both monetary and fiscal, followed in the United States. I do not believe that the relatively minor fraction of fluctuations in nominal GNP growth that can be accounted for by procyclical fluctuations in the growth rate of the money supply in postwar U.S. business cycles is sufficient evidence to dismiss this latter contention. Let me say, however, that there are enough potential "surprises" or "shocks" to the economy that the case for abandoning "gross-tuning" is far less compelling than for abandoning "fine-tuning."

Gordon goes on to describe the basic characteristics of postwar U.S. business cycles. He then provides an interesting interpretation of these events based on econometric estimates (primarily his own) of the relationships among the variables he discusses. He presents alternative scenarios for the paths of inflation and unemployment in a simulation based on his inflation equations. His primary conclusion—that the Federal Reserve must decelerate the growth rate of nominal GNP as the economy nears its natural rate of unemployment—is plausible given his model and estimates. Yet other models and estimates, no more implausible, give somewhat different results, and obviate the need for the type of "glide path" that Gordon advocates.

Gordon correctly dismisses the substantial concern with short-run budget deficits, emphasizing a potential crowding out of private investment (and I would add, of housing and state and local government capital spending) when the economy returns to its potential GNP. That is, the composition of output may well be affected, with too large a share of consumption and too small a share of private investment in GNP.

Gordon also properly points out that some government expenditure is investment, and that one needs to compare overall rates of return to decide whether more private or more government investment is called for. Of course, government nonmilitary investment has fallen precipitously in the United States in the past thirteen years. Whether the rate of return on the types of increased spending Gordon advocates would be sufficient to offset the costs is a matter of substantial dispute. I would also echo his interpretation of protectionism, industrial policy, and regulation. The overvalued dollar is clearly much more at cause for our net trade deficit than any set of export subsidies provided by foreign governments. Gordon also suggests loosening various institutional constraints, as in the recent financial deregulation undergone in the United States. I applaud these suggestions.

What, then, is the relationship between Gordon's analysis and alternative suggestions to speed recovery and real output in the United States, or to "manage" economic fluctuations, and economic growth?

First, there is the undeniable short-term loss of real output from the worldwide recession. Whether this loss of output could have been ameliorated substantially either by a different disinflation process producing the same reduction in inflation, or by accommodating the inflation is a somewhat more subtle point than is usually discussed by macroeconomists. It is not clear to me that long-run potential output is unaffected by even the modest types of inflation we have had in the United States. Gordon himself points to a variety of aspects of this in our institutional arrangements: e.g., our unindexed tax rules for depreciation, capital gain, and interest, among others. There can be no doubt that these have had some influence on the reduction in real net capital formation. Gordon's reading of the evidence notwithstanding, I consider rising real tax rates on capital income to have reduced investment. This reduction is important in explaining the slowdown in productivity growth (and has been so signified by several econometric studies). Further, there may well be reasons to believe that the type of inflation the United States was experiencing was not stable. The alternative of avoiding so severe a recession by keeping an inflation rate of 10 or 12 percent might not have been available; instead, ever-worsening inflation might have occurred as various periodic episodes made it necessary to stimulate nominal GNP to prevent a decline in real output. At that point, one is led to ask what the (largely unmeasured) loss in real output is in an economy where a large fraction of its citizens devote much of their time and energy to "betting against" inflation in borrowing and lending activities, for example, rather than in the direct production of goods and services. I do not believe contemporary macroeconomics has an adequate answer to the question of whether the appropriate measure of the loss of real output is the short-run deviation from the apparent short-run sustainable level of real output in the course of a recession, or whether this measure must be adjusted for an inevitable loss in future real output, discounted of course to the present. These concerns have led economists from Hayek to Fellner to question not only the minimization of the cost of inflation, but the actual measures of potential output that are used in calculations of this sort.

Deep recessions can have deleterious effects on long-term growth in a variety of ways. A long-lasting recession can seriously disrupt the human capital formation of an entire vintage of workers, leading them to experience different career paths and productivity growth. It can have similar effects on the capital stock. While it has become fashionable to speak of the substantial increase in risk for long-term investment that inflation had in the United States in the 1970s, it is clear that frequent and substantial fluctuations in real output and employment likewise lead to substantial risk to the economy. But recessions, for all the costs and suffering involved, also are a time of substantial reorganization of resource allocation in an economy such as the United States, and while it is perhaps inertia and inflexibility in various institutions and markets that dramatically quicken the pace of this reallocation, it may well be that some (hopefully modest) fraction of that "lost output" is necessary to improve future productivity.

What then about long-term economic growth in the United States? After over two decades of super-normal economic growth — an average 2.5 percent annual rate of increase in real terms in private nonfarm business productivity, averaged over business cycles—the growth of output per worker slowed noticeably in the late 1960s. Just as much and perhaps more is at stake in such long-term productivity-growth slowdowns as in whatever fraction of the conventionally measured lost output could have been avoided. Consider what small differentials in growth rates have done to the relative wealth of societies over the space of a couple of generations.

Much has been written about the determinants of long-term growth in the United States and elsewhere. Much attention also is focused on the causes of the productivity-growth slowdown in recent years in the advanced world. No definitive answers can be given to questions such as how we can partition the growth slowdown into its various contributing factors; and what would happen to the long-term growth rate if policy X were changed to produce outcome Y. Unfortunately, the U.S. political economy tends to operate with an implicitly enormous rate of time preference: short-term benefits and costs are weighed heavily, and long-term benefits and costs are highly discounted. The long-term effects of policies that chip away at the foundation of economic growth—a high quality and growing rate of capital per worker; improved knowledge, skills, and motivation of our labor force; institutions that allow resources to allocate themselves efficiently—tend to be ignored. Thus heavy taxation of capital income in the 1970s interacted in an insidious way with the unindexed tax system to raise dramatically the marginal tax rates on investment income. This was no doubt one of the reasons for the reduced rate of net capital formation and the shift away from investment in structures to investment in shorter-lived assets.

Capital formation and technological progress are at least two determinants of economic growth that most economists would consider important, though they would differ with respect to the quantitative significance attached to each. It is important to note that there are at least two potential links between the two. If new technology is much more cheaply embodied in new capital than in old, then a very low rate of investment means that technology is being diffused through the capital stock at too low a rate. Second, if there is a substantial amount of learning by doing—that is, if in the course of the investment process new products and processes become known and available—then the social rate of return exceeds the private rate of return in investment. Both of these reasons, which admittedly are difficult to document empirically, lead me to believe there is a strong feedback between the low rate of capital formation in the U.S. and the low rate of technological progress. I also believe that a substantial increase in the rate of capital formation is a necessary, but not sufficient, condition to increase the *long-term* growth rate of productivity. It is clear that this is one of the primary purposes of the structural revisions in the 1981 tax laws as amended in 1982. The accelerated cost recovery system (ACRS) was designed, albeit imperfectly, to redress the substantial erosion of depression allowance generated by the high inflation of the 1970s. However, the high before-tax cost of capital has more than offset the tax reductions, and thus, even when capacity utilization is once again within reach, it is not clear that the investment rate will be any higher than it was prior to the recession. In fact, it has been at a postwar low for the last two years.

Gordon properly emphasizes the potential role of human capital formation and the potential role of government in financing it. I have indicated that recessions can have potential long-term impacts on productivity-enhancing experience, but it is also clear that there are many other factors potentially affecting the rate of human investment. While I suspect that cultural and sociological factors are quite important in the decline of the quality of educational outcomes in the United States, it is clear that a variety of institutions are not functioning very well. For example, the tax system now taxes investment in human beings more heavily than investment in physical equipment.

Restoring long-term productivity growth in the United States to anything like its historical level for the past hundred years, or even to levels sufficient to make each generation noticeably better off than that which preceded it, has much more importance than the policy attention it receives. We must find some way of evaluating sensibly the long-term benefits and costs of these government policies and giving them equal weight with attempts to do something about fluctuations in the short-term performance of the economy.

Let me conclude by restating that I do believe that the world-wide recession, which Gordon attributes primarily to U.S. monetary policy (I would spread the blame to other central banks and to the worldwide inflation of the 1970s as well), certainly caused substantial disruption in economic activity and a substantial short-term loss in real output. Whether the present value of the ultimate course of real output has been decreased by the recession is another story. But in the United States, at least, substantial offset in terms of high future productivity growth is likely, due to anticipated higher rates of investment and technical change resulting from a combination of the reduction of inflation and of the disincentives to invest and innovate that are embedded in the tax laws.

III

Developing Countries: Case Studies in Progression and Retrogression

7

UMA LELE

Tanzania: Phoenix or Icarus?

Since President Nyerere's Arusha Declaration in 1967, Tanzania has rivaled only India before the mid-1960s and China since then in the attention its development strategy has received in the international development community.[1] This high visibility has produced high expectations of performance and substantial scrutiny of the country's development strategy.[2]

Tanzania is now suffering its worst economic crisis since independence. The magnitude of its problems is indicated by the fact that in the decade between 1971 and 1981, per capita income in the country's monetized sector declined nearly by half; and despite official rhetoric of self-reliance, dependence on food and financial aid has increased and shows signs of becoming permanent. In the wake of these severe economic difficulties, the

---

The views expressed in this paper are those of the author and they should not be interpreted as reflecting the views of the World Bank.

159

fascination with Tanzania's exciting "experiment" has not only begun to wear thin, but growing disenchantment has set in, even among the country's long-time admirers.[3]

It is not surprising that Tanzania's sympathizers and critics emphasize different things in judging the underlying causes of the current economic crisis. Admirers, as one would expect, share the view articulated by President Nyerere about the adverse effects of international events, which are beyond the control of government policymakers. These include the roles played by the drought in 1973−74, the break-up of the East African Community in 1977, the Ugandan War in 1979, and the two oil price increases in 1974 and 1979.[4] The primary commodity market slump, following the beverage boom in 1976−77, has also been unexpectedly long. All of these events cost the Tanzanian economy an estimated U.S. $1.7 billion[5]—compared to its 1980 GDP of U.S. $4.3 billion.

While critics of the government acknowledge the role of these external events, they place a considerable measure of blame on failures of the government's own domestic economic policy—not just problems of implementation (as President Nyerere has argued), but defects in the government's basic development strategy.[6] Critics argue that the willingness to face flaws in the underlying strategy is long overdue, and that fundamental reforms in the strategy are urgently needed to reverse the present decline in the country's production and productivity. While acknowledging Tanzania's substantial social achievements, critics note that the country has been one of Africa's largest recipients of foreign aid,[7] and that total aid of about U.S. $2.7 billion during the 1971−81 period[8] far exceeds the cost of the external events mentioned above.

The debate continues about where and how far Tanzania needs to depart from its declared development strategy to alleviate the present crisis and restore the Tanzanian economy to a path of stable growth. In this chapter, we will first consider Tanzania's socioeconomic structure and then examine its recent economic performance. By exploring the causes of the recent economic crisis, we may clarify our understanding of policy reforms that are necessary to end the current crisis.

The Socioeconomic Setting

Tanzania, which had a population of about 19 million in 1982, is classified as a "least-developed" country.[9] Agriculture is the most important sector. It provides livelihood for about 80 percent of the population and contributes between 35 and 45 percent to gross domestic product (GDP). Agro-based exports constitute 80 percent of total exports and are an important source of government revenue. Agriculture has been the major source of food and raw materials for the small but expanding modern sector; it is also the most important market for goods and services produced in the industrial sector. Agriculturally led growth is thus crucial to achieving overall economic growth, and especially to achieving broad participation in that growth. The current macroeconomic crisis in Tanzania is largely an agricultural crisis.

Tanzania's present agricultural production structure may be classified into five major categories: peasants owning under 10 hectares of land, medium-scale farmers with up to 100 hectares, large-scale tractorized commercial producers with over 100 hectares, private estates, and nationalized estates and the newly established state farms. Estimates of their respective shares in agricultural production are shown in table 1.

Since World War I, the largely subsistence peasant agricultural sector began to commercialize, with its rapidly growing production of export crops such as coffee, tea, tobacco, and pyrethrum. These crops formerly had been the exclusive domain of the European estate sector. By the time independence was won in 1961, there had been considerable diversification in crops, with the introduction of such new crops as cotton, cashews, cardamom, and oilseeds grown almost entirely by the peasant sector. Export-crop production grew by about 3.5 percent annually from the 1930s to early 1950s,[10] accelerated to about 6 percent in the 1950s, and the growth rate remained at that level until the late 1960s.

Throughout the postwar period, a grassroots peasant cooperative movement had made impressive inroads into a largely Asian-dominated agricultural trading sector. By the time of independence, peasant smallholders were a dynamic force in the economy.

Tanzania's extremely low level of manpower and institutional development at independence was reflected in its mere handful of

Table 1

Distribution of Crop Production by Type of Farming Unit (1970s)

(as percentage of total crop marketed through official channels)

	Producers				
	Peasant (under 10 hectares)	Medium (10–100 hectares)	Large (100+ hectares)	Private estate	Public estate
Food crops					
Maize	85[a]	10[a]	5[a]		negligible
Rice	50				50
Wheat			—— 5[b] ——		95
Drought staples	95[a]	5[a]			
Sugar	15[c]	5[a]	5[a]		85
Legumes	90[a]	5[a]	5[a]		
Export crops					
Coffee	85[d]			10	5[d]
Cotton	95[a]	5[a]			negligible
Sisal				50	50
Cashews	100				negligible
Tobacco	90	5[a]		5[e]	5[d]
Tea	25[d]			70	
Pyrethrum	100				
Seed beans	100		—— 100 ——		

[a]Rough estimates; no precise breakdown available.

[b]In the early 1970s, marketed production from large and private estates accounted for over 90 percent of the total official procurement.

[c]Peasant outgrowers at public estates.

[d]Estimated breakdown between smallholders and public estates.

[e]In the early 1970s, output from private estates accounted for over 25 percent of the total marketed output.

Source: World Bank estimates.

university graduates. There was no significant domestic educational institution beyond the secondary level. Despite the vibrance of the African entrepreneurial class in the traditional sector, neither it nor the intelligentsia was large enough to build a modern economy quickly. Europeans managed the estate sector and the top levels of the government administration. The service sector and the minuscule manufacturing sector were mainly in the hands of the Asian community. This division of economic activity along racial lines, and especially the commercial dominance of the Asian community, have posed serious sociopolitical problems for Tanzania. While the new leadership idealized the building of a multiracial nation in the years following independence, it also faced a strong political need to "Africanize" quickly. The effect of these social considerations in formulating economic policy has received relatively little attention from Tanzania's analysts—in contrast to their concern about the serious ideological difficulties posed by the existence of a private sector.

In shaping development policies, considerations of tribal integration and development of a national identity have been far more significant among Tanzanian policymakers than is typical in Africa. Though Tanzania's African population has not been dominated by a few major tribes to the extent that it has in Kenya and many other African countries, at independence the Hayas and the Chaggas were agriculturally the most prosperous, and were represented in the government service because of their better educational background. Tanzania's achievements in tribal integration are underscored by the fact that both education and economic activity are now far more diversified. Tanzania also stands out among African nations for its virtual absence of overt tribal or racial conflicts. Once again it seems that while Tanzania's gains in the more direct areas of social welfare are frequently scrutinized, its successful national integration is less commonly noted. The adverse economic consequences of its policies to achieve regional equity must therefore be viewed in the context of this major sociopolitical achievement. As I will point out, however, both the degree to which economic policies have been distorted, and the type of political and bureaucratic interventions that have been followed to achieve these social objectives have now made the Tanzanian strategy so unviable economically as to threaten its major achievements.

The role of foreign aid in Tanzania's development should similarly be noted at the outset. Some may argue that foreign aid is simply a rather inefficient transfer payment to compensate for the injustices of the international economic order. From a different perspective, however, the financial aid received has been clearly disproportionate to Tanzania's limited absorptive capacity. Nor has the form in which aid has been given been helpful in improving this capacity. The project-by-project approach followed by donors has not been the result of a critical assessment of the feasibility of the overall development strategy. There has been inadequate examination of the ways in which foreign assistance could be used to increase the very limited local financial, manpower, and institutional capacity. Donors have taken the government's rhetorical statements about development objectives largely at face value, and they have competed with each other for a limited number of project ideas. This has led to a rapid buildup of the public sector. The resulting imbalance in the productive and service sectors has contributed—albeit inadvertently—to the considerable inefficiency of resource use.

I do not mean to suggest that no lessons have been learned by donors from their experiences in administering aid. Attempts have been made to simplify projects and to emphasize institutional and manpower development. During periods of economic crisis, donors have shifted project aid to program assistance. There is greater awareness of the importance of a constructive policy and institutional environment. But there has been relatively little questioning of the implications of past experience with foreign aid on the form that aid takes, or even of the way these forms themselves have affected domestic developmental priorities. None of these problems with aid is unique to Tanzania. Their general applicability to other least-developed countries highlighted the urgent need for an examination of ways to increase the effectiveness of foreign assistance.

Economic Performance

Because of deficiencies in data, especially those related to the subsistence sector, assessment of the performance of the GNP over time is neither possible nor desirable. Instead, a more disaggregated picture of economic performance is presented below.

External trade and balance of payments. Appendix table A-1 presents the balance-of-payments picture for the last fifteen years, a good indicator of the relative importance of the various domestic and international factors that have influenced Tanzania's economic performance since the mid-1960s. Before the first oil price increase and the major drought in 1973–74, the Tanzanian balance of payments was not in any major difficulty. Small current-account deficits were offset by aid receipts, while good harvests were reflected in record export volumes. From 1973 on, however, export volumes stagnated or declined. The import composition changed and import prices increased. These various factors led to a steadily deteriorating balance of payments, with a temporary respite in 1976 and 1977 due to high coffee prices. Since then large deficits have appeared in the current-account balance, and external reserves have long since been exhausted. Payment arrears have been persistent not simply on commercial imports but also on debt service. These are likely to have a serious adverse effect on Tanzania's ability to mobilize external resources. Restrictions on imports have been in effect since 1974, with a brief period of liberalization during 1977–78 in the wake of the coffee boom. A devaluation of the Tanzanian shilling (Tsh) by 10 percent vis-à-vis the Special Drawing Rights (SDR) took place in the same year. The shilling was further devalued by 10 percent in relation to the U.S. dollar in 1982.

During the 1970s the government succeeded in marshalling an increased inflow of concessionary foreign assistance to counter the current-account deficit. Close to 40 percent of aid in 1981 came in the form of program assistance, mainly to finance food and maintenance imports.[11] The symbiotic relationship of aid with the distorted domestic resource allocation will be discussed later.

Despite current debt-servicing problems, Tanzania's commercial borrowings and debt-service ratios are low, and are not the cause of the present difficulties.[12] Nor is the deterioration in any significant measure a result of the declining prices of Tanzanian exports in relation to imports (appendix table A-2). Though the current low level of commodity prices compared to those of

manufactured goods is causing difficulties for most primary commodity exporters, Tanzania's terms of trade did not decline substantially between 1970 and 1981 (appendix table A-1). On the
other hand, there has been a major decline in the volume of
agricultural exports. By 1980, export volumes were less than half
those of 1970 (appendix table A-2). There also has been a substantial deterioration in the quality of agricultural exports, with
coffee, tobacco, and cotton receiving between 10 to 30 percent
quality discounts in the late 1970s compared to the earlier
period.[13] If export volumes had been maintained at the peaks
reached in the 1970s, the balance-of-payments crisis clearly would
not have reached current proportions. A 2 to 4 percent rate of
growth in exports similar to that existing since the 1930s—and
far lower than that in the 1960s—would have averted the current
crisis altogether.[14]

Three characteristics of Tanzania's exports give it an advantage
over many other developing countries. First, the export sector is
highly diversified and reflects the country's substantial physical
potential. Coffee, tea, cotton, sisal, tobacco, cashews, and cloves
together constitute about 70 to 80 percent of total exports (appendix table A-2). This provides Tanzania considerable protection
from individual commodity price fluctuations. Second, its small-
market share allows it an elastic demand for most of its exports
with the exception of sisal, and coffee in the quota market. Third,
only a quarter to a third of the land classified as cultivable in
Tanzania is now under production, providing it with tremendous
potential for increasing production and exports. An aggressive
and diversified export-crops production strategy would have led to
substantial overall economic growth. This would have compensated for the little control Tanzania has over the prices of its exports and especially its imports.

The value of imports increased more than fivefold from the late
1960s to the early 1980s (appendix table A-1). However, with a
brief exception in 1977–78, real imports declined by an estimated
37 percent between 1970 and 1980 (appendix table A-3). By 1981,
real imports were lower than in 1978, and were almost half those
of 1970.

Despite the decline in imports, capital goods' share of total imports increased from over 30 percent in the early 1970s to 47 per-

cent in 1979 (appendix table A-3). This reflected the substantial needs of Tanzania's import-substituting industrialization strategy, which has been pursued vigorously since 1975. In contrast, imports of manufactured goods, which had accounted for over 30 percent of imports in 1970, decreased throughout the 1970s to 17 percent in 1980 (appendix table A-3). Nonproject and nonoil imports declined even more drastically than these overall figures suggest; their volume decreased by 37 percent and 23 percent in 1980–81 and 1981–82 respectively.[15] The decreasing import of manufactures, combined with the low-capacity utilization of the domestic manufacturing industry implicit in the shrinking category of free imports, explain the growing shortages of consumer goods experienced since the late 1970s. This has had a serious impact on agricultural producer incentives. There also has been a severe shortage of critical agricultural inputs and spare parts for transport and processing in the agricultural sector. The number of new tractors entering Tanzania dropped from around 800–1000 per year in the early 1970s to 400–500 per year in the late 1970s.[16] Dealers reported receiving less than 20 percent of their import requirements for agricultural machinery spares in 1979 and 1980, and the operating tractor fleet declined by nearly 50 percent in the 1970s.

The extreme deterioration in the transport and processing sectors was noticeable in the case of crops that had not benefited from donor-assisted projects. By 1981, much of the existing cotton or sisal production could not be transported or processed. In the cashew- and tobacco-processing sectors a major expansion had occurred through donor-assisted projects in the 1970s, but production lagged due to poor agricultural policies and a lack of local financial and manpower resources, leading to substantial underutilization of processing capacity.

The cost of oil was of course partly responsible for the constraints on other imports. Oil had accounted for about 8 to 11 percent of total imports in the early 1970s (appendix table A-3). Despite little change in volume since 1974, the share of oil and oil products in total imports reached over 20 percent in the 1980s.

Commercial food imports accounted for 4 to 12 percent of total imports during the 1970s (appendix table A-3). In the drought of 1975 the share of food imports reached 18 percent. Thanks to rising levels of food aid, such high commercial food imports were not necessary in the early 1980s (table 2).[17] Even though food imports in this period reached the levels of the 1973−74 drought period, domestic food shortages had become extensive.

Agricultural performance before and after the 1970s. Most of Tanzania's food crops are consumed domestically (especially sorghum, millets, and cassava) and some are marketed locally through unofficial channels. Maize, wheat, and rice are the major officially traded food items, although maize and rice are also sold in the unofficial market. The share of this market is not known, but usually seems to be inversely related to the excess supply in the domestic market. The data on officially marketed volumes are therefore not an adequate indicator of total food production.

Almost all of the export-crop production requiring further processing is marketed through the official monopoly marketing channels, although there is some illicit trade in coffee and cotton. Thus official data generally are a good indicator of export-crop output. Table 3 shows the officially marketed output of major food and export crops from 1970−71 to 1981−82.

The performance of marketed agricultural production in the 1970s is in sharp contrast to the annual growth rate of 3.5 and 6 percent for the 1933−1953 and 1953−1973 periods referred to

Table 2

Tanzania: Net Imports of Grains (Maize, Wheat, and Rice)

	Volume (000 tonnes)			Value (U.S.$ million)		
	Commercial	Aid	Total	Commercial	Aid	Total
1970−71	—	—	(12.9)	—	—	(0.8)
1975−76	116	73	189	19.7	9.6	21.7
1976−77	40	41	81	5.4	5.0	10.4
1977−78	27	97	124	12.4	17.3	29.7
1978−79	41	66	103	9.4	12.8	22.2
1979−80	37	83	120	5.7	25.0	30.8
1980−81	202.3	186.2	388.5	27.8	42.8	70.6
1981−82	38.5	349.4	387.9	10.7	88.9	99.6

Source: World Bank estimates.

Table 3
Tanzania: Volume of Officially Marketed Production of
Principal Export Crops and Food Crops
(thousands of tonnes, figures are rounded)

	1970–71	1975–76	1976–77	1977–78	1978–79	1979–80	1980–81	1981–82
Export crops[a]								
Cotton	78	42	67	50	56	61	56	44
Coffee	50	55	49	52	50	48	63	63
Sisal	202	119	113	105	92	80	86	86[c]
Tea	8	13	15	18	18	17	17	16
Cashews	111	82	98	68	57	41	57	42
Tobacco	12	14	19	18	17	17	17	17
Pyrethrum	2	4	3	2	2	2	2	2
Index of export crops	100	87	96	90	86	83	87	83
Food crops[b]								
Maize[d]	186	91	128	213	220	162	105	94
Paddy and rice	94	16	19	44	43	41	15	16
Wheat	43	25	23	35	28	26	28	23
Cassava	—	17	20	37	64	44	8	10
Sorghum	—	3	10	34	59	21	19	11
Finger millet	—	2	4	22	23	16	1	—

[a]Quantities for coffee, cotton, cashews, and tobacco are for crop year indicated, the rest of export crops are in calendar years.

[b]Food crops quantities are for crop year July through June.

[c]Estimate.

[d]Purchases by the National Milling Corporation (NMC).

Source: International Monetary Fund data.

earlier.[18] Of course, acreage expansion following population
growth of about 2.5 percent annually was an important factor in a
land-surplus economy in the earlier period. However, the 6 percent annual growth realized from the 1950s on indicates that
agricultural productivity had undoubtedly increased. In contrast
to this earlier period, export-crop production generally either stagnated or declined in the 1970s (table 3).

Food-production performance had begun to change course even
prior to the 1970s. Although production had grown, there was a
minor but clear trend of increasing food imports even before that
decade. The performance of food crops in the seventies was mixed.
Official sales of wheat and rice—the grains preferred in urban
areas—declined sharply. Official sales of maize—also a preferred
cereal—and of the less preferred sorghum, millet, and cassava
recovered after the 1973–74 drought but has declined again in
more recent years (table 3). This was due largely to the growing
parallel market in food crops, both internally as well as across
Tanzania's vast international borders. There was also a shift in
the 1970s in the sources of official sales, with increased quantities
coming from the remote high-cost regions and from the relatively
inefficient state farms. The declining volumes of official sales
have meant erosion of the official economy because of their adverse effect on official foreign-exchange earnings, government
revenues, and urban food supplies.

As I will show later, a variety of pricing and resource-allocation
decisions made by the government, together with institutional
changes, have led to the declining official sales and the declining
share of private producers in favor of state farms.

Performance of the social sectors. The causes of poor
agricultural performance cannot be understood without an examination of the other elements of Tanzania's development
strategy. The emphasis on meeting the basic needs of its population has been an important reason for the international attraction
to Tanzania. In the area of social services, its most important
achievement has been in the field of primary education.[19] Il-
literacy is reported to have declined from 75 percent in 1962 to as
low as 10 percent in the most recent surveys. In 1979, primary
school attendance was reported to be universal among eligible stu-

dents (ages 7—14). However, the growth of free primary education has not been without cost to secondary and higher education: the percentages of secondary school and university students in Tanzania are among the lowest in Africa, with only 4 percent of the 12—17 age group and less than half of 1 percent of the 20—24 age group enrolled in these institutions respectively. These percentages are also small in comparison with other African countries that started at similar levels at independence.[20] The supply of secondary school graduates has been especially small in relation to the vast increase in the demand for formally educated manpower generated by the rapid growth of the public sector, leading to a serious adverse impact on productivity.[21]

Tanzania's record on improving its water supply system has been far less impressive than on primary education, despite substantial foreign assistance channelled in this direction. In 1970, an estimated 9 percent of the rural population had access to a piped water system.[22] Ten years later, between 20 and 30 percent of the 8300 registered villages were said to have been provided with clean, potable water. Evaluation studies show, however, that less than 50 percent of these systems (i.e., in only 10 to 15 percent of all villages) are in working condition, due to lack of fuel, maintenance, and repair facilities. The net effective increase in the provision of rural water supply thus seems to have been minimal.

Achievements in the health sector have been better, but not without major problems.[23] In 1962 there was one physician for every 21,000 Tanzanians. By the late 1970s this had increased to one per 18,000. More significantly, the ratio of registered nurses in rural areas is estimated to have increased from one per 10,000 to one per 3,000 over the same period. In both cases, the ratio is some 40 percent better off than the average for low-income sub-Saharan African countries. There also has been a large increase in physical facilities with increased capital allocations to health care. Life expectancy has gone up from 42 at independence to 52 in 1980, five years higher than the average for low-income sub-Saharan African countries and equivalent to that of middle-income African countries. Yet the health sector still suffers from extreme shortages of personnel and a chronic scarcity of drugs and medical equipment.

Industrial production. As was the case for agriculture, manufacturing production showed substantial growth in the 1970s (table 4). The production of consumer goods was the dominant activity, accounting for more than half of the value added and two-thirds of employment in manufacturing in the mid-1970s. With the Arusha Declaration and the proclamation of the Basic Industries Strategy in 1975, however, the government gave priority not only to industries meeting mass consumption needs but to the more basic intermediate-goods industries as well. During 1976–80, the textile industry expanded from 90 million to 200 million square meters' capacity, the cement industry from 340,000 tons to 1.1 million tons, and the fertilizer industry from 105,000 tons to 134,000 tons.[24] A pulp and paper mill was also being built. Yet manufacturing value added grew by only 1.7 percent per year in real terms during the 1973–79 period, compared to 7.8 percent in the 1966–1973 period.[25] This reflected the government's growing commitment to capital- and foreign exchange–intensive industries, and the consequent shortages of foreign exchange for importation of raw materials and for maintenance needs in periods of falling real earnings. An unweighted average of fifteen major industries showed an estimated 45 percent capacity utilization in 1980.[26] Some indications show a substantial further decline in capacity utilization since then.

Fiscal, monetary, and exchange-rate performance. Severe deterioration in the government's fiscal position also occurred in the 1970s because of the decline of revenue from exports.[27] While budgetary revenue increased by about 16 percent annually during the 1970s, government expenditures grew at an annual rate of 21 percent. This rapid growth in expenditure was the result of a combination of industrial and social-sector expansion and defense expenditures during the Ugandan war that were not cut back or adequately compensated by other measures. Despite increases in foreign grants and nonbank financing, bank borrowing grew substantially, leading to growth of the money supply at about 20 percent a year during the 1970s. The number of items under price controls increased from about 400 in 1973 to 3,000 in 1976. Their number was then reduced to about 500 in 1981. The official national consumer price index rose only by about 12 percent an-

Table 4

Tanzania: Indices of the Volume of Manufacturing Production

(1975=100)

Commodity	1970	1975	1976	1977	1978	1979	1980
Consumer goods							
Cigarettes	74	100	105	114	122	118	135
Beer	60	100	108	117	127	117	99
Textiles	—	100	95	90	83	97	95
Shoes	78	100	137	234	236	213	153
Batteries	30	100	115	128	141	142	157
Intermediate goods							
Cement	66	100	92	93	94	112	107
Rolled steel	—	100	99	105	156	173	175
Iron sheets	69	100	101	100	118	117	60
Aluminum	83	100	106	123	125	121	123
Other							
Fishnets	144	100	118	251	223	253	146
Fertilizers	—	100	71	62	75	78	86
Petroleum	102	100	112	91	88	70	92
Sisal ropes and twines	—	100	166	143	123	149	124
Pyrethrum extract	8	100	73	52	38	27	25

Source: For 1976 to 1980: International Monetary Fund data. For 1970 to 1975: World Bank data and Bank of Tanzania, *Economic Bulletin*, March 1980 (converted into 1975 base).

nually during the 1970s, while actual inflation has been substantially greater, especially since 1979, as the parallel-market share in total transactions has increased rapidly. Open-market food crop prices were reported to be between two to six times the official prices in 1979.[28] In all likelihood these disparities grew in 1980 and 1981.

The nominal value of the Tanzanian shilling was broadly maintained in terms of the U.S. dollar during the 1970s. But due to the far more rapid rates of domestic inflation, the effective real exchange rate has appreciated sharply. Between 1970 and 1981, the real import-weighted effective exchange rate appreciated by 46 percent. Its appreciation was as high as 71 percent against the Kenyan shilling and 78 percent against the U.S. dollar.[29]

Causes of Poor Performance in the 1970s

The present economic crisis highlights four dilemmas Tanzania has been facing in its development strategy, namely between (1) agriculture and industry, (2) growth and equity, (3) short- and long-term objectives, and (4) the private- and the public-sector roles.

These dilemmas have not only affected pricing and investment decisions, they also have led to a massive and frequent overhaul of key institutions. Changes in all these directions have been most noteworthy since the Arusha Declaration. Some of the post-Arusha policy initiatives go back to the earlier period, however. For instance, village settlements were initiated in the mid-1960s on the advice of the first World Bank mission in 1961, but were abandoned in the late 1960s as being too capital intensive.[30] Similarly, coercion of the peasantry into following certain agricultural practices was prevalent throughout the colonial period. The exceptional performance of the agricultural sector prior to the 1970s was the result of a large number of positive policies that more than compensated for the weaknesses on a few fronts. These included strong agricultural incentives, investment in rail and road transport—although at independence Tanzania still had one of the poorest physical infrastructure services in Africa—rapid growth of rural private trade and a voluntary cooperative movement. These all led to an improved access to inputs, consumer goods, and produce marketing facilities for a growing proportion of the peasantry.[31]

Since the Arusha Declaration, however, Tanzania has concentrated its political energies and economic resources in the pursuit of two principles: socialism and self-reliance. Socialism has been interpreted to mean public control over the nation's resources through nationalization of most major industries, commerce, real estate, and agricultural estates, and the establishment of a single publicly owned commercial bank. While equity may have been an initial consideration in increasing public control, the desire to curb the role of the Asian community also played a part. As will be illustrated later, public control had ended up becoming an end in itself—though perhaps inadvertently—rather than a means to an end. The investment program has been the other major instrument of a socialist development strategy.

Self-reliance has been a more elusive concept. Self-sufficiency in food has certainly been one of the objectives, although the policies to achieve it have hardly been articulated, leading to a growing dependence on food aid. The most significant step towards achieving self-reliance has been the adoption of the Basic Industries Strategy, which was intended to industrialize the economy in a short period of twenty years. Self-reliance was to be realized in two ways: first, by meeting domestic needs for intermediate and consumer goods through domestic production; and second, by lessening the country's dependence on primary-commodity exports, which were seen as putting developing countries into an unfair trading relationship with the industrialized world.

Agriculture vs. industry and the rural vs. the urban sectors. The industrialization strategy and associated urbanization have tilted the balance of public investment and the physical infrastructure away from agriculture. In this process, Tanzania has relied on two sources of support: foreign donors and, by implication, the agricultural sector. The share of public-sector development expenditures on industry increased from 2 percent at the beginning of the 1970s to 17 percent at the end of the decade table 5). In comparison, the share of agriculture declined from 21 percent in the mid-1960s to 10 percent by the end of the 1970s. It was as low as 5 percent in 1981. The share of transport, which was

Table 5

Tanzania: Actual Capital Expenditures of the Government

(figures are rounded)

	1965–66	1972–73	1975–76	1976–77	1977–78	1978–79
Tsh million						
Agriculture[a]	49	139	387	344	411	418
Industry	1	19	83	377	561	746
Transportation[b] and infrastructure	30	120	228	406	374	576
Total	230	956	2,234	2,764	3,163	4,286
Percentage of total						
Agriculture[a]	21	15	17	12	13	10
Industry	negligible	2	4	14	18	17
Transportation[b] and infrastructure	13	13	10	15	12	13

[a]Includes livestock.

[b]Includes road, waterway, rail, and any other communication expenditures.

Source: World Bank estimates.

about 18 percent[32] soon after independence in the early 1960s, had declined to a steady range of 10 to 15 percent in the 1970s (table 5). Even this reduced budget underestimates the actual allocations in support of agriculture, since a major portion of these funds went to the Tanzania Zambia Railway Authority (TAZARA) railway in the early 1970s (which hardly serves the Tanzanian agricultural sector), and to an international airport in Dar es Salaam in the early 1980s. That the budget for transportation is far lower than Tanzania's requirements is evident from the rapid deterioration of its transport and communications system in the 1970s. Transportation's share of expenditures is also far lower than that spent by neighboring Kenya, Malawi, and Zambia, all of which have less geographical dispersion of their production base.[33]

The large extent of donor support for industrialization can be readily seen in table 6. Between 1975–1976 and 1981–82 industry and its supporting infrastructure were together the largest recipient of donor finance. Whereas the proportion of all aid allocated to industry was less than 10 percent in 1975–76, by 1978–79 this had jumped to over 20 percent of a larger aid volume, and remained at about this level for the rest of the period. Among the major donor-assisted industrial projects were a fertilizer plant financed by the Federal Republic of Germany; a cement plant established by DANIDA; the textile mill established with World Bank assistance; the pulp and paper mill financed jointly by the World Bank, SIDA, and others; a ceramic plant set up with Czechoslovakian assistance; and a machine tool factory provided by Bulgaria. At the same time the share of aid going to agriculture dropped sharply from 40 percent in 1975–76 to 17 percent in 1976–77, and remained at around 10 to 12 percent for the rest of the decade (table 6).

Negative value added has hurt several of Tanzania's capital-intensive industries, such as the steel-rolling mill and the fertilizer factory. But the undervaluation of the foreign-exchange rate and the distorted domestic prices of inputs and outputs have concealed the inappropriateness of these capital-intensive investments at this early stage of Tanzania's development. These industries have not only been uneconomic in themselves; they have also diverted local financial, manpower, and institutional resources, scarce foreign exchange, and especially domestic policy attention away

Table 6

Tanzania: Share of Total Aid Resources Allocated to Major Ministries
(percent, figures are rounded)

	1975–76	1976–77	1977–78	1978–79	1979–80	1980–81	1981–82
Industry	9	12	19	22	23	24	21
Water, energy, minerals	25	12	21	17	14	15	12
Transport/communications	0	3	8	21	11	12	10
Agriculture/livestock	40	17	14	10	12	12	10
Works	8	13	6	5	13	13	15
Finance/planning	1	20	17	11	8	7	9
Education	8	8	7	5	5	5	7
Natural resources	3	6	4	3	4	6	5
Land/housing/urban development	3	2	2	1	2	2	1
Capital development	0	—	—	1	3	3	2
Other	3	2	4	4	5	2	6
Total	100	100	100	100	100	100	100

Source: World Bank data.

from the key needs of the agricultural sector, thus accelerating its decline.[34]

That basic industrial investments have taken place at the expense of the agricultural sector can be seen from agriculture's unsatisfied requirements. In the early 1980s, when it was receiving a far lower level of import allocations, the amount of recurrent foreign-exchange inputs needed to maintain the current level of agricultural production was estimated at about U.S. $200 million on an annual basis.[35] These estimates overstate agriculture's routine requirements because they include the costs of investment and maintenance deferred over a number of years, and are based on current levels of capital-intensive technology and low efficiency in the public sector. Even so, agriculture's recurrent foreign-exchange needs are no more than 20 percent of Tanzania's total imports. They are thus not excessive when considered in terms of agriculture's major role as an earner or saver of scarce foreign exchange. However, so large are the needs of the government's existing public-investment program that Tanzania's flexibility to release foreign exchange for agriculture's needs has been greatly reduced. In the face of declining export earnings, increased funding for agriculture will not be possible without mothballing many of the existing unproductive industries or ongoing investments. Simply postponing future planned investments will not be enough.

Diversion of very scarce trained manpower away from agriculture also should be noted. Despite 45 percent share in GDP, the agricultural sector had only 45 qualified accountants in 1980, compared to 139 in industry, whose share in GDP was less than 10 percent.[36] Agriculture's accounting needs are of course far greater than even its share suggests, due to its decentralized, atomistic nature. Reorientation of scarce resources in favor of agriculture now poses difficult decisions for the government and the donors. Without such reorientation of priorities, however, repeated rescue operations would be needed through external assistance.

The urban bias associated with the growing role of the public sector has been an additional source of anti-agricultural policies. Producer pricing has been a major instrument of resource mobilization in favor of the growing urban public sector. Appendix table A-4 and figures 1 and 2 show the real official producer prices of major food and export crops and marketed production since

Figure 1

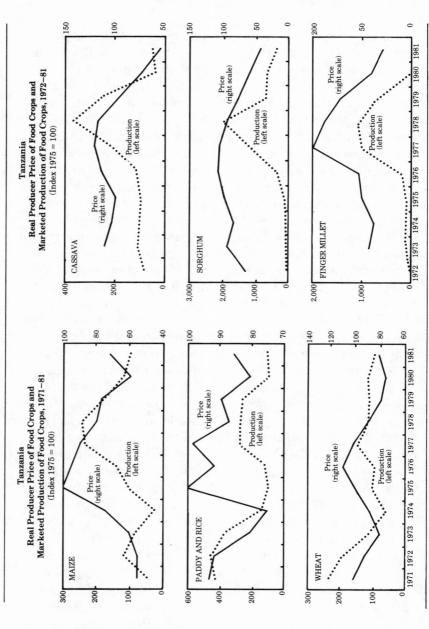

Source: International Monetary Fund data.

Figure 2

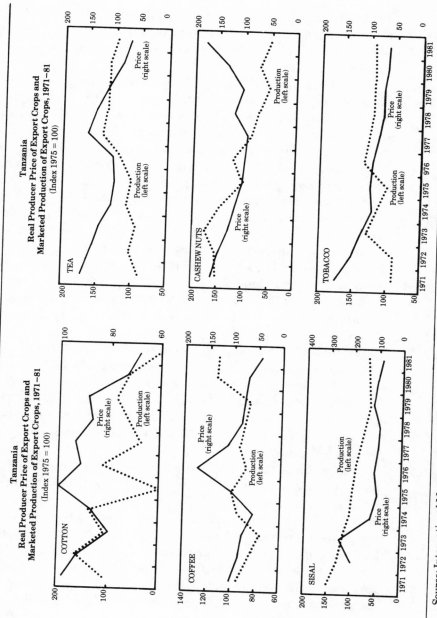

Source: International Monetary Fund data.

1971−72. Official prices play an important role in Tanzania due to the government's monopoly in agricultural marketing. It can be seen from these charts that marketed output closely followed the movement of prices.

While the relative producer prices of food and export crops were adjusted to reflect changing international prices and growing domestic food shortages, appreciation of the Tanzanian shilling led to a substantial taxation of export crops. In addition, the high costs of marketing parastatals—publicly owned institutions which operate with some autonomy from the government bureaucracy—and their growing losses have led to a considerable reluctance on the part of the government to raise producer prices. In 1980−81, subventions to parastatals already constituted 11 percent of the budget of the Ministry of Agriculture, and were expected to reach 20 percent in 1981−82.[37] In addition, large overdrafts on the banking system also have been necessary to support growing parastatal deficits. In 1981−82, agricultural marketing parastatals lost TSh 680 million, or 17 percent of the value of their combined turnover. Their losses were expected to be larger in 1982−83.

Concern for maintaining urban incomes has furthermore led to a reluctance to increase official consumer prices. In 1981−82, the margin between producer and consumer prices covered only a fraction of the parastatals's actual marketing costs. Only 33 percent of the marketing costs for maize, 20 percent for rice, 40 percent for cassava, and between 30 to 50 percent for sorghum and millet were covered.

Until recently, the government also has followed a system of uniform producer prices. The purpose of this measure was to achieve regional equity and to ensure supplies to Dar es Salaam. Since a number of distant border regions produce low-value food crops with high transportation costs, the uniform pricing policy has encouraged substantial production of such crops for the official market. It has raised incomes in these remote regions, but it has also raised the operating costs of the marketing parastatals. The government recently changed the uniform pricing policy, but instead of adjusting it to reflect transportation costs, it undertook to pay higher prices to regions with the most productive potential so as not to risk a lack of supplies to Dar es Salaam.

Growth vs. equity and the public- and private-sector roles. Tanzania's pursuit of equity is strongly evident in the range of policy instruments it has used for this purpose. Public expenditures have been one such instrument. The recurrent resource needs of social programs have been substantial, even though their investment requirements have been low. Education, health, and water supply together consumed 65 percent of the regional budget in 1981—82.[38] In a system of decentralized administration, each region is largely responsible for the implementation of its field services. Rural education alone used 40 percent of the regional recurrent budget in 1981—82. This constituted a real increase of 21 percent since 1974—75, while the recurrent budget as a whole had declined by about the same proportion in real terms, as had the budget for agriculture.

Donors have facilitated the priority placed on social services in two important ways: by undertaking regional integrated rural development programs (RIDEPs) involving provision of both directly productive and social services, and through direct support for regional social-sector activities. Eleven of the twenty administrative regions in Tanzania currently have donor-assisted RIDEPs. Experience indicates, however, that the implementation of directly productive programs such as agricultural research, extension, or input supply has either not begun or greatly lagged behind. The more popular social service programs, on the other hand, have surged ahead because local political leaders have used them for patronage distribution.

Other equity-oriented and allocative policies have involved public-sector priority to investments in poorer regions such as Kigoma, Lindi, and Mtwara, and opening up the previously unexploited high-potential Southern Highlands with the introduction of coffee and hybrid maize. These policies have certainly helped Tanzania to move in the direction of regional equity, and may have been important politically in the early years of independence. But they have frequently been implemented at the cost of the traditionally more productive and agriculturally advanced regions such as Arusha, Kilimanjaro, and Iringa, all of which have experienced a decline in their marketed agricultural production over the 1970s.[39]

The most significant aspect of the equity-oriented approach has been substantial and frequent institutional change in an environment of fragile institutions and highly restricted supply of the trained manpower needed to implement such change. The more direct institutional steps taken to prevent the creation of a rural capitalistic class included nationalization of large private sisal, tea, and coffee estates in the early 1960s; establishment of large state farms was then considered necessary to generate marketed surpluses that until then had come from the commercial producers under a market-oriented system.

The Ujamaa policy involved the movement of almost the entire rural population of nearly 12 million into some 8000 villages in less than a decade after the Arusha Declaration. Because of the need to meet target dates for the establishment of Ujamaa villages, the movement often ended up being forced on a reluctant peasantry unconvinced of its benefits. The relocation to villages, or "villagization" initially was seen both as a way to promote rural political mobilization and to ensure a broad-based provision of rural services. However, it quickly degenerated into a means of political control by the local party and government officials. The nonvoluntary nature of the relocation may have contributed to the serious long-term costs by eroding the confidence of the peasantry. The disruption in production following villagization has not been temporary. There is growing evidence in cotton- and tobacco-growing areas that overcrowding through villagization is accelerating a process of soil degradation already underway through increasing population pressure. Walking distances to fields have increased greatly, adversely affecting the availability of labor for critical agricultural operations. Some de facto de-villagization is taking place where local officials permit, but such movement is highly limited and an overt policy retraction may not be easy for a government highly committed to the policies associated with Ujamaa villages.

Cooperative farming also was introduced following the establishment of Ujamaa villages.[40] This has now been almost completely abandoned due to village apathy or resistance, although in recent years the Party frequently has given consideration to creating village farms, for which there seems to be equally limited local enthusiasm.

Like the Ujamaa villagization policy, the decentralization of the government administration was undertaken in 1972 to increase local political participation in decision-making. This involved disbanding the system of local government and giving more power to the regional administration. But since decentralization spread thinly the very limited quantity of trained manpower among the many regions, it greatly undermined the effectiveness of the central functional ministries, such as agriculture. At the same time the importance of central ideological and bureaucratic influences in decision-making increased as the role of the Party and the Prime Minister's Office grew, and the original intention of fostering local participation thus fell by the wayside. So great is the disenchantment with the decentralized administration that the government is once again on its way to reestablishing local government.

Still other measures undertaken to avoid exploitation of the peasantry include the discouragement of private ownership of tractors, private transporters, large-scale private estates (even where surplus agricultural land is available), the largely Asian-operated private retail shops, and hired labor for agricultural production. Directives have been given to field services to address agricultural extension messages to the village units as distinct from previous attention focused largely on commercially-oriented farmers. There also have been specific crop-production and procurement targets and directives to peasants regarding the use of particular agricultural practices. In contrast to colonial times, however, these directives have been less the result of concern for sound agricultural practices than of the desire of zealous Party officials to increase output. By frequent invocation of national interests, production directives are expected to counter the lack of adequate economic incentives.

Still another drastic change was the abolition of the marketing cooperatives in 1976. The grassroots cooperative movement had earlier received active government support with a view to countering the largely Asian-dominated private trade in agricultural produce. To ensure their rapid spread throughout the rural sector, the cooperatives were brought under government control through Compulsory Marketing Orders in the 1960s. Over time, however, concern grew over increasing corruption—itself a result of their rapid spread—and over avoiding their control by commercially oriented peasants. In agriculturally advanced regions where cooperative growth had been particularly noteworthy the latter was perceived as a serious problem. Party control of cooperatives increased in the early 1970s to curb what was seen as the clear tendency of the movement to improve the political importance of the rural elite. By the mid-1970s, however, it was evident that neither the extensive corruption[41] nor the increased political manipulation of cooperatives by the rural elite could be avoided. As a result, cooperatives were replaced by a public-sector monopoly of agricultural parastatals in 1976.

These "crop authorities" have set back the cause of rural equity by fostering the vested interests of the bureaucratic and urban groups, i.e., traders, government and party officials, etc. In addition to their legal monopoly over procurement of almost all crops, they have controlled much of the agricultural research, transport, processing and distribution of inputs, agricultural credit, and retailing of consumer goods. These and other public enterprises grew from just under 70 in 1967 to almost 400 in 1981. Public employment grew at an annual rate of 10 percent during the last half of the 1970s.

As in the case of industry and social services, donors have actively supported the growth of parastatals through financial and technical assistance. The World Bank provided loans and credits of U.S. $174 million for six of the eleven major agricultural parastatals during the 1970s.[42]

As a result of the growing disenchantment with the quality of parastatal services and their uncontrollable financial losses, the government is once again considering handing over many of their responsibilities to cooperatives. Whether grassroots cooperatives will be allowed to evolve remains to be seen. Cooperatives dominated by the rural elite are likely to be seen as encouraging the development of a rural capitalistic class and as an alternative political force. Already the cooperative legislation includes troublesome forebodings of compulsory membership and universal coverage of services. In any case, given the history of their drastic abolition, a genuine cooperative movement will take a long time to emerge. In the meantime, a serious institutional vacuum exists in rural areas despite the massive growth of institutions and public-sector employment in the 1970s.

Short- and long-term objectives. These various policies, investment priorities, and institutional choices together help to explain the declining volume of agricultural production and its increased diversion to the parallel market. The urban industrial sector has clearly benefited from the modernization policies in the short run. Not only has there been expansion in industrial activity, but wages have been pegged at artificially high levels under minimum wage laws, reducing their competitiveness. Studies of the cashew industry have shown that at the official exchange rate, Tanzania's minimum wage was about three times as high as India's in the mid-1970s, whereas labor productivity was about a third of India's.[43] Similar wage and productivity differentials can be documented in other industries. The poorer rural classes have similarly benefited from many of the policies in the social sector, from investments in previously backward regions, and from the pricing of agricultural produce. Such a broad-based distribution may have been important for the government to achieve political legitimacy and to create an African middle class for national economic and political management. On the other hand, the shrinking size of the economic pie has now made it impossible for the government to continue these policies. Real urban incomes have declined by nearly 50 percent since the mid-1970s as wages have stagnated and dependence of the urban population on the parallel market for basic supplies has increased. The Asian community is no longer the sole beneficiary of the current policies, although that is frequently the official perception. The size of the Asian community was halved through emigration in the 1970s, and flight of capital has reduced their share in manufacturing and trade even further. The new beneficiaries of these policies are a growing class of African producers and traders who have shown a remarkable tendency to respond to economic incentives. Thus the racial overtones of a market liberalization policy are now less serious than they were before. This does not mean that what remains of the Asian community will not benefit handsomely from the policies of liberalization; Asian interests may even grow once again if the investment and immigration climate improves. But the sociopolitical developments in the post-independence period should allow more containment of such claims by minorities.

One of the dilemmas the government faces thus arises from the

desire to provide the necessary incentives to its agricultural
population without allowing the emergence of a rural capitalistic
class. This goal may turn out to be impossible to achieve. The other
dilemma arises from the emergence of a new class of bureaucratic
elite that has become well-entrenched. The present conflict is
largely between the needs of this elite and those of the low-income
regions and classes on the one hand, and on the other hand the requirements of a large and productive African peasantry to achieve
growth. Tanzania also finds itself locked in various vicious circles.
For instance, due to increasing price distortions, the share of the
parallel market has been growing, reducing the tax base and requiring more inflationary finance to keep up public-sector real expenditures. Yet because the government is reluctant to adjust
nominal prices to the extent needed to have any real impact, the
inflationary pressures of government expenditures further aggra-
vate the price distortions. Similarly, the growing role of foreign aid
has encouraged foreign-exchange intensity of investments without increasing the country's foreign-exchange earning ability,
thus increasing further the dependence on foreign aid. These
dilemmas have led the government in the opposite direction of its
primary goals, namely those of achieving self-reliance and of
using the public sector to achieve equity with growth.

Implications and Prospects for a Recovery

Three major implications are self-evident from this analysis. First,
without the restoration of agricultural growth as a major priority,
there is little scope for an economic recovery in Tanzania. This
restructuring of priorities would require not only curtailment of
the future investment program and its reorientation to meet critical needs of the agricultural sector, but also closing down many
unproductive investments, especially in the basic industrial sector, in order to provide more recurrent resources to fill the urgent
needs of agriculture. The public investment program also would
need to be redirected to support agriculture and its related sectors.

Second, producer incentives need to be augmented. Beyond
simply adjusting the exchange rate and the official prices of commodities to reflect their scarcity value this would require
liberalizing markets for goods and services, which would also

mean a substantial alteration of the government's monopoly position in most activities so that it would become an actor of last resort. Instead of preempting functions best performed by the private or the cooperative sector, the government would need to concentrate its efforts on the services traditionally provided by the public sector, such as transport and communications, agricultural research, and manpower training, all of which have received little attention in the post-Arusha period. Whether there is enough flexibility at the top policy level to meet the policy and institutional requirements of the peasant agricultural sector remains to be seen.

Third, the donor community would need to reorient its policies and actions in various ways. In the short run, this might involve:

- Far greater coordination among donors in working with the government to help articulate a development strategy led by agriculture;

- Abandoning the past tendency of donors to encourage domestic overcommitment in sectors that divert attention and scarce resources away from the development of an efficient agricultural sector;

- Modification of the project-by-project approach in favor of program, sectoral, and subsectoral loans that support the critical recurrent and investment needs of agriculture and its supporting sectors, such as processing, storage, transport, and manpower;

- A long-term aid commitment in support of such a strategy; and

- Aid commitments more directly related to the implementation of a mutually agreed-upon development strategy between the government and the donors.

The three areas with clear priority from a long-term point of view are (1) development of secondary and higher education and training; (2) the building of an agricultural research system; and (3) development of the transport and communications network needed to develop agriculture. In addition, through long-term support of critical ministries such as agriculture, education, and transport, donors can help create a strong pro-agricultural lobby of national professionals in the government. The role of U.S.

bilateral assistance to India in initiating technological change demonstrates the contribution that donors can make in this regard.

This approach implies substantial change in the policies of both the Tanzanian government and the donors. But without an emphasis on improvement of the policy environment and the human and institutional capacity, even larger amounts of foreign aid probably will be needed to keep the modern sector functioning, even though, as the experience of the past decade has demonstrated, they are unlikely to achieve much in the way of long-term development. Perhaps the current crisis will lead both the government and the donor community to reexamine their respective roles.

Appendix
Table A-1

Tanzania: Balance of Payments
(Tsh million, 1975=100, figures are rounded)

	1965	1970	1973	1974	1975	1976	1977	1978	1979	1980	1981[a]
Goods											
Exports	1,400	1,713	2,553	2,851	2,764	4,108	4,220	3,571	4,243	4,187	4,430
Imports	-1,335	-2,232	-3,533	-5,422	-5,710	-5,355	-6,161	-8,798	-8,965	-10,003	-9,298
Trade balance	65	-519	-980	-2,571	-2,946	-1,247	-1,941	-5,226	-4,722	-5,816	-4,868
Services (net)	-71	226	190	182	466	602	156	208	306	156	333
Transfers (net)	33	92	35	351	759	464	962	1,273	1,447	2,376	2,883
Private and parastatal	—	79	-101	-81	85	98	162	176	242	181	202
Central government	33	12	136	432	674	366	800	1,097	1,205	2,195	2,681
Current account balance	27	-201	-755	-2,037	-1,721	-181	-823	-3,746	-6,769	-3,284	-1,652
Capital account											
Government loans[b] (net)	-9	-56	-254	-80	-45	-41	-118	-109	-71	-99	-70
Inflow	124	458	830	750	1,091	831	722	765	1,141	925	1,244
Outflow	134	513	1,084	830	1,136	872	840	874	1,212	1,024	1,314
Parastatal loans[b] (net)	c	—	-11	-15	-58	-113	-133	-169	-125	-139	-102
Inflow	c	—	70	160	210	55	150	378	601	667	1,010
Outflow	—	—	80	175	268	168	283	547	726	806	1,112

Table A-1 (cont'd)
Tanzania: Balance of Payments and Terms of Trade

	1965	1970	1973	1974	1975	1976	1977	1978	1979	1980	1981[a]
Private loans[b] (net)	-63	54	d	d	d	d	38	-58	115	87	80
Inflow	—	—	d	d	d	d	55	118	143	118	99
Outflow	—	—	d	d	d	d	-17	-175	-28	-31	-19
Other capital movements	—	—	-95	119	225	-327	-94	-162	-84	-151	-50
Exceptional financing	—	—	—	51	265	—	44	124	213	132	49
Errors and omissions	-99	-425	181	56	-89	-124	906	461	86	162	-387
Overall balance	-11	-114	-230	952	-284	-259	943	-2,238	-897	-1,461	294
Net change in reserve	11	114	230	-952	284	259	-943	2,238	897	1,461	-294
Terms of trade[e]	—	150	115	106	100	147	195	166	145	136	132

[a]Preliminary.

[b]Including medium- and long-term loans.

[c]Included in net private loans.

[d]Included in other capital movements.

[e]The Terms of Trade are the ratio of the index of export prices to that of import prices.

Sources: For balance of payments, 1965 and 1970, World Bank, "Tanzania: Basic Economic Report, Main Report," December 1977, p. 154; 1973 to 1981, International Monetary Fund data. For terms of trade, International Monetary Fund data.

Tanzania Exports: Share, Real Exports, and Index of Export Prices
(Share in percentage, figures are rounded)

	1970	1975	1976	1977	1978	1979	1980a
Primary products	76.0	78.6	82.8	85.5	83.6	76.3	72.5
Major items	59.2	66.3	73.4	77.9	71.1	62.7	59.8
Coffee	17.1	17.5	31.2	41.0	35.4	27.0	24.4
Tea	2.3	2.9	3.3	3.9	4.6	3.6	3.8
Cotton	13.6	11.2	15.4	11.9	11.4	10.9	8.3
Sisal fiber	9.7	10.8	5.8	5.0	5.9	5.7	5.1
Cashews	6.2	6.3	3.2	4.1	4.4	3.2	1.2
Cashew kernels	1.2	1.6	1.9	1.9	1.8	1.8	2.6
Tobacco	3.2	4.4	6.3	4.7	6.0	3.3	2.2
Cloves	5.9	11.5	6.3	5.4	1.6	7.3	12.2
Minor items b	16.8	12.3	9.4	7.6	12.5	13.5	12.8
Manufactured products c	23.2	19.5	15.9	12.9	15.4	21.7	25.9
of which:							
Sisal cordage and twines	1.5	3.2	2.6	2.7	3.1	4.8	4.8
Diamonds	8.7	6.4	4.3	4.5	6.6	7.7	7.5
Re-Exports	0.9	1.9	1.3	1.5	1.1	2.0	1.6
Total exports	100.0	100.0	100.0	100.0	100.0	100.0	100.0
Real exports (1975 prices)	515	327	307	262	231	241	206
Index of export prices (1975=100)	46	100	150	215	201	214	248

aPreliminary.

bIncluding cereals and cereal preparations, animal feed, meat and meat preparations, vegetables, sugar, oil seeds, hides, skins and furs.

cIncluding paper and paper goods, textiles, nonmetallic mineral goods, iron and steel, nonferrous metals, metals, and miscellaneous goods.

Sources: World Bank and International Monetary Fund data.

Table A-3

Tanzanian Imports: Share, Real Imports, and Index of Import Prices
(share in percentage, imports in 1975 prices, 1975=100, figures are rounded)

	1970	1975	1976	1977	1978	1979	1980[a]	1981[a]
Food and live animals	7.7	17.7	8.2	8.7	5.6	3.4	11.7	—
of which: Cereals	2.4	15.3	3.9	5.5	3.0	1.8	0.1	—
Beverages and tobacco	0.9	0.1	0.1	0.1	0.0	0.0	0.0	—
Raw materials	1.4	1.6	3.0	2.0	2.1	1.6	1.5	—
Mineral fuels and lubricants[b]	8.5	11.9	17.7	14.4	11.2	15.7	23.1	21
Animal and vegetable oils	1.2	1.7	2.9	2.3	1.7	1.4	1.1	—
Chemicals	10.0	11.8	10.9	11.6	11.5	9.5	10.9	—
Capital goods[c]	35.2	30.8	32.7	37.1	43.6	46.8	34.2	—
Manufactured goods	27.7	20.9	21.0	20.1	20.0	18.1	14.5	—
Miscellaneous manufacturers	6.7	3.4	3.2	3.7	4.0	3.3	2.9	—
Others	0.8	0.1	0.2	0.1	0.0	0.0	0.0	—
Total[e]	100.0	100.0	100.0	100.0	100.0	100.0	100.0	—
Real imports	1,058	736	626	674	945	739	668	613
Index of import prices	31	100	102	110	121	147	182	183

[a]Preliminary.
[b]Excluding re-exports of crude oil.
[c]Including machinery and transport equipment.
Sources: World Bank and International Monetary Fund data.

Table A-4
Tanzania: Real Producer Prices of Selected Food Crops and Export Crops
(in US cents per kg, 1980–81 prices)

	1971–72	1975–76	1976–77	1977–78	1978–79	1979–80	1980–81	1981–82	Percent change 1971–72 to 1980–81
Food crops									
Maize	93	163/174	159	151	134	129	100	121	7.5
Paddy	202	217	199	213	189	194	175	186	−13.4
Wheat	221	217	239	222	197	174	165	178	−25.3
Weighted average price	128	187	177	170	151	146	121	139	−5.5
Cassava	—	87	99	106	103	84	65	49	—
Sorghum	—	163	179	177	158	129	100	71	—
Finger millet	—	174/185	189	355	315	258	150	106	—
Export crops									
Cashews	368	228	219	204	268	232	300	404	−18.5
Cotton	426	435	398	408	379	387	320	299	−24.9
Coffee	1,744	1,739	2,982	1,931	1,431	1,316	1,220	767	−30.0
Sisal	—	352	405	358	335	431	377	310	−47.2
Tea	283	174	179	266	237	194	150	121	−47.0
Tobacco	2,550	1,522	1,471	1,312	1,167	1,135	1,050	1,018	−58.8
Pyrethrum	1,105	869	795	709	726	774	750	808	−32.1
Cardamom	—	2,609	2,982	4,432	7,098	5,806	4,500	3,635	—
Cocoa	—	—	795	975	1,262	1,290	1,100	888	—
Castorseed	190	163	149	177	158	129	120	137	−36.2
Weighted average price	1,045	894	1,238	828	788	744	663	517	−36.5

Source: International Monetary Fund data.

COMMENTS

Knud Erik Svendsen

The reasons for discussing the bad shape of the economy in Tanzania instead of in countries like Kenya or Zaire are often political. The experience of the 1970s is used to prove that the Tanzanian type of development strategy cannot succeed.

It is not quite clear to me whether Uma Lele is going this far. But she is at least rushing to general policy conclusions that are in line with the World Bank's analysis for all of sub-Saharan Africa. Her paper comes close to being an argument for a radical break with the principles of the Tanzanian development strategy rather than for an adjustment of this strategy.

While agreeing with much in her paper, I am opposed to such a use of the Tanzanian record. The material from the short history of this young state does not permit such general conclusions. Having criticized major points with regard to the implementation of the strategy in the past, I suggest another reading of the evidence based on a different approach to the relationship between politics and economics in Tanzania.

Let me begin with the relative roles of external and internal factors in producing truly miserable economic conditions in that country. It is true that the Tanzanian authorities have shown a tendency to seek the causes of crisis in factors beyond their control. Since 1981 this has changed. Efforts have been made by a national task force to initiate a change in policy, resulting in 1982 in a structural adjustment program of severe financial cuts and guidelines for a new agricultural policy.

I believe Uma Lele is downplaying the negative role of external factors in Tanzania's recent history. To compare, as she does, the estimated losses from exogenous factors—including the war with Idi Amin—with the admittedly large inflows of aid to Tanzania

197

does not make sense. The external losses hit certain parts of the economy, while the aid on the whole went elsewhere. Foreign aid put additional pressure on the financial situation. The main problem is that neither the aid donors (including the World Bank) nor the government responded satisfactorily to the adverse conditions.

The external strains on the economy added to a number of internal strains, caused mainly by many rapid institutional changes, such as decentralization of public administration, movement of the peasant population to villages, expansion of the state sector as part of a new industrial strategy, and dissolution of the cooperative unions, just to mention the major ones. All of these policies had costs in terms of negative effects on agricultural development. Given the economic and social structure of the country, such costs can fall only on agriculture. I am ready to concede that there were arguments in favor of each of these policies, even if I do not agree with all of them, but in the long run they were brought about too quickly and were not implemented well.

Under better external conditions—without the droughts, the breakup of the East African Community, and the war—these policies would have worked better. The negative impact on agriculture could have been softened. Equally important, there would have been a greater possibility of adjusting these policies in line with experience gained as to their effects. It is generally more difficult for a less-developed country to adjust economic policy to changing economic realities; it has little to do with the "fine tuning" mentioned in connection with the industrialized countries. The data base is weaker, and year-to-year fluctuations in agriculture are larger. The role of expectations is decisive, whether they relate to weather, the hope for an economic upturn (shared by most in 1977–78), or to more general changes in the international economic order.

The macroeconomic signals to the political leadership were very erratic during the 1970s, and the leadership was able to sustain the optimistic idea that the difficulties were transitional—that is, until things really went downhill in 1979. Take foreign reserves: they went down and up and down and up. In fact, on advice from outside, the year of 1978 became a spending year, giving rise to the idea that the economy had been able to absorb the many policy initiatives. But this was not so. The agricultural basis had been weakened. And aside from the reasons for this enumerated in Uma Lele's paper I would add ecosystem problems for crops like cotton, and the implementation of the village policy.

Tanzania's experience does not argue against political initiatives or political mobilization, if you will. But there is an argument for not overstraining the economy in a country like Tanzania, and for keeping reserves in many forms. Because of the nature of the monetary productive economy, and its dependence on inflows of foreign exchange, it is easy for the economy to turn into a downward spiral: excessive shortages of foreign exchange lead to cuts in exports, and the vicious circle begins.

Uma Lele concludes her paper with some observations on the consequences of foreign aid to Tanzania. While I agree with the broad priorities she defines, I have some doubts about her strong call for far greater coordination among donors. I would emphasize rather the need for some pluralism in this area. The record of foreign aid to Tanzania has shown success mainly in the areas of education and health, where major progress has been made. But overall the donor community has no reason to be too proud of its understanding of Tanzania's problems. Some humility on its part—and on the part of the World Bank in particular—would be in order. On the whole, the Bank has pushed Tanzania in the wrong direction during the 1960s and 1970s. It is extremely difficult to find the right balance among the different kinds of change required to revive agriculture. Producer prices are very important, for example, but an all-consuming belief in their importance will induce strong inflationary pressures in the short run and have little effect on real output. An adjustment of the nominal exchange rate is also called for, but it will not have positive effects without measures to remove other constraints on the supply of export crops. Institutional changes will be needed that relate to the role of the various forms of production in agriculture, and they are under way. More important, foreign exchange is needed to turn the downward into an upward spiral. In general, the main problem remains to arrive at a better interaction between public initiatives and market forces.

8

MICHAEL ROEMER

Ghana, 1950–1980: Missed Opportunities

At its independence in 1957, Ghana was probably the richest and most educated country in black Africa.[1] Its 1960 per capita income of about $500 (in 1980 dollars) would have placed Ghana in the World Bank's category of middle-income countries. In the 1950s, Ghana's exports amounted to more than 30 percent of gross domestic product (GDP), and the value added in exports was probably a very high fraction of the total.

Despite its promising beginning, Ghana today reflects only a history of shattered dreams. Over thirty years of trying to realize its development potential, alternately by interventionist and by (timidly) liberal measures, Ghana has managed only a *decline* in GNP per capita of 0.7 percent per year. By 1980, its capital investment as a percent of GDP had fallen from 20 percent in the 1950s to only 5 percent. Its exports as a share of GDP were only 12 percent. And its continuing decline may soon push Ghana into the ranks of the poorest countries in the world.

The story of Ghana's debacle is partly the story of discredited theories of development, especially the "big push" and import-substitution approaches that were popular in the 1950s and 1960s. In important ways, Ghana was a model for such development strategies, which include central planning of economic activity and especially a strong commitment to industrial development protected by high trade barriers—thus substituting inefficient domestic production for foreign imports, which would otherwise be financed by more efficient production for export.

The misallocations and inefficiencies that resulted were made even worse by an almost complete lack of fiscal management, as Ghana pressed on with a program of domestic investment in publicly owned firms, with little regard for project efficiency. Toward the middle of the 1960s, mounting losses from state-owned firms coincided with explosive public spending to bring the country close to bankruptcy.

The high point of these policies was reached in the latter half of Kwame Nkrumah's regime, between 1961 and 1966, but they have been substantially continued ever since, interrupted by tentative attempts at liberalization and reform.

Reviewing the record, it is hard to avoid the conclusion that Ghana, in many respects, has turned out to be a model of how *not* to develop. It thus provides a valuable case study from which to understand why some countries, especially in East and Southeast Asia but including Kenya and the Ivory Coast in Africa, have maintained strong economic growth rates over long periods, and why many others have not.

Although the proximate causes of its poor economic record have been economic policies that discourage efficient utilization of Ghana's resources, the underlying causes are political. As in most countries, political considerations have confounded economic policymaking, but over the past several years political instability in Ghana has made it impossible for that country to have any economic policy at all.

The Thirty-Year Record

In reexamining Ghana's thirty-year record of missed opportunities, it is best to begin with an overview. As noted, Ghana's

GDP per capita declined 0.7 percent a year between 1950 and 1980. Although the 1970s were a decade of especially poor performance—GDP per capita fell by about 2.5 percent a year—the previous two decades were hardly models of development. GDP grew at about 4 percent a year in the 1950s (though population grew faster, probably due partly to migration from neighboring countries) and at just over 2 percent a year in the 1960s. The only period of satisfactory growth since 1950 occurred in the second half of the 1950s, when GDP grew by almost 6 percent a year (table 1). But this was accomplished by an unsustainable use of accumulated resources, albeit under a liberal regime. The overthrow of Nkrumah in early 1966 marks one of the more easily identifiable policy turning points in Ghanaian history. The rhetoric of economic policy changed substantially, economic management improved, and economic growth did increase after 1966. But post-1966 policies had some crucial similarities to Nkrumah's regime, while growth rates in the late 1960s were still modest and were not sustained.[2]

The impression conveyed by movements in GDP is confirmed by indicators of structural change. The share of agriculture in GDP was the same during the 1970s as during the 1950s—41 percent—and the share of manufacturing remained at about 10 percent (table 2). Although there was some shift of the labor force during this period, in 1980 over half of the work force remained in agriculture, and only 20 percent were engaged in industry (including mining, construction, and utilities).

Ghana's former prosperity was based on its primary exports—predominantly cocoa, but also minerals and timber. The major cause of the country's stagnation and decline has been inadequate diversification of its exports. As noted, its exports fell from more than 30 percent of GDP in the 1950s to only 12 percent in 1980. During the Nkrumah period, export volumes grew rapidly (over 7 percent a year from 1955–65), but cocoa prices fell by over 50 percent and consequently export revenues did not keep pace with GDP.

In the post-1974 world of high petroleum prices and global inflation, it is customary to seek reasons for declining exports in adverse terms of trade, especially for primary exporting countries. Yet Ghana's export prices were buoyant in the 1970s. In 1977,

Table 1
Growth Rates, Ghana
(percent per year)

		Nkrumah period			NLC/PP governments		NRC government
	1950–77	1955–60	1960–65	1960–66[a]	1965–71	1966–71[a]	1971–77
GDP (market prices)	2.7	5.9	3.1	1.8	2.8	4.3	–0.2
Agriculture	NA	NA	NA	NA	4.1	4.6	–2.0
Manufacturing	NA	NA	NA	NA	10.0	12.3	–6.9
Imports	–0.6	7.0	0.6	–1.1	–5.1	0.0	–14.4
Exports	–1.4	7.4	7.3	4.0	–3.2	–1.6	–13.5
Investment	–0.7	12.6	2.1	–3.7	–2.3	3.9	–15.6

[a]Nkrumah fell in early 1966, a year in which GNP declined. To include 1966 in the Nkrumah years makes the post-Nkrumah period look better by comparison.

Source: World Bank, *World Tables*, 2nd ed. (Washington, D.C.: World Bank, 1980), pp. 86–87.

Table 2
Structural Characteristics, Ghana
(as percent of GDP, current prices)

	1950	1960	1965	1971	1977
Agriculture	NA	41	41	44	38
Manufacturing	NA	10	10	11	9
Imports	22	35	27	20	8
Exports	34	28	17	16	8
Investment	15	24	18	14	5

Source: World Bank, *World Tables*, 2nd ed. (Washington, D.C.: World Bank, 1980), pp. 86–87.

unit values (free on board [f.o.b.]) for cocoa exports, which constitute about 60 percent of total exports, were six times the level in 1971, which was itself a good year (table 3). And the cocoa terms of trade, using import unit values for non-oil-exporting less-developed countries (LDCs), stood at 193 in 1977 (1975 = 100), compared to 96 in 1971 and only 53 in 1960.[3] (Since 1977, cocoa wholesale prices have remained above—sometimes substantially above—the 1977 level.) Yet the volume of cocoa exports plunged during this period: in 1977, tonnage was less than half that in 1970 and substantially below that of any year during the 1960s. Other exports did not perform much better. Cocoa revenues retained their share of Ghana's total export revenues throughout the period, and the share of nonprimary exports fell from 10 percent in 1960 to only 1 percent in 1978.

It is not surprising that other macroeconomic aggregates declined along with exports. Without any compensating change in either foreign aid or investment, Ghana's imports plummeted along with exports, dropping to only 12 percent of GDP in 1979, compared to 31 percent during the 1950s. Nor, evidently, did import-substituting industries make up much, if any, of the difference, because manufacturing value added grew by just over 1 percent annually from 1965 to 1977. Gross domestic investment, which averaged 20 percent of GDP during the 1950s, plunged to only 5 percent by 1980. Reports from Ghana suggest that disinvestment is palpable in deteriorating roads and in the breakdown of much other infrastructure.[4]

Table 3
Price Indicators, Ghana
(1970=100)

	1950	1955	1960	1965	1971	1977
GDP deflator	40.5	47.6	50.4	72.9	105.3	702.8
Foreign exchange rate (cedi/$)	0.714	0.714	0.714	0.714	1.029	1.150
Cocoa prices						
Nominal unit value	NA	77	52	34	77	466
Nominal producer prices	65	113	87	70	100	NA
Real producer prices	160	237	173	96	95	NA
Real effective exchange rates[a]						
Imports	NA	128	121	106	97	NA
Noncocoa exports	NA	108	101	71	NA	NA
Cocoa exports	NA	61	83	33	NA	NA

[a]1969 import rate = 100; in 1969, the noncocoa export rate index was 75 and the cocoa export rate index was 39.

Sources: World Bank, World Tables, 2nd ed. (Washington, D.C.: World Bank, 1980), pp. 86–87 (GDP deflator and exchange rate); International Monetary Fund, International Financial Statistics Yearbook 1982 (Washington, D.C.: IMF, 1982), pp. 206–7 (cocoa unit values); International Monetary Fund, Surveys of African Economics, vol. 6 (Washington, D.C.: IMF, 1975), p. 99 (cocoa producer prices); and J. Clark Leith, Foreign Trade Regimes and Economic Development: Ghana (New York: Columbia University, Press for the National Bureau of Economic Research, 1974), p. 42 (real effective exchange rates).

Upon gaining independence in 1957, Ghana probably had the most educated population in black Africa.[5] Since then it has almost doubled the share of eligible population enrolled in primary school to 36 percent of the eligible age group. Some aspects of health status also appear to have improved: life expectancy has risen modestly, from 40 to 49 years from 1960 to 1980, and infant mortality has dropped by about 28 percent. The number of doctors per capita has doubled and the number of nurses per capita has risen ninefold in twenty years. However, in 1977 caloric intake was only 85 percent of "requirements."[6]

Its early investment in human capital should have improved Ghana's development prospects. Yet Ghana was favorably endowed at independence only in relation to other African countries, and some of the better-performing African states have improved relatively more than Ghana. Even in 1980, the better-performing African countries were educating a substantially smaller fraction of their populations through secondary school than was true for countries in Asia and Latin America. Moreover, given the political upheaval that has plagued Ghana, especially since 1977, it is doubtful whether the figures on education and health mean much, whether improvements have been sustained, and whether the quality of these services has been maintained, whatever the levels of inputs.

Changing Policy Environments, 1950–80

Recent Ghanaian economic history can be divided into four reasonably distinct periods of differing policy environments. During the 1950s, as Kwame Nkrumah led Ghana through internal self-government and into independence, the Ghanaian leader had not yet put his stamp on economic policy and the economy remained substantially in its colonial mold. In 1961, Nkrumah turned to economic policy as a prime focus and began to move towards a protectionist, industrializing, and socializing policy framework. This period was ended abruptly in early 1966 with a coup that brought the military to power under the National Liberation Council (NLC) and continued with the Progress Party (PP) government of Kofi Busia, elected in 1969. These were years of relative economic stabilization and then partial liberalization. The Busia government was ousted in turn by a second military government, the National Redemption Council (NRC) in January 1972, less than three weeks after a major devaluation, the high-water mark of the liberalizing period. The NRC returned to the controls of the Nkrumah period.

A fifth period, from 1978 to the present, is a jumble of political instability, including a palace coup within the NRC, the first coup by Flight Lieutenant Jerry Rawlings just before scheduled elections, the short-lived civilian government of Hilla Limann, and the second Rawlings coup in 1981. As poor as performance was until 1978, it has been worse in the political anarchy that has obtained since then, and no coherent economic policy can be discerned. It will be the better part of kindness to ignore the recent period.

The early Nkrumah years, to 1961. Until 1961, Nkrumah's
economic policies, whatever his rhetoric, were relatively liberal
and internationally oriented.[7] Ghana was in the sterling area,
within which trade and payments were relatively unencumbered,
though there were restrictions on payments outside the area. The
average rate of tariff collections on imports (cost, insurance, and
freight [c.i.f.]) was 17 percent from 1955 to 1960, and no other
taxes or restrictions were imposed. However, cocoa exporters paid
heavy taxes, ranging from 13 to 50 percent of the f.o.b. value of exports.[8] The cocoa rate varied because farmers were paid a fixed
price, so in effect the short-term marginal tax rate was 100 percent. The level of farmer prices for cocoa is one of the pivotal
policy variables in the economy. In both nominal and real terms
the producer price was high during the 1950s but declined during
the early 1960s (table 3).[9] The Korean War—induced commodity
boom raised world cocoa prices dramatically during the early
1950s, and Ghana's buoyant cocoa earnings permitted a rapid
building of reserves, which became one of Ghana's important
legacies at independence. At the end of 1956, the year before independence, net reserves stood at $252 million, equivalent to 17
months' imports. By 1961, reserves had been cut in half, while imports grew, so reserves covered only four months of imports.[10] The
reserve accumulation of the early 1950s permitted both an expansionist and a liberal policy regime.

During the 1950s, investment constituted a high and rising
share of GDP, averaging 20 percent for the decade. The capital
stock appears to have increased by about two-thirds between 1955
and 1961.[11] The latter half of the decade was, in fact, the only
period of moderately rapid growth in the past thirty years, with
GDP expanding at 5.9 percent a year. Yet the capital stock was
growing much faster and the incremental capital-output ratio
from 1955 to 1961 was 3.6, excluding cocoa (or 4.3 including it).[12]
The high ratio reflects three factors. First, cocoa itself requires a
large investment of labor to clear the forest for planting, and also
of time—five years or more—until new trees begin to bear fruit.
Second, during the liberal, expansionist phase, Nkrumah
emphasized infrastructure as a leading sector, and the government overbuilt transport, utility, and other services as a means of
stimulating directly productive activities later. Third, it is undoub-

tedly true that in such an expansionist mode, project design and analysis were not carefully done, a failing that became intense in the early 1960s.

Nkrumah's big push, 1961–66. It appears that the year 1961 marked the major turning point in Nkrumah's economic policies.[13] Until that year, his government had run the economy more or less as the colonial government had done, though perhaps with a greater willingness to spend accumulated foreign currency reserves and to finance development expenditures with domestic borrowing. By 1961, however, despite good growth during the late 1950s, Nkrumah evidently sensed a need to deliver more of the economic changes he had promised with independence, and he began to implement his visionary strategy of an integrated pan-African market, led by Ghana.

Nkrumah's new path was, in effect, laid out by the most influential development economists of the day.[14] The strategy of the early 1960s was based on the notion of a "big push" of massive investment that would break the "vicious circle of poverty" and propel a "takeoff" into self-sustained growth. It was an unbalanced growth strategy; import-substituting industry was the leading sector operating behind a high protective barrier, and agriculture yielded its labor surplus to man the new factories. Nkrumah was determined to shuck the colonial shell that encompassed Ghana's economy. He meant to depend less on primary exports and increasingly on Ghanaian manufactures. National planning was to center on the allocation of public investment, with a growing share of resources allocated by government; industry was to be built with sufficient capacity to supply the emerging Africa-wide market.

Nkrumah's strategy is recognizable as the consensus development economics of the era. He borrowed, if a bit eclectically, from Harrod and Domar, Scitovsky, Rosenstein-Rodan, Hirschman, Lewis, Prebisch, Singer, Nurkse, Kaldor, and others whose work was required reading for students of development during the 1950s. Lewis, Kaldor, and Dudley Seers actually advised Nkrumah at one time or another.[15] However, two elements of Nkrumah's approach were more controversial. First, as a socialist, he used public enterprise as a central instrument in implementing development plans. State-owned enterprises sprang up in all fields, but made their greatest (largely detrimental) impact in manufacturing and agriculture. State firms were charged to generate employment, not only for workers in general, but particularly for the young school-leavers who formed one of Nkrumah's most vociferous constituencies.[16] The results were predictably bad. Second, although Nkrumah distrusted local entrepreneurs and dismissed them as instruments of development, he tried to encourage foreign investors. By such means as the 1963 Capital Investments Act, fiscal incentives were granted to investors. The largest and in many ways most successful project of the period was the Volta dam and its associated Valco aluminum refinery, in which a consortium of Kaiser Aluminum and Reynolds played the central role.

Once a government has decided on its economic goals and preferred (or acceptable) means of achieving them over any period, the twin tasks of economic management are macroeconomic consistency and microeconomic efficiency. Nkrumah's government failed on both counts. External deficits had begun to plague Ghana before 1961; the drawdown of reserves has already been mentioned. But cocoa prices fell precipitously during the early 1960s, with unit values in 1965 at only half the 1959 level, and export earnings remained stagnant despite a doubling of cocoa export volumes. Ghanaian economic policies have always been hostage to the severe volatility of cocoa prices, and Nkrumah's regime probably suffered from this menace more than most governments. The import demands of the "big push" put an intolerable strain on external payments: over the 1960–65 period, despite the imposition of new import taxes and controls, current account deficits averaged 15 percent of GDP, peaking at 20 percent in 1965, and only half of those deficits were financed by long-term capital inflows.[17] By 1965, there were no net reserves left.

Fiscal management was little better. On the basis of recorded budget data,[18] Nkrumah's fiscal performance appears responsible enough. The government made a determined effort to raise taxes to finance its big push of industrialization, and noncocoa revenues rose from 9.4 percent of GDP in 1961 to 14.7 percent in 1965, while recorded government outlays remained around 25 percent of GDP over the period from 1961 to 1965. However, these outlays did represent a leap from the 21 percent average of 1960 and earlier years, and were accompanied by declining cocoa revenues. More telling, though, was the unrecorded expenditure on development projects.[19] The cumulative government deficit from 1960 to 1965 was almost 50 percent higher than the recorded deficit, and averaged 12 percent of GDP. The difference was financed by short-term suppliers' credits from equipment manufacturers and others. (This use of short-term borrowing to finance long-term structural adjustment became a characteristic of Ghana's economic management and exacerbated later payments crises.) The government was not only increasing its control over resources; it was also putting inflationary strains on the economy and, perhaps most damaging, shielding a substantial fraction of its development projects from even rudimentary scrutiny by the budgetary process. Inflation, which had been under control before 1960, jumped to an average of 7.6 percent a year from 1960 to 1965, based on the GDP deflator.

The shielding of many investment projects from serious professional appraisal was one important kind of microeconomic mismanagement during the later Nkrumah years. Although much of the evidence for this is necessarily anecdotal, the stories of white elephants are too numerous to dismiss: they include state farms designed to cultivate relatively abundant land intensively using scarce imported capital equipment; a pharmaceutical plant that cost ten times as much as a feasible alternative; a sheet-glass plant designed to produce for three times the local market, which was then converted to a bottle-making plant; a footwear factory designed to produce four kinds of shoes, two of which were not consumed domestically; a tannery in the south of Ghana, 500 miles from the northern meat factory that was to be its source of hides and 200 miles from a footwear factory that would use the leather; sugar factories completed before their plantations; a tomato- and mango-canning plant built to accommodate the output of 2,500 acres of these crops — in a region that grew neither of them commercially and could not begin to do so for at least five years; and so on.[20] Incremental capital-output ratios moved steadily upward from the 2.5 to 3.0 range before 1961 to 6.1 between 1960 and 1965.[21] Although related macroeconomic forces and slow growth could have been responsible for these figures, the proliferation of bad projects must have played a role.

Increasingly, government's investment was being channeled

through newly created public enterprises, from state farms to gold mines to manufacturing companies and trading organizations. Of twenty-two of these enterprises in 1964–65, thirteen made losses.[22] The National Trading Corporation, which benefited from preferential access to import licenses, made the only large profits, 6.5 million cedis (¢), while the State Farms Corporation lost ¢12.7 million. Overall, the state firms lost ¢14.1 million that year. State companies had on average less than half the value added per worker of private firms.[23] In gold mining, the private Ashanti Gold Fields worked ore at one-third the unit cost of the state gold mines. And, most critically for economic performance, small private farms convincingly outperformed the State Farms Corporation, with almost five times the yield and over five times the labor productivity of state farms.[24]

To some extent, the state companies bore higher costs because they carried the additional burden of social goals, especially the creation of employment and Nkrumah's vision of a pan-African market, for which some of Ghana's overlarge factories were supposedly planned. But given the haphazard, almost wanton mishandling of state projects, there is a strong presumption that poor management and a detrimental incentive system were root causes of inefficient production.

During the 1960s, Nkrumah's government began to tamper with the microeconomic price environment in ways that further worsened allocational inefficiency. The relatively liberal trade regime of the 1950s became increasingly burdened by higher tariffs, rising from average duty collections of 17 percent in 1960 to 26 percent in 1965, and the addition of other taxes that together totaled 22 percent in 1965.[25] Import licensing began in late 1961. These import-limiting devices had multiple economic objectives: restriction of import expenditures as export revenues stagnated; protection of domestic manufacturing to stimulate import-substituting industrialization; and, in the case of import taxes, increased revenues to replace falling cocoa receipts and to finance growing investment.

In some respects the new trade system accomplished its goals. Although trade and current account deficits did grow, imports were restrained in the sense that their ratio to GDP fell from the 30-plus percent levels of 1960 and 1961 to roughly a 24 percent average over the next four years. Import substitution took place and dramatically changed the composition of imports: consumer goods, which constituted well over half of imports by end use in the 1950s, fell to 30 percent of the total by the late 1960s, while imported producer materials rose from about 25 percent to almost 40 percent of the total, and capital goods imports from about 15 percent to around 25 percent.[26] The Nkrumah program must be given substantial credit for the 10.3 percent annual growth of manufacturing from 1962 to 1966, a pace that continued through the second half of the decade, at a time when GDP was growing at only 2.1 percent a year.

But Nkrumah's trade policy ultimately failed to produce sustained growth, for reasons that are now familiar to development economists. While import-substituting industries were stimulated, exports were discouraged. In the face of a fixed exchange rate and annual domestic inflation of 7.6 percent during the early 1960s, the price-deflated effective exchange rate declined for all commodities. For imports the average price-deflated effective exchange rate fell from ¢0.84 per dollar to ¢0.73 (in 1960 prices). This meant that the highly differentiated, erratic protective structure bore a relatively greater weight in investment and production decisions. For noncocoa exports, the fall in the effective exchange rate was relatively greater, and although the noncocoa export rate was only 16 percent below the import rate in 1960, it was 33 percent lower in 1965 (table 3).[27] Cocoa producer prices fell by a third in nominal terms from 1959 to 1965, reducing growers' incentives. But world prices, as measured by Ghana's unit values, fell by half, so not all of the world price disincentive was transmitted to growers. Thus, as export revenues stagnated, the government reduced the incentive either to diversify exports or to increase them. Because these figures exclude the effects of import quotas, they overstate the decline in the import rate and hence understate the relative disincentive to invest in exports.

The protective duties imposed during these years were highly differentiated, and import licensing—especially as corruption made the impact of quotas more unpredictable—added variability to produce a chaotic system whose complexity could not have been intended. Effective rates of protection ranged from zero or negative effective protection for several export industries to over 200 percent for such sectors as fruit and vegetable processing, biscuits and confectionery, knitting, clothing, footwear, and radios. Industries such as cocoa-processing (which used subsidized inputs), distilling, handbags and luggage, and paints all used material inputs that, at world prices, were worth more than their outputs.[28] There was even greater variability at the plant level within sectors.[29]

Policies towards factor prices exacerbated the adverse impact of Nkrumah's system of trade incentives. A combination of minimum wage legislation, controlled interest rates, an overvalued exchange rate, duty-free import of capital equipment, and tax-reducing investor incentives all conspired to make labor artificially expensive relative to capital, and thus to encourage capital-intensive choices of technology and industry. From 1960 to 1965, the ratio of wages to capital rentals rose by 8 percent for foreign-financed investments if they paid income taxes and by 24 percent if they enjoyed tax holidays, and by 23 percent for domestically financed investments without tax holidays;[30] a rise of 25 percent in the wage-rental ratio could, over a five-year period, reduce job creation by 20 to 25 percent in a country like Ghana.[31] Real interest rates ranged from −2 to −23 percent a year from 1961 to 1965, reinforcing the dual nature of financial markets.[32]

As 1966 began, Nkrumah's policies had pushed Ghana to virtual international bankruptcy, with an overstimulated economy that could no longer be contained by import and price controls, an enlarged public sector that could not be managed effectively by available Ghanaian manpower, an economic structure unsuitable to Ghana's endowments, and a price structure that promised no solution to Ghana's emerging stagnation. In early 1966 the military overthrew the government in the first of what has become a tiresome series of coups.

Stabilization and liberalization, 1966–71. The National Liberation Council (NLC) was forced to concentrate on restoring internal and external macroeconomic balance to the economy. For the six years from 1966 to 1971, the NLC and the succeeding Progress Party (PP) government of Kofi Busia, elected in 1969, kept government consumption, gross domestic investment, and imports below the real levels reached in Nkrumah's last full year. Although export volumes also declined, these governments were blessed with rising cocoa prices until 1971, so the current account balance narrowed steadily and substantially through 1970, when net reserves increased for the first time in a decade.

The NLC also began the process of decontrolling the economy, and the PP government was committed to completing the task. Import controls were the principal target, and a 43 percent devaluation of the cedi–dollar exchange rate in 1967 was the key instrument. Although devaluation was accompanied by some trimming of duties and other charges on imports, the effective exchange rate for imports rose by 39 percent and for exports by the full 43 percent. However, continued reduction in import taxes and the persistence of inflation, which accelerated to 12 percent a year, eroded the relative price impact of devaluation completely within two years.[33] Although erosion of the effective exchange rate put the trade balance about where it was in the early 1960s, the situation would have been much worse without devaluation.[34] Central to this conclusion is the judgment that the inflation of 1968–69 was not caused by the devaluation, which was probably deflationary on balance, but by expansionary fiscal policies relative to those of 1966–67.

Despite the erosion of the 1967 devaluation, import liberalization proceeded. By 1970, 60 percent of the goods previously under license had been removed from the list.[35] A surcharge and a sales tax increase, along with taxes of 10 to 25 percent on service payments, were imposed on imports by the Busia government in 1970 and 1971. Those, together with a proposed (but ineffectively implemented) bonus on noncocoa exports, simulated a rather ragged devaluation. But these measures were inadequate to dampen import demand in the face of reduced quantitative restrictions and continuing, although abated, inflation. Imports, which had been reduced 16 percent in 1968 by the devaluation and the continued partial controls, increased 21 percent in real terms from 1968 to 1970. It took a doubling of cocoa prices (in unit values) from 1967 to 1970, and a substantial increase in foreign aid following devaluation, to stave off a balance-of-payments crisis until 1971.

The Progress Party government came to power in October 1969. It was committed to continuing the liberalization begun by the NLC, but with a more ambitious program for development. Its finance minister, J. H. Mensah, who had been Nkrumah's chief planner, was determined to accelerate growth through higher investment and expanded exports, to stimulate employment creation, and to correct perceived disparities in rural and urban standards of living.[36] The most tangible manifestation of this policy was a dramatic expansion of capital outlays, which almost doubled over two years (though gross domestic investment remained below Nkrumah's highest levels in real terms). Buoyant cocoa revenues and increased foreign aid financed this expansion and left the budget close to balance until late 1971, when cocoa prices declined sharply. The PP government spent all its cocoa receipts during the boom period. When cocoa prices began falling in 1971, Ghana still had virtually no net reserves and was spending at a rate that pushed its 1971–72 budget deficit to 6 percent of GDP.

Mensah's views on income distribution are interesting, both because he was an early advocate of redistributing income in favor of rural dwellers and because his perceptions of inequality, though consistent with conventional wisdom, may have been wrong. In 1971, Mensah enunciated the view that, in Ghana, the lower-paid urban workers were really the lower stratum of a "relatively wealthy urban minority," while farmers and other rural residents were really the poor class.[37] He was in part reacting to the legacy of the Nkrumah years, when minimum wages were imposed to protect urban workers against capitalists, and cocoa prices and incomes were depressed to squeeze surplus from the rural areas to finance industrialization. He may also have been recognizing the electoral politics of the Progress Party, whose main bases of support coincided with the cocoa-growing areas. The difference in economic policies may also be explained along tribal lines: cocoa growers are largely Ashanti and allied ethnic groups; Nkrumah had wanted to break Ashanti political power, on which the Progress Party was largely based. Mensah acted upon his view of income distribution dramatically in his 1971 budget: he imposed a 5 percent "development levy" on the incomes of urban workers (perhaps the most unpopular measure of his tenure), reduced civil service and military incomes by about 25 percent through a reduction in perquisities, and also cut the military budget by 12 percent.[38]

Mensah's perception of Ghanaian income distribution appears to have been incorrect. Total payments to all cocoa farmers, deflated by the consumer price index, did decline from an index of

100 in 1960 to a low of 34 in 1966, but they had risen to 62 by the time of the PP electoral victory.[39] Moreover, the minimum wage also declined in purchasing power, from 100 in 1960 to a low of 56 in 1966, but unlike cocoa prices, the minimum wage did not recover significantly during the late 1960s; real average wage and salary payments declined very little over the decade. Finally, although cocoa farmers suffered declines in real prices and incomes, the bulk of farmers, who produce food, probably enjoyed relative income gains over the 1960s, as their terms of trade rose from 100 in 1960 to peaks of 132 in 1966 and rose again in 1971. It also appears that rural laborers had incomes not very different from lower-paid urban workers.

Thus, the popular view that Nkrumah's policies favored urban workers over farmers is probably wrong, whatever the government's intentions. In fact, much of the drop in cocoa producers' incomes can be traced to the fall in world prices rather than to domestic policies, since the producer price fell by less than world prices. On the whole, under both Nkrumah and succeeding governments, rural dwellers evidently improved their relative position, largely because food prices rose relative to other prices.

The economic policies of the NLC–PP governments and those of Nkrumah reveal more continuity than change.[40] Efforts to abandon controls were partial and tentative. Substantial import liberalization did not come until the Busia administration, two years after the 1967 devaluation and after its effects had been dissipated by inflation. The import surcharges then imposed added only 6 percent to the average cost of imports—woefully inadequate to ration imports to sustainable levels once the cocoa price boom had ended. Domestic price controls were never dismantled and continued to be taken seriously by policymakers throughout the period. The NLC did close some state farms, sell some state enterprises, and reorganize many of the rest, but it accepted the need for continued state management of many industrial firms. Although the NLC broke with Nkrumah's fiscal policy and tried to restrain government expenditure and aggregate demand, under Busia and Mensah the government expanded development expenditures, albeit at real levels lower than those reached by Nkrumah. Neither post-Nkrumah government seriously challenged the relatively high consumption levels to which Ghanaians had become accustomed: from 1965 to 1971, public plus private consumption averaged close to 90 percent of GDP and never fell below 87 percent.

Whether the stabilization-liberalization period succeeded in improving growth performance depends on the base year chosen. From 1965 to 1971, GDP grew at only 2.8 percent a year, slightly below the 3.1 percent registered from 1960 through 1965. But 1965 was a year of unsustainable expenditure that led directly to the recession of 1966. If the latter is used as the base, growth was a modestly better 4.3 percent a year, or almost 2 percent per capita.

The devaluation of 1971. The one truly pivotal period after the coup against Nkrumah was the second half of 1971, when an impending balance-of-payments crisis led to a devaluation that intensified the government's commitment to liberalization. But Ghana's second military coup followed two weeks later, and since then market forces have not been employed as a major tool to promote growth and development. Because the devaluation was a watershed in modern Ghanaian economic history, it is worthwhile analyzing that decision and its implementation in some detail.[41]

The 1971 crisis began to break just after Mensah's budget speech in July 1971. Although imports had been substantially liberalized, the real effective exchange rate stood 30 percent below its 1967 post-devaluation level and imports began rising to unsustainable levels. As Ghana fell further in arrears on trade credits, in September suppliers began warning of a cutoff in credit-financed imports. Cocoa prices had begun to retreat from their 1970 highs toward levels much closer to their long-run average (the wholesale price declined 26 percent on average from 1970 to 1971), and a steep slide was forecast for the coming year, with little prospect of early recovery.[42] The need to stimulate noncocoa exports was widely recognized. When Prime Minister Busia, alarmed at the growing crisis, sought additional aid and debt relief, the large donors demanded major policy changes that would correct the impending payments imbalance and reinforce the commitment to liberalization. An unrelated incident intensified the sense of crisis: members of the Trades Union Congress (TUC) struck in protest of the new development levy and the declining real minimum wage. In response, the government disbanded the TUC, further alienating urban workers.

In November the cabinet met to consider the crisis. The finance minister was opposed to any major policy change, especially devaluation, which he felt would jeopardize his development goals. Mensah alone believed that cocoa prices would soon recover, though he gave no reasons for thinking so. The prime minister, virtually committed to dealing with the crisis forcefully, then turned to the governor of the central bank, J. H. Frimpong-Ansah, to organize a team of economists to consider policy options and report to the cabinet. A team of Ghanaian and foreign economists was hastily assembled and began to work intensively, pulling together work that had been going on over the past few months. They sought to arrive at a set of policy recommendations sufficient to close a projected ¢100 million deficit in the basic balance of payments over a two- or three-year period. Three options were considered: a return to import licensing, a large increase in tariffs, and a devaluation. It was clear that the latter dominated the other two in economic terms and was the only option seriously considered by the cabinet, although tariff increases were given brief consideration at one point. Licensing went too strongly against the government's commitment to liberalization to be taken seriously. Although the issue was seen largely as a medium-term payments problem by most policymakers, the economists were deeply conscious of the need for policies to promote long-run structural change, especially export diversification and growth and a more efficient allocation of resources.

Although the economics literature offered compelling reasons for believing a devaluation was the correct instrument for the situation, it provided little guidance on the extent of the devaluation. The committee's attempts to make econometric estimates of the relevant elasticities foundered because history had not been kind enough to produce the needed experiments. In particular, the dominance of import controls for so many years and the lack of data for earlier years made it impossible to estimate demand elasticities for imports. The committee had to rely on guesswork for its data and projections.

The committee estimated that a 50 percent devaluation, to ¢1.52 per dollar, would correct the payments imbalance in two to three years, given the indications from donors of increased aid flows. This would, however, require substantial cuts in government expenditure to reduce absorption and contain inflation, and would permit little in the way of "sweeteners." But the cabinet was willing to undertake devaluation only if certain compensating changes would be made. First, government expenditure cuts were to be resisted. Instead, devaluation's impact on government cocoa revenues and import tax revenues would have to balance the budget. Second, government's electoral strategy and commitment to rural development meant that the cocoa producer price should be raised. And third, to quiet labor unrest, there should be some increase in the minimum wage. To accomplish these objectives, the cabinet seemed willing to effect a devaluation of as much as 100 percent. It seemed to view devaluation as a soft option, relieving constraints all around. Despite the economists' attempts to convey the need to reduce real incomes (especially consumption) to make devaluation work, the policymakers never showed that they accepted this imperative. Perhaps the most deeply entrenched feature of Ghana's political economy has been the primacy of consumption, regardless of the political regime and its stated intentions.

Charged with the task of recommending a devaluation that could accomplish both external and domestic—mostly fiscal—aims, the committee of economic advisers proposed a 75 percent devaluation in the cedi–dollar rate; the elimination of import surcharges, export bonuses, and the development levy; a 25 percent increase in the cocoa producer price; a 14 percent rise in the minimum wage; and expenditure cuts of ¢48 million. The technical committee had prepared a note warning that there would be losers from devaluation (the urban middle class, food farmers, and traders) as well as gainers (cocoa farmers, other exporters, import substituters, and government workers). No one then thought to include the military in the list. But it is not clear that the cabinet, whose grasp of the technical issues was shaky at best, ever understood or even saw this memorandum. It is evident from later speeches that many of them badly misinterpreted such key estimates as the likely rise in import prices.[43]

The final decision to devalue had its ironic elements. Faced with the inevitable, the finance minister suddenly opted for a higher adjustment—82 percent—and retention of both the import surcharges and export bonuses. A stunned cabinet readily agreed. And since the rate was pegged to the recently devalued dollar, the overall trade-weighted rate was devalued by 92 percent, far in excess of the estimated need for the balance-of-payments correction. The decision, made before Christmas, was almost announced on Christmas Eve, but it was then postponed to the following week.

The initial public reaction was favorable, but the mood changed quickly once traders began raising prices or removing goods from the shelves. Although traders probably overreacted and prices might well have come down eventually, the government's dilatoriness exacerbated the reaction in two respects. First, it had been the practice to pass 180-day trade credits on to importers, who purchased their foreign exchange from the central bank only when the credits fell due. Hence, many goods already sold or on the shelf had not been paid for, and traders assumed they would have to buy foreign exchange at the higher exchange rate. Early in January the government finally announced that such credits could be repaid at the old rate, but it was hard to erase the public's impression of wild price increases. Second, because the government was slow to eliminate or adjust price controls, many merchants simply removed controlled goods from the shelves until action was taken, intensifying the atmosphere of scarcity. Nor did good news come in time from overseas. Busia acted—against advice—before he could secure additional aid or debt relief from any source. Although Busia had indications that some assistance would be forthcoming from the United Kingdom, the United States, and the World Bank, none of these donors made any commitment after the devaluation. The consuming public had become sensitive to the possibility that a reduction in their living standards was necessary to repay loans to foreigners; some public announcement from the donors to the contrary might have improved the climate in Accra.

The subsequent coup took place at a time when public opinion was hostile to the government. The first pronouncement of Colonel Ignatius Acheampong did not mention the economy or the devaluation, but concentrated on mistreatment of the army. Only later in the day, after the military leaders of the coup had talked to civilian supporters, was the devaluation trotted out as an ex-

planation. In fact, the coup had been plotted for several months
and was not the only conspiracy afoot at the time. Acheampong's
group used the post-devaluation discontent—and Busia's absence
for medical treatment in England—as the occasion to preempt
competing usurpers.

The devaluation may have been good electoral politics for Busia.
It favored groups (such as cocoa farmers) that had voted for his
party; it may have assuaged the workers; and it could have produced some visible success by the next election. But it was no
deterrent to a military coup, which succeeds more easily when urban dwellers are unhappy with the government. The devaluation
hit hardest at the urban middle class, who welcomed the coup. In
the short run, before supply elasticities become large, even those
who will eventually benefit from the devaluation may not realize
it, while the losers are painfully aware of the consequences.

The stagnant seventies. The Acheampong government, styled
the National Redemption Council (NRC), revalued the cedi in
stages back to ¢1.15 by 1973 (perhaps the only deficit country to do
so in recent history); it abrogated, and eventually was successful in
renegotiating, much of the hated Nkrumah debt; and it generally
went back to controls and exhortations as economic policy tools.
The economic history of these years has not been written (or at
least not published), and this is not the place to undertake that
task. It may be enough to point out that despite record cocoa prices,
there was virtually no growth in GDP from 1970 to 1977; the real
value of exports and imports fell by about 10 percent a year; and
gross domestic investment dropped by almost 9 percent a year.

The cocoa price boom of 1973 to 1979 was unprecedented and
confounded the sophisticated forecasts of 1971. Cocoa unit values
more than quadrupled from 1971 to 1977, enough to improve
Ghana's terms of trade by one-quarter for that period, despite the
first oil price increase. It is a testimony to what must have been
colossal mismanagement by the NRC that it was unable to capitalize on such favorable circumstances. It is also ironic that the
civilian government that eventually saw a need for a major
devaluation-liberalization lacked the power to sustain it, while the
military government that had the power lacked the understanding or perhaps the will. After seven years of 30 percent inflation,

the NRC (no longer under the deposed Acheampong) finally devalued the cedi massively, to ¢3.58 per dollar. In light of current and continuing inflation, even that proved woefully inadequate. The 1978 devaluation and Busia's death did inspire a spate of revisionist editorials recalling that Busia had tried to convince the Ghanaian public of the need for devaluation in 1971.

Subsequent political instability has made a mockery of economic policy. Those who deposed Acheampong did so in order to rid the army of the burden of governing. Before they could accomplish a return to civilian rule, Flight Lieutenant Rawlings staged the first of his two coups, ruled for a month, and then turned the reins over to the newly elected Limann government. Two years later, just as the civilians were rumored to be coming to the same decision as Busia in 1971, Rawlings interceded again. He ruled for two years before adopting any discernible economic policy to halt the continuing decline of living standards. In the meantime, inflation continued at triple-digit rates, production declined, and the black market exchange rate climbed to many multiples of the official rate.

Lessons for Ghana and Africa

Ghana's choice of economic strategy is severely constrained by its lack of trained and experienced policy analysts and public managers; in addition, its brain drain has intensified in recent years. Neither economic controls, nor extensive dependence on public enterprises, nor highly differentiated incentive systems can be managed effectively under such manpower constraints. In these circumstances any government—whatever its ideological persuasion—must depend on the market as much as possible, and on intervention as little as possible, to manage its economy. Moreover, its market-oriented policies need to be simple and sweeping, not detailed and differentiated.

Fortunately, Ghana and most African countries have market participants who can make such a strategy work. The image of traditional farmers and subsistence economies, borne of the colonial era and perpetuated by some development economists in the 1950s, is more myth than reality. Considerable economic and anthropological history now documents the existence of well-functioning, long-distance markets in foods, raw materials, and simple manufactures long before the advent of the colonial period.[44] In Ghana, the migration of cocoa farmers in response to economic incentives at the turn of the century, and the highly effective retail and wholesale trade run by market women, attest to the presence of agents capable of taking advantage of market opportunities. It is probably true that there are limits to what African entrepreneurs can accomplish in modern economies until they have had greater exposure to them, but in Ghana and elsewhere these limits have hardly been tested. Instead, the market women are often set up as scapegoats for poor government policies and seen as enemies rather than potential agents of development. And cocoa farmers have borne the heaviest taxes in Ghana, so that they exercise their ingenuity by smuggling headloads of cocoa out to neighboring countries where cocoa taxes are lower.[45]

I have argued elsewhere (as have others) that a liberal, internationally-oriented development strategy would benefit most African countries with greater growth, employment creation, and more egalitarian distribution of the benefits.[46] Ghana's experience from 1950 to 1980 provides no evidence to test this hypothesis. While economic controls have been thoroughly discredited, liberal policies were tried only for a short period—and then rather hesitantly—and were cut off before their usefulness could be judged. The most rapid growth in Ghana since 1950 (and even this was modest by East and Southeast Asian standards) came under the liberal though expansionist policies during the second half of the 1950s, and that growth was not sustainable. Although a case could be made that the stabilization-liberalization period of the late 1960s also induced slightly greater growth, this is based on shaky evidence, and in any event there was no dramatic change from the early 1960s. So the case for a liberal economic regime in Ghana must be based on *a priori* considerations and on the experience of other countries.

Ghana's recent history reinforces what we already know: the passage from a controlled regime to a liberal one is dangerous for any government. Those with a stake in the control regime, who have risen to relative wealth and power under it, will see immediately that their interests have been threatened by liberalization and the accompanying adjustments in relative prices. The new regime will eventually have its own constituents, but it takes time for these to emerge, for new agents to see the opportunities and seize them. Moreover, in many African countries (including Ghana), these agents may be small farmers, traders, and manufacturers whose power will never be as great as the less numerous agents who benefit from favoritism under control regimes. The now-demonstrated political instability of Ghana and other African countries will discourage an early response in any case, because the expectation is that governments cannot sustain radical changes in policy. To be effective, the new policies must be maintained for a time under difficult circumstances. It takes strong governments to institute such changes; so far in Africa there have been few such governments whose leaders also understand the need for liberal policies. The irony of the Ghanaian experience is typical: those with the vision lacked the power, and vice versa.

Finally, in the face of continuing political instability, there is little role for economic policy. It is unfortunate that badly managed economic policies can contribute to sustained political instability, but good policies cannot cure it. In Ghana today, it is hard to imagine that good policies can emerge, or if they do, it is hard to imagine that they can end the disruptive series of coups. In Ghana, as in Uganda and Chad, a political solution must precede effective economic policies. And on a reduced scale, the same applies to other countries on the continent. The only hope for Ghana is that the country be some day blessed with a strong government that understands the need for economic liberalization.

COMMENTS

Yaw Ansu

The outstanding feature in Ghana's economic record is the extreme rigidity of its economic system. The Ghanaian government has almost no room to use economic instruments to deal with economic problems because almost all important economic issues are transformed into political crises. Although the state *appears* to exercise extensive control over the country's economic activity, in reality the experience of successive governments shows that the state has no real control. What accounts for this paradox?

The paradox is perhaps most evident in situations where the government is the major employer in the economy (see table 1). Consider the problem of trying to reduce aggregate real consumer spending, which, as Michael Roemer notes, the government after Nkrumah had great difficulty doing. Reduced spending can be accomplished either by increased taxes or devaluation (if much of the consumer spending is on imported goods), both of which will reduce spendable income. The effectiveness of this policy will depend on the ability of employers to resist demands for wage increases. When the government is the employer, what is primarily an industrial dispute can become a political crisis, with one arm of the government adopting measures to reduce consumer spending and another arm doing battle with workers to translate those measures into real cuts.

As Michael Roemer's account of the 1971 devaluation dramatically shows, the result is a juggling act: how much compensation can be given to each group in the form of pay increases and subsidies? In such situations it may be difficult to resist the temptation to print more money to satisfy all the powerful groups, and the crisis is then rolled over.

Table 1

Public Employment

(as a percentage of total work force)

1964	64.8%
1966	72.9
1968	72.6
1970	70.1
1974	72.7
1976	76.1
1978	77.8

Sources: Killick, (1978), p. 314 for 1964–1970 data; Central Bureau of Statistics, 1981, p. 218 for data from 1974–1978.

Regardless of the problem of allocating pay increases, an even more important consideration is access to consumption. In a system where resources are allocated by rationing rather than by prices, the relationship between income and command over goods is a loose one. In the Ghanaian system the government controls (nominally, at least) the distribution of importables, which comprise a significant part of consumption. Whenever import controls are tightened, the various governments customarily have made special provisions for government workers. This imposes special penalties on rural cocoa farmers, for instance, who have little access to such privileges and thus must purchase goods on the "parallel markets"—those that trade illegally in currencies, smuggled imports, and goods "diverted" from government shops. Under these circumstances, export smuggling becomes very attractive to cocoa farmers, as it provides them with the opportunity to maintain their purchasing power in terms of the parallel-market prices they face. Table 2 shows that the producer price of cocoa, at official exchange rates, has been higher in Ghana than in the Ivory Coast for most years since 1977, a fact that should imply greater producer interest in selling output in Ghana than in the Ivory Coast. Yet smuggling into the Ivory Coast is rampant, because the Ghanaian currency is enormously overvalued, and at black-market exchange rates, cocoa prices are higher by a factor of ten or more in the Ivory Coast than in Ghana (see table 2).

Table 2
Cocoa Prices and Black-Market Exchange Rates
(produce price per metric ton—cedis)[a]

| | | In the Ivory Coast | |
	In Ghana	At official exchange rates	At black-market exchange rates
1977	944	927	7,115
1978	1,778	1,678	9,637
1979	3,333	3,400	16,867
1980	4,000	3,905	31,240
1981	5,333	3,036	45,450
1982	12,000	2,511	n.a.

[a]Conversion from the CFA franc into cedis is via the dollar exchange rates for both official and black-market rates.

Sources: For producer prices, Gill and Duffus, Cocoa Market Report No. 304, November 1982; for official exchanges, International Monetary Fund, *International Finance Statistics, 1982;* black-market exchange rates from *Picks Currency Yearbook* and *Economist Intelligence Unit,* various issues; the table is adapted from Ansu's paper, where earlier years are also considered, and comparison with Togo is given. Estimates of smuggling are also provided.

When government workers put up direct resistance to cuts in real consumption, the cut tends to be transferred to weaker groups, such as cocoa farmers, who happen also to be among the more productive segments of the population. The larger the group exempted from cuts, the higher the burden that falls on the rest— and the greater the incentive to resist indirectly by smuggling, refusing to harvest cocoa plantations, or by replacing cocoa trees with other crops that don't have to be sold through the government.

For political reasons, the government cannot lay off its employees. But beyond this, it seems the government cannot even control its hiring rate. Since 1974 government employment has been increasing not only absolutely, but also as a fraction of the total work force—at a time when output of government goods and services, including the maintenance of physical infrastructure, have all been declining.

On the face of it, the Ghanaian government appears to control a great deal of economic activity, but in reality it controls very little. Ghana today is so overcontrolled that much productive enterprise is driven underground. There is thus little hope for the economy until the government relaxes its controls and allows the productive energies of the country to resurface.

9

MALCOLM GILLIS

Episodes in Indonesian
Economic Growth

Indonesia is the fifth most populous nation in the world, and the 147 million inhabitants of this tropical archipelago nation represented 43 percent of the population of OPEC member countries in 1980. Annual rates of income growth averaged 7.9 percent over the period from 1971 to 1981, allowing a doubling of real gross domestic product (GDP) and a 70 percent increase in real GDP per capita (see table 1), to U.S. $520.[1] Economic growth in this later period was well above that experienced in the decade after independence and contrasted sharply with economic performance in the turbulent, hyperinflationary years of 1960 through 1965, when real GDP per capita declined marginally.

Until relatively recently, it was popularly assumed that oil wealth furnished a virtual guarantee of steadily rising prosperity

This paper represents the author's own views, and not necessarily those of the Harvard Institute for International Development.

232   MALCOLM GILLIS

Table 1
Average Annual Growth in Real GDP,
Population, and Per Capita GDP,
Indonesia
(percent)

	Real GDP	Population	Real GDP per capita
Annual growth rates:			
1952–59	3.2	2.0	1.2
1960–65	2.0	2.1	−0.1
1966–71	6.0	2.1	3.8
1972	9.4	2.3	6.9
1973	11.3	2.3	8.8
1974	7.6	2.3	5.2
1975	5.0	2.3	2.6
1976	6.9	2.3	4.5
1977	8.8	2.3	6.4
1978	6.9	2.3	4.5
1979	5.4	2.3	3.0
1980	9.6	2.3	7.1
1981	8.5[a]	2.3	6.1[a]
Average growth			
1967–73	7.1	2.2	4.8
1974–81	7.4	2.3	5.0
1971–81	7.9	2.3	5.5

[a]Preliminary.

Sources: For years prior to 1967: Anne Booth and Peter McCawley, "The Indonesian Economy since the Mid-Sixties," in *The Indonesian Economy During the Suharto Era*, ed. Anne Booth and Peter McCawley (Kuala Lumpur, Malaysia: Oxford University Press, 1981), table 1.1, p. 4. For 1967–1981: Indonesian Central Bureau of Statistics (Biro Pusat Statistik), *Pendapatan Nasional Indonesia* (various issues).

for the few countries so blessed. While this view is less widespread than before the problems encountered by such oil exporters as Mexico, Ecuador, and Nigeria in 1981 and 1982, it is perhaps not altogether clear that the Indonesian growth experience is of any particular relevance to those of the many oil-importing less-developed countries (LDCs) in general, for this nation has historically been the sixth largest producer among OPEC's fourteen members. The following three observations, in fact, suggest that the Indonesian economy bears but faint resemblance to stereotypical images of OPEC nations.

First, when viewed in appropriate perspective, the nation's oil wealth is quite limited relative to other OPEC members. In 1980, Indonesian oil production per capita was but four barrels per year, or about 1 percent of per capita production in Saudi Arabia. More to the point, Indonesia's annual per capita oil production was one-twelfth that of another middle-income OPEC member, Venezuela, and but 40 percent of that of Mexico.[2] Second, Indonesia experienced high rates of economic growth for several years prior to the first oil boom in late 1973. From 1966 through 1973, when oil exports averaged less than 20 percent of total export earnings (table 4), real GDP rose at an average annual rate of 7.1 percent, not much below rates recorded during the oil booms. Third, middle-income oil-exporting nations as a group grew no more rapidly during the seventies than did middle-income oil importers. Real growth in Indonesia in the decade 1970 to 1980, however, was some 40 percent higher than that for middle-income nations in general.[3]

As in other rapid-growth countries, the sectoral composition of Indonesian GDP altered substantially over the period from 1965 to 1980 (table 2). At the nadir of Indonesian economic development in 1965, the agricultural sector accounted for slightly over half of GDP. Although the food and tree-crops subsectors experienced, by worldwide standards, strong growth over the next fifteen years, by 1980 agriculture was but 31 percent of GDP, owing to very fast growth in other sectors (particularly construction and manufacturing).

The most recent decade in Indonesian history began and ended with the highest rates of economic growth since independence. The prior decade, however, yielded very different results, and is of general interest both because of the vigor of economic recovery after 1966 and because the economy resisted collapse for so long after 1959. In subsequent sections economic growth over the past thirty years will be seen to have been materially affected by policy choices and, in one particularly turbulent period, paralysis in such choices.

While growth in many countries has proceeded episodically in the postwar era, the boundaries between episodes are rarely drawn as distinctly as those for Indonesia since 1950. In what follows, the principal focus is upon the role of economic policy in each of four such episodes. However, the reader should be mindful

Table 2
Sectoral Composition of GDP 1965–1980, and
Real Growth Rates 1971–80: Indonesia
(at 1973 constant prices)

Sectors	Real growth rate (%) 1971–80	Sectoral share in GDP (%) 1965	1974	1980
1. Agriculture:	3.9	52	39	31
Food	4.3			
Smallholder and estate crops	4.2			
Forestry	1.4			
Livestock	3.1			
Fisheries	3.7			
2. Mining:	7.3	4	12	9
Oil and gas	6.4			
Nonfuel minerals	8.6			
3. Manufacturing:	13.8	8	10	14
4. Services:	10.1	36	39	46
Utilities	13.5			
Construction	15.6			
Trade	7.6			
Transport/ communication	12.3			
Banking	13.8			
Ownership of dwellings	15.2			
Public administration	12.9			
Other services	2.5			
Total GDP growth	7.9			
Growth in nonmining GDP	8.0			

Sources: *Tabel-Tabel Pokok Pendapatan Nasional Indonesia 1977–80* (Jakarta: Biro Pusat Statistik, revised July 22, 1981) and various issues of same publication in earlier years.

that, to an extent seldom exceeded elsewhere in recent decades, Indonesian economic development has been particularly reactive to political stability or its absence, perhaps for no other reason than the fact that the extremes between stability and instability have been so pronounced. Comparative advantage in assessing the effects of political development on the economy (and vice versa) lies with others,[4] and no such assessment is made here. About all that can be safely claimed is that during the first two decades of Indonesian independence, the interplay between political stability and economic growth tended to run somewhat more from the former to the latter, rather than the other way around. This was arguably true at least up through 1963, by which time economic conditions had deteriorated so markedly that major political consequences of economic distress were inevitable. Political developments in the late fifties and early sixties that were not obviously rooted in economic problems and grievances, such as the campaign to reclaim Irian Jaya from the Dutch as well as a military confrontation with Malaysia, clearly helped set the stage for economic decline from 1960 to 1965. But there were other political developments perhaps more deeply grounded in economic conflict that also, in the end, severely undercut prospects for orderly growth in the young nation. These included a series of regional revolts in 1956–57, particularly in Sumatra and Sulawesi, and the abrupt nationalization of Dutch properties in 1957 (itself directly related to the Irian Jaya problem). These political developments affected economic progress in many significant ways, not the least of which were their implications for military spending, as Indonesia experienced a series of large budgetary deficits in the decade after 1957.

Economic Growth from Independence to 1957

By 1952 Indonesia had begun to recover from the privations and sporadic destruction of both wartime occupation and the struggle for independence. Although three centuries under Dutch domination had left the country with but a tiny cadre of trained indigenous officials (including only one Ph.D. economist, who served often as a cabinet member during three decades), the initial phases of the transition to Indonesianization of policymaking, particularly in economic policy, was by most accounts unexpectedly smooth.[5] But the new nation inherited another legacy from the Dutch that was to have great importance in the unfolding of Indonesia's development over the next thirty years: a pervasive system of government controls affecting virtually all aspects of economic life. The so-called "Ethical Policies" of the Dutch colonial administration in the early 1900s provided the initial philosophical basis for extensive government regulation of the economy—a basis that was later reinforced in the thirties by the administration's acceptance of the doctrines of dualism and the economically unresponsive peasant. Timmer has argued persuasively that this *Weltanshauung* strongly conditioned the policy responses of a whole generation of Indonesian leaders after independence.[6] The regulatory system initially involved price controls on rice and then other commodities. With the passage of time, an increasingly elaborate apparatus came to include government regulation of entry and exit in industry and trade, and extensive licensing and controls on both interprovincial and international trade.

Growth in real GDP from 1952 to 1959 was not substantially lower than in most other newly independent, primarily agricultural countries (table 1), three factors notwithstanding: (1) the problems implicit in rebuilding a physical infrastructure neglected under three years of wartime occupation and four years of revolution, (2) the drop in prices of the nation's commodity exports after the end of the Korean War, and (3) the burdens of a complex regulatory environment. Trade contributed to gradually rising prosperity: even by the end of 1959, foreign exchange reserves stood at $300 million, a level not surpassed for another thirteen years, and the central government was collecting as much as 14 percent of GDP in primarily trade-related taxes (table 3). Inflation was held in check through much of the first half of the decade, but it was later to erupt with corrosive force, and by the period between 1957 and 1959 it had spurted to an annual rate of 25 percent (table 3). The mechanism whereby inflation was restrained before 1957 merits special emphasis, given that a variant of that mechanism was resurrected after the economic debacle of the mid-sixties.

Many knowledgeable commentators have argued that neither

Selected Economic Indicators: Inflation, Exchange Reserves, Tax Ratios, Liquid Assets

	(1) Annual inflation[a] (%)	(2) Net official gold & foreign exch. reserves[b] (U.S. $million)	(3) Reserves in months of imports	(4) Total central govt. taxes[c] (% of GDP)	(5) Oil taxes[c] (% of GDP)	(6) Liquid assets[d] (% of GDP)
1953–59	25	n.a.	n.a.	n.a.	n.a.	n.a.
1960	19	301	n.a.	13.8	n.a.	n.a.
1961	72	122	—	13.2	n.a.	n.a.
1962	160	94	—	5.4	n.a.	n.a.
1963	128	−16	—	5.1	n.a.	n.a.
1964	135	−49	—	4.2	n.a.	n.a.
1965	596	−73	—	3.9	n.a.	n.a.
1966	636	−77	—	4.0	n.a.	n.a.
1967	111	−78	—	7.1	0.9	6.1
1968	84	−93	—	7.2	1.2	5.4
1969	10	−86	—	9.0	1.7	5.5
1970	9	−52	—	10.3	2.0	9.4
1971	4	−106	—	11.7	3.0	11.8
1972	26	422	3.0	13.0	4.3	15.1
1973	27	649	3.5	14.3	5.1	14.6
1974	33	1,203	2.4	16.4	9.0	13.6
1975	20	490	1.2	17.7	9.8	15.8
1976	14	1,226	2.8	18.8	10.4	17.5
1977	12	2,423	3.4	18.6	10.2	16.5
1978	7	2,580	4.3	19.0	10.2	17.0
1979	22	4,145	5.6	21.6	13.7	16.8
1980	16	6,480	6.5	23.4	16.0	17.6
1981	7	7,366	6.0	n.a.	n.a.	n.a.

[a]Jakarta cost of living index, year-end to year-end. Source: Bank Indonesia, *Annual Reports* (various issues).

[b]Gold & foreign exch. reserves of monetary authorities each Dec. Source: *International Financial Statistics* (various issues). Source: *Nota Keuangan* (various issues from 1969–1981).

[c]Source: *Nota Keuangan* (various issues from 1969–1981).

[d]Liquid assets = money + quasi money. Source: Bank Indonesia, *Indonesian Financial Statistics* (various issues 1972–81).

Table 4
Indonesian Exports
(U.S. $million)

	(1) Total exports[a]	(2) Net oil and LNG[b]		(3) Rubber[a]		(4) Timber[a]		(5) Manufactures[c]	
		Amount	% Exports	Amount	% Exports	Amount	% Exports	Amount	% Exports
1968	647	78	12.0	232	35.8	15	2.3	20	3.0
1969	660	112	17.0	307	46.5	34	5.1	n.a.	n.a.
1970	761	152	20.0	259	34.0	130	17.1	n.a.	n.a.
1971	896	135	15.0	223	25.0	170	19.0	n.a.	n.a.
1972	982	192	19.5	211	21.5	275	28.0	n.a.	n.a.
1973	2,546	641	25.1	483	19.0	720	28.3	77	3.0
1974	4,671	2,638	56.4	425	9.0	615	13.1	114	2.4
1975	5,011	3,138	62.6	381	7.6	527	10.5	144	2.8
1976	6,573	3,710	56.4	577	8.7	885	13.5	196	3.0
1977	7,859	4,445	56.5	608	7.7	943	12.0	245	3.1
1978	7,764	4,013	51.7	774	10.0	1,130	14.5	360	4.6
1979	12,479	6,975	55.9	1,101	8.8	2,165	17.3	996	8.0
1980	14,929	10,601	71.0	1,077	7.2	1,658	11.1	1,092	7.3

[a]Source: Ministry of Finance, *Nota Keuangan* (various issues). Original series given by *fiscal*, not calendar, year.

[b]Net oil = gross oil exports minus oil product imports and profit repatriation by oil companies.

[c]Source: The World Bank, *Indonesia: Development Prospects and Policy Options* (1981), Analysis and Projection Appendix tables.

economic growth nor control of inflation were primary economic or political concerns for Indonesia's leaders (particularly President Sukarno) in the 1950s, preoccupied as the leaders were with countering secessionist movements and with the larger international political arena. However, until 1957 Indonesian governments were limited in their ability to employ deficit financing by legal restraints in the Central Bank Act: the government's indebtedness to the Central Bank was limited to an amount not to exceed five times the country's gold and foreign exchange holdings.[7] This restriction could be breached only under emergency provisions, which required approval by a reluctant Parliament. But in 1957, Parliament allowed modifications such that "the effectiveness of the limitation on government prodigality virtually broke down altogether."[8] And after "Guided Democracy" was proclaimed by Sukarno in 1958, Parliament ceased to be a check on spending of any kind.

Growth under the Guided Economy

Policy orientation. The ending of legal restraints on public spending, together with the necessity of financing growing military operations, first in secessionist-leaning provinces and then later against the Dutch in Irian Jaya and in the "confrontation" with Malaysia, set the stage for later economic chaos in the urban and monetized sector. But the recipe for chaos required two further prime ingredients: a tax system dependent upon international trade for about 60 percent of revenues, and a succession of strongly interventionist government trade and financial policies that yielded, among other problems, steady deterioration in exports, therefore in imports, and therefore in tax collections.

Although government economic officials in the early days of the republic through 1958 were clearly influenced by the *dirigisme* traditions of Dutch colonial administration, particularly the assumption of the economically unresponsive peasant, this view was not consistently reflected in economic policies adopted by the government. Much depended upon who happened to be finance minister at the time.[9] The full flowering of the Indonesian version of *dirigisme* came only after the proclamation of "Guided Democracy"—meaning, principally, drastic centralization of all deci-

240   MALCOLM GILLIS

sionmaking authority in the hands of Sukarno. Naturally enough, this was accompanied by a shift to a "Guided Economy." Under the "Guided Economy," whatever vestiges of the market mechanism that remained in 1958 were to be replaced by government planning, implemented by bureaucratic judgments.

Whereas under later Dutch rule small farmers were considered unresponsive to price signals, this trait was now deemed to be not only typical of all economic agents in both the traditional and modern sector, but desirable. It was expected that exhortation, symbolism, and ideological fervor would, along with government planning and an elaborate regulatory structure, replace the market system in directing economic behavior in the "Guided Economy," with more acceptable spiritual and social—if not economic—results.

Although the principles underlying the "Guided Economy" were never set down in what might be recognized as a formal structure of thought, the underlying assumption was that there is an "Indonesian Economics" that is fundamentally different from economics elsewhere. Indeed a recurrent theme in the rhetoric of the later Sukarno period was that "Indonesia defies the rules of conventional economics." While there remain some Indonesian economists who believe this to be so, policies followed under the "Guided Economy" yielded results that "conventional economists" would find supremely unsurprising.

For example, after 1959 the government refused to recognize any role for exchange rates in encouraging exports or in restraining imports. After a major (300 percent) devaluation in that year, the rate was held constant through mid-1963. By that time, the domestic price index stood at six times its 1959 level, reserves were nonexistent, and devaluation was unavoidable. The exchange rate had been persistently, but not as deeply, overvalued since 1955, but the consequences of overvaluation before 1961 were much less serious than in 1961–65. Before 1961 the government had ample foreign exchange reserves so that declining exports did not necessitate declining imports, thereby allowing continued high import duty collections and thus manageable deficits (see table 3). But net reserves began to fall at a rapid pace in 1960, turning negative in 1963. As exports declined with growing overvaluation, administrative curbs on imports were further tightened, causing both higher budget deficits and bottlenecks in import-intensive production—and, of course, higher inflation, which then led to further overvaluation and completion of the vicious circle. In sum, there was a precipitous fall in the tax ratio, from 13.2 percent in 1961 to 4.0 percent in 1966 (table 3). This, coupled with rising military spending, led to deficits on the order of 3 to 4 percent of GDP and, given the shallowness of the nation's financial system at the time, a doubling (and later tripling) of liquidity.[10]

Economic performance. Indonesian national income data for 1960 through 1965 are even more suspect than for earlier and later years, largely because of an almost complete breakdown of statistical data-gathering. Even so, there is little doubt that levels of economic well-being had deteriorated notably by the end of 1965. The nation's physical infrastructure lay almost in ruins through lack of maintenance and repair. Standards of service in water supply and electric power had declined to levels probably inferior to those available in the thirties; the road, rail, and irrigation network was to require nearly a decade of expensive restoration after 1965. Although the annual decline in real GDP per capita from 1960–65 (table 1) was not nearly as great as suffered by Ghana and Jamaica in the 1970s, any continuing decline in income was a serious matter for farmers in rural Java (with about half the nation's 1965 population), so close to bare subsistence was this group.

Inflation accelerated every year during the period, rising from 19 percent in 1960 to a peak of about 600 percent in both 1965 and 1966 (column 1, table 3), while net foreign exchange reserves fell steadily, to *minus* $75 million. Still the economy resisted complete collapse, as farmers and businessmen circumvented the pervasive web of administrative controls through barter, smuggling, and black markets. Indeed, production in some sectors—particularly agriculture—continued to grow, although not by much. In the end, the intricate system of controls proved no less vulnerable to hyperinflation and economic chaos than most private institutions. A paradoxical result, in the view of one analyst, was that in 1965 Indonesia was "becoming a thoroughly *laissez-faire* economy, *faute de mieux*, despite all the talk to the contrary," with the further result of a "growing gulf between rich and poor."[11]

Years of economic decline coupled with steadily rising social and
political tensions culminated in tragic political upheaval in the
months after August 1965. Not until almost mid-1966 had it
become clear to the outside world that the Indonesian government
had reconstituted itself under General (later President) Suharto.
What became known as the "New Order" government prepared to
change course on many, but by no means all, of the political and
economic policies followed by the "Old Order." Former students of
Indonesia's first Ph.D. economist (and frequent cabinet member),
all trained abroad in the early sixties, were to play a significant
role in many of the changes that followed. Most have remained in
positions of economic leadership (primarily in the cabinet)
through 1983. The long tenure of this group provided a type of continuity in those aspects of economic policy entrusted to them that
has rarely been matched elsewhere. Beginning in 1967, this group
of eight or so economists became known as the "economic team,"
the label that will be applied in this paper rather than the more
popularly applied sobriquets, "technocrats" or "Berkeley Mafia"
(after the university where many were trained).

Growth under the New Order

Macro reforms, micro *dirigisme*. Much of the complex
mosaic of controls and regulations of the era of the "Guided Economy" and earlier *dirigiste* instruments of Dutch colonial administration remained intact after 1966. To be sure, some sizeable sections of that mosaic were replaced over the next few years. Most of
them were by and large in the nature of macro "rules of the game"
that define the broad parameters under which economic activity
takes place. These rules govern policies affecting basic macro
prices, including exchange rates, rice prices, interest rates,
domestic energy prices, tax and duty rates, and prices of key inputs, such as fertilizer. In addition, a series of reforms has led to
application of new rules for taxation, government consumption
spending, and much of government investment spending save a
few very large capital-intensive projects in fields such as
petrochemicals. The economic team has been the custodian of
these rules since 1966, and has applied them more or less successfully—particularly in times of economic distress, as in the

years 1966 through 1968, 1972, 1974, 1978, and 1982 (see below). In periods of apparent prosperity, such as immediately after the two "oil booms" of the 1970s, some of the rules have proved rather more difficult to implement effectively. Hence, some key macro prices, including those for foreign exchange, money, and energy, have been allowed to diverge so far from their scarcity values that later painful corrections became unavoidable.

At least through 1982, two principles have been applied with particular tenacity. The first is the so-called "balanced budget rule," intended as a means of maintaining fiscal discipline in both good times and bad. In the revenue-short years of rehabilitation and recovery (1966–73), adherence to this rule required avoidance of *actual* budget deficits. In the years of high real oil prices and revenues (1974–77 and 1979–81), the rule was interpreted to mean avoidance of *projected* deficits (or surpluses) for any particular year. Actual spending could then be adjusted to generate the accumulated actual budget and foreign exchange surpluses that, through early 1983, provided an essential cushion from the worst shocks of a softening world oil market. The second rule has been followed rather more relentlessly than the first: avoidance of any form of quantitative controls on the foreign exchange market. Experience with the futilities and complexities of the "Old Order" system of exchange controls ultimately led one member of the economic team even to refuse to listen to discussion of this tool.

Liberalization of macro rules has, however, not been accompanied by any significant dismantling or relaxation of the pervasive system of "micro controls" built up from the beginning of the century. That is to say, there remains a large sphere wherein *dirigisme* thrives. In this sphere, one finds not "rules of the game," but rather "games of rules." Before 1983 there were few changes—though not for lack of trying—in ponderous systems regulating terms of entry into or exit from business, in Byzantine procedures for licensing operations in general, or in systems of credit allocation incorporating every known technology for fine-tuning of directed credit. Identification of the stifling effects of *micro-dirigisme* on growth has been largely dependent upon abundant anecdotal, rather than empirical, evidence. This is because an investment not made, a plant not opened, or a technology not tried due to regulation never shows up in any statistical series. In-

deed, the relatively high growth rates of the Indonesian economy
since 1966 might be cited as an example of how fairly consistent
application of sensible macro policies can counterbalance the ill
effects of *dirigiste* micro policies. Before turning to a discussion of
these policies, it is useful to examine some of the principal
features of Indonesian growth after 1966. Although rates of income growth before and after the first oil boom in late 1973 were
similar, there are enough differences both in other indicators of
economic performance and in policy orientation to justify separate
discussion of the two periods.

Stabilization, rehabilitation, and growth: 1967–73. The luster of
achievements in the reversal of Indonesia's economic fortunes in
the years between 1967 and 1973 is in no way diminished by the
observation that there was little out of the ordinary in the policy
measures initially adopted to arrest the hyperinflation and then
initiate economic rehabilitation and recovery. What was unusual
was, first, the tenacity with which the policies were implemented,
and second, the virtually complete absence of any empirical basis
for predicting their success or failure. The reforms that were
adopted were chosen not after examining the results of simulations of alternative policies in an econometric model, but because
the training and experience of members of the economic team led
them to expect that economic agents would ultimately respond to
liberalized policies in ways beneficial to the economy.

It was recognized that the first order of business was containing
the large budgetary deficits of the years of hyperinflation. On the
expenditure side, tight austerity measures were adopted. These included a virtually complete ban on construction of government
buildings, halting of various showcase industrial projects of previous governments, and sharp increases in prices charged by previously heavily subsidized, state-owned enterprises. On the
revenue side of the budget, it was recognized early on that quick
reversal of the long erosion in the tax ratio was out of the question,
and that both a series of devaluations and sizeable foreign assistance were essential not only to bolster revenues, but also—because of the precarious reserve position—to allow vital imports of
foodstuffs and spare parts. Flows of foreign savings were reiniti-
ated in 1967, first almost exclusively in the form of foreign aid,

later principally in the form of foreign investment (table 5). Indeed, in the first three years after 1966, foreign aid accounted for 28 percent of government spending.[12] But at the same time, domestic tax collection efforts were intensified, resulting by 1969 in a near-doubling of the share of taxes in GDP to 9 percent, still well below the share in 1960 (table 3).

Another set of policies involving financial reform was intended both to help bring inflation under control and to foster resource mobilization through the organized financial system. Here, as in their efforts to generate support for other reforms, the economic team drew on lessons from experience elsewhere; they were able to point to the positive results of financial liberalization programs undertaken in Taiwan in the 1950s and in Korea between 1964 and 1965.[13] These "conventional" measures, and others affecting foreign exchange, agricultural, and public enterprise policy all combined, with help from accelerated inflows of foreign aid, to bring inflation under control by the end of 1968. Over the subsequent three years, inflation was never greater than 10 percent, and it bottomed out at 4 percent in 1971 before spurting again to over 25 percent from 1972 to 1973.

Such was the momentum of the economy in the early 1970s that not even a "rice crisis" in 1972–73 (caused both by a 4 percent drop in production and by counterproductive policy responses to that drop) in this quintessentially rice-conscious society served to derail rapid growth in this period,[14] although at the time the crisis was viewed as virtually a make-or-break situation for the policies of the economic team. Instead, 1972 and 1973 turned out to be the two years of highest growth since such records were first kept in Indonesia. The rehabilitation period between 1967 and 1973 was, overall, one of very strong economic growth, averaging over 7 percent for the period as a whole.

Even from the vantage point of 1984, it is difficult to determine the sources of finance for the rapid growth in investment for the period. Indeed it is not clear how much investment did expand, as the investment figures shown in GDP accounts are still subject to wide margins of error, with a probable downward bias.[15] Still, the official estimates do show an almost uninterrupted rise in the share of total gross investment in GDP, from 8 percent in 1967 to almost 18 percent in 1973 (table 5). Information on inflows of private and official foreign capital is somewhat more reliable. Even recognizing that the total investment figures are understated, it is clear that foreign savings played a significant role in investment finance both during the period from 1966 to 1973 and in the 1974–80 period of high oil prices. In the early years of recovery (1967 to 1969), apparent domestic savings were about two-thirds of gross investment, while foreign aid was virtually the sole source of foreign savings. Private domestic savings apparently accounted for a much larger share of investment finance before 1974 than after, and was virtually the only source of domestic savings until 1970. It is likely, however, that relatively high ratios of private savings to GDP between 1967 and 1972 reflected primarily repatriation of capital by Indonesian residents once political stability was restored after 1966. Government savings, virtually nonexistent before 1969, grew steadily thereafter, primarily as a result of continued restraints upon spending combined with intensified collection of non-oil taxes.

Oil-fired growth? 1974 to 1981. Oil exports and oil taxes played a relatively modest role in the period of recovery ending in 1973. Before 1974, the share of oil in total export earnings averaged about 17 percent. For the remainder of the decade, oil typically accounted for between one-half and three-fifths of total exports (table 4). Oil taxes, never more than one-fifth of total taxes before 1971, rose to one-third by 1972, to one-half by 1974 and, in 1979, to two-thirds. From 1974 onwards, growth in oil taxes was almost wholly responsible for growth in government savings, which by 1980 was almost half of reported gross investment.

Inflation quickened in the early stages of the first oil boom in 1973–74, but held at levels near world inflation rates from 1979 to 1981, after the second large oil price increase. And inflows of new chunks of oil revenue, *qua* inflows, had little to do with inflation in either period. In the early years of the first boom, monetary and budget policies were loose; in the period between 1979 and 1981, growth in liquidity was more restrained and large budget surpluses were generated.[16] Incidentally, it is interesting to note that the inflation rate declined every year following the first oil boom until a major devaluation occurred in late 1978, and declined in both 1980 and 1981 after the onset of the second boom (table 3).

For the entire period of so-called "oil-fired" development ending in 1981, the inflation rate averaged 16.1 percent.

Real GDP growth was 7.4 percent over the period containing the two oil booms, only marginally higher than in the rebuilding years after 1965. The lesson that some observers have drawn from this period is that large oil windfalls are of dubious value to the nations that receive them. Whether this is true or not depends, first, on how such revenues are used, not on the fact that they proceed from oil. It also depends, as noted later, on exchange rate policy. Another lesson to be drawn from recent Indonesian experience is that oil windfalls may not contribute to general prosperity in cases where the government-as-stockholder allows state oil enterprises to elude and abuse their fiscal and financial obligations. By 1975 the state oil firm PERTAMINA had, through what is most charitably termed financial adventurism, accumulated short- and medium-term debt equal to about one-third of GDP.[17] The government's efforts to cover the legitimate external debts of the enterprise in the years 1975 and 1976 meant, among other problems, that international reserves failed to rise from 1974 through 1976 (table 3) even with an increase in exports of 41 percent.

In spite of both PERTAMINA and (until 1978) ever-growing overvaluation of the exchange rate, growth in income and investment was substantial over the period, although not nearly as vigorous as in the pre-oil "recovery" era. By 1980, the share of gross investment in GDP had risen to nearly 22 percent (table 5), nearly half of which was financed by government savings. Inflows of foreign capital accounted for nearly 40 percent, and apparent private domestic savings the remainder. Other than the relatively low share of private domestic savings in the total, the most striking feature of investment finance over the period was the sharp decline in the contribution of non-oil direct foreign investment, which by 1980 amounted to only 0.5 percent of GDP. Weak world markets for Indonesian hard mineral resources explain part of the decline; the rest is probably best attributed, in about equal parts, to the unintentional disincentives implicit first in an ever more unwieldy licensing and regulatory system, and second, in policies designed to extract greater nonfinancial benefits from foreign investment projects.

Policies: confocal aims, discordant instruments. Successive five-year development plans for Indonesia, first formulated in 1968, lack both the sophistication and the pretensions of similar planning documents of many other nations. The plans do, however, contain unapologetic expressions of the importance of growth in satisfying other social objectives. In fact the main proximate, but not necessarily overriding, objective stated for all economic policies has been that of furthering growth. It is not much of an oversimplification to say that among principal policymakers, there are at least two distinct perspectives regarding what is and is not helpful to growth. Interpretation of recent Indonesian economic history would be greatly simplified if the policies favored by both schools consistently reflected underlying attitudes; but consistency has never been as highly valued as pragmatism in the post-Sukarno era. Nonetheless, most Indonesian policymakers, and their advisors, may be found along a continuum between the two dominant views sketched below.

Both schools display nationalistic plumage to one degree or another; both have sizeable constituencies within the bureaucracy, the military, and business. The major differences lie in underlying attitudes toward the role of price signals in guiding economic behavior, the contribution of international trade to economic development, and the efficacy of centralized industrial planning. At one end of the continuum is a group of engineers, academics, and career civil servants in the so-called "sectoral" ministries. This group tends to be profoundly pessimistic as to the responsiveness of economic agents to market signals. The strongly held "elasticity pessimism" of this group reflects the enduring influence of the economic philosophy of the later Dutch Colonial administration and the fixed coefficient outlook characteristic of much of the literature of economic development of the 1950s and 1960s. The policies favored by this group display many of the earmarks of inward-looking "Big Push" industrialization strategies, with autarkic undertones—even though this group has been a fairly consistent proponent of foreign investment.

The other school exhibits a rather more incrementalist approach to industrialization, and a more outward-looking focus on issues pertaining to international trade. Policies associated with this group tend to be premised on the assumption that producers and consumers, as well as savers and investors, are sensitive to changes in relative prices: only in the very short run are elasticities of demand and supply assumed to be near zero. The essential elasticity optimism of this school is reflected in a series of policy measures affecting basic macro prices over the period between 1967 and 1981, and in particular in most of the policy reversals of the late 1960s.

Policy reforms. The high-water mark for policies geared to elasticity optimism came in the first period of vigorous growth under the new government, before 1974. Some of these policies fell into disuse in the years of high oil prices before 1983, but even in that period there was intermittent resort to several that had proved effective in the period 1966 to 1973, usually with some success.

- Foreign exchange policy—Indonesian economic policymakers have since 1966 exhibited in their actions a strong aversion to foreign exchange controls; none has been employed since 1970. There has been no such aversion to the use of exchange rate adjustments to further national economic goals. The role of devaluations in restoring fiscal revenues and export incentives in the years just after 1966 was cited earlier. Major exchange rate adjustments were undertaken on two other occasions between 1970 and 1980, and again in March 1983. The latest devaluation was too recent to allow for informed discussion, but the first two illustrate well the basic premises of decision-makers responsible for macro prices since 1966.

  By mid-1971, the steady improvement in Indonesia's negative reserve holdings since 1966 had come to an end, largely because continued robust growth in imports required for economic reconstruction was accompanied by weakening world market prices for rubber, coffee, tea, tin, and timber, commodities accounting for over half of export earnings. Prospects were for further declines in all non-oil export prices in 1972, an expectation that in fact was realized, except for timber. Policymakers concluded that a devaluation was in order. While it was clear that short-term elasticities of supply for the nation's export commodities were low, it was believed that with achievement of virtual price stability by 1971 (table 3), devaluation would create conditions for beneficial supply responses in 1972 and 1973. And in any event, the short-term elasticity of demand for imports was thought to approach −0.5. Thus, amidst public speculation that a revaluation was in the offing, in August the rupiah was devalued by 10 percent. Imports responded essentially as hoped, while the short-term response of exporters exceeded expectations. The volumes of several important export items, including rubber, palm oil, and copra cake, actually grew appreciably in 1972,[18] even though world prices in that year declined, in some cases (palm oil, copra cake) sharply. By the end of 1972, reserves had risen by $528 million over late 1971.

The 1971 devaluation was undertaken primarily to strengthen a precarious reserve position. The second devaluation of the decade, in 1978, came at a time of high and rising reserves, again amid widespread speculation of an imminent revaluation. By the beginning of that year, reserves stood at nearly $2.5 billion (table 3), and they continued their slow growth throughout the year. Still, in November 1978 the rupiah was devalued by 33 percent. Three principal factors underlay the reasoning behind this large adjustment. First, while there were no firm devotees of purchasing power parity doctrines among the economic decision-makers, it was clear that because the pace of internal inflation since 1971 had so far outrun world inflation (and particularly that of Indonesia's principal trading partners and competitors), the rupiah had become seriously overvalued, perhaps by between 40 and 60 percent, depending on the gauges followed.[19]

Second, it appeared in September of 1978 that the era of rising prices for petroleum had ended. Moreover, it was recognized that the strongest potential for employment growth lay not in the relatively capital-intensive import substitution industries, but in the substantially more labor-intensive export sector.[20] Deep overvaluation had severely hamstrung this sector, as indicated by the fact that by 1977 manufactured export values had reached less than $250 million, and constituted the same share of total exports (3 percent) as they did ten years before (table 4). Also, the long-declining rubber export industry was a source of particular concern inasmuch as it was the largest employer in the country outside of food grains.

Finally, 1979 was to be the first year of the Third Five-Year Plan. Because collections of non-oil taxes had proved unresponsive to income growth, and because the Third Plan was to emphasize major new programs in education, water supply, and health, decision-makers saw devaluation as the least painful among several unattractive means of adhering to the balanced budget rules that had undergirded fiscal policy for a decade. The government as a major exporter could, through devaluation, turn the internal terms of trade in its own favor, at the expense of the private sector.

As in previous devaluations in the late 1960s and in 1971, policymakers had only limited empirical evidence as to the likely short- and long-term supply responses for exportables. And, as in 1971, the temptation to assume high short-term elasticities was foresworn. Virtually no short-term volume response was expected for traditional commodity exports, although a modest medium-term elasticity, perhaps 0.5, was assumed for manufactured exports. The devaluation was not geared to short-term objectives. Rather, the measure was seen as a necessary condition for refurbishing the enfeebled smallholder rubber and coconut palm sectors over the long term, while also providing a strong impetus to the heretofore struggling manufactured export sector.

Because both inflation and liquidity growth had abated significantly in the months prior to November 1979 (table 3), it was thought that any inflationary consequences of a major devaluation could be contained. As the results unfolded over the next two years, the relatively modest expectations were more than amply fulfilled, in spite of a short-lived attempt to impose price controls in December. Real values of imports fell by 15 percent in six months. Manufactured exports tripled in value by the end of 1979; rubber exports, benefiting from both devaluation and higher world prices, exceeded $1 billion for the first time (table 4) and, more significantly, increased in volume by 10.3 percent in the space of twelve months. Several categories of manufactured exports expanded at remarkable rates, albeit from small bases: woven cotton fabrics increased by 684

Table 5
Gross Investment and Sources of Finance as Percent of GDP,[a] Indonesia

	I	II Foreign savings					III Domestic savings			
	Gross domestic investment[b]	Oil co. investment[c]	Other foreign investors[d]	Recorded commercial borrowing inflows[e]	Foreign aid inflows[f]	Total foreign inflows (2+3+4+5)	Government savings[f]	Apparent private domestic savings (incl. PEs)[g]	Total domestic savings (7+8)	Domestic savings as % of gross investment (9÷1)
	1	2	3	4	5	6	7	8	9	10
1967	8.0	n.a.	0.0	0.0	3.0	3.0[i]	− 1.2	6.2	6.2	77.5
1968	8.8	n.a.	0.0	0.0	2.8	2.8[i]	0.0	6.0	6.0	68.2
1969	11.7	1.1	0.1	0.0	3.3	4.5	1.0	6.2	7.2	61.5
1970	13.6	1.3	1.4	0.0	3.6	6.3	1.7	5.6	7.3	53.7
1971	15.8	2.3	2.5	0.0	3.7	8.5	2.2	5.1	7.3	46.2
1972	18.8	2.2	3.1	0.0	3.5	8.8	3.4	6.6	10.0	53.2
1973	17.9	2.5	2.0	1.3	3.0	8.8	3.8	5.0	8.8	50.8
1974	16.7	3.1	0.8	0.9	2.2	7.0	6.9	2.8	9.7	58.0
1975	20.3	3.5	1.8	4.0	3.9	13.2	7.2	0.0	7.2	35.5
1976	20.7	3.0	1.1	2.4	5.1	11.6	8.3	0.8	9.1	44.0
1977	20.1	1.9	0.6	1.7	4.1	8.3	7.3	4.5	11.8	58.7

1978	20.8	1.9	0.9	1.2	4.6	8.6	6.8	5.4	12.2	58.6
1979	21.6	2.2	0.6	2.0	4.5	9.3	8.5	3.8	12.3	56.9
1980	21.7	3.0	0.5	1.2[h]	3.4	8.1	10.1	3.5	13.6	62.2

[a]GDP at current prices.

[b]Source: Biro Pusat Statistik, *Pendapatan Nasional Indonesia* (various issues).

[c]Source: U.S. Embassy, "Indonesia's Petroleum Sector" (various issues, 1976–81).

[d]Source: Bank Indonesia, *Report for the Financial Year* (various issues).

[e]Source: Ministry of Finance, The World Bank, *World Debt Tables* (Washington, D.C.: November 15, 1980), p. 73. (Almost wholly government borrowing.)

[f]Source: *Nota Keuangan* (various issues). Government savings defined as current tax receipts minus government consumption.

[g]This column is merely a residual, found by taking the difference between column I minus the sum of foreign savings and government savings. Since government savings in Indonesia do not include savings of public enterprises, this column is gross of public enterprise (PE) savings.

[h]Estimated (preliminary).

[i]Exclusive of foreign investment by oil companies in 1966 or 1967.

percent, exports of apparel rose by 341 percent, exports of other textiles by 500 percent, exports of furniture and other processed wood products by over 80 percent, and exports of cement by nearly 1,000 percent.[21]

Inflation in the year following the devaluation was 22 percent, some 12 percent above the world rate, but in 1980 and 1981 it declined to 16 percent and 7 percent respectively. And it was not wholly coincidental that, while real growth in 1979 slowed to about 6 percent, the years 1980 and 1981 marked the strongest growth performance since 1972 and 1973, particularly in the industrial sector.

• Financial policy and liquid asset demand—In the period from 1967 to 1974, the conduct of at least one aspect of financial policy illustrated well the essential elasticity optimism of key policymakers; from 1975 through 1982, the deployment of this important set of policy tools would suggest otherwise. But even before 1975, policymakers displayed a curious bifurcation of attitudes concerning the use of financial policy: the adverse consequences of sharply negative real rates of interest were readily recognized for deposits, but not for loans.

Until well into the 1970s, there was but one interest-bearing liquid asset enjoying wide acceptance among savers: insured time deposits of the five state-owned banks. Even as late as 1971, there was still a complete absence of credible empirical evidence on factors affecting the demand for liquid assets in Indonesia. Nevertheless, policymakers viewed the demand for such assets as significantly interest-elastic, but they did not overlook the convenience properties of money and quasi-money balances. Consequently, the real deposit interest rate became a significant issue in policy choice: steeply negative real rates were thought inimical to both stabilization and growth; mildly positive rates were seen as helpful to both. A reversal of the high negative real rates of 1966 and 1967 was thought essential for curbing velocity and dampening inflationary expectations. Once a modicum of price stability was achieved, avoidance of negative real rates would, it was expected, allow significant growth in the real size of the organized financial system, thereby facilitating the flow of resources from savers to investors.

Policies premised on these assumptions were enacted with particular success both in the years 1967 through 1969 and again in early 1974. In 1968, in the midst of continuing hyperinflation, nominal interest rates on one-year time deposits were increased to 6 percent *per month,* and were held near that level until early 1970 when they were reduced to 2 percent. The effects were immediate and sizeable: within a year the public was holding about 25 percent of its liquid assets in such deposits.[22] This set of policies, together with others involving monetary restraint, was followed consistently until 1975. One result was that the ratio of liquid assets to GDP rose from below 6 percent in 1968 to almost 16 percent by 1975 (table 3).

In 1974 deposit rates, and to a lesser extent lending rates, were again sharply adjusted for purposes of stability and growth. In the six months prior to April 1974, inflation was running at an annual rate of 42 percent. As part of a draconian stabilization package involving a doubling of reserve requirements on time deposits and marginal increases in bank lending rates, the highest deposit rate for time deposits was doubled, to 30 percent. Again, the public responded as expected, and time deposits expanded 62 percent over the year. Inflation for the twelve months following these measures was slashed to 17 percent, while real GDP growth held at a respectable 7.6 percent.

In spite of the rather successful experiences in deploying financial policy for stabilization and growth before 1975, this tool was shelved through 1982. For most of the period between 1975 and 1982, real deposit rates were negative, as every change in nominal rates was downward. Then again, abundant oil revenues throughout that period meant that efforts to mobilize resources through the financial system lacked the urgency of earlier years.

* Pricing of domestic energy—Throughout the 1975–82 period, in decisions concerning exchange rates, interest rates, and financial and (ultimately) agricultural prices, policies premised on producer and consumer responsiveness to price signals prevailed more often than not.[23] But it was not until the late 1970s that domestic demand for oil products came to be viewed as significantly price-sensitive, and even then actions on this conviction were infrequent and subject to long delays.

From 1970 onward, Indonesia priced most oil products sold domestically at levels well below world prices (and in 1974 at levels below costs of production). The resulting losses on domestic sales by the state oil enterprise were covered by direct subsidies from the budget. Budgetary oil subsidies had reached 3 percent of domestic tax revenues by 1978 and 9 percent by 1980. By 1980, budgetary subsidies on oil consumption were $1.6 billion, but the much higher economic cost of the oil subsidy (export prices minus domestic prices) was nearly 5 percent of GDP, or about $3.7 billion.[24] The subsidy grew rapidly from 1978 to 1982 because domestic oil prices increased by only about 110 percent, while world prices increased by 160 percent over the four years. For most years, kerosene and diesel fuel accounted for about 80 percent of the total subsidy; other refined products were much less heavily subsidized. One consequence of the oil subsidies was, of course, that consumption of refined products grew at very rapid rates—more than twice as fast as per capita GDP growth rates over the period from 1970 to 1981. At this rate of consumption growth, the country would have likely become a net importer of petroleum by the early 1990s. In addition, plans for large-scale government investments in new refining capacity were being formulated on the assumption of vastly increased domestic refined product needs by that time.

For over a decade, proposals to increase domestic oil prices to levels closer to their opportunity costs had been countered with four arguments: first, that price increases would not have any significant effects in curbing growth in consumption; second, that subsidies on kerosene (and hence diesel fuel, for kerosene could be used in diesel engines) were effective in redistributing income to the poor; third, that they were likewise effective in reducing deforestation (a serious problem on Java); and fourth, that they also helped control inflation. When it was shown that the subsidy program was in fact an ineffective method for achieving income redistribution, preventing deforestation, and controlling inflation—and led besides to deadweight resource loss of perhaps 0.5 percent of GDP[25]—key officials from several agencies still stoutly opposed, over several years, any price increases for oil products on the grounds that demand was insensitive to price changes. Thus, price increases would have little effect on conservation or the need for new refineries. Once again, Indonesian consumers were held to "defy the rules of conventional economics."

Another view, however, ultimately prevailed. Domestic oil prices were increased by 60 percent in 1982. When consumption growth responded by falling by about what was projected, prices were again increased by 70 percent in January 1983. Indonesian consumers of refined products were shown to be not materially different from their counterparts elsewhere.

• Other policy reforms—Reforms in foreign exchange and financial and energy policy illustrate the enduring, if sometimes intermittently applied, elasticity optimism of policymakers entrusted with these tools. Those were not necessarily the most important changes in economic policymaking in the post-Sukarno era; rather, they are better understood by this author than are other, essentially market-oriented adjustments in rice-pricing policy and in other agricultural policies. Still other changes, in customs and tax administration and in policies toward state enterprise, were less far-reaching in significance. These are discussed below.

Expansion of rice production—indeed, rice self-sufficiency— has been one of the principal objectives of government policy since 1966. If policy could be assessed strictly on the basis of contribution to progress toward this goal, rice policy would have to be labeled as successful. In any case, the underlying premise of this aspect of agricultural policy has been for over a decade that farmers do respond to price incentives, not only in use of fertilizer, but in area planted and labor applied to paddy. Both average yields and area planted have responded strongly to government programs. For example, very heavy subsidies on fertilizer usage,[26] particularly from 1977 until 1983, combined with deft management of price and institutional supports and the virtual completion of restoration and expansion of irrigation networks in Java, resulted in very rapid rates of growth in rice production. Output growth peaked at 13.4 percent in 1980 after growing at almost 4.5 percent over the previous decade, in spite of serious pest infestations between 1974 and 1977.

Reforms in customs and tax policy have proved more difficult to implement, although not for lack of effort. Still, change has consistently been in the correct direction, if reduction in resource waste and tax evasion is what is wanted. Over the period from 1968 to 1973, customs duties were significantly reduced on eight occasions; the ludicrously high levels of nominal and effective protection of the Sukarno era (and intense smuggling activity) were brought down to levels not dissimilar to those of most of Latin America. Confiscatory levels of personal and corporate income tax rates were brought down to enforceable levels in 1970, and state enterprises became major taxpayers after 1968. And in 1979 Indonesia became one of the few countries in the world to recognize the ravages of inflation on the corporate tax, by allowing virtually complete revaluation of business assets for inflation after 1970. Still, as of 1983 the fiscal system remained laced with ineffective, often redundant incentives and essentially unadministerable taxes. Nevertheless, serious efforts at reform were, here too, under way in 1982 and early 1983.

Interventionist policies: regulation, licensing, and protectionism. Although memories of the outcome of the *dirigiste* policies of the Sukarno years have yet to fade, an abiding distrust of the market is still widely discernible not only among academics, but among many managers, military officers, and of course civil servants. This accounts for the persistence of both strong protectionist policies and the ponderous and restrictive system of licensing and regulation that intrudes upon virtually every significant private sector investment decision and also generates high rents for regulators and not a few regulatees. It also accounts for the reversion, after 1974, of credit allocation policies to a system of detailed fine-tuning seldom, if ever, matched in other mixed economies. In part, too, it accounts for the marked bias, in many sectoral departments, toward large, lumpy, natural resources investments, based on the belief that more local processing is always better. All of the above institutions and policies have implications for growth, unless one believes that the resources thereby wasted lacked alternative uses elsewhere in the economy. Because of limitations of space, only the first two policies are discussed in any detail, but they well illustrate the tenor of enduring interventionism.

The present regulatory and licensing system would tend to retard growth even if it only postponed implementation of investment, as it surely does. To illustrate, merely to add an additional product line in an already established plant may require an approval process of two years' duration. Two and more years of delay in securing approval for investment in new projects, whether domestic or foreign, is common in many fields.

The essence of the regulatory process is to discourage, not promote, competition. Many investment applications have been denied, or at the least delayed, for years on grounds that "sufficient capacity already exists" in that industry. The apparent purpose is that of protecting already established firms. Some regulators, however, go as far as to say that the system is also designed to protect prospective investors (even foreign investors) from themselves, by preventing them from entering "already saturated industries." Little more need be said of the motives for or consequences of this system, except that each time the government attempts to reform and simplify the process, it has by most accounts become more, not less, restrictive and complex.

Customs policy is in the hands of the Department of Finance; import quotas, bans, and other quantitative restrictions are the responsibility of the Department of Industry (for industrial projects), the Department of Agriculture (for agricultural and forest products), and the Department of Trade (other products). At the beginning of the 1970s, very few items were subject to bans and/or quotas. As customs policy was gradually liberalized through 1973, sectoral departments countered with a growing number of quotas and bans, and proposals for same. Imports of finished sedans were banned in 1974, and bans and quotas later extended to a few other industrial goods, such as newsprint, some textiles, and motorcycles. Faced with these protectionist countermoves, liberalization efforts in customs policies came virtually to a halt.

The successive reductions in tariffs after 1968 were not at all uniform across industries. Coupled with wide variations in domestic value added for protected industries (very low for automobiles, very high for cigarettes), wide differences in nominal rates yielded a pattern of effective protection that, while not high (by world standards) on the average, is highly variable across activities. Recent estimates by Mark Pitt (author of an earlier study for 1971) done

for IBRD show an average level of effective protection for 1975 of
almost 30 percent, but with some rates as high as 4,000 percent
(tires) and as low as minus 35 percent (batik apparel).[27]

Significantly, the most robust employment growth within the
manufacturing sector tended to occur not in the most heavily protected industries, such as textiles, apparel, and vehicles, where
rates of effective protection in 1975 were 298 percent, 192 percent,
and 718 percent respectively, but in lightly protected labor-
intensive industries, such as the cigarette industry (5 percent effective protection). This latter industry, together with other tobacco-
processing industrial activity, still accounted for 17.5 percent of
total employment in the large- and medium-scale industrial
sectors in 1979, indicating something of both the character of
industrialization and the failure of import substitution policy to
provide employment gains.

The welfare costs of protection as high as that for textiles,
apparel, and vehicles cannot help but be considerable. Annual
costs to consumers are also not trivial. Protection of the textile
and footwear industries has been particularly costly, with few
employment benefits. Recent estimates indicate that for 1978,
protection of the textile and footwear industries cost Indonesian
consumers a total of $435 million, or about 44 percent of their
outlays on those items. Even under the extreme assumption that
the total change in employment in the fast-growing textile
industry (14 percent per annum) over the period 1974–79 was due
solely to protection, then the cost to consumers for each job
protected was $3,400, or 5.5 times the annual wage in this
industry.[28]

Growth, Equity, and Social Development

There is general agreement among Indonesia scholars that slow
and negative growth before 1967 hampered the achievement of
social goals in income redistribution, health, education, and nutrition. Therefore, the limited discussion of this section may be confined to the social implications of post-1966 growth.

There are no figures for, and thus no reliable studies of, national
income distribution. There are, however, a series of four surveys of
the distribution of consumption expenditures since 1970. Several

attempts have been made, including those by Booth-Sundrum[29] and Dapice, as well as by a Fiscal Studies group organized by the author, to use consumption data in income distribution studies by adjusting them in some reasonable way for savings. For what they are worth, the results do suggest a worsening in income disparities through 1978, with some improvement by 1980. The income share of the top decile may have fallen from nearly 45 percent in 1978 to about 41 percent in 1980. However, since 1970, the coverage of consumption in the surveys has been deteriorating steadily. Thus the results do not inspire confidence.[30]

Almost no one doubts that urban disparities increased through 1978. But it now appears that income inequality may have narrowed in rural areas of Java, an island with nearly two-thirds of the nation's population. As to absolute impoverishment, a strong refrain among both domestic and foreign critics of government policy through much of the 1970s was the claim that the "poor are getting poorer." However, many of these critics, and certainly the most persistently vocal among them, have lately concluded that at least since 1978, "there appear to have been some dramatic changes in rural Java," such that for the first time, "the combination of [several favorable] trends appears to be bringing about a major economic advance."[31] That particular author attributes much of the improvement in the lives of the rural poor to substantial growth in government expenditures for just that purpose. Indeed, any plausible assumptions about the incidence of taxes and expenditures by income class would indicate (for any recent budget) some significant positive budget impact on the lower deciles. This is altogether consistent with, for example, the large and growing outlays for primary education (now almost universal in the relevant age group) and the fact that owing to oil, other taxes are very low on all income groups, including low-income families. In any case, virtually any statements regarding income distribution in Indonesia are best received with even more than the usual skepticism one reserves for studies of trends in income distribution in almost any setting.

Other indicators of social development are founded upon better statistical evidence. Here are five conclusions indicating a rather mixed record in promotion of employment growth over the past decade, taken from a comparison of the 1970 and 1980 censuses:[32]

1. The modern sector, and particularly the modern industrial sector (medium- and large-scale firms) contributed very little to employment growth over 1971—80. In particular, the modern *industrial* sector contributed only 0.5 percent of total job gains over the period. Taking modern industry together with the mining, utilities, and finance sectors, these four modern fast-growing sectors combined generated only 2.5 percent of total new jobs.

2. By far the largest job gains were reported in the cottage and small-scale industry sector, in which 1.4 million new jobs were added.

3. All net job gains have come from self-employed workers, while the number of employees in 1980 was about the same as in 1971.

4. Overall job creation *did* match the growth in the labor force, largely because of growth in small-scale and cottage industry employees and in the number of self-employed workers.

5. The census data show a sharp drop in numbers of agricultural employees and agricultural family workers. This was offset by a reported rise in the number of self-employed in agriculture.

The above depicts a record not of remarkable success, but of the ability of a rapidly growing economy to generate jobs in spite of capital-intensive, big-project bias in several *dirigiste*-oriented agencies in government.

Other social indicators, including those pertaining to education, nutrition, crude death rates, and infant mortality rates,[33] indicate steady but not spectacular inroads in several areas of long-standing concern. From 1971 to 1980, the crude death rate fell from 17 to 14 per 1,000 population, while the infant mortality rate declined by 30 percent. There is now virtually complete primary enrollment, and enrollment rates in junior and senior secondary levels both doubled in that past decade, to 35 percent in the former and 19 percent in the latter.

Growth over the past fifteen years has made possible sizeable expansion in public and private spending for the improvement of education, health, nutrition, and housing. In addition, a few people have become very wealthy. While much can be learned from efforts to determine more accurately how the gains from recent growth have been distributed, perhaps the greater challenge in the coming decade will be that of maintaining growth at rates not materially below the past decade, in a world where world oil prices may be stagnant at best. Indonesia did achieve relatively high rates of growth without large infusions of oil revenues in the seven years before 1974. Oil revenues after 1973 did not appreciably increase growth; rather, they provided a cushion against both the consequences of both external shocks and policy error—a cushion that may be unavailable over the next few years.

Postscript

This article was essentially completed in March of 1983, just following a year (1982) in which real GDP growth had slowed to 2.5 percent, the lowest rate in fifteen years. Although up until early 1983 Indonesia had managed to escape the worst of the severe economic maladies befalling other middle-income oil-exporting countries after 1980, the outlook for the coming years was at least as dim as at any time since 1966: international reserves were dwindling rapidly and large prospective budget deficits appeared inevitable. In order to forestall the types of trauma faced by Mexico, Nigeria, Venezuela, and Ecuador in 1981–83, and to position the domestic economy to capitalize on the long-awaited recovery in the world economy, policymakers adopted in rapid succession a series of five major policy strokes in the ten months beginning in March 1983. These were (1) a 28 percent devaluation of the rupiah in late March 1983; (2) in mid-May, cancellation or postponement of several large capital-intensive government projects involving several billion dollars; (3) in early June, a fundamental reform of financial policy involving virtually complete deregulation of interest rates; (4) in October–December, adoption of a radical reform of income and sales taxes, intended not only to replace declining oil taxes but to rid the tax system of glaring inequities and barriers to efficiency; and (5) in early January 1984, a further marked reduction in subsidies to domestic energy consumption, through sharp increases in petroleum product prices.

Whether these very recent measures will in the end prove effective in assuring a return to vigorous growth is still unknowable.
Nevertheless, all of these reforms appeared, in early 1984, to be
working just about as expected.

10

GLADSTONE G. BONNICK

Jamaica: Liberalization to Centralization, and Back?

Many people believe that since the mid-1960s, economic policies in Jamaica have swung to and fro with its politics: that the Labor Party pursued generally liberal and free trade policies until 1972; then the (socialist) People's National Party changed course and established rigid central control of the economy; and finally the Labor Party returned triumphant in 1980 to decentralize the economy again. In this scenario, it is common to regard the middle period as an anomalous era, during which policies biased toward public-sector expansion brought on economic disaster.

The economic collapse between 1973 and 1980 is certainly a matter of record. Real GDP, which had grown an average of more

The views expressed are those of the author based on his experiences and interest in Jamaica, and do not necessarily relect those of the World Bank or the United Nations Development Program.

265

than 6 percent per year between 1966 and 1972, actually declined every year between 1974 and 1980—leaving total GDP 18 percent lower that year than its peak in 1973. This period was also marked by huge increases in government spending, ruinous inflation rates, exploding public deficits, and increasing unemployment. It is not clear, however, whether a radical change in economic policy was responsible for the collapse.

Even up to the present, economic policymaking in Jamaica has been more consistent over time than is generally acknowledged. Restrictions on trade, prices, and imports have been in place since the more prosperous 1960s. A reluctance to allow prices to reflect relative scarcities of resources and a wish to minimize cost-of-living pressure on poor consumers have been traditional in Jamaica and transcend political changes in the country.

Current Labor Prime Minister Seaga may point with pride to modest improvements—reduced public spending, lower inflation, and some positive real growth in GDP. But once oversimplified views of economic liberalization versus centralization have been dispensed with, real changes are more difficult to find. It remains to be seen whether the Seaga government has truly diverged onto a path of new free-market reform.

Economic Trends since the Mid-1960s

Real gross domestic product (GDP) in Jamaica grew at an average rate of 6.5 percent between 1966 and 1972, slowed abruptly to 2.8 percent in 1973, and afterwards declined every year up to and including 1980, when total GDP was 18 percent below the 1973 peak. In 1981 the economy achieved positive growth of about 2 percent, and preliminary estimates suggest that there was slight positive growth again in 1982. Among expenditure components, real gross domestic investment reached a peak in 1973, but by 1977 fell by over one-half of the 1973 level. Although there was a slight recovery in the ensuing five years, in 1980 the level of real investment was only two-thirds that in 1966. Private consumption (in real terms) rose by one-half to a peak in 1975, but by 1980 fell back almost to its 1966 level. Significantly, public-sector consumption rose continuously to a peak in 1978–79 (see tables 1 and 2).

Most major productive sectors showed the same pattern as that

Table 1
Gross Domestic Product
(at constant 1974 prices)

	Total GDP	Growth Rates of GDP
1970	1,980.8	12.0
1971	2,042.9	3.1
1972	2,231.8	9.2
1973	2,263.9	2.8
1974	2,170.0	−5.4
1975	2,157.3	−0.6
1976	2,026.4	−6.1
1977	1,992.9	−1.7
1978	1,985.9	−0.3
1979	1,956.8	−1.5
1980	1,850.8	−5.4
1981	1,888.5	2.0

Source: Department of Statistics, Jamaica; (National Income and Product 1981).

Table 2
Private Consumption and Public Consumption
and Gross Domestic Investment
(at constant 1974 market prices, J$ million)

	Private	Public (gen. govt.)	Total consumption	Gross domestic investment
1966	1069.6	140.3	1209.9	392.5
1968	1106.0	176.0	1282.0	519.5
1970	1266.4	256.9	1523.3	589.9
1972	1593.5	293.1	1886.6	521.6
1973	1431.3	351.4	1782.7	606.3
1974	1482.0	386.1	1868.1	539.2
1975	1609.4	392.3	2001.7	535.5
1976	1460.0	446.4	1906.4	386.3
1977	1423.1	451.3	1874.4	245.4
1978	1280.2	468.8	1749.0	264.5
1979	1224.5	467.7	1692.2	308.7
1980	1111.7	440.2	1551.9	257.4

Source: Department of Statistics, Jamaica.

of overall GDP, rising to a peak during the early- to mid-1970s and declining through 1980. The bauxite/alumina sector grew at an average of 6 percent per annum from 1966 to peak year 1974, and declined at nearly 4 percent per year during the period between 1974 and 1979. Major factors accounting for the decline were the tendency of aluminum producers to diversify their sources of alumina, weak demand due to recession in the industrial countries after 1974, and reaction to the levy imposed by the government of Jamaica in 1974. Total manufacturing production reached a peak in 1973. The subsequent decline has been attributed mainly to the shortage of foreign exchange to buy imported inputs, but wage-price movements adversely affecting profitability may have contributed. Construction activity reached its peak in 1971, after which the boom in alumina plant and hotel construction ended, housing projects stalled, and—with the general decline in investment—the sector's contribution to real GDP in 1980 was only 37 percent what it had been in 1971. Electricity and water reached maximum contribution to GDP in 1976. While GDP arising from government services grew throughout the 1970s, other services grew only up to 1972 and declined afterwards.

Unemployment, (which in the Jamaican definition relates unemployed job seekers wanting work and nonseekers available for work to the total labor force) has been regarded as the most serious problem in Jamaica. It became worse in the 1973–79 period, increasing from 21 percent to 28 percent. At the same time, a chronic shortage of high-skilled workers appears to have worsened due to the emigration of professionals.

Jamaica experienced a sharp increase in average inflation rates after 1973. From an average of 7.5 percent between 1966 and 1973, the consumer price index increased at an average of 21.5 percent from 1973 to 1980. This sharp rise in average inflation was not associated with a uniform rise from year to year. After reaching a peak of 27 percent in 1974, the rate declined for the next three years to 9.8 percent in 1976. It increased in 1977, and in 1978 jumped to 49 percent under the impact of the devaluation of the Jamaican dollar and the elimination of some consumption subsidies. After falling back to 35 percent in 1979, reached 25 percent in 1980 (see table 3). A single digit inflation rate of 6.2 percent was achieved in 1982, according to the Economic and Social

Table 3
Consumer Price Index (All Jamaica)
(average rate of change, percentages, January 1975 = 100)

	Total	Food and drink	Fuel and household supplies	Housing	Household furnishings and furniture	Personal clothing and accessories	Personal expenses	Transpor- tation	Miscel- laneous
1973	17.6	24.7	12.3	16.3	6.8	8.1	14.6	4.5	7.8
1974	27.0	29.0	36.9	32.1	26.9	19.4	23.3	32.0	12.5
1975	17.4	17.8	15.1	15.3	27.6	16.5	17.1	18.5	16.4
1976	9.8	8.9	8.3	13.3	15.6	11.4	8.9	5.3	12.8
1977	11.1	9.4	8.1	5.3	14.9	9.7	9.5	13.4	30.2
1978	35.0	36.8	39.1	11.2	54.9	40.3	36.4	61.0	20.4
1979	30.9	35.5	48.3	16.9	29.7	27.5	28.5	23.3	11.7
1980	25.1	31.4	37.7	11.5	15.6	18.9	18.5	11.1	12.9

Source: Department of Statistics, Jamaica.

Survey 1982, published by the National Planning Agency,
Jamaica.
    Jamaica's public finances deteriorated significantly during the
second half of the 1970s. The overall deficit, which was 2.25 percent of GDP in 1966, increased to over 19 percent of GDP in 1976.
Under adjustment programs negotiated with the International
Monetary Fund (IMF) this deficit fell to nearly 12 percent in 1979,
but it shot up to 18 percent in 1980 when the programs were suspended. Under the new program in 1981 the deficit was reduced to
13.5 percent of GDP, but there was no further reduction by the
end of March 1983. It can be seen from table 4 that the ratio of
central government expenditures to GDP grew by over 60 percent
between 1973 and 1976 while the ratio of current revenues rose by
less than 12 percent. At the end of 1982 the outstanding public
external debt reached 44.5 percent of GDP according to National
Planning Agency estimates. With the rest of the public sector also
in a worsening financial situation, loans became an increasingly
important source of funds for use in the public sector as a whole.
Between 1973 and 1980 the outstanding public external debt as a
ratio of GDP rose from 10.6 percent to 40.5 percent; and the cost of
servicing the debt as a percentage of earnings from the export of
goods and services tripled.
    In contrast to the 1966–71 period, during which net interna-
tional reserves of the Central Bank doubled, between 1973 and
1980 Jamaica's balance of payments was under continuous pressure; since 1976 net international reserves of the Central Bank
have been negative. During the years 1966 to 1973 the current account deficit rose from 4 percent of GDP to 14 percent, but capital
inflows were adequate to offset this problem. After 1973 capital
inflows fell considerably due to declining foreign investment in
the domestic economy and to rising capital flight. This, in conjunction with falling real exports (table 10) not always offset by rising
prices, made it necessary to borrow, and when this was unsuccess-
ful, to curtail imports. The deficit on current account reflecting
the tightness of the foreign exchange constraint fell to less than
1.5 percent of GDP in 1977, a year of low exports and few loans;
but it rose to 15 percent in 1981 after the change in government
and the negotiation of a new arrangement with the IMF.

Table 4
Public Finance (Central Government)
(percentage of GDP)

	Expenditures		Central government revenues		Overall deficit	
1966	17.6		15.1		−2.5	
1968	20.5		17.2		−3.3	
1970	23.1		19.9		−3.2	
1972	26.8	(25.0)[b]	21.7	(20.3)[b]	−5.1	(−4.7)[b]
1973	27.6	(25.5)[b]	21.9	(20.1)[b]	−5.7	(−5.5)[b]
1974[a]	34.6		25.9		−8.7	
1975	35.7		24.5		−11.2	
1976	41.7		22.4		−19.3	
1977	38.9		21.8		−17.1	
1978	41.7		27.6		−14.1	
1979	38.7		26.3		−12.4	
1980	43.1		25.1		−18.0	
1981	42.8		29.3		−13.5	
1982	43.1		29.3		−13.8	

[a]Series revised in 1974.

[b]Figures in parentheses consistent with series revised in 1974.

Source: Bank of Jamaica and Ministry of Finance.

Liberalization and Centralization as Explanation of Trends

Many economists, political analysts, and newspaper and magazine columnists have sought to link the behavior of the Jamaican economy to the policies followed by successive governments. Because of the marked difference in political rhetoric with each change in leadership, the tendency has been to assume that the policy mix of one government was distinct from the other and in each case was consistent with its rhetoric. The government formed by the Jamaica Labor Party, which was in office from 1962 to 1972 and has been in office since November 1980, is free enterprise—oriented in its rhetoric. The government of the (Socialist) People's National Party, which was in office between 1972 and 1980, favored a mixed economy with state enterprises operating in areas where market competition is inadequate to assure efficiency and reasonable pricing of goods and services, and also advocated a fair degree of central planning and direction. It is not surprising, then, that the behavior of the economy has usually been explained in terms of the differential impact of liberal policies before 1972 and since 1980 and centralizing policies during the period between 1972 and 1980.

Indicators of the shift toward centralization. There is some factual and analytical justification for this explanation. Factors that one might cite include the importance of the public sector relative to the private sector in resource use and allocation, and in contribution to gross product; the use of direct controls to regulate private activity; and the range of public-sector activities of a commercial nature. First, there has been a profound change in the allocation of resources away from the private sector toward the public sector. The data in table 4 show that the ratio of central government expenditure to GDP averaged 21 percent during the 1966–70 period and 36 percent during the 1972–80 period. Central government revenue was 18 percent of GDP from 1966 to 1970 but nearly 24 percent from 1972 to 1980, actually averaged 26 percent during the period from 1977 to 1980, and was 29 percent in 1981. The shift in resources toward the public sector was accomplished partly through redistribution of domestic credit, following an amendment of the Bank of Jamaica Law in 1977 to expand the Central Bank capacity to lend to the government and to put use of that capacity under the control of the Ministry of Finance. Between 1966 and 1971, banking system net credit to government varied between 7 percent and 14 percent of total credit, but in 1977 credit outstanding to government came to exceed that to the private sector—i.e., over 50 percent—and this situation has persisted. In addition to borrowing short-term from the banking system, the government increasingly preempted other domestic loanable funds. While it is impossible to determine the shares, the growth of the internal national debt can give an indication. At the end of 1971 the internal national debt was 13 percent of GDP, but by the end of 1976 it had risen to 23 percent, and it reached 49 percent at the end of 1980. The contribution of the sector 'producers of government services' to GDP can be a useful indicator of the importance of public production in the economy even though in the national accounts some public-sector output is included elsewhere, e.g., electricity and water; transportation,

Table 5
Contribution of Public Administration to GDP
(constant 1974 prices, value in J$ million)

	Public Admin.	GDP	%
1966	100.6	1593.5	6.31
1972	207.2	2231.8	9.28
1977	328.3	1992.9	16.47
1978	344.1	1985.9	17.33
1979	363.8	1956.8	18.59
1980	366.7	1850.8	19.81
1981	372.6	1888.5	19.73

Source: Department of Statistics, Jamaica.

storage, and communications. The producers of government services (public administration and defense) contributed 6 percent of GDP (constant 1974 prices) in 1966 compared with 9 percent in 1972, with 19 percent in 1979, and 20 percent in 1981 (see table 5).

Second, controls over private-sector activities were intensified in the 1970s. The main controls were quantitative restrictions on imports, exchange controls, and price controls including wage and income guidelines. Data compiled by Mahmood Ayub (table 6) indicate that a major increase in the control of imports occurred between 1964 and 1968, when 86 additional items were restricted, and again between 1973 and 1980, when a further 179 items were restricted.

Table 6
Number of Items under Quantitative or Absolute Restriction

	Consumer goods	Intermediate goods	Capital goods	Total
1961	44	3	3	50
1964	58	5	9	72
1968	128	15	15	158
1973	164	16	21	201
1979	272	26	36	334
1980	310	30	40	380

Sources: Mahmood Ayud, *Made in Jamaica,* and World Bank estimates.

Exchange controls have been used in Jamaica since the devaluation of the pound (sterling) in 1949 and have typically followed the British pattern. However, Jamaican controls were made more comprehensive and were more vigorously enforced as balance-of-payments problems grew worse in the 1970s, and by 1976 many capital remittances had been suspended and waiting periods imposed on others. The stated objective was to reserve scarce foreign exchange for high-priority imports and for the servicing of the public sector's external debt. Price controls on a limited range of necessities date back to World War II; and a Prices Commission to set and monitor prices was set up after the devaluation of 1967. In 1975–76, a package of measures was passed to set up an Economic Stabilization Commission to determine prices policies and to guide wage tribunals. All prices were brought under control in 1975–76 when, after an initial general freeze, goods were put in three categories: those with prices fixed by the Prices Commission within guidelines set by the Economic Stabilization Commission, and that could be changed only with prior approval; those with prices subject to review by the Commission (that is, a change notified to the Prices Commission by the vendor would come into effect if the commission did not object to it within a stated period); and those with prices subject to general guidelines, which could be changed within the guidelines without approval of the Prices Commission. The main change in the 1970s could be seen in the number of items under price control and the superimposition of a centrally planned pricing authority over a formerly private sector–dominated statutory board.

Third, during the 1970s there was a significant increase in public-sector involvement in the ownership and operation of commercial entities. While for over thirty years statutory bodies controlled most primary exports (coffee, cocoa) and operated an edible-oil-processing and soapmaking plant, in the 1970s government became involved in the ownership of hotels; commercial banking; importation of petroleum, lumber, wheat, and a wide range of necessities; secondary real estate development; sugar manufacturing; and even off-course betting—to name only the main areas. In some instances the public sector operated in direct competition with the private sector, while in others—e.g., public utilities—the public sector acquired control of existing monopolies. Public-sector acquisition of land formerly dictated by the pace of land reform programs was accelerated in 1974 by arrangements for reversion of ownership of bauxite-bearing lands to the government, in order to permit a more rational exploitation of the mineral. But this reversion, along with the acquisition of some sugar lands for setting up sugarcane worker cooperatives, had the effect of making the government the largest landowner and the largest holder of idle lands.

The relationship to growth. While the foregoing indicates that some facts support the thesis of a shift toward economic centralization, it is necessary to analyze the relationship between these indicators and the performance of the economy. The relationship between centralization of resource use and GDP growth depends on the impact of centralization on the level and composition of investment and on the relative efficiency of resource use in the public and private sectors. While it is difficult to isolate the impact of centralization on the level of investment, the data are generally consistent with the view that after the ratio of central government expenditures to GDP and central government revenues to GDP shifted upward after 1973, the ratio of central government capital formation to GDP shifted upward with a slight lag, while private capital formation to GDP shifted downward. The rise in central government capital formation (proxy for public sector) did not offset the fall in private capital formation (due to rising public-sector consumption that did not reach a peak until 1979 and that was largely responsible for the upward shift in the ratio of total consumption to GDP after 1974), with the result that total investment fell (see tables 4 and 7). In short, the diversion of resources from the private to the public sector was associated with a fall in total investment. Although the data do not permit analysis of the change in composition of investment, it is reasonable to assume that the public sector's investment—being more concentrated in infrastructure and primary development with longer gestation periods than private investment—would have had a smaller impact on GDP and growth would have slowed. It was also the case that a not insignificant part of public-sector capital expenditures went to pay off the debts of private enterprises that were acquired by government. These "investments"

Table 7
Consumption, Gross National Savings, Gross Investment
(ratios to GDP)

	Consumption		Savings		Investment	
1966	76.9		14.7		20.3	
1967	78.4		13.3		22.3	
1968	79.6		14.6		26.6	
1969	77.7		13.9		26.7	
1970	80.2		11.3		25.7	
1971	80.2		11.7		26.1	
1972	82.1	(81.0)	10.3	(19.1)	24.0	(27.3)
1973	81.5	(78.3)	13.1	(21.6)	26.3	(31.2)
1974[a]	86.0		17.2		24.2	
1975	84.7		15.8		25.6	
1976	90.6		7.0		18.2	
1977	89.3		10.8		12.2	
1978	83.6		11.7		15.1	
1979	82.7		13.1		18.9	
1980	86.7		9.5		15.4	
1981	88.8		6.1		21.1	

[a]Series revised in 1974.

Source: Department of Statistics, Jamaica.

to change the ownership of existing assets generated no incremental GDP (table 8).

Most "free enterprise" economists would be tempted to conclude almost as a matter of doctrine that the intensification of controls very likely contributed to the slowdown in growth during the mid-1970s. However, some controls—e.g., on foreign exchange—reflected underlying resource constraints on growth and did not represent an extension of state control for its own sake. One could argue that the government of the day chose to keep the exchange rate overvalued, thereby taxing exports and foreign exchange earning activities and subsidizing imports. The response to an initial shortage of foreign exchange pointed therefore in a direction that would have aggravated the shortage and constrained growth. Plausible though the superficial arguments are, one must admit that there are underlying assumptions regarding supply elasticity of exports and elasticity of overseas demand for Jamaican exports that may not have obtained in real life. Detailed studies have been illuminating. The decline of banana exports was probably more

Table 8

Private Capital Formation

	Gross domestic investment (GDI)	GDP	GDI/GDP	Central government capital formation (% GDP)	Derived private capital formation (% GDP)
1972	394.2	1438.8	27.4	2.6	24.8
1973	541.6	1735.1	31.2	2.9	28.3
1974	525.1	2170.0	24.2	3.9	20.3
1975	670.1	2614.7	25.6	6.3	19.3
1976	494.4	2715.3	18.2	9.5	8.7
1977	365.1	2994.1	12.2	8.2	4.0
1978	568.7	3763.7	15.1	8.2	6.9
1979	813.5	4301.2	18.9	5.8	13.1
1980	733.9	4757.2	15.4	6.5	8.9
1981	1120.9	5309.8	21.1	10.0	11.1

Source: Original data provided by Department of Statistics, Jamaica, adjusted to put GDP in market prices.

responsible for the fragmentation of certain estates on the death of the former generation of growers than was the exchange rate; and with the importance of the foreign exchange earnings, it is not clear that the availability of foreign exchange over a short period benefited from devaluation. Thus, if devaluation is the alternative to rationing through foreign exchange controls, it is by no means certain that such controls reduce GDP growth.

These arguments have relevance only to the current account. The intensification of controls could have discouraged capital inflows, which may have assisted growth; but the recession of the industrialized countries after 1974, among other considerations, makes it doubtful that capital flows were otherwise poised to enter Jamaica. Price controls were rigorously applied to imports in order to prevent profiteering made possible by shortages. Margins in distribution of imported goods were squeezed and contribution of the sector as a whole to GDP suffered as some import houses went out of business and others reduced employment. It is not clear that price controls are to blame for the slowdown. If prices were not controlled, the shortage of foreign exchange would still have meant a reduction in quantity of imported goods for distribution and employment, and GDP would have fallen. Price controls were less rigorously applied to domestic production. In the case of agricultural output no new price controls were imposed, while in the case of manufactures, traditional profit margins were generally allowed. Although guidelines on pricing of services were mentioned in numerous political speeches, no attempt was made to implement them.

Guidelines for income and wage adjustments were discussed in 1975 and simply announced in subsequent years. Some attribute the rise in emigration of professionals and the fall in availability of some services, such as dental and medical, to the fear that an absolute ceiling on earnings would be imposed; but no ceiling was imposed outside the public service sector.

In any case, economic theory does not provide a basis for predicting how workers would respond to a curtailment of wage rates; they may all find leisure more attractive as it becomes cheaper, but some may work more in order to maintain their current real income. So even if controls in this area had been effective, which by and large they were not, the effects on GDP would have been of uncertain direction and probably insignificant.

Did the shift toward centralization really occur? While it is likely that the shift of resources to the public sector restrained growth and—although the case is less clear—that foreign exchange and price controls could have had a similar effect, this conclusion assumes that there was in fact a distinct change in policies in the 1970s that can be construed as constituting a shift from liberalization to centralization. There is evidence, however, to suggest that policies essentially continued along their postindependence trends while the accompanying political rhetoric changed. Certainly foreign exchange and price controls had been in use for many years; they were simply intensified in 1967 in response to changed external circumstances (the devaluation of the pound sterling) and justified to the citizenry as minimizing cost-of-living pressures and ensuring that the import of necessities had priority access to foreign exchange to protect the poor consumer—one of the traditional imperatives of Jamaican politics. Another traditional imperative—the creation of employment—was the *raison d'être* of the quantitative restrictions on trade, to protect and so encourage the development of local manufacturing, which was largely responsible for much of the industrial expansion between the mid-1950s and 1970. By 1970 it was generally conceded that the easy options for import substitution had been taken, and further restrictions for this purpose were never imposed. Indeed, part of the argument for a Caribbean free trade area in 1967—68 and its upgrading into a Common Market in 1972 was that protected industries would be subjected to increased competition. Intensification of trade restrictions and foreign exchange controls in the mid-1970s was not regarded as new policy, but as the reorientation of existing policy to deal with an unemployment crisis. Formerly protected industries based on the use of imports had to be assured of continuing supplies in order to preserve jobs, an assurance to come at the expense of imported luxury-type final goods and capital outflows of emigrants. The employment objective remained uppermost and the intensification of restrictions and trade controls did not constitute a policy shift toward centralization.

The shift of resources to the public sector was only superficially an indicator of a shift toward centralization. If the revenue from the new bauxite taxes introduced in 1974 is not included, the ratio

Table 9

Current Revenues of the Central Government

(percentage of GDP)

FY	Current revenue	Bauxite levy	Non-bauxite
1970/71	18.6	—	18.6
1971/72	20.3	—	20.3
1972/73	20.3	—	20.3
1973/74	20.0	—	20.0
1974/75	26.0	6.0	20.0
1975/76	26.2	5.6	20.6
1976/77	22.3	2.9	19.4
1977/78	21.8	3.7	18.1
1978/79	27.6	7.1	20.5
1979/80	26.4	5.4	21.0
1980/81	25.3	4.9	20.4

Source: Bank of Jamaica, Kingston, Jamaica.

of central government current revenues to GDP can be seen to have undergone no significant change that would indicate a conscious intent to shift resources from the remainder of the Jamaican private sector to the public sector (table 9). Indeed the decision to place economic burdens on the foreign-dominated mining sector, and to restore its lands to Jamaican control as well as permit government participation in ownership, may have been motivated by nationalist concerns similar to those of the 1960s, when the previous administration decided to Jamaicanize commercial banks and insurance companies. The shift in the use of resources indicated by the expenditure ratio partly reflects the superior external borrowing power of the public sector. To the extent that the government took an increasing share of the banking system's credit, there is the temptation to conclude that the private sector was being squeezed, yet for much of the post-1975 period commercial banks held liquid reserves well in excess of the required minimum. A rising ratio of central government expenditure to GDP was motivated mainly by the need to compensate for a faltering economy. The Special Employment Program, which cost over J$50 million per year during the mid-1970s, is one example of a populist program's response to the number one political imperative.

The expansion of government ownership of commercial productive activities—e.g., hotels and banks—is only superficially an indication of centralization. Acquisition of hotels was in many cases the result of a policy of the 1960s and early 1970s to encourage tourism through tax incentives for hotel construction and the granting of government guarantees for the debt-financing of private hotels. In other cases it was the result of secondary "seed" developments planned at the time of primary urban developments in the late 1960s, when the free enterprise–oriented government started the "Urban Development Corporation." In the face of the recession of 1975 and after, the downturn in tourism aggravated by adverse publicity in certain markets created a situation in which most hotels could not service their debt, and the government had to honor guarantees, thereby acquiring an interest in them. There was no guarantee of commercial banks, but in order to avoid a serious disturbance in the financial sector after a real estate boom broke in 1974, the government decided to acquire some banks (many with large Jamaican shares since the movement toward Jamaicanization in the late 1960s) that were in trouble. Thus it can be seen that what appears on the surface as a shift toward centralization was largely an outcome of the management of a crisis in which the government had inherited from its predecessor a large contingent liability.

The return to liberalism? The government formed by the Jamaica Labor Party since November 1980 has shown no consistent or persistent tendency away from centralization. The public sector continues to absorb a large share of total resources. Central government expenditure was 42.8 percent of GDP in 1981—not significantly below the peak of 43.1 percent reached in 1980. Central government revenue at 29.3 percent of GDP in 1981 was well above the previous peak of 27.6 percent achieved in 1978. In 1982 the ratio of revenues to GDP remained at 29.3 percent. The public debt held by the Bank of Jamaica increased by J$100 million in 1982, indicating that the distribution of bank credit continued to facilitate public-sector access to resources. Significantly, the new government has not repealed the 1977 amendments to the Bank of Jamaica Law that permitted heavy recourse to money creation to finance budgetary deficits in the late 1970s.

The use of direct controls on prices, importation, and foreign exchange has not undergone profound change, although under IMF arrangements constant attention should lead eventually to some liberalization. As late as mid-1982 the Bank of Jamaica reported that "the regulations introduced under the Ministry paper of January 1977 have remained in effect," and the government's new import-licensing policy outlined in a Ministry paper presented to Parliament promised only progressive liberalization flowing from a constant review of items on the "restricted" and "banned" lists. In 1982, under an adjustment program negotiated with the IMF, the government agreed to allow commercial banks to operate in the unofficial exchange market to which it has consigned some transactions formerly in the official market. Recent tightening of controls to ensure that the foreign exchange earnings from tourism go into the official market appear to tilt back toward centralization. In early 1983, when the parallel market rate rose steeply, the prime minister persuaded the bankers to resist rate increases or risk formal intervention. His efforts were only temporarily successful, but they injected a note of ambiguity in the announced return to a free-market economy. The recently legislated Rent Act continues detailed control of rents by setting them at specified percentages of the government's assessed valuation.

A similar situation obtains regarding government involvement in commercial activity. Although it has announced a program to divest itself of hotels, the government has recently acquired the oil refinery formerly owned by Esso, justifying its action as necessary to protect consumers from unwarranted price increases and to save foreign exchange remitted as profits by the foreign company. Significantly, the government has not announced that it will divest itself of large acreages of idle agricultural land that were acquired by the previous administration. Such divestment could not only continue needed land reform but would signal clearly the return to private control of a sector dominated by many small producers.

The economic strategy of the present government has emphasized foreign borrowing to bridge the gap between imports and exports, rather than focusing on adjustments to favor an increase in the level of exports and/or a contraction in the level of imports. There has been a reluctance to allow prices to reflect the relative scarcity of resources, including that of foreign exchange, and a tendency artificially to restrict movement in the general price level, thereby giving the impression that a better standard of living is generally achievable than is realistically the case. For employment reasons, among others, restraint on public expenditure has been delayed. In 1983 the public-sector deficit was estimated to be in the range of 13 to 15 percent of GDP. These components of strategy clearly indicate the continuation of populist policies oriented more to short-term political objectives and less to economic development over the medium to long term.

An Alternative Explanation of Trends

In approaching the formulation of a more adequate explanation of Jamaican economic performance during the 1970s, care should be taken to avoid the major deficiencies examined above. Some of these are:

- failure to take into account the development path along which the economy was moving and the effect this would have on subsequent performance;

- failure to take adequate cognizance of the role of external shocks;

- failure to take into account the impact of noncentralizing policies;

- failure to pay adequate attention to internal nonpolicy factors affecting performance;

- the adoption of a simplistic approach to a complicated phenomenon.

The development path. Jamaica's rapid economic growth between 1955 and 1972 was due mainly to the existence of primary resources that were attractive to foreign entrepreneurs and the existence of a domestic market for certain manufactured goods that could be produced on a relatively small scale using a technology within the capability of Jamaican labor. Bauxite resources attracted international aluminum companies and beautiful beaches attracted hotel developments. Domestic manufacturing was protected by tariffs and encouraged by tax incentives. Traditional exports (table 10) of sugar, bananas, coffee, and cocoa earned enough foreign exchange to pay for the imported inputs required by import substitution industries. Toward the end of the 1960s, investments in mining and tourism began to level off and the opportunities for import substitution in the domestic market became fewer. With the impending and eventual entry of Great Britain into the European Economic Community, the protected market for Jamaica's traditional exports was threatened. Clearly the easy phase of economic expansion was drawing to a close as the decade ended, and government policies reflected concern with this fact. Participation in the Caribbean Free Trade Area (later to become a Common Market) was seen as a means of continuing import substitution on a regional scale, thereby creating industrial opportunities formerly beyond the reach of individual members. The government legislated more generous incentives, undertook primary physical developments in urban and resort areas, and offered guarantees to investors in certain types of secondary developments. But by 1972, economists analyzing the Jamaican situation were unable to foresee what would provide the impetus to further expansion. At the same time it was also recognized that the benefits of the expansion of the 1960s had not trickled down to the masses, who still suffered from high and growing unemployment and underemployment, and that the situation had the potential for social unrest. Clearly, the development path on which the Jamaican economy was moving at the beginning of the 1970s led toward a slowdown in growth. This situation required favorable changes in external circumstances to create new opportunities and the correction of internal weaknesses in economic structure and the policy environment if a reversal of direction were to be achieved.

External shocks. The changes in external circumstances during the 1970s were generally adverse to the expansion of the Jamaican economy. Indeed the increases in food prices in 1973 as a result of worldwide crop failures, the increases in petroleum prices beginning late in 1973 and repeated later in the decade, recession in the industrial countries, worldwide inflationary pressures, and the surge in international interest rates during the second half of the 1970s have had such a staggering impact on so

Table 10
Exports of Sugar, Bananas and Nontraditional Products
(value in US$ million; volume in thousands metric tons)

	Sugar		Bananas		Nontraditional exports
	Value	Volume	Value	Volume	Value
1970	35	299	14	132	68
1971	39	294	15	124	72
1972	42	271	15	125	70
1973	40	257	18	106	78
1974	82	266	13	71	78
1975	154	250	16	67	96
1976	61	226	13	75	101
1977	63	210	14	75	115
1978	60	193	17	73	106
1979	57	188	18	64	126
1980	54	132	11	31	149

Source: Department of Statistics, Jamaica.

many economies that an explanation of economic performance in any country must be immediately suspect if it fails to pay specific attention to these changes. Jamaica is highly dependent on food imports, primarily cereal and feed grains, vegetable oils, and dairy products; and the massive price increases early in 1973 significantly added to the food import bill and caused an increase of 25 percent in the cost of food (which, accounting for over 50 percent of average household expenditures, contributed to the 18 percent jump in the cost of living in that year). From the outset, Jamaica, which derives nearly 100 percent of its energy requirements from imported petroleum, was included by international experts in the category of "most seriously affected countries." Table 11 shows that Jamaica's fuel import bill increased by 167 percent in 1974 and by 600 percent by 1980, rising in seven years from 11 percent to 38 percent of the total value of imports. The impact was not only to divert scarce foreign exchange from inputs but also to involve the public sector in petroleum trading under bilateral arrangements for exporter financing of part of the fuel bill. The recession in industrial countries retarded the growth of mining and tourism and interfered with the penetration of Jamaican manufactures into these markets. The shocks did much to widen the trade deficit, and with rising indebtedness overseas, the sharp increases in international interest rates multiplied the debt-service burden and exacerbated the scarcity of foreign exchange available for supporting productive activities. Beyond question, then, external circumstances did not change to create new opportunities for Jamaica; instead, the shocks must have contributed greatly to the dismal growth performance and also must have been largely responsible for starting severe inflationary pressures.

Internal policies affecting performance. Jamaica is a classic case of adherence to undesirable policies that, *quite apart from any centralizing effect,* helped to undermine economic performance during the 1970s. A few examples can be cited in support of this contention:

- The extension of minimum wage legislation and the setting of a national minimum wage well above rates prevailing in many industries must be credited with the flight of a substantial part of the export-oriented garment industry to Haiti and other locations—clearly making worse the problem of unemployment and foreign exchange scarcity.

- Failure to adjust exchange rates soon after 1974 because of the effects of the bauxite levy on earnings caused a "Dutch disease" effect among other exports, which became increasingly uncompetitive both abroad and at home.

- Protectionism was not avoided, although trade controls were replaced by exchange controls. The main problem for resource allocation derived from the fact that effective protection has been uneven. The manufacturing industry has been overprotected while agriculture has been underprotected because of a policy encouraging cheap food imports. The result has been the relative impoverishment of the agricultural sector, and continued dependence on imported food with attendant vulnerability to international food price shifts.

- In the public sector, time and resources have been wasted in pursuit of large projects expected to provide "single stick" solutions to the economic problems of unemployment and weak balance of payments. One project such as the Luana Oil Refinery was pursued for political reasons long after economic analysis showed it to be submarginal, while another cotton/polyester textile mill was made submarginal by politically motivated, inappropriate siting. This project also suffered from inadequate protection since remnants and ends were imported at low tariffs in order to keep down the cost of living.

- Some politically motivated programs of dubious economic merit were continued and expanded during the 1970s. The Special Employment Program, on which the government spent over J$50 million per year after 1974 without proper planning, selection, and supervision of projects, simply provided income support for thousands without enhancing real capital formation and any increase in the productive capacity of society. This program, though somewhat reduced, still continues.

Unsettled industrial relations. An explanation of economic performance in Jamaica would be incomplete if it failed to recognize the importance of industrial relations. Jamaica has for thirty

years suffered from competitive political trade unionism. The
rivalry seems to be most keen during recessions, when job open-
ings are fewer. During most of the 1970s, recession plus exaggerated polarization of political philosophy and propaganda transformed rivalry into hostile confrontation, occasioning delays and
cost overruns in new construction—especially of major projects.
While no major project has ever been completed without at least
one prolonged strike, several were simply abandoned in the 1970s.
The outstanding example was the expansion of the nation's only
cement plant, which was designed, planned, and had equipment
imported for implementation in 1975. Violent rivalry between the
major unions stalled the project at its inception. After seven years,
the crates of machinery are gathering dust at dockside near the
project site, while in the interim Jamaica spent scarce foreign exchange revenue to import cement from Cuba and other Caribbean
sources. The governments of the two political parties, depending
as they do on support from affiliated unions, have failed to introduce legislation aimed at procuring adequate discipline in industrial relations.

In searching for explanations of the poor performance of the
Jamaican economy during the latter half of the 1970s, one cannot
ignore the high degree of ideological polarization of the society
and the uncertainty created as the interpretation of the "democratic socialism" of the governing party shifted leftward from its
Fabian roots. The response of entrepreneurs and many professionals was to emigrate, withdrawing not only their marginal
product but also aggravating the scarcity of foreign exchange by
illegally financing, through the black market, the exportation of
their accumulated physical capital. The chance that the People's
National Party with its philosophy of democratic socialism may be
returned to office in the near future and continue its policies constitutes a source of uncertainty that could frustrate the present
government's efforts to induce the return of Jamaican entrepreneurs and capital from abroad.

Policy Prescriptions

The initial development path; external shocks; defective internal
policies, programs, and projects; unsettled industrial relations;

and uncertainty deriving from political conditions all seem to have played a part in the poor performance of the Jamaican economy during the 1970s. To ignore them in the interest of simplicity is to lose sight of the complicated nature of the development process and to risk ill-considered choices for the future. Clearly all the factors affecting the behavior of the economy cannot be taken into account if the analysis is to remain manageable, but the economist must judge which of those factors are the most important.

As we have seen, the explanation of Jamaica's recent economic history that focuses on shifts of internal policy from liberalization to centralization and back would appear to leave out too many important factors and to confuse the shifts in political rhetoric with real shifts in policy. A more adequate explanation would be that centralizing shifts in policy should be included as having played a part, but a more important role must be attributed to the structure of the economy at the beginning of the 1970s and the dependence on foreign exchange as a critical determinant of the level of domestic productive activity.

Reorientation of policies toward the private sector must be perceptible as such. The movement must be positive and unambiguous, and above all internally consistent. Clearly, the share of the public sector in total resource use must be reduced over time. Direct, distorting controls over private economic activity must be dismantled to the maximum extent possible. Recent legislation on rent should be abandoned or it will throttle investment in real estate, depress construction, and lead to further urban deterioration and blight. Government's direct involvement in commercial activity should be reduced. Divestment of agricultural land should begin now and continue until only the forest estate, lands needed for watershed protection, and land for agricultural experimentation remain in public ownership.

The reorientation of policies toward the private sector will not be sufficient; management of the economy must generate appropriate signals to private decision-makers by removing and minimizing distortions wherever these exist. Of prime importance is the removal of disincentives to foreign exchange—earning activities and of encouragements to foreign exchange—using activities. Also important is the removal of subsidies to food prices. These may appear desirable to keep down the cost of living, but they tend to depress local agriculture and increase dependence on food imports, initially through low prices but ultimately by altering tastes. Minimum wage legislation may well be having the effect of supporting wage rates, and ultimately the cost of labor, above free-market levels: this has a deleterious effect on production and employment.

Jamaica's longer-term progress cannot be assured if the present system of competitive political trade unionism continues. Unfortunately, there appears to be no clearly feasible way of changing this situation. In the past, the government made efforts to soften union pressure for pay increases by holding discussions with labor leaders to sensitize them to the weakness of the economy. These discussions have not been successful because, motivated by political considerations, opposition unions have been uncooperative. Since the present opposition labor union is likely to behave in the same manner as the former one, the outlook for conciliatory moves is unfavorable. Perhaps only a prolonged downward spiral in economic activity coupled with widespread layoffs can lead to a restructuring of the Jamaican labor movement to make it less a political tool and more a champion of working-class interests that sees the need for more jobs and not only for higher wage rates.

The climate of uncertainty is likely to continue as long as the two dominant political parties have divergent views on the role of the market and private enterprise in the economy, and as long as a democratic political system gives both parties the opportunity to constitute the government. It may very well be that the country will have to suffer through a rapid succession of reversals in policies with attendant lack of growth until gradually the opposing political philosophies drift closer together and policy reversals cease. It would of course be regrettable if an easing of uncertainty came only at the expense of a democratic process that now permits a choice between parties and economic systems.

In sum, Jamaica's poor economic performance of the 1970s reflects the need for a fundamental restructuring that is not yet clearly under way, and its full realization may not be possible without significant dislocation in the near to medium term.

Table 11
Imports
(US$ million)

	Current prices			1974 prices		
	Total	Fuel	Nonfuel	Total	Fuel	Nonfuel
1970	522	33	489	1181	158	1023
1971	553	52	501	1147	198	949
1972	588	56	532	1161	146	1015
1973	677	73	604	971	139	832
1974	936	195	741	936	195	741
1975	1123	215	908	979	200	779
1976	913	204	709	743	170	573
1977	747	235	512	582	153	429
1978	865[a]	194	671	665	146	519
1979	1003[a]	331	672	593	178	415
1980	1173[a]	451	722	544	146	398

[a]There is a discrepancy with balance-of-payments data due to inclusion of payments for freight and insurance made to residents.

Source: Department of Statistics, Jamaica.

COMMENTS

Michael Connolly

We are indebted to Gladstone Bonnick for his careful, reasoned documentation of the recent Jamaican economic record. In some cases the figures really do speak for themselves. In the 1970s gross domestic product (GDP) per capita declined 40 percent, government consumption expenditures rose from 14 to 21.5 percent of GDP, and net foreign reserves fell from 10 percent to a minus 27 percent of GDP.[1] That is not a very good economic record for the People's National Party. The new government of the Jamaica Labor Party inherited these economic problems. While this is an important experiment, it is far too early to draw conclusions for the 1980s.

I will mainly try to complement the analysis by Bonnick here and focus some attention on the adjustment problems faced by Jamaica that were inherited from the 1970s. Five main points deserve some attention.

First, Jamaica's economic record from 1972 to 1981 is comparatively far worse than that of other Caribbean economies. Table 1 compares the level of 1981 real GDP per capita to the 1972 level for Caribbean countries reporting their data to the International Monetary Fund (IMF). Barbados and Haiti showed mild rises in per capita income of 16 and 13 percent respectively, while Trinidad and Tobago, an oil exporter, showed a large increase of 30 percent. In the Bahamas per capita income was unchanged, while in the Dominican Republic and Jamaica the declines were 20 and 38 percent respectively. Thus the decline in the standard of living in Jamaica has been dramatic and far exceeds that of other Caribbean economies.

Table 1

Caribbean Real Income and Growth Rates, 1972–1981[a]

	Real GDP per capita 1981 / Real GDP per capita 1972	Per capita growth rate (percent per year)
Bahamas	1.00	0
Barbados	1.16	1.6
Dominican Republic[b]	.80	−2.7
Haiti	1.13	1.5
Jamaica[c]	.62	−5.4
Trinidad and Tobago[d]	1.30	4.3

[a]Since in some cases 1981 data were not available, column 1 uses the most recent year for which data are available as end year. Consequently, some of the per capita growth rates in column 2 differ slightly from the natural log of column 1 divided by 9.

[b]Decline due solely to population growth.

[c]Population growth was 1.4 percent while GDP fell 4 percent per year.

[d]In 1979, 90 percent of exports were petroleum. All others are oil importers.

Source: Calculated from *International Financial Statistics, 1982 Yearbook.*

Second, not all external shocks to the Jamaican economy have been unfavorable. Table 2 reports selected commodity price indexes from 1972 to 1981. While the petroleum price index shows a rapid rise, accounting for many problems of small oil-importing Caribbean economies, the prices of most Jamaican export goods rose substantially during this period. Bauxite prices in particular rose. This is especially important since Jamaican exports of bauxite and aluminum far exceeded oil imports. Furthermore, world demand for bauxite did not appear weak; bauxite prices rose rapidly from 1974 on, both in absolute terms and relative to the U.S. consumer price index. It is thus surprising that mining and quarrying production declined 20 percent in 1975 and a further 21 percent in 1976. It seems reasonable to attribute the decline to domestic factors, such as the bauxite levy imposed in 1974, and possibly exchange controls. This levy was substantial, as it represented 6 percent of GDP in 1974–75. No other sector, apart from construction, showed a similar decline (chapter 10). Thus world

Table 2

Selected Commodity Price Indexes

	Bananas	Bauxite	Cocoa	Coffee	Sugar	Oil	U.S. consumer price index
1972	66.0	50.6	51.6	69.5	35.8	21.8	77.7
1973	67.3	57.6	90.8	85.8	46.7	32.7	82.6
1974	75.2	68.3	125.2	93.8	146.4	94.0	91.6
1975	100.0	100.0	100.0	100.0	100.0	100.0	100.0
1976	105.6	111.4	164.2	195.9	57.0	103.6	105.8
1977	111.6	128.0	304.3	316.1	39.9	114.1	112.7
1978	117.0	131.4	273.3	213.9	38.6	114.1	121.2
1979	132.9	144.9	264.3	233.9	47.6	154.1	134.9
1980	153.1	201.7	209.0	207.9	140.9	253.5	153.1
1981	158.7	205.4	166.7	159.8	83.3	294.3	169.0

Source: *International Financial Statistics, 1982 Yearbook*, pp. 82–85; for the U.S. consumer price index, *ibid.*, p. 467.

demand for bauxite was high while production slumped dramatically. Prices for other Jamaican export goods displayed a similar rise over the period, with the notable exception of sugar.

Third, the large increase in the government sector was financed mainly by the printing of new money and by drawing down on foreign exchange reserves. In the Bank of Jamaica Law (Section V), the bank's objectives in this regard were clearly set out:

... to issue and redeem notes and coins, to keep and administer the external reserves of Jamaica, to influence the volume and conditions of supply of credit so as to promote the fullest expansion of production, trade and employment, consistent with the maintenance of monetary stability in Jamaica and the external value of the currency.[2]

In 1961 the issue of Jamaican pounds was backed initially by sterling holdings, and monetary policy was dictated by the maintenance of a fixed exchange rate—first to the pound sterling and then, since the middle of 1969, to the U.S. dollar. Table 3 reports changes in the Bank of Jamaica's holdings of Treasury debt, as a percent of government consumption in column 1, and as a percent of GDP in column 2. The use of the printing press began in 1972, accelerated in 1975 and 1976, but was temporarily halted in 1977. It is probably no coincidence that there was, in Bonnick's words, "an amendment of the Bank of Jamaica Law in 1977 to expand the Central Bank capacity to lend to the government and to put use of that capacity under the control of the Ministry of Finance." The printing press was set in motion again in 1978, reaching a maximum of 62 percent finance of government consumption. This represented 13 percent of GDP financed by the issue of new money.

The creation of domestic credit by the Central Bank naturally caused a loss of reserves. Column 3 of table 3 illustrates the fall from net reserves equivalent to 11 percent of GDP to negative 27 percent of GDP over the 1972–1981 period. With a world interest rate of about 10 percent, servicing this debt would require 2.5 percent of Jamaican income. In short, Jamaica, and particularly its government, financed high expenditures by drawing down on its reserves. This can be done only once. Thereafter, expenditures must fall relative to income when a deficit can no longer be financed from existing reserves or increased borrowing from abroad.

Table 3
Loans to Treasury and International Borrowing by The Bank of Jamaica

	Change in Bank of Jamaica's claims on government		Foreign assets minus foreign liabilities as percent of GDP
	As percent of GVT consumption	As percent of GDP	
1970	1	0	10
1971	3	0	11
1972	11	2	8
1973	7	1	6
1974	5	1	6
1975	23	4	2
1976	55	11	− 5
1977	−7	−2	− 6
1978	20	4	−15
1979	36	7	−18
1980	62	13	−20
1981	37	8	−27

Source: Calculated from *International Financial Statistics, 1982 Yearbook*, pp. 266–69.

The fourth point to be made is that the adjustment process will be painful for Jamaica, as it will involve a combination of further exchange-rate depreciation and the dampening of absorption relative to income. Figure 1 illustrates the initial situation of early deficits financed by a combination of drawing down on reserves and increased foreign borrowing. The value of the deficit is equal to *CP* in terms of traded goods (or dollars). The smaller production frontier is 60 percent of the larger one, roughly corresponding to the decline in GDP per capita from 1972 to 1981. Had Jamaica adjusted in 1981, further depreciation of the Jamaican dollar would shift production toward traded goods, and consumption away from them. It would also dampen expenditures, which would have to be reinforced by other measures to cut domestic absorption—particularly reductions in government expenditures. The cut in the Jamaican standard of living is thus much larger than indicated by

Figure 1

Hypothetical Comparison Between 1972 and 1981 Production and Consumption Patterns

(with debt repayment and a 40 percent reduction in real GDP per capita)

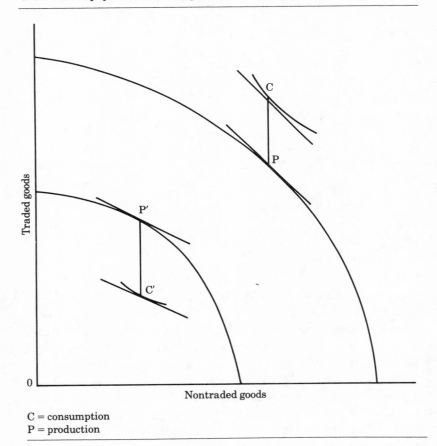

C = consumption
P = production

the 38 percent decline in per capita income, since there are no
reserves to cushion the drop and new borrowing is more difficult.
In other words, the new government inherited an economic mess
of gigantic proportions, for which adjustment measures cannot be
popular.

Finally, import substitution used to create employment is export
substitution, which destroys employment. If unemployment exists
in import-competing industries, a production subsidy—not a tariff
—is the optimal solution. We owe the theorem on the symmetry
between import and export taxes to Abba Lerner's elegant 1936
proof.[3] Simply put, if resources are drawn to the import-competing
sector by tariffs and quotas that raise the relative price of importables, they are pushed out of the export sector by the equivalent
decline in the relative price of exportables. It is a pity that in his
otherwise excellent treatment of the problem, Gladstone Bonnick
fails to criticize more vigorously the 1970s policy of "the creation
of employment—the *raison d'être* of the quantitative restrictions
on trade, to protect and so encourage the development of local
manufacturing." It is not clear to me how a country can increase
employment by specializing in the areas in which it has a comparative disadvantage. Ricardian theory tells us that specialization in the wrong direction is costly. It would seem that if employment is to be increased, it would be less harmful to pursue export
promotion.[4] Harry Johnson has further shown that a solution to
unemployment in import-competing industries brought about by
rigidity in real wages and immobility between import and export
sectors is a wage or production subsidy, not a tariff or quota. The
reason for this is that a tariff unnecessarily taxes the consumer,
since it is equivalent to a production subsidy plus a consumption
tax.

11

S. C. TSIANG

Taiwan's Economic Miracle: Lessons in Economic Development

During the past thirty years Taiwan, South Korea, Hong Kong, and Singapore have become widely considered as models of economic growth for developing countries; and rightly so. To take the case of Taiwan, it is a small island of 13,900 square miles with very high population density but few natural resources. Yet it achieved a fivefold increase in real income per capita from 1952 to 1980 in spite of a more than doubling of its population (from 8.14 million to 17.8 million). This record is all the more remarkable in light of Taiwan's need for constant military preparedness. Throughout the period, no less than half a million soldiers have been under arms at all times.

Taiwan's remarkable experience was built on her rejection of certain fashionable postwar development theories and her embrace of more traditional strategies based on market allocation of resources. In fact, the postwar development experiments have now run long enough to compare the results of these two very different strategies. The results are very clear. Taiwan languished when she followed the once-fashionable practices of using quantitative restrictions and tariff barriers to ensure a sheltered domestic market for import-substituting industries, and of keeping interest rates low by strict regulation of banks and other financial intermediaries. In the mid-1950s, however, Taiwan implemented fundamental reforms in policy, liberalizing trade restraints, promoting exports at an equilibrium exchange rate, and encouraging private saving and efficient allocation of capital funds by a market-determined interest rate. These policies produced enormous changes in the composition of outputs in Taiwan's economy, in addition to encouraging very rapid income growth together with substantial income equality. By encouraging movement of inefficient agricultural production—in which land-poor Taiwan had no comparative advantage—into industrial production of low capital intensity, Taiwan's foreign trade increased more than 200 times between 1954 and 1980. In that time, agriculture declined from about 90 percent of exports in the early 1950s to about 10 percent in 1980, while industrial exports rose from 10 percent to 90 percent.

These increases in industrial output were fueled by enormous increases in private saving in response to policies that encouraged savings. In the same period, domestic saving increased from about 5 percent of the national income in the early 1950s to almost 35 percent at the end of the 1970s.

This basic strategy has provided the basis for Taiwan's rapid economic development over the past thirty years; and the same strategy, undertaken several years later, has produced the same results for South Korea and other Pacific Basin countries. These consistent successes contain important lessons for other countries, whose growth experience, influenced by development theories once in fashion, has been disappointing. To understand the nature of those lessons more clearly, we would do well to reexamine closely how the market-based strategy helped produce Taiwan's "economic miracle."

Immediate Postwar Experience

Taiwan's economic picture after World War II looked extremely bleak. The major industries of the island had suffered severely from bombing during the war, and the island population had suddenly increased when nearly two million soldiers and civilian refugees from the Communist takeover of the mainland joined the roughly six million islanders.

The industries the Japanese had left were mostly oriented to supply the Japanese market (e.g., the sugar and rice industries) or to provide for the needs of the Japanese military, with no independent economic basis (such as the aluminum refinery). Other industries were very small-scale factories supplying the crude daily necessities of the local population. Some cotton and woolen textile factories were brought over by refugee industrialists and established in Taiwan with government help.

The pressing fiscal need of supporting a large military force plus the urgent necessity of restoring the infrastructure of the economy made it impossible to balance the budget. Rapid inflation was thus inevitable in the early postwar years.

At that time, the economic authorities of the Republic of China in Taiwan were laboring under two popular misconceptions in development policy that were highly fashionable among academic circles as well. These were, first, that the best way to develop the infant industries of a developing country was to shelter the domestic market behind a wall of high tariffs or quantitative import restrictions; and second, that interest rates should be kept low even in the face of considerable inflation, thus alledgedly insuring a cheap supply of credit to the new industries at home. These twin policies, unfortunately, are both harmful, and developing countries that persisted in following them are now sadly lagging in their performances.

Taiwan was one of the first countries to break away from this strategy. It did so first by abandoning the low interest-rate policy in the face of inflation. Then, shifting the emphasis of her industrialization from import substitution to export promotion, it devalued its currency to a realistic level—which obviated the need for quantitative restrictions and prohibitive tariffs.

The Failure of Import Substitution Development Strategies

The most naive argument for this strategy is that industries in developing countries, apart from the traditional raw material producing agriculture and mining industries, stand no chance in competition with industries in developed countries. Therefore, if a developing country is to diversify into other fields than its traditional raw material producing roles, it must provide strong protection to its nascent industries.

This argument in its simplest form virtually denies the existence of comparative advantages for developing countries. The confusion may lie in the fact that when the exchange rate is overvalued, one might confuse the apparent absence of absolute advantages in any industry with the absence of *comparative* advantages for any industry at all. In the end, however, imports can only be paid for with exports; and it is thus impossible for there to be *no* industries with comparative advantages, or for there to be *no* industries with absolute cost advantages if the exchange rate is adjusted to the appropriate level. Of course it is possible that the traditional export industries may be so productive that even under free trade and equilibrium exchange rates, they would show up as the only industries with both comparative and absolute cost advantages. In that case, they should indeed be the only exporting industries, unless it could be shown that they had hidden external diseconomies or that they were based on rapidly exhausting natural resources, like the oil industries. In the latter case the appropriate policy would be to impose an appropriate export duty on the relevant traditional export industries and to let the exchange rate of the domestic currency devalue; some new export industries with absolute cost advantages might then manifest themselves.

A more sophisticated version of the import substitution argument holds that world demand for the exportables of the developing countries is likely to be inelastic. If so, devaluation, coupled with the removal of protective tariff barriers or quantitative restrictions on imports, might lead to such a deterioration of the terms of trade that the welfare of the country may actually suffer in spite of some increase in exports.

As later events have shown, this elasticity pessimism (as it has come to be known) is totally unwarranted. In fact this assumption has proved so wrong that the latest academic fashion seems to have swung to the opposite extreme, treating all "tradeable goods" from a small country as enjoying a perfectly elastic world demand. Of course, neither of these cases is strictly true, but countries that actually accepted elasticity pessimism certainly missed an excellent chance to improve the real productivity of their available resources through reallocation and trading. They missed the powerful boost Taiwan and other newly industrialized East Asian countries enjoyed in their efforts toward economic takeoff.

In the early 1950s, Taiwan followed the prevalent development strategy of the time, viz., letting her currency be grossly overvalued while inflating domestically, but keeping her balance of payments in balance by means of strict quantitative controls and a high tariff wall. Under these policies, Taiwan's exports were merely the few traditional ones—sugar, rice, pineapples, plus a few minor items—going chiefly to markets established through prewar trade relationships (e.g., Japan). New export industries and new markets for exports simply could not be developed. Industrial development efforts were therefore limited to the industries producing cheap consumer products for the highly protected—but relatively small—domestic market. Given the country's low per capita income, industries for import substitution necessarily operated at scales far below efficient levels.

Devaluation and Liberalization

Economic development required that Taiwan recognize that it could exploit comparative advantage; it had to specialize, and it had to seek broad foreign markets for exportable goods in order to bring its industries to economical scales of production. Thus when the government of the Republic of China called upon the late Professor T.C. Liu and me to advise on economic policy in the summer of 1954, we immediately sought to persuade the government to adopt a policy of devaluation coupled with trade liberalization; i.e., to devalue the exchange rate of domestic currency to a realistic level that would ensure the balance-of-trade equilibrium without the need for stringent quantitative restrictions and high protective tariffs.

At that time, sugar and rice together accounted for nearly 80 percent of the value of exports. Taiwan's sugar exports were practically fixed for her by the international sugar agreement that allotted world market share annually for each participating sugar-producing country. Her rice export went exclusively to Japan, and the quantity and price (in terms of U.S. dollars) were fixed each year by direct negotiation between the two governments. Thus these two major exports were confronted with literally zero demand elasticity with respect to the exchange rate. Taiwan appeared to be a typical case of a developing country capable of producing only a few traditional export products facing what appeared to be extremely inelastic world demand. Devaluation, according to then-current wisdom, would only worsen the terms of trade, drive up the domestic prices of imported goods, and thus add fuel to domestic inflation.

Nevertheless, we persisted in arguing that even if the traditional major exports were confronted with foreign demands of little elasticity, there must be hundreds of new products that could be produced with cheap labor supply and readily sold in countries with relatively scarce labor, provided that the relative abundance and cheapness of labor in Taiwan was not artificially covered up by the overvaluation of her currency.

As against the view that devaluation would surely spur domestic inflation, we pointed out that domestic market prices of imported goods are not determined by their landed costs when their supplies are quantitatively restricted. Rather, their market prices tend to be determined by the strength of domestic effective demand and the quantities allowed to enter. With a devaluation and trade liberalization, assuming foreign demand for all potential exports in the aggregate were not inelastic, export proceeds would rise, and hence the quantities of imports permitted could also increase. On the other hand, if imports were allowed to expand *pari passu* with exports after devaluation and liberalization, trade would continue to balance, and there would be no expansion in aggregate effective demand in monetary terms attributable to the devaluation. Thus there is no reason at all why the prices of imported goods should rise if devaluation is coupled with trade liberalization.

Indeed, so long as the implicit tariff on imports implied by the initial quantitative restrictions plus the existing explicit tariff is higher than the so-called "optimum tariff rate"—and there is every reason to believe that they would be higher, since the elasticity of world demand for a small country's exports as a whole is likely to be very elastic, which would imply a very low, if not zero, optimum tariff rate—real income of the country will certainly increase as resources are allocated more efficiently with simultaneous and equal expansion of both exports and imports. Provided that no monetary expansion is inadvertently permitted during the process of resource reallocation, the general price level is more likely to fall than to rise.

Fortunately, our argument slowly and gradually won the approval of the government. The principle of devaluation coupled with liberalization of trade was finally adopted as a conscious policy goal to be achieved gradually in April 1958. In that month, the basic exchange rate was devalued from NT $15.55 to NT $24.58 buying and NT $24.78 selling. What was more significant was that thereafter exporters (except those of sugar, rice, and salt) would be awarded exchange surrender certificates representing the full amount of their export proceeds surrendered to the Bank of Taiwan. They could sell these certificates on the market to importers, who would have to present these certificates in the amount of the foreign exchange they wished to purchase from the Bank of Taiwan for their imports. At the same time, to make the market demand for exchange certificates correctly reflect the market demand for imports, the quota restrictions on all types of permissible imports were boldly removed, although importing what were classified as luxury goods was still forbidden. In general, the existing high tariffs on imports were still maintained, but the 20 percent defense surcharge, which used to be assessed on the basis of the value of imports, was thereafter assessed on the basis of the duty payable. Thus the market-determined price of the certificates would constitute a flexible margin to be added to the fixed basic rate. The resulting effective rate would approach the equilibrium exchange rate under the existing tariff system and adjust automatically to changes in supply and demand conditions.

The same effective rate thus obtained was gradually made applicable to all imports and to most remittance and transfers. The complicated multiple exchange rate system was at last unified. In

August 1959, in compliance with the regulations of the International Monetary Fund (IMF), the Bank of Taiwan stopped separating the effective exchange rate into two components (the basic rate and the price of exchange certificates) and declared that the exchange rate of the new Taiwan yuan was to be NT $38.08 to one U.S. dollar buying, and NT $38.38 selling. This rate was allowed to creep up to NT $40.00 to one U.S. dollar in 1960, where it was pegged until February 1973.

The effect of this policy of devaluation and liberalization on the foreign trade of Taiwan has been truly remarkable, as can be seen from table 1. The devaluations and tax rebate on exports started in 1955 were certainly effective in reviving export trade from its low point of 1954 in spite of the predictions of elasticity pessimists. But it was only in the 1960s, after the exchange rate was linked with the liberalized demand for imports, that the expansion of exports really took off. By 1970, the U.S. dollar value of Taiwan's exports had already increased to U.S. $1,469 million, a 15.3-fold in-

Table 1

Merchandise Trade of the Republic of China (Taiwan)

	Exports (in millions of U.S.$)	Average annual rate of growth of the decade	Imports (in millions of U.S.$)	Average annual rate of growth of the decade	Trade balance (in millions of U.S.$)
1950	93.1		123.9		−30.8
1955	127.1	5.8%	184.7	8.7%	−57.6
1960	164.0		286.5		−122.5
1965	450.8	24.5%	517.2	16.9%	−66.4
1970	1,468.6		1,363.4		105.2
1971	2,047.2		1,754.6		292.6
1972	2,979.3		2,331.9		647.4
1973	4,476.0		3,741.8		766.0
1974	5,592.0		6,422.4		−811.9
1975	5,304.1	29.6%	5,558.6	30.4%	−254.5
1976	7,809.6		7,125.0		699.9
1977	9,517.2		8,316.9		1,214.7
1978	12,602.0		10,367.4		2,234.6
1979	15,828.9		14,421.3		1,407.6
1980	19,575.0		19,428.0		147.0

Source: *Financial Statistics Monthly, Taiwan District, The Republic of China,* The Central Bank of China, various issues.

crease in sixteen years. The annual rate of increase during the 1960s averaged 23.6 percent. The rapid expansion continued in the 1970s so that by 1980, the dollar value of Taiwan's exports reached U.S. $19,575 million, which was more than 200 times that of 1954. The average annual rate of increase during the 1970s was 29.6 percent.

The rapid expansion of exports under trade liberalization and more realistic exchange rate implied that the economy of Taiwan had been enabled to concentrate on industries in which Taiwan could use her resource endowment to the greatest advantage and avoid industries in which she was handicapped. This showed up in the changes in the structure of her exports as well as her industries.

Agricultural products and processed agricultural products together constituted 91.9 percent of the total value of her exports in 1952. By 1970 the combined share of these two groups had dropped to 21.4 percent and by 1980 it was merely 9.2 percent. Conversely, the share of industrial products in exports rose sharply from 8.1 percent in 1952 to 78.6 percent in 1970 and to 90.8 percent in 1980 (table 2).

History shows, then, that for a congested small island with only one-third of its area arable and an overall population density greater than that of the Netherlands, agricultural products certainly offered no clear comparative advantages. Rather its com-

Table 2
Relative Shares of Agricultural and Industrial Products in Exports of Taiwan

	Agricultural products[a]	Industrial products
1951	91.9	8.1
1955	89.6	10.4
1960	67.7	32.3
1965	54.0	46.0
1970	21.4	78.6
1975	16.4	83.6
1980	9.2	90.8

[a]Including processed agricultural products.

Source: *Taiwan Statistical Data Book,* Council for Economic Planning and Development, 1982

parative advantages lay with those industries requiring relatively large amounts of labor, little land space, and moderate amounts of capital to produce. Thus textile products, clothing, shoes, umbrellas, toys, and other products of light industry seemed to suit her endowment conditions nicely at the early stage. The agricultural products that remained on Taiwan's export list had also changed character. Instead of products that required relatively more land to produce, such as rice and sugar, the new agricultural exports tended to be very labor-intensive but relatively land-economizing, such as mushrooms, asparagus, and in later years, eels for Japan and edible snails for France.

Limited Elasticity of World Demand

The apparent ease with which Taiwan had dramatically expanded her exports after devaluation and liberalization soundly refutes the elasticity pessimism that prevailed in the early postwar years. On the other hand, the experience of Taiwan does not really endorse the new fashion among many economists who assume an infinitely elastic world market demand for a small country's "tradable goods." For although Taiwan's total exports expanded by leaps and bounds after devaluation and liberalization, particular items frequently encountered foreign protectionism. The foreign demand curve for each export product would suddenly turn from a nearly horizontal and infinitely elastic curve into a downward vertical curve of zero elasticity. When the competing domestic producers of a foreign country began to feel threatened, they would petition their government to impose quantitative restrictions (sometimes under the euphemism of "voluntary restraint") on the import of the product concerned. In such cases, Taiwan could only try to discover new export markets for that product (only to run into similar quantitative restraints when too many inroads were made into the new markets) or to find new products to produce for export.

This process is well illustrated by the development of both agricultural and manufactured exports of Taiwan. Increasing population density very quickly made rice production for export unprofitable. Instead, Taiwan had developed mushrooms as the new export crop, since they could be produced in stacked layers in small sheds and thus took relatively little land area. This new crop quickly expanded into a major export item worth more than a hundred million dollars a year. However, soon the United States imposed what was called a voluntary restraint on Taiwan's export of mushrooms into the U.S. Taiwan then had to find a new outlet for her mushrooms in the European Common Market, and at the same time develop a new export crop in asparagus. The same story, however, was repeated with asparagus, for very soon the U.S. as well as the Common Market began to impose quantitative restraints on asparagus exported from Taiwan as they did on her mushrooms. Taiwan had therefore constantly to develop new export products and discover new markets, such as eels and onions for the Japanese market and edible snails for the French market.

The expansion of her manufactured exports has followed a similar process. For instance, her textile exports, shoes, umbrellas, television sets, and mechanical and electronic toys have in turn been put under restraints both in the U.S. and in Western European countries. Only by constant development of new export products and the discovery of new markets has Taiwan been able to expand her total exports at such a remarkable rate.

Thus the world demand confronted by a small, developing country for its exportable products is neither as inelastic as assumed by the early elasticity pessimists, nor infinitely elastic as assumed by modern textbook writers on international trade and finance. The aggregate demand curve faced by such a developing country is likely to be highly elastic over a certain range (i.e., to have a nearly horizontal stretch) that terminates abruptly into a vertical bend downward. However, if the entrepreneurs of the country are sufficiently ingenious and resourceful, they will soon discover new products for export or new markets for their old products, and there will be another stretch of nearly horizontal demand curve, which however is likely to end again in a vertical bend downward, and so on. Thus the aggregate world demand curve for the exportables as a whole might be conceived as a sort of step function. When the entrepreneurs of the country are resourceful enough, these horizontal steps may be spaced very closely in the vertical dimension but stretched out rather widely in the horizontal dimension, and the resulting aggregate demand curve may approach a highly elastic smooth curve. If the entrepreneurs of the country are not very resourceful, these steps will be rather steep and rather far apart vertically. The resulting aggregate demand curve would amount to a relatively inelastic curve. Taiwan was very fortunate to be endowed with an ample supply of capable entrepreneurs, but it should be emphasized that proper incentive afforded by realistic exchange rate, which could reward the exporters with the full market equilibrium value of the export proceeds they earned, was also very important. Furthermore, Taiwan's openness towards foreign direct investment and foreign participation in domestic industries was useful, for foreign investors would often bring new ideas about products and have new connections in untapped markets as well.

The profound changes in the composition of exports and the rapid increase in the relative importance of production for export naturally brought about corresponding changes in the structure of Taiwan's economy. In 1951, agricultural output made up 35.5 percent of the gross domestic product while industrial output (including mining, manufacturing, utilities, and construction) was only 23.9 percent. In 1970, the share of agricultural output had already declined to 15.5 percent while that of industrial output had climbed up to 41.3 percent. This trend continued, and in 1980 cultural products composed only 7.7 percent of the GDP while industrial products further rose to a 52.2 percent share (see table 3).

Table 3
Relative Shares of Agricultural and Industrial Products in Gross Domestic Product of Taiwan

	Agricultural	Industrial[a]	Service
	(as percentages of gross domestic product)		
1951	35.5	23.9	43.6
1955	29.2	26.4	44.4
1960	28.7	29.6	41.7
1965	23.7	33.9	42.4
1970	15.5	41.3	43.2
1975	12.8	45.9	41.3
1980	7.7	52.2	40.1

[a]Including agricultural produce processing industries.

Source: *National Income of the Republic of China*, Directorate-General of Budget, Accounting and Statistics, 1982.

This shifting of weight in gross domestic product away from agriculture to industrial production was of immense importance to the steady improvement of the per capita real income and the standard of living of the people of Taiwan. For on a congested island like Taiwan, agriculture is inevitably subject to the relentless law of diminishing returns. The only way to circumvent this law on a large scale is to shift labor away from agriculture, where land is the limiting factor. This reallocation of productive resources from agriculture to industrial production, and the ability to concentrate on those industries in which Taiwan had true comparative advantage, allowed Taiwan not only to support a much larger population (which had grown from 8.13 million in 1952 to 17.81 million in 1980) but also to provide it with a per capita real income five times higher (see table 4).

Interest-Rate Policy and Inflation

The major difficulty of a developing country in its effort to break loose from the poverty trap and to rise in self-sustained growth is generating enough savings, in spite of the existing miserably low income per head, to finance the necessary investment in capital equipment such that productive capital per unit of labor can continously increase even with an expanding population. As Professor W. A. Lewis put it:

Table 4
National Income of Taiwan at Market Prices
(at constant 1976 prices)

	Aggregate national income		Per capita income	
	Amount (NT$ millions)	Index (1976=100)	Amount (NT$)	Index (1976=100)
1952	87,308	13.5	10,222	25.9
1955	112,760	17.5	11,895	30.1
1960	151,718	23.5	13,601	34.5
1965	240,229	37.3	18,582	47.1
1970	387,166	60.1	26,582	67.4
1975	558,598	86.7	34,910	88.5
1980	879,139	136.4	49,832	126.3
1981	918,899	142.6	51,161	129.6

Source: *Taiwan Statistical Data Book,* Council for Economic Planning and Development, Executive Yuan, 1982.

The central problem in the theory of economic growth is to understand the process by which a community is converted from being a 5-percent to 12-percent saver (investor)—with all the changes in attitudes, in institutions and in techniques which accompany this conversion.[1]

Unfortunately, the prevailing academic fashion in monetary theory in the 1950s and 1960s suggested a totally misguided monetary policy, which would discourage rather than promote savings by the public. That is, under the prevailing influence of Keynesian economics, most developing countries had been induced to keep the interest-rate structure of their domestic banking systems at the low conventional levels of developed countries—where the capital supply is more abundant and prices are more stable. Supposedly this policy was necessary for stimulating real investment and growth as well as for preventing the cost-push inflation alleged to ensue from increased interest rates. In fact, such a government-enforced low interest-rate policy in the face of inflationary conditions and great scarcity of capital at home would fuel domestic inflation by creating an enormous excess demand for bank credits, while retarding real capital formation at home. It would discourage the inflow of genuine savings into organized financial intermediaries and encourage the public to hoard precious metals and foreign exchange, or to direct personal investments into real estate or other nonproductive channels.

Taiwan was probably the first among the developing countries boldly to abandon the almost universally approved low-interest policy by raising the interest rate on savings deposits to approximately the prevailing rate of price inflation. In March 1950, a special system of savings deposits, called the Preferential Interest Rate Deposits, (PIRD) was introduced by the Bank of Taiwan, which offered the hitherto unheard of nominal rate of interest of 7 percent per month, which, when compounded monthly as stipulated, would come to a remarkable 125 percent per annum.

The high-interest policy quickly had the desired effect. As the appendix shows, total savings and time deposits rose from a meager NT $6 million, or barely 1.7 percent of the contemporary money supply (currency plus demand deposits) at the end of March 1950, to NT $28 million at the end of June, which was approximately 7 percent of the money supply at that time. Even more remarkable, price inflation was rapidly brought to a halt. Whereas the average monthly rate of price inflation in Taiwan during the first three months of 1950 was as high as 10.3 percent per month, it dropped dramatically to only 0.4 percent in the second quarter. Indeed, after May 1950, prices were actually declining a little. This incredible turnaround happened before the resumption of U.S. aid to Taiwan in July, soon after the outbreak of the Korean War.

Partly encouraged by the immediate success and partly fearing that the 125 percent annual interest rate would be intolerable with stable prices, the government sharply cut the interest rate payable on one-month deposits in July by half, to 3.5 percent per month, and again in October to only 3 percent. The public, taken aback by the abrupt reversal of the government's high-interest policy so soon after its inauguration, reacted by stopping the flow of new savings into the banking system and even started to withdraw its deposits. By the end of December the same year, total savings and time deposits had fallen to only NT $26 million or 4.5 percent of the current money supply. And prices resumed their rapid rise, until in February 1951 they were 65 percent higher than in July 1950, when the first cut in the interest rate was announced.

Alarmed by the prospect of renewed rampant inflation, the monetary authorities were obliged on March 26, 1951, to raise the monthly rate on one-month deposits from 3 percent to 4.2 percent (equivalent to an annual rate of 64 percent). Apparently the public was then sufficiently appeased, and the flow of savings into the banking system resumed at such a spectacular pace that one year later total savings and time deposits had already reached NT $271 million, or 31.2 percent of the contemporary money supply, and six more months later, they rose further to NT $541 million or 56.4 percent of the contemporary money supply. Prices then were once more completely stabilized (see appendix).

Thenceforth, the monetary authorities gingerly lowered the interest rate step by step whenever they felt that price stability warranted it. Owing to the lack of a free money market at that time, however, these successive downward adjustments were guided only by the subjective feelings of the monetary authorities about the public's expectation of future price inflation. Frequently they would overestimate the public's confidence in price stability and its willingness to supply savings to the banking system, and would thus make overly precipitous cuts in the interest rate that would send prices on the upward climb again. However, when the interest rate was raised again prices would once more stabilize as the upward trend of the savings and time deposits in the banking system resumed.

One incident is especially worth noting here. In 1972 and 1973, the worldwide inflation gave Taiwan two successive years of big trade surpluses, amounting to U.S. $647 million and U.S. $766 million, respectively. Since the Central Bank is required to absorb all the surplus supplies of foreign exchange, the domestic money supply increased by 38 percent and then 49 percent in these two years, although the target rate of money supply expansion was often announced to be 20 percent (see table 5). As a result, prices started to rise, first by 7.3 percent in 1972 and then by a further 40.3 percent in 1973.[2] The spectre of inflation was still fresh in the public memory, and the annual rate of increase of savings and time deposits dropped from 40 percent in 1971 to 21.5 percent in 1973. Had no quick action been taken, the rate of increase could readily have turned negative. The monetary authorities finally reacted by raising the interest rates on one-year savings and time deposits from 8.75 percent to 9.5 percent in July 1973, then to 11 percent that October, and again to 15 percent in January 1974 in the hope of arresting the declining tendency of the rate of increase of such deposits.

These efforts finally proved successful. During 1974 aggregate savings and time deposits increased NT $44.9 billion or 37.3 percent over the balance at the end of the preceding year, compared with the increase during 1973 of only NT $20 billion or 21.5 percent. This increment of NT $44.9 billion in savings and time deposits was equal to approximately 50 percent of the total money supply (M_1) in 1974. This, therefore, constituted a major anti-inflationary force that was to be added to that year's big trade deficit of U.S. $811.9 million (equivalent to NT $30.9 billion). The trade deficit was only partly due to the world recession in that year; the government had also relaxed the restrictions on imports of luxury goods, including foreign luxury automobiles, and had encouraged private manufacturing firms to import more raw materials and machinery. These two hefty anti-inflationary forces

Money Supply, Savings and Time Deposits, Interest Rate, and Wholesale Prices

End of period	Money supply (in millions of NT$)	Savings & time deposit (in millions of NT$)	Column 2 as % of column 1	Interest rate on one-year time deposits (annual percentage)	Average rate of price increase over the preceding year (percent)	
1955	2,555	993	38.9	20.98	14.08	
1960	6,037	4,536	75.1	18.43	14.51	
1965	16,194	21,602	133.4	10.80	-4.66	
1970	32,035	60,378	188.5	9.72	2.72	
1971	39,980	79,222	198.2	9.25	0.02	
1972	55,126	101,837	184.7	8.75	7.25	4.45[b]
1973	82,310	120,450	146.3	11.00[a]	40.34	22.86
1974	88,079	165,387	187.8	13.50[a]	14.87	40.58
1975	111,780	212,313	189.9	12.00[a]	-0.60	-5.07
1976	137,560	270,367	196.5	10.75	4.50	2.76
1977	177,575	360,579	203.1	9.50		2.76
1978	238,079	467,950	196.6	9.50		3.54
1979	254,703	514,504	202.4	12.50		13.84
1980	305,444	631,752	206.8	12.50		21.54

Sources: *Financial Statistics Monthly, Taiwan District, The Republic of China*, The Central Bank of China, various issues; *Quarterly Economic Trends, Taiwan Area*, The Republic of China, DGBAS; *Monthly Statistics of the Republic of China*, Directorate-General of Budget, Accounting, and Statistics, various issues.

[a]The interest rate was first raised to 9.5 percent on July 26, 1973, then to 11 percent on October 24, 1973, and finally to 15 percent on January 27, 1974. On September 19, 1974, however, it was lowered to 14 percent on December 13, 1974, to 13.5 percent, on February 22, 1975 to 12.75 percent; and on April 21, 1975, to 12 percent.

[b]The figures in this column are the new revised wholesale price index for the whole island. The figures in the preceding column are presumably for the Taipei area.

were powerful enough to curb increases in the money supply and to bring the increase down to only 7 percent during 1974. Price inflation was promptly reduced to 14.9 percent during 1974 according to the prerevision wholesale price index, and 1975 showed no inflation at all (table 5).

Taiwan's experience repeatedly and convincingly demonstrated that adequate interest rates on savings and time deposits are necessary to attract the public's voluntary savings into the banking system, and that they constitute a significant anti-inflationary instrument. The cost-push inflation theorists were dramatically mistaken in their claim that raising the officially controlled low interest rates would increase domestic inflation.

Savings and "Economic Takeoff"

The relative stability of prices and the fairly attractive interest rates for savings deposits restored and stimulated the traditional thrifty habit of the Chinese people. But additional tax measures were also adopted to encourage savings and investment, such as exempting from personal income tax the interest income from savings and time deposits with maturity terms of two years or more, and exempting from corporation income tax profits that were plowed back for investment. These and other inducements brought about a rapidly enlarged inflow of voluntary savings, which provided noninflationary financing for the domestic investment opportunities created by the new export-encouragement policies. The investments made possible by these noninflationary sources of finance brought about the rapid growth in productivity per worker and hence the growth of per capita real income since 1960. The rapid growth in real income in turn made savings relatively easy and effortless because of the natural tendency for consumption to lag behind rising income. In this way, Taiwan was rapidly converted from a country with a very low propensity to save into a country with a remarkably high saving propensity.

In 1952, only 5.2 percent of national income was saved in Taiwan. In 1963, that figure had risen to 13.2 percent, surpassing both the United Kingdom (9.8 percent) and the United States (9.1 percent). Since 1971, the percentage of national income saved in Taiwan began to surpass even that in Japan, which used to be the highest in the world. In 1978, the percentage saved in Taiwan climbed to as extraordinarily high a level as 35.2 percent, compared with 20 percent in Japan, 8.3 percent in the United Kingdom and 6.5 percent in the United States (table 6).

Taiwan presents an excellent example of W. W. Rostow's "economic takeoff"—which he defines as occurring when an underdeveloped country with a growing population overcomes the tendency for its standard of living to decline on account of the increasing population pressure, and achieves instead rapid self-sustained growth in real income per capita, with or without foreign assistance. The continuous increase in real productive capacity must be achieved with continuous investment in productive capital, financed by savings, as Taiwan's experience shows (table 7). Thus W. A. Lewis once treated a 12 percent or higher propensity to save as the hallmark of success in economic development.[3] However, I have argued elsewhere[4] that the basic condition for economic takeoff is achievement of domestic saving per capita that is more than sufficient to maintain a steady increase in the capital/labor ratio in the face of population increase: the percentage saved out of the net national product should exceed the

Table 6

Net Domestic Saving as Percentage of National Income

	Taiwan	Japan	U.K.	U.S.
1952	5.2	24.1	6.4	10.4
1955	4.9	20.4	9.8	12.2
1960	7.6	27.7	10.9	8.6
1961	8.0	29.9	11.0	8.4
1962	7.6	28.4	9.4	9.0
1963	13.4	26.6	9.8	9.1
1964	16.3	25.2	11.2	9.8
1965	16.5	23.3	12.4	11.5
1970	23.8	30.5	13.6	7.6
1975	25.3	21.4	5.3	3.8
1978	35.2	20.0	8.3	6.5
1979	34.9	—	—	—
1980	32.9	—	—	—

Sources: For Taiwan, *Taiwan Statistical Data Book,* 1981; for other countries, *Yearbook of National Accounts Statistics,* 1979, United Nations.

Table 7
Estimation of the Approximate Year of The Economic Takeoff of Taiwan

	Capital/output ratio $\dfrac{K}{Y}$	Rate of growth of population $\dfrac{\dot{L}}{L}$	Column I · Column II $\dfrac{K}{Y} \cdot \dfrac{\dot{L}}{L}$	Saving/Income ratio $\dfrac{S}{Y}$	Column IV − Column V $\dfrac{S}{Y} - \dfrac{K}{Y} \cdot \dfrac{\dot{L}}{L}$
1952	6.0	3.3	19.8	5.2	14.6
1955	4.8	3.8	18.2	4.9	−13.3
1960	3.7	3.5	13.0	7.6	−5.4
1961	3.6	3.3	11.9	8.0	−3.9
1962	3.4	3.3	11.2	7.6	−3.6
1963	3.2	3.2	10.2	13.4	3.2
1964	2.9	3.1	9.0	16.3	7.3
1965	2.7	3.0	8.1	16.5	8.4
1970	2.2	2.4	5.3	23.8	18.5
1974	2.1	1.8	3.8	31.5	27.7
1978	2.0	1.9	3.8	35.2	31.4

Sources: *Taiwan Statistical Data Book*, Council for Economic Planning and Development, 1981. The ratio (K/Y) is the estimate of Professor R. I. Wu, of the Chung-Hsing University of Taiwan, and myself.

capital/output ratio multiplied by the rate of population growth.[5] This condition for takeoff was far from satisfied before the devaluation and trade liberalization policy was carried out gradually in the late 1950s. When trade liberalization and the consequent export expansion went into full gear, and the sensible interest-rate policy had restored the traditional thrifty habit of the Chinese people, however, the propensity to save in Taiwan went up by leaps and bounds. And in 1963 domestic saving propensity began to exceed the requirement for investments to maintain a constant capital/labor ratio in the face of population growth. Although the excess for that year was at first quite minor (only approximately 3 percent in 1963), the excess grew progressively thereafter. In the 1970s, the saving propensity of Taiwan continued to rise rapidly and climbed well above 20 percent, eventually reaching an incredible 35 percent. This implies that Taiwan is now fully capable of achieving a continuous and fairly satisfactory rate of growth in real income per head even without the assistance of foreign capital.

Before the presumed takeoff year of 1963, Taiwan had to rely very heavily on foreign aid and capital inflow for her capital formation. Until 1962, in fact, aid and capital inflows constituted no less than 30 to 50 percent of gross capital formation (table 8). After 1963, however, there was a sharp decline in foreign capital inflows and transfers, as U.S. aid to Taiwan was rapidly diminishing until its termination in 1965. Fortunately, in 1963 the economy took off and thereafter domestic savings not only successfully

Table 8

Sources of Funds for Gross Domestic Capital Formation in Taiwan

	Gross domestic capital formation	Gross domestic savings	Foreign capital inflow
1952–55	100	59.3	40.7
1956–60	100	60.0	40.0
1961–65	100	85.1	14.9
1966–70	100	95.0	5.0
1971–75	100	97.4	2.6
1976–80	100	106.0	−6.0

Source: *Taiwan Statistical Data Book*, 1981.

322   S. C. TSIANG

filled the gap left by foreign aid but also sustained domestic capital
formation at an increasing rate. After 1975, Taiwan showed signs
of becoming a capital-exporting country.

Income Distribution

One beneficial effect of Taiwan's development strategy is that in
spite of her very rapid rate of industrial growth, income distribution became more equal at least until 1978 (table 9), contrary to
the view of many eminent development economists that there
might be an inevitable trade-off between growth and equity.[6] In
hindsight, it is not difficult to explain this phenomenon of rapid
growth with improved equity, since the twin pillars of Taiwan's
development strategy in the past could both be expected to contribute to the improvement of income distribution in favor of
labor. First, the trade liberalization and export promotion policy,
after proper adjustment of the exchange rate, induced a vast shift
of labor supply from land-intensive agriculture, which inevitably
suffered from diminishing returns because of the limitation of

Table 9
Changes in Income Distribution in Taiwan
Percentage Shares in the Aggregate Income
of the Quintiles of Families

Quintiles of families (from lowest to highest income)	1964	1970	1974	1978	1979
First quintile (lowest income)	7.7	8.4	8.8	8.9	8.6
Second quintile	12.6	13.3	13.5	13.7	13.7
Third quintile	16.6	17.1	17.0	17.5	17.5
Fourth quintile	22.0	22.5	22.1	22.7	22.7
Fifth quintile (highest income)	41.1	38.7	38.6	37.2	37.5
Ratio of income share of the richest to the poorest quintile	5.3	4.6	4.4	4.2	4.4

Source: *Report on the Survey of Personal Income Distribution in Taiwan area, Republic of China (1977),* Directorate-General of Budget, Accounting and Statistics,
Executive Yuan, 1981.

land, towards the new labor-intensive export industries, in which Taiwan obviously had comparative advantages. This big shift of labor supply naturally implied a big net increase in the marginal productivity of labor and hence in the real wage rate.

Second, the abandonment of the artificial, government-enforced low interest-rate policy enabled Taiwan to avoid selecting excessively capital-intensive and labor-saving methods of production, or industries using such methods of production. Many other developing countries had been tempted to adopt these methods and industries by the false cheapness of capital (as well as by considerations of national prestige); their erroneous yet highly popular low-interest policies tended to reduce greatly the number of workers who could be employed productively with a given amount of investment, thus leaving a large portion of the labor force to wallow in the traditional low-productivity employments. In addition, such policies reduced the inflow of savings into financial institutions and thus reduced the supply of noninflationary funds available for investment. By avoiding such common mistakes, Taiwan was able to provide rapidly increasing new employment opportunities to her labor force in her expanding export industries, with resultant rapid increases in the real income of her working class.

In sum, Taiwan's experience of rapid economic growth with equity offers a good example that should stand other developing countries in good stead. It has demonstrated how sustained rapid growth without tears and bloodshed can be achieved in a peaceful and humane way based on sound classical economic principles. Especially for those developing countries that are on the verge of embracing socialist totalitarianism in their desperation with the persistent failure of misguided development policies, the experience of Taiwan may indeed be recommended as a good example of an alternative.

Appendix

Money Supply; Savings, Time, and PIR Deposit; Interest Rates; and Wholesale Prices

End of period	Money supply (in millions of NT$)	Savings, time & PIR deposits[a]	Column 2 as % of Column 1	Monthly interest rate on one-month PIR deposits	Monthly rate of price inflation during the quarter (%)
1950					
March	348	6	1.7	7.00 effective	10.3
June	401	28	7.0	7.00 (Mar 25)	0.4
Sept.	595	36	6.1	3.50 (July 1)	6.0
Dec.	584	26	4.5	3.00 (Oct. 1)	5.4
1951					
March	732	30	4.1	4.20 (Mar. 26)	4.8
June	942	59	6.3	4.20	3.9
Sept.	687	164	23.9	4.20	1.8
Dec.	940	163	17.3	4.20	3.9
1952					
March	867	271	31.2	4.20	2.6
June	942	494	52.4	3.80 (Apr. 29) 3.30 (June 2)	−1.0
Sept.	959	541	56.4	3.00 (July 7) 2.40 (Sept. 8)	−0.4
Dec.	1,336	467	34.9	2.00 (Nov. 30)	0.0

1953					
March	1,074	499	46.5	2.00	1.5
June	1,198	640	53.4	2.00	1.4
Sept.	1,292	671	51.9	1.50 (July 16)	1.6
Dec.	1,683	599	35.6	1.20 (Oct. 10)	0.5
1954					
March	1,622	667	41.1	1.20	0.0
June	1,809	747	41.3	1.20	−1.4
Sept.	1,923	782	40.6	1.00 (July 1)	−0.6
Dec.	2,128	765	35.9	1.00	1.3
1955					
March	2,300	816	35.5	1.00	2.7

[a]Preferential Interest Rate Deposits Scheme was phased out in March 1955. Afterwards the former PIR deposits were merged into ordinary savings deposits and the name was abolished.

Sources: *Financial Statistics Monthly, Taiwan District, The Republic of China,* The Central Bank of China, various issues and *Taiwan Commodity Prices Statistics Monthly,* Bureau of Accounting and Statistics, Taiwan Provincial Government, various issues.

COMMENTS

Lawrence J. Lau

By any yardstick, the performance of Taiwan's economy during the past quarter of a century must be regarded as a great success. Real per capita GDP grew at an average rate of 7 percent per year. The inflation rate was moderate. Income distribution was among the most equitable in the world, and the balance of payments was favorable. The exchange rate was stable and closely approximated the equilibrium rate.* After 1965 Taiwan did not receive any foreign aid, and accumulated only a very small foreign debt.

What is the secret of Taiwan's success? We are very fortunate to have with us today Professor S.C. Tsiang, who, together with the late Professor T.C. Liu, was the principal architect of the economic development strategy pursued by Taiwan. Professor Tsiang has presented an excellent in-depth analysis of the Taiwan experience. In particular, he has identified the two most important components of the Taiwan strategy: first, the liberalization of the international sector, and second, the liberalization of the credit sector. In this case, liberalization of the international sector meant the setting of an exchange rate that approximated the equilibrium exchange rate (thus obviating any discretionary allocation of foreign exchange), and the reduction and elimination of import tariffs and quotas. For a small economy such as Taiwan's, such a liberalization necessarily implied a policy of export promotion rather than import substitution. Liberalization of the credit sector meant the setting of an interest rate that approx-

---

*Since 1960, the new official Taiwan dollar/U.S. dollar exchange rate has been adjusted very infrequently and never has gone below NT $36/U.S.$ or above NT $40/U.S.$. In addition, the black-market exchange rate has seldom deviated more than a couple of percentage points from the official exchange rate except during brief abnormal periods of crises caused by adverse international political developments.

328 LAWRENCE J. LAU

imated the equilibrium rate and, in particular, yielded a positive real rate of return to holders of savings deposits in formal financial institutions. It is of interest to note that both of these measures were diametrically opposed to the twin policies of import substitution and low interest rate that were widely advocated and regularly prescribed by economists to promote economic growth in developing countries in the 1950s and 1960s. Since then, the essential correctness of the Taiwan strategy has been clearly vindicated.

The Taiwan experience should not be regarded as an isolated case. Similar strategies embodying to a greater or lesser degree the liberalization of the international and credit sectors have been pursued in Hong Kong, Singapore, and South Korea. These three economies also have been very successful. Between 1960 and 1980 the real per capita GDPs of these countries grew at an average rate of about 7 percent per year—very impressive indeed.

What can one learn from the experience of Taiwan, Hong Kong, Singapore, and South Korea? Obviously the liberalization of the international and the credit sectors has worked in all these cases—even though the process might be far from complete. The most interesting question, however, is whether the Taiwan strategy is applicable to other economies, especially to those attempting to make a start today. It is beyond the scope of these comments to consider whether a Taiwan-like policy is either necessary or sufficient for a developing country to enter into a period of self-sustaining economic growth. Instead, I shall focus on additional factors and circumstances that were integral to the Taiwan experience.

First, Taiwan, as well as Hong Kong, Singapore, and South Korea, was a small economy as it began its economic-development drive. The domestic market, limited by both the size of the population and the level of disposable income, was by itself too small to permit economies of scale to be exploited effectively. There was also little monopoly power over the commodities being imported and little monopoly power over the commodities being exported. Under these circumstances, the benefits—if any—of restraints on trade (export taxes, import tariffs, quotas) most likely would be very small, and the costs in terms of efficiency losses would be quite substantial. Thus, for similarly situated economies, a

Taiwan-like strategy not only makes sense but may well be the only viable strategy.

Second, Taiwan had the good fortune to be able to achieve a relatively high saving rate at a relatively low level of per capita national income. In 1965, when per capita national income was approximately U.S. $350, the net domestic saving rate as a percentage of national income was 16.5 percent. The saving rate kept rising as national income grew. In the seventies, Taiwan's net domestic saving rate averaged more than 30 percent, whereas the comparable figure for Japan, whose citizens are well known for their high savings, was only around 25 percent; for the U.K. and the U.S. it was less than 10 percent. Professor Tsiang has constructed an elegant model illustrating the critical importance of a sufficiently high saving rate. It is a precondition for self-sustaining economic growth that the net domestic saving rate be high enough to enable the maintenance of capital available per unit of labor in the presence of population growth.

However, a high saving rate alone is not sufficient to guarantee that an economy will take off into self-sustaining growth. Take the case of mainland China. During the period 1960–1980, China's saving rate averaged approximately 30 percent of her national income. The performance of the Chinese economy was nevertheless quite disappointing. A high saving rate only ensures that resources will be available for investment; it does not ensure that the right investments will be made, or that once made, they will be used efficiently.

Third, Taiwan, along with Hong Kong, Singapore, and South Korea, had a substantial pool of labor. The literacy rate was high, and the labor force had both the incentive and the ability to acquire new skills. In addition there was a good supply of entrepreneurs, many of whom were immigrants. The high literacy rate in these countries facilitated the acquisition of new skills by the labor force—crucial for the success of a policy of export promotion. A high literacy rate alone is not sufficient however—witness the case of Jamaica.

The fourth factor, and in my opinion the most important one as far as domestic factors are concerned, is the existence (and continual maintenance) of a stable and competitive free-enterprise environment. The word "competitive" is chosen rather de-

liberately. It is used to signify a low degree of economic con-
centration and government intervention. Compared to Japan and
the United States, economic power in Taiwan is quite diffused, a
fact that also accounts partly for Taiwan's relatively equitable distribution of income. In addition, the labor unions have been far
from being militant. Thus the markets, including labor markets,
are generally quite competitive. Exit and entry are relatively easy
for most industries, and individuals and firms are free to seek
their own self-interests. There is thus a great deal of room for individual initiative motivated by profit. In such an environment,
distortions tend to be minimized, inefficient operations are
naturally weeded out, and "ingenious and resourceful"
entrepreneurs, in Professor Tsiang's words, can take full advantage of the new opportunities created by the liberalization of the
international and credit sectors.

Finally, one must take into account the external environment.
Taiwan and the other three countries got started at a time when
total world trade was growing by leaps and bounds and there was
relatively little protectionist sentiment in developed countries.
During the past two years, however, the growth of world trade has
slowed considerably and protectionist sentiment has gained much
currency. It is not clear whether a Taiwan-like strategy would
work as well today as it once did, as Michael Roemer has pointed
out. I believe, however, that there is always room for the exploitation of comparative advantage, although slower growth in total
world trade will certainly mean slower growth in the exports of
developing countries and correspondingly reduced benefits for a
policy of export promotion.

There are two points on which I do not agree completely with
Professor Tsiang, however. First, I am prepared to accept the
possibility that a comparatively disadvantaged industry
(statistically) may be transformed into a comparatively advan-
taged industry over time, through such effects as learning by
doing and scale expansion. But in this case, some form of *interim*
protection for such an industry—preferably a production subsidy—may well be justifiable. This is the standard "infant industry" argument. The critical qualification, however, is in the adjec-
tive "interim." Any such protective measure must have an explicitly specified time schedule by which it will be phased out.

Second, I think it is useful to distinguish between savings deposits held in formal financial institutions and savings per se. Professor Tsiang had presented convincing evidence that the volume of savings deposits held in financial institutions is extremely sensitive to the rate of interest paid and particularly to whether or not that rate of interest is positive. However, the evidence is not as clear concerning the sensitivity of *total* savings to the rate of interest paid by formal financial institutions, since saving also may be held in informal financial institutions. It is nevertheless true that any reduction in the rate of interest paid by formal financial institutions below the equilibrium rate can only decrease total savings, whether held in formal or informal institutions. Additional efficiency gains also accrue to the economy if the rate of interest paid by the formal financial institutions is equal or close to the equilibrium rate rather than substantially below it; the latter necessitates some form of credit rationing.

12

FRANCISCO GIL DÍAZ

Mexico's Path from Stability to Inflation

Mexico has accomplished a continuous record of economic development and social progress since the 1930s, with some variations in economic performance throughout the period.[1] In the 1940s and early 1950s there was per capita growth, inflation, and instability. From the mid-1950s up to 1971, inflation was controlled and per capita growth improved. Finally, the decade between 1973 and 1982 has witnessed a resumption of inflation, somewhat less growth, the reappearance of oil, and a shaky legacy at the end of the decade for economic and social well-being in the 1980s. Yet despite the ups and downs, one can observe a policy continuum from the early 1940s up to the end of the 1960s.

The late 1920s and the 1930s witnessed the foundation of Mexico's current institutional framework. Confidence in the currency was restored through the 1930s and inflation was gradually controlled in the 1940s and early 1950s, setting the stage for the emergence of a financial system.

The country underwent radical changes in a relatively brief period while experiencing rapid population growth. A revealing index of how fast and far Mexico came out from an almost feudal situation into a modern economy and society is the change that took place in the rural-urban composition of the population.

In 1900 only 12 percent of the population was urban (table 1). Thirty years later the situation had not changed much: 80 percent of the population still lived in the countryside. Furthermore, 66.5 percent lived in communities of fewer than 2,500 inhabitants and agriculture absorbed 69 percent of the labor force. Economic life for these people was circumscribed to self-subsistence with little contact with the rest of the economy or society. By 1940 the situation had changed only slightly, but in twenty more years it was dramatically different.

By 1960 the urban population was close to 40 percent, an important part of the agricultural sector had been modernized and was prosperous and growing, and most economic activities were not only national in scope but intertwined in many ways. The same trend continued up to 1980, when an astounding 60 percent—perhaps too large a share of the population—had been urbanized.

One measure of economic improvement in recent decades is the purchasing power of a monthly minimum wage. Compared with 1950, a worker in 1982 could purchase 4.6 times as many tortillas, 3 times as many beans, 2.7 times as much rice, twice as much milk, 8 times as much bread, 1.63 times as much beef, the same amount of eggs, 4.5 times as many shirts, and almost 10 times as many irons. If quality were taken into account, the comparison would be even more favorable in most cases. Growth has trickled down then, but relative income distribution has remained about the same[2]—a situation perhaps best explained by the vast insufficiency of educational resources, as will be discussed later.

One measure of the success of economic performance is the growth in per capita income (table 2). From 1940 to 1954 per capita income grew at 3 percent per year. These results were improved upon as per capita income grew at 3.3 percent from 1955 to 1972, despite a recession in 1971. Finally, the 1973–82 decade showed the lowest per capita rate of growth of 2.8 percent, even though this was a period of abundant foreign credit and rising oil prices.

Table 1
Rural-Urban Population Structure in Mexico
(millions of persons)

	Total		Urban			Rural		
	Population	Rate of growth	Population	Rate of growth	Share	Population	Rate of growth	Share
1900	13.7	—	1.7	—	12.2	12.0	—	87.8
1930	16.6	0.7	3.3	2.3	19.8	13.3	0.4	80.2
1940	19.7	1.7	4.3	2.8	21.9	15.4	1.5	60.7
1960	35.0	3.1	13.8	6.3	39.3	21.2	1.5	78.1
1980	67.6	3.3	40.7	5.5	60.2	26.9	0.7	39.8

Source: *La Economía Mexicana en Cifras*, Nacional Financiera, Mexico, 1980.

Table 2

Growth in Real Income in Three Key Periods

	Growth in real income	Per capita real growth
1940–1954	5.9	3.0
1955–1972	6.7	3.3
1973–1982	6.8	2.8

Sources: *Producto Interno Bruto y Gasto*, Banco de México, Mexico, 1979; and *Sistema de Cuentas Nacionales de Mexico*, Budget and Programming Secretariat, Mexico, 1980; population data come from *La Economía Mexicana en Cifras*, Nacional Financiera, Mexico, 1980; *Indicadores Económicos*, Banco de México.

The country has come a long way in forty brief years, and its new situation offers opportunities for continued growth and modernization. However, it has also become an increasingly vulnerable and delicate economy, as perhaps all modern industrial-service, world-inserted economies are. Growth and prosperity in the 1970s and in the first two years of the new decade were more fragile than in the past, as the outcome of 1982 has shown.

The situation in Mexico at the end of 1982 was very discouraging. Inflation was close to 100 percent; there was widespread and growing unemployment, falling production levels, an immense public foreign debt, and a lack of confidence and even despair among savers and investors; and a private foreign debt of 20 billion dollars was complicated by a devaluation of 300 percent in the controlled exchange rate. After so many years of fairly continuous growth, a crisis of this magnitude raises many questions.

The case study of Mexico provides an excellent opportunity not only to pose these questions and to examine its economic policy of the past twelve years, but also to compare these last difficult years with periods in which economic policy was more successful. Policymaking in the 1950s and 1960s in Mexico was considered an exemplary model by some countries; it has even been given a name—"stabilizing development," or SD. At the time, we became so conceited and confident about SD's outcome that we developed a theory around it and offered it to others as a possible model.

Everything was not perfect, of course. At the end of the 1960s, poverty and even misery still existed for large numbers of the population. Middle-class discontent had surfaced violently with the 1968 student movement. Even though the so-called SD model was still working, its whole approach was questioned, and—incredible for a politician—the president who took office in December of 1970 was willing to experiment with a new approach, even though the former one was still in effect. Thus, sometime during 1972, economic policy in Mexico underwent a deep transformation.

The new strategy was devised more as a negative reaction to the past than as a coherent set of policies. Moreover, the reaction to past policies was partly framed on a flawed criticism of the SD model, especially of an outline of that model that Finance Secretary Ortiz Mena presented in 1969 in a now-famous monograph.[3] This erroneous diagnosis is as much a result of some misleading information in the Ortiz Mena document as a fault of his critics, who took it at face value. The attempt by Ortiz Mena to rationalize and provide a coherent framework for his policies (he was finance minister for almost twelve continuous years, from 1958 to 1970) helped to legitimize some myths about the epoch that are now considered axiomatic, with no need of verification.

The curious and imaginative name of "stabilizing development" thus became the stamp of a period blamed with failure to achieve a better income distribution. The alleged unchanging—or for some authors worsened—income distribution, was partly blamed on the encouragement believed to have been granted to private capital accumulation. Despite the impotence of recent policies to eradicate the alleged ills of SD, the word "stability" still arouses strong feelings: some almost consider it a dirty word.

By understanding both the strengths and weaknesses of SD, we may get a better grasp of the dilemma facing the Mexican economy today and of the possibilities to return Mexico to a path of renewed economic growth.

Basic Misconceptions about SD

The policy ingredients and objectives singled out for SD by Ortiz Mena are (a) measures to stimulate voluntary savings, through a low inflation rate, a stable exchange rate, positive real interest rates, and low taxes on interest income; (b) taxing to promote the reinvestment of profits (through tax exemption for productive investments); (c) a reduction in the real price of energy and in the prices of other services provided by the public sector; (d) support of agricultural prices to compensate for deteriorating terms of trade; (e) a controlled government deficit, preventing an inordinate expansion of the money supply; (f) import substitution through tariffs and selective licensing, with a bias favoring domestic production of consumer goods.

The above list includes many items indeed, but only a few were truly essential. From this standpoint, the outstanding features of the stabilizing development period were: (a) a low and stable ratio of government deficits to gross domestic product (GDP); (b) a stable ratio of public external debt to GDP; (c) internal inflation comparable to world inflation; (d) positive real returns to savers; and (e) a fixed nominal exchange rate.

But since on balance the period was favorable, it seems that all sorts of policy measures were thrown in by Ortiz Mena to provide an exhaustive and systematic picture of policymaking. Not all that is alleged about the period, however, was as Ortiz Mena or his critics described it; nor were some of the enunciated policies conducive to healthy economic development. Before going into a deeper analysis of what happened, we need to get rid of some basic misconceptions that, because of their political content, helped set the stage for a rejection of the good features of the scheme— throwing out the baby with the bath water, as it were. Take, for instance, the argument that preferred treatment was given to interest income in order to foster savings. While it is true that the nominal income tax on real returns to savers was low throughout most of the period, taxation calculated as the percentage of taxes plus the inflation tax with respect to the gross nominal interest rate was far from minimal. As shown in appendix table A-1, the tax on interest was near or above the maximum marginal personal income tax in twelve out of the seventeen years of the SD period. It exceeded 100 percent even in 1955, when inflation was high while the economy was coming out of the 1954 devaluation, although it never reached the consistently excessive level of taxation evidenced in the period between 1973 and 1982.

Another assertion with high political content is that private investment had been subsidized. Actually, corporate income taxes went steadily up from 1.16 percent of GDP in 1954 to 2 percent of

GDP in 1970. With 1971 being a recession year, the ratio to GDP of the corporate income tax fell below 2 percent, but the it quickly went back to normal.

How can a rise of 72 percent in real terms in corporate income tax collections and of 168 percent in real terms in personal income taxes from 1954 to 1971 be regarded as subsidizing? In 1972 Mexico, with corporate income tax receipts of 2 percent of GDP, exceeded in this regard such countries as Belgium (0.9), Chile (1.2), Germany (1.0), Sweden (0.5), and Switzerland (0.5).[4] It fell short, but not by much, of the fractions registered by Japan (3.2), the U.K. (2.5), and the U.S. (3.1).

And what about the argument that agricultural prices had to be supported to compensate for deteriorating terms of trade? Take the 1960s, to which the Ortiz Mena document refers. From 1960 to 1965, product prices rose at an annual rate of 4 percent and input prices rose at 1.7 percent per year. From 1966 to 1970, input prices grew at 1 percent per year and output prices at 0.3 percent— hardly a devastating trend that needed to be compensated for with support mechanisms. But artificial prices did create some important distortions, discriminating against exports, reducing the overall value of agricultural production, and inducing a less labor-intensive structure of production.[5]

Mexico's overall terms of trade show a remarkable and continuous decrease over the 1950–71 period, with the index going from 147 in 1950 to 100 in 1960. Despite this, and contrary to the folklore of development economics, real per capita income increased. From 1960 to 1970 the terms of trade improved slightly, reaching 110 in 1970, and thereafter they improved considerably up to 1980, when the index attained 160. What then were the true rights and wrongs of SD for the extended period from 1955 to 1972? To better understand these years, it will prove useful to look briefly at policies immediately preceding SD.

One of the most striking features of government policy in the 1940s was the almost continuous reduction of foreign public debt as a proportion of GDP (table 3). Because of previous debt accumulation and default, foreign public debt in 1939 had reached an incredible 46 percent of GDP. Through some repayments (negative net borrowing), it was kept at basically the same amount (valued in current dollars) throughout the 1940s up to the

Table 3
Public External Debt
(millions of dollars)

	Debt	Debt[a]/GDP ratio		Debt	Debt[a]/GDP ratio
1938	652.5	43.2	1971	4,673.3	12.6
1939	650.3	46.0	1972	4,827.5	11.3
1940	645.6	44.8	1973	6,455.3	12.4
1945	611.2	15.3	1974	9,380.3	13.8
1950	647.7	14.0	1975	13,711.5	16.5
1955	733.3	10.8	1976	18,852.7	22.5
1960	1,251.6	10.4	1977	21,840.0	28.3
1965	2,192.1	10.9	1978	24,428.8	25.3
1966	2,427.8	10.8	1979	27,763.8	21.9
1967	2,966.5	12.1	1980	31,873.8	18.2
1968	3,337.6	12.3	1981	50,160.8	22.2
1969	3,818.6	12.7	1982	55,798.9	36.5
1970	4,262.0	12.7			

[a]In order to obtain a long series of public external debt, balance-of-payments flows of net borrowing were accumulated to or subtracted from a base debt for 1970, taken from the Ministry of Finance. This indirect method results in figures slightly different from the official ones, which are available for only a few years. The differences are less than 10 percent.

Source: Estadísticas Históricas de Balanza de Pagos, Banco de México, Mexico, 1981; *La Economía Mexicana en Cifras*, Nacional Financiera, Mexico, 1980.

beginning of the 1960s, when it reached a manageable 11 percent of GDP.

Active foreign borrowing reappeared in 1955. However, as the economy kept growing, the proportion of foreign public debt to GDP was sustained at a steady 11 to 12 percent of GDP. Use of foreign savings was thus a fairly constant and reasonable proportion of GDP. Basically, this was accomplished through very able handling of the public finances. In table 4, we see the federal government generating a surplus every year from 1935 through 1952. Deficit spending first emerged in 1953, but it remained very moderate up to 1971.

If private savings and investment behave in a stable manner, the deficit in the current account of the balance of payments should reflect the government budget deficit. Prudent aggregate

Table 4
Federal Government Revenue, Spending, and Deficit
(as percentage of GDP)[a]

	Revenue a	Spending b	Deficit b−a		Revenue a	Spending b	Deficit b−a
1935	10.1	7.5	−2.6	1964	8.0	10.0	2.0
1936	7.6	6.6	−1.0	1965	8.7	10.4	1.7
1940	7.7	6.7	−1.0	1966	8.7	9.6	0.9
1945	7.3	5.4	−1.9	1967	8.9	10.6	1.7
1949	11.1	8.5	−2.6	1968	9.4	10.4	1.0
1950	8.9	7.8	−1.1	1969	9.5	10.8	1.3
1951	9.5	7.0	−2.5	1970	9.6	11.6	2.0
1952	9.8	8.2	−1.6	1971	9.4	10.1	0.7
1953	8.4	9.2	0.8	1972	9.7	12.5	2.8
1954	9.3	10.5	1.2	1973	10.2	13.4	3.2
1955	9.3	9.5	−0.2	1974	10.5	13.7	3.2
1956	9.3	9.4	0.1	1975	12.3	16.5	4.2
1957	8.4	9.2	0.8	1976	12.6	17.4	4.8
1958	9.3	9.9	0.6	1977	13.2	16.7	3.5
1959	7.9	8.6	0.7	1978	13.8	16.8	3.0
1960	8.5	10.2	1.7	1979	14.3	17.4	3.1
1961	7.5	9.1	1.6	1980	17.0	20.0	3.0
1962	7.9	9.4	1.5	1981	17.1	23.8	6.7
1963	8.4	10.1	1.7	1982	17.9	30.4	12.5

[a]In tables 4, A-4, A-5, the figures used for GDP were calculated applying the growth rate of the new GDP series calculated by the Budget Department to the Banco de México figure for 1970. Figures are rounded.

Source: *Estadísticas de Finanzas Públicas,* Ministry of Finance, Mexico, 1981.

demand management and a fairly constant real exchange rate kept the deficit on current account at a moderate fraction of GDP, averaging only 2.76 percent of GDP during this period, and rarely reaching a figure as high as 4 percent. This combination of policies helps to explain the good macroeconomic performance of SD.

Relative Price Policies during SD

One of the policies described by Ortiz Mena that data confirm as having been implemented is that of lowering the relative prices of energy inputs and other goods supplied by the public sector. The relative price of electricity, rail transportation, and petroleum products gradually decreased throughout the period; however, the finances of the public sector did not deteriorate, since total government expenditures were kept under control.

But the secular deterioration of the income of these firms together with a constant share in the ratio of government spending to GDP meant that debt was increasingly contracted to finance growing current government expenditures, which crowded out government investment. This gradual erosion in the provision of public capital would prove expensive in the long run, as declining educational performance and agricultural production later showed.

In figure 1, where relative price indices of electricity, gasoline, and petroleum are plotted, only industrial electricity holds its own. Petroleum products other than gasoline start a secular decline in 1959, while the decline of gasoline prices starts in 1960 and that of household electricity in 1963. Even though this policy did not become an important source of budget deficits or credit expansion during SD, it was the start of a very serious future weakening of public finances. The failure to recover costs through adequate pricing, to maintain real prices, or, in some cases, to reflect international prices became gradually entrenched as a political given.

Some important commodity prices were also fixed in nominal terms, driving out marginal private producers and eventually intramarginal ones as well. This drove the government first into supporting faltering firms with credit supplied by public banks, and eventually into taking them over as they went under. A classic case was that of the sugar industry, which by the end of the SD period was practically state-owned. As bad management and corruption became endemic, production levels fell. Despite massive transfusions of cash, Mexico went on to become an importer of sugar, having previously been an important exporter. These distortions became even more acute after SD. The policy of fixing nominal prices for as long as possible had been set, but creeping inflation made the cost much higher.

Another important matter related to price-fixing is the efficient allocation of investment resources when the prices of important energy sources are distorted. Under SD, the distortion was not so severe. However, even when real prices are drastically reduced— as they generally were in the latter decade, and even more so

Figure 1

Wholesale Relative Price Indexes

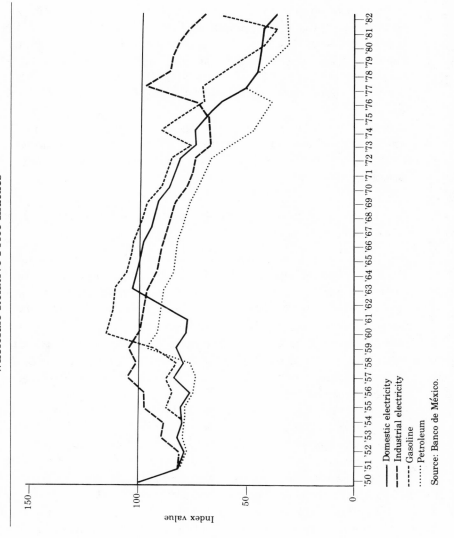

Source: Banco de México.

under some regional development schemes adopted in the late 1970s—the question remains of how permanent private investors expect the subsidy to be.

If private investment is promoted through cash bonuses or faster depreciation, the investors (or landowners) will take advantage immediately. But when the outcome depends on an energy input price being kept artificially low for many years, a high risk is involved that may render the subsidy ineffective. To this extent the distortive consequences of the subsidies may not have been too serious.

Price distortions are important and have many dimensions. They were perhaps the gravest venial sin of SD, becoming a mortal one later on. The seed had been planted, and it would germinate ferociously when inflation set in.

Exchange Rate and Budgetary Policies, Balance of Payments

The exchange-rate experience of Mexico in this century has been rich indeed. There was the revolutionary period that destroyed the flimsy confidence the public had begun to acquire regarding paper money. Eventually the exchange rate was set in terms of gold, but silver coins were the main medium of exchange and fluctuated with regard to gold. This peculiar situation, which prevailed from the mid-1920s up to the early 1930s, has been likened to a flexible exchange rate because of imperfect international arbitrage on silver coins.[6]

At any rate, Mexican financial authorities realized early that fluctuating exchange rates, free convertibility, and the convenience of seigniorage from paper money did not go well together. An attempt in 1930 to establish exchange controls failed quickly and completely;[7] the failure was immediately recognized, however, and the controls were eliminated.

A fixed nominal exchange-rate regime was a logical answer for a country of a relatively small size neighboring the most important currency area in the world—that of the U.S. dollar. How else could demand for a national paper currency be maintained? Mexican authorities eventually realized this and started to set a nominally fixed price for the U.S. dollar. After intermittent devaluations, they eventually succeeded. The peso-dollar nominal rate changed every year from 1925 to 1934. In the 1930s, however, authorities fixed a rate and were able to keep it for a little over seven years. The start of the 1950s brought a renewed attempt at fixing it, with only one interruption in 1954; after which the nominal rate was again fixed, this time to last up to 1976. With the sole interruption of 1954, then, we have a fixed nominal rate going from the 1950s through the 1960s and halfway through the 1970s.

One approach to the nominal exchange rate is to regard it as something to be modified, watching constantly the relation between domestic and world prices and preventing the real exchange from becoming overvalued. The difficulty with this method is to select the appropriate price indices and to value adequately relative productivity changes among different countries. This is the usual problem associated with any situation in which a policymaker simulates the working of the market. If he fails, he will have found the surest and fastest road to perdition.

If a mistake is made and the exchange rate becomes permanently undervalued, the outcome will resemble what happens when monetary policy aims to hold real interest rates—or real wages, or unemployment—below their equilibrium market-clearing level: hyperinflation. An undervalued exchange rate will raise the internal price level above whatever trend it was following as a result of other pressures. Such a rise in domestic prices will signal authorities (wrongly) that the exchange rate is becoming undervalued, and if they follow the rule of keeping it constant in real terms, they will react by devaluing it still more to prevent it (in their view) from becoming undervalued. The additional devaluation will generate more price increases that in turn will provoke another devaluation. This process can be seen as conducive to hyperinflation if a fixed real exchange rate is truly maintained.

A fixed nominal exchange rate may work because, even if the nominal rate is set by the authorities, the real rate will be determined by market forces. If external inflation begins to rise above domestic inflation, it will eventually seep into the country. If domestic inflation is higher, it will not remain so for a long time. Higher internal prices will induce a lower rate of increase of domestic aggregate demand through a flow of international currency reserves out of the country.

The automatic mechanism can be short-circuited temporarily if the government keeps on stimulating aggregate demand, if it has sufficient international credit and/or foreign currency reserves. During most of SD, care was taken to prevent the creation of domestic credit from getting out of hand. But it will be seen that under a fixed nominal exchange rate, even when credit undergoes a strong expansion, there is not as much room as some might believe for internal prices to get out of line. Tables 5 and A-2 are quite revealing in this respect. They show the calculation of a real exchange rate for Mexico using a trade-weighted method.[8]

The figures in table 5 and A-2 show that the index was 100 in 1953. The budget deficit had been rising sharply after 1951, and the current account deficit had risen strongly even in 1951 and had remained high. Appendix table A-3 shows a longer history of trade deficits. Looking at the "usual computation" column, we can see that the current account deficit may have appeared quite large for the years 1951 to 1954, since the 1948 and 1949 devaluations were made to correct a current account deficit of 3.9 percent of GDP in 1946 and 1947.

These deficits may have loomed large in the minds of the public and policymakers after years in which the current account had balanced on the average. They again must have seemed substantial in the early 1950s, hitting 4.3, 3.4, 3.7, and 3.7 percent of GDP from 1951 to 1954. Perhaps because of these deficits—despite the fact that the parity index appeared to be in equilibrium—the devaluation was undertaken. Another concurrent reason for the devaluation may have been the rapid rise in the budget deficit, which went from a surplus of 2.5 percent of GDP in 1951, to a surplus of only 1.6 percent in 1952, to a deficit of 0.8 percent in 1953, and to a deficit of 1.2 percent in 1954 (table 4). The era of budget surpluses had ended, and one of moderate manageable deficits was about to start.

The real exchange rate shows an impressive central tendency. After the 1954 devaluation, the real exchange rate took about ten years to return to parity. It did so around 1963, when it started gradually to become overvalued, only to come back to parity again in 1973, to take off again, and to reach 112.2 in August of 1976, before the September 1 devaluation. Again, in 1981 it showed a substantial margin of overvaluation, which led to the dramatic

Table 5
Parity Index for the Peso

	Parity index		Parity index
1948	125.5	1966	100.6
1949	104.2	1967	103.4
1950	86.5	1968	104.1
1951	95.0	1969	103.1
1952	100.0	1970	104.6
1953	100.0	1971	104.1
1954	84.4	1972	100.2
1955	85.7	1973	100.0
1956	86.8	1974	102.7
1957	88.1	1975	105.4
1958	91.9	1976	99.7
1959	92.7	1977	90.3
1960	96.9	1978	94.0
1961	97.5	1979	98.1
1962	99.0	1980	102.8
1963	99.1	1981	114.8
1964	102.6	1982	84.9
1965	102.0		

Source: *International Financial Statistics,* International Monetary Fund, Data Resources files.

changes in the nominal exchange rate that occurred in 1982. This took the nominal exchange rate from 26.22 pesos per dollar on January 1 to 150 on the free market at the end of 1982.

Table A-3 shows a closer look at the recent devaluations, revealing some interesting information. The current account deficit of the balance of payments is presented as usual, but it is also corrected for inflation. In an inflationary environment, nominal interest rates rise, as they did worldwide with the onset of global inflation in the 1970s. However, the higher interest rates are misnamed as such, and some inflationary accounting reclassification becomes necessary.[9]

The correction on the current account is done in the third and last columns of table A-3. Looking at the figures for the 1970s, the correction on interest payments seems to put numbers into a better perspective; 1971 and 1973 do not look so bad anymore. But it is beyond doubt that the current account worsened significantly in 1974 and 1975, leading to the 1976 devaluation.

The differences between the usual and the corrected figures are more striking for the second half of the 1970s and the 1980s. Apparently high current deficits in 1978, 1979, and 1980 appear significantly less so when properly adjusted for real interest payments; however, 1981, which looks similar to the previous years when uncorrected, actually shows a dramatic worsening when the corrected deficit of 5.2 percent of GDP is compared with the 3.9 figure for the previous year, thus leading again to the devaluations of 1982.

Aside from the convenience of having an appropriate definition of interest in the national accounts, it seems that in the case of Mexico the reclassification allows as well for a better interpretation of the facts.

The parity index and the adjusted current account move contemporaneously to suggest that the prevailing nominal exchange rate may no longer be one of equilibrium. The reason in this case is the destabilizing force of the basic source of disequilibrium. For the period concerned, this force was the pressure of the budget on aggregate demand, and therefore on the prices of nontradeables.

Since the increase in the budget over the long term can be misleading when the size of the public sector is rising, use will also be made of the government's deficit taken by itself, of the ratio of public expenditures to GDP, of the behavior of revenues, and, for the latter years, of the role of Pemex, the government oil monopoly. (It would have been desirable to use a single concept such as the growth and allocation of total credit to both the private and public sectors, but the breakdown is available for only a few recent years.)

It was previously seen how, after the surpluses of the 1940s and early 1950s, the subsequent government deficit did not go above 2 percent of GDP until 1972, and has not come down since (table 4). The year 1972 shows a striking rise in this figure—an increase of 300 percent from 0.7 tercent of GDP. The deficit rises slightly more in 1973 and 1974, goes up again by 31 percent in 1975, and then rises slightly more in 1976. From this evidence, it could be argued that instead of 1973, 1972 should be the departing point for the new strategy. But after so many years of stability, an unexpected and drastic change in economic policy takes some time to modify expectations and therefore to produce real effects.

Given such rises in the public deficit and in public expenditures, it is not surprising that the prices of nontradeables eventually rose, leading to an overvalued exchange rate in 1975 and 1976 (up to the devaluation) when the 12.5-pesos-per-dollar exchange rate was finally abandoned.

Essentially the same story is told by the public-sector deficit (appendix table A-4), although in this case the rise in the deficit is more dramatic in 1975, going up 63 percent from 4.9 to 8 percent of GDP. Despite significant world inflation in the first part of the 1970s, the peso-dollar exchange rate finally became significantly overvalued after twenty-two years of holding its own.

To see why the real exchange rate so quickly returned to parity after the substantial 1976 devaluation, it is helpful to look at the path followed by government income and expenditures. Despite common notions about the subject, the public deficit did not rise significantly during most of the López Portillo administration, which began in December 1976. The usual public deficit computation shows an important drop in the public deficit after 1976, from 7.6 percent to 5 percent of GDP in table A-4. Actually, the decline is more striking if one looks at the inflation-adjusted figures in appendix table A-5. The inflation adjustment follows the procedure explained above for the current account of the balance of payments, since higher nominal interest rates due to inflation are not an increase in current government expenditures, but a capital amortization.

The adjusted figure in table A-5 provides a better overall view of the historical sequence of deficits and also of the close coincidence between sharp rises in properly measured public deficits and economic crises. The series of the total adjusted deficit also shows a clear pattern of large deficits from 1972 onward, an important increase of 146 percent in the deficit in 1972, and a sharper rise (79 percent) than the one shown by the other series (63 percent) in 1975. It also shows much more strikingly the important reduction in the deficit achieved from 1977 through 1980. This reduction, albeit to a still high level, permitted an internal rate of inflation within world bounds, as the parity index in tables 5 and A-2 show. However, the deficit was still high by historical standards, and it kept up the pressure on aggregate demand.

Government expenditures had kept a very fast pace, as had private investment and consumption. The only reason the adjusted public deficit showed some improvement was the sharp rise in income from oil exports and prices.

Table A-4 shows how external public revenue (mainly oil exports) reached 9.1 percent of GDP in 1980 from a level of only 1 percent in 1975. This same table provides an interesting separation of public income and expenditures, according to whether they originate in the country (revenues) or spill out (expenditures). This separation was important during the oil-exporting years because a large chunk of oil export revenue was not converted into aggregate demand within the country, but rather went out as the import content of petroleum-related expenditures; oil-refining, exploration, and exploitation rose significantly with the discoveries of the new reserves announced at the end of 1976. Even adjusting for these effects, however, the additional pressure on local resources brought about by larger deficits was significant when the crisis erupted.

Up to and including 1977, expenditures by the public sector outside the country had almost always exceeded exports channeled through the public sector. In 1978 the two concepts became equal and the internal and total deficits coincided. Thereafter, the expansion in imports—though substantial—has been unable to match the rise in foreign income that has gone mainly to finance a sustained upward trend in internal expenditures. By 1981 these were about double the amount they averaged during SD. Nor can the rise in expenditures be ascribed totally to oil expansion. As table 6 shows, oil-spending went up only from 4.66 percent of GDP in 1976 to 10.56 percent in 1981, as compared with a rise in total public spending from 32.8 to 43.7 percent of GDP.

Perhaps a brief summary is in order, since so many tables and classifications have been combined to describe events in the 1970s. First of all, the adjusted public deficit became entrenched at much higher levels in the 1977–80 period than during SD. Second, the 1976–80 levels of the adjusted public deficit were significantly lower than during the former administration (1972–76), so that some effort was made to correct public finances. However, once the oil effect is taken away, the picture is not so favorable for the latter years, even after adjusting interest expenditures for inflation, because the adjusted internal deficit is seen to emerge

Table 6
Income and Expenses of Pemex
(as percentage of GDP)

	Total income	Total expenditures	Surplus or deficit (−)
1965	3.44	3.14	0.30
1970	3.29	3.21	0.08
1971	3.19	3.45	−0.26
1972	3.06	3.29	−0.23
1973	2.87	3.40	−0.53
1974	3.74	4.03	−0.29
1975	3.53	5.16	−1.63
1976	3.80	4.66	−0.86
1977	4.96	5.97	−1.01
1978	5.12	6.63	−1.51
1979	6.44	7.76	−1.32
1980	9.04	10.52	−1.48
1981	8.31	10.56	−2.25

Source: *Estadísticas de Finanzas Públicas,* Ministry of Finance, Mexico, 1981. Data for 1981 from *"Memorias de Labores 1981,"* Petroleos Mexicanos, Mexico, 1981.

again in 1979 and 1980, with ratios to GDP of 4.5 and 6.2, respectively. Third, everything fell apart in 1981 when, whatever the definition or explanation, there was an astounding surge in the public deficit.

Everything combined in 1981 to explode the deficit. Total expenditures went from an already high level of 30.3 percent of GDP in 1980 to the still higher level of 37.7 percent. External revenue dropped from 9.1 to 7 percent of GDP because Pemex was forced by the government to price itself out of the world market, with the result that oil exports took a nose dive. Revenue from internal sources fell from 24 to 21.5 percent of GDP, mainly because the real price of public sector goods and services did not keep up with rising domestic inflation, and because tax revenues went down about 1 percentage point of GDP as a result of exempting all food products (starting January 1) from the value-added tax.

As has already been mentioned, the exchange rate during the year became substantially overvalued, with the parity index hitting 114.8, a level it had not reached since 1948. The corrected balance-of-payments deficit went up by 33 percent to its second highest historical level of 5.2 percent of GDP (the highest was in 1975, when it reached 5.4 percent of GDP).

The ratio of public debt to GDP, which had been decreasing since its peak of 28.3 percent in 1977, rose sharply again to 22.2 percent in 1981 from the 1980 level of 18.2 percent. In 1981, the keg had been filled with powder and the fuse had been set; it was to be lighted in 1982. Notwithstanding this conglomerate of un-favorable events was compounded by a world recession, 1982 began with still more expenditures, lesser revenues, and a fixed nominal exchange rate. Miraculously, the exchange rate had not exploded in 1981, but it did in 1982 and with a big bang, increasing sixfold within the year.

Public policies had without question been setting up such a scenario since the 1970s and, in some cases, even before with the secular weakening of public prices. However, there is no denying that private investment also played a role. After the reduced rate of growth induced by the corrective measures that followed the 1976 devaluation, private investment began to surge in the second half of 1977. It did so with a vengeance. It grew so fast that private firms went far beyond the means of the Mexican financial system to provide the resources.

The oil boom persuaded international bankers of the firms' ability to pay. Unfortunately, expectations were not realistic on the average. Entrepreneurs proceeded as if the cost of capital were limited to the interest rate on dollar loans, without creating a reserve to cover a possible devaluation of the peso.[10] This potential reserve was considered by many firms as a normal profit to be in-vested, with some additional foreign currency leverage if possible.

It could be argued that these firms incurred loans from the devaluation because there was no active futures market in foreign currencies to allow them to hedge their debts. But such an argu-ment would be incorrect, since the Central Bank had, since 1977, allowed any taker willing to pay the prevailing peso interest rates to convert dollar debts into peso debts.[11] Few took the opportunity; most preferred the gamble, and most of the private sector ended 1982 in a poor financial situation.

To end this section, a closer look at the final year of this difficult decade is warranted. At the beginning of 1982 the pressures on the peso intensified. International oil markets were weak, dollar interest rates remained extremely high, and the U.S.—Mexico's principal trading partner—had not come out of its prolonged recession. By February, capital flight reached massive proportions. These developments led to the floating of the peso. On February 18 the exchange rate was depreciated by 57 percent, reaching 45 pesos to the dollar.

Immediately after the fall of the peso, a cut of 3 percent in the federal budget was announced, and import tariffs for some 1,500 items were reduced. At the same time, more flexible interest-rate and exchange-rate policies were adopted in an attempt to stop capital flight and the dollarization of the system. The program almost succeeded. Dollarization started to reverse itself and the program seemed credible until a sudden, unexpected, and large wage increase (30 percent) was granted to most workers. The new wage, the impact of the new exchange rate on dollar-linked expenditures, and reduced fiscal revenue as a result of the weakening economic situation again pressured the budget deficit upward.

Expectations of an even higher rate of inflation that would bring about further devaluations of the peso were reinforced. Firms began to face increasing difficulties in obtaining fresh foreign credits, as well as in rolling over existing debt, adding to the serious lack of foreign exchange.

In view of the erosion of the country's foreign currency reserves, and to seek a reduction in inflationary pressures, a two-tier exchange system was adopted on August 5. The system established a preferential rate of 49.13 pesos to the dollar, to be used in transactions related to debt-servicing and to high-priority imports. A second exchange rate to be determined by market forces would apply to all other transactions. Inflationary pressures were certainly not abated through this measure and the dual exchange rate led the public to expect, correctly as it turned out, the likelihood of exchange controls, thus precipitating additional pressures on international reserves.

On August 13 dollar-denominated accounts in Mexican banks —the so-called "Mexican dollars," which had reached $12 million —were made payable only in pesos in order to eliminate the risk of additional transfers of foreign currency abroad. On the same day, the foreign exchange market was temporarily closed and a 90-day extension of public external payments on the principal of the public debt was obtained while negotiations with the International Monetary Fund got under way. After transactions in foreign currency were suspended for six days, they were resumed with a 69.50-peso-to-dollar rate for Mex-dollars, and a free-market rate that fluctuated between 100 and 120 pesos to the dollar.

In September Mexican private commercial banks were expropriated and, for the first time in Mexico's modern history, exchange controls were established. Immediately afterwards, a peso market developed abroad. Most of the private-sector foreign currency receipts and purchases were channeled through this market, making the lack of foreign capital for imports and debt-servicing even more serious. Capital flight became more acute, taking the form of a lack of sale of dollars by private exporters. Imports were financed through a sharp increase in suppliers' credits and by drawing on dollar deposits abroad. The reason foreign creditors were willing to increase their exposure was the imminence of a new government in December of 1982.

Part of the sad outcome of 1982 has already been mentioned in the introduction. Total output fell one-half of a percentage point, the budget deficit reached 19 percent of GDP (its highest historical level),[12] unemployment was rampant and output levels were declining in the last third of the year, and the inflation rate reached 238 percent, judging by the 10.7 percent monthly change in the December increase in the Consumer Price Index. The lesson from 1982 is perhaps that it should be viewed not in isolation, but as the culminating year of a ten-year process that dates from the start of 1973.

Public Pricing

It is truly striking, though perhaps not surprising, that the bulk of present problems could have been considerably mitigated had pricing policies for government-provided goods and services—so proudly announced as a pillar of SD—not been so consistently followed in the last decade.

A few comments have already been made concerning the distortions introduced in private and public decisions because of the downward bias the public ownership of firms introduced in their prices. Later on we shall advance some hypotheses on the "why" of their behavior; for now, let us consider the budgetary consequences of their income policies.

A numerical exercise was performed to adjust the figures of oil, electricity, and railway firms from 1965 up to 1980 to calculate the subsidies implicit in their pricing policies. In the case of oil products, the average U.S. retail price is used as the relevant benchmark. For the electric and railway firms, the only adjustment to their actual prices is to add on to them the cost of capital. The results of these adjustments appear in appendix table A-6. Column (a) shows the additional income that would have been provided had actual cost-pricing policies been followed. Simple zero elasticity of demand was assumed in making calculations. Revenue would not have been as high had the quantity demanded been lower as a consequence of higher prices, but expenditures incurred to provide an increased distorted demand would also have been lower. In the case of oil, higher internal prices would have provided more revenues than those implied by zero demand elasticity, since excess supplies could have been exported at world prices.

Higher revenues also would have meant lower interest payments on the marginal external public debt. This calculation is shown in columns (b) and (c). The lower interest expenditures would have reduced the deficit during the period in which the public price is assumed to be increased and in subsequent periods as well, due to the lower foreign public debt carried over.

The reduction in the deficit in columns (a) and (c) is shown in column (e). Finally the actual deficit is corrected, and the result appears in column (f). Although this estimate is on the low side because many other public services are left out of the calculations, the results are impressive. In fact, with the exception of 1975 and 1976, every year would have shown a budget surplus had adequate pricing policies been followed. And as column (f) shows, the surpluses would by no means have been marginal, reaching as much as or more than 3 percent of GDP in some years.

For a double check on the argument, see the available subindexes of the wholesale price index (figure 1). The relative price of gasoline can be seen reaching its peak in 1960 and going steadily down thereafter, with a few discontinuous jumps hardly denting the overall trend. The same basic story is told by the price of home electricity and the prices of petroleum products. Such disastrous pricing policies by government-owned firms may have been caused by political resistance, or they may have come simply from fear of making continual price adjustments, or from the way public firm managers view their roles. In any case there can be little doubt that the policies actually pursued involved exchanging successive short-run postponements for enormous long-run costs.

In Mexico most of the investment of public firms was financed by foreign debt, and these firms view their cost of capital as, at most, the dollar interest rate, since the government has absorbed foreign exchange losses. But that is not all. No effort is made to impute depreciation and interest user charges on the net stock of capital, leading them into larger and larger appropriations of public funds. The ill consequences of these policies go beyond insufficient revenues and distorted consumer and investment decisions; they affect as well the optimal labor-capital combination as seen by the managers of these firms, who tend to prefer capital over labor inputs.[13]

Financial Intermediation

Perhaps one of the significant achievements of SD was the creation of a financial market. Certainly, it was desirable to have a legal framework conducive to the development of financial institutions and to the gradual creation of stable economic expectations, which induced the trust of economic agents. But as will be seen, the additional necessary ingredient, facilitated by low inflation, was positive real interest rates.

As happens with most good things, it took a long continuous effort to get financial intermediation to a reasonable level, though the change was modest by international standards. By the end of the unstable period in 1954, the ratio of financial intermediation to GDP was a meager 9.9 percent (table 7). This ratio started to increase in 1955 and from then on it went up almost every year, until it reached its maximum historical level in 1972 at 32.5 percent —a little over three times its 1954 value.

Financial intermediation has been likened to saving, but it is more related to efficient asset transactions or to the best channeling of savings to their most productive users and uses. It performs

Table 7

National Currency Financial Intermediation Coefficient and the Real Interest Rate

(as percentage of GDP)

	Financial intermediation[b]	Real interest rate[c]
1950	12.2	−1.0
1951	11.0	−12.7
1952	9.9	4.4
1953	11.4	10.4
1954	9.9	−1.1
1955	10.5	−4.7
1956−1960[a]	10.1	4.2
1961−1965[a]	15.7	7.1
1966−1970[a]	25.3	7.0
1971	31.7	5.0
1972	32.5	4.2
1973	29.2	−2.1
1974	26.4	−9.7
1975	27.3	−2.2
1976	21.0	−2.8
1977	20.2	−12.6
1978	22.4	1.2
1979	22.8	−1.6
1980	23.0	−1.5
1981	23.9	7.0

[a]Five-year averages are presented for periods in which the real interest rate was positive in every year and in which the financial intermediation coefficient showed a reasonable upward trend.

[b]Current accounts and saving deposits in private and mixed banks.

[c]Maximum capitalized interest rate for bonds or deposits of one year or less. Inflation for 1950 to 1968 taken from the wholesale price index, and since 1969 from the consumer price index.

Source: *Estadísticas Históricas de Moneda y Banca y Banca*, Banco de México.

a role similar to that of the introduction of money into a barter economy, liberating real resources used up in achieving a double coincidence of needs and wants. Financial intermediation enables the separation, impersonally and efficiently, of the saver from the investor; it obviates the need for asset barter, and its growth is a reflection of how savings-investment transactions, formerly performed directly, become intermediated.

Part of the success of SD may lie in the combination of budget and exchange-rate policies, which were mutually consistent and at the same time produced positive real interest rates. Significantly high real interest rates coincided with increases in financial intermediation and with a more efficient allocation of capital resources as well.

Another important aspect of financial policy was that lending rates were unregulated. This characteristic prevailed throughout the 1970s and the 1980s, with the brief exception of a three-month period in 1982. This part of credit policy was essential during the period of negative real interest rates, to prevent far-reaching misallocations of capital resources. However, liberalized lending rates have applied only to the so-called "unregulated" portfolio of banks. As government credit needs grew throughout the 1970s, the percentage of total credit absorbed by the government increased as well.

Table 8 contains the series of the ratio of reserves to deposits from 1950 to 1981. It can be seen how this ratio started going steadily up after exhibiting a fairly constant average of 32.5 percent from 1955 to 1970. Its rise was a consequence of the need to finance the rapid rise in government expenditures that started in 1972. Such an absorption of total credit at a time when private investment perked up, as it did beginning with the second half of 1977, could lead only to high levels of foreign private indebtedness.

Foreign credit was available throughout the 1970s for both the public and the private sectors because of the huge increases of cash reserves in the oil-producing nations, which had to find a place in the trade and budget deficits of other countries. The unregulated bank portfolio shrank partly because of increased government use of total credit, but also because of funds channeled to government trust funds established to promote all sorts of activities, such as foreign trade; internal commerce; low- and middle-income housing; small, medium, and large industry; communal agriculture; and private agriculture. As inflation grew in the 1970s, so did the subsidies granted through financial channels. This combination had the double effect of magnifying budget deficits and making more acute the misallocation of resources created by unrealistic (negative) real rates of interest. The transfer

Table 8
Private and Mixed Banks Reserve Ratio

	Monetary and savings instruments offered to the public[a] a	Banking reserves[b] b	Ratio b/a
1950	4,234	2,059	48.6
1955	8,131	2,834	34.9
1960	17,418	5,691	32.7
1965	44,562	15,542	34.9
1970	118,095	35,910	30.4
1975	260,534	117,245	45.0
1976	275,318	140,056	50.9
1977	373,711	192,201	51.4
1978	520,328	257,941	49.6
1979	722,500	355,000	49.1
1980	1,001,700	661,100	66.0
1981	1,495,500	747,100	50.0

[a]Does not include capital and interbanking operations; does include national and foreign currency.

[b]Includes cash deposits in Banco de México and government bond holdings.

Source: *Estadísticas Históricas de Moneda y Banca*, Banco de México; *Informes Anuales*, Banco de México.

of funds to people with little or no need for subsidies was another corollary of these policies.

Perhaps the increase in subsidized loans was to some degree inevitable, since continued inflation caught policymakers unprepared to face some of its distortions, paramount among them the shortening of credit pay periods implied by the combination of high inflation, increased nominal interest rates, and formulae for determining annuities and payments designed for stable prices. As is well known, in countries that have experienced prolonged inflation, new payment mechanisms have to be devised; otherwise the present value of payments becomes so concentrated in the first payment periods that firms may go broke and middle-class individuals become priced out of middle-term and mortgage credits. The effects of this combination of events on the housing market can be disastrous, since the classic annuities formula can imply initial payments that absorb more than 80 percent of an individual's salary with an inflation of 60 percent.[14]

Table 9 contains some figures showing the impact of interest payments on the cash flow of firms. The leverage of these firms rose 27 percent in four years but the proportion of their sales eaten up by interest payments went up by 156 percent, from 3.18 percent of sales in 1978 to 8.15 percent in 1981. This increase occurred in spite of the fact that lower-interest dollar liabilities accounted for an impressive proportion of total debt by 1981. In fact, dollar debt for this sample of large firms went up from less than one-third of total debt in 1978 to 63 percent in 1981.

These figures confirm how the crowding out by the government of private borrowing from commercial banks drove them into dollar borrowings on a large scale. Firms, on the other hand, were willing to take the risk, both because their investments were rising and because of the strangling of liquidity that was provoked by the combination of high nominal interest rates and payment mechanisms on peso loans.

This combination of events set the stage (in both the business sector and the overall economy) for the collapse of 1982. Maybe there is a lesson to be learned here concerning the need to weigh heavily the distortive effects inflation has upon an economic system whose institutions have been established under the expectation of stable prices. Such consequences can be serious indeed, even if inflation is not chronic.

Table 9
Debt Growth in a Sample of Private Firms

	Debt equity	Dollar debt total debt	Financial expenditures sales
1978	0.9341	30.0	3.18
1979	1.0016	33.7	3.41
1980	1.1458	52.6	6.48
1981	1.1902	62.8	8.15

Source: Sample of 2,200 firms taken by the Office of Advisors to the President.

Commercial Policy

Among the policy areas of the greatest strategic importance for healthy, sustained economic growth, trade policy surely must rate high. In the case of Mexico, one can trace a very definite pattern of trade policy that has had a clear-cut effect on the structure of output, as well as on the balance of trade and on the country's dependence on foreign supplies.

Before going into a deeper analysis of some structural changes influenced over the years by trade policy, we should make some brief remarks about the issue of dependence in light of Mexico's most recent experience. One could say that Mexican policy has been influenced by the popular notion that selective import barriers promote domestic industrial growth, a concept obviously favored by so-called nationalistic entrepreneurs. Protectionist barriers also have a flavor of autarchy; they are implemented, so they say, to insulate the country from unfavorable dependence on the world economy, which is associated with deteriorating terms of trade from traditional export prices versus the rising prices of industrial imports.

In fact, trade policy in Mexico has favored the installation of many medium-sized industries with high unit costs unable to compete in world markets. That is not all, however; these industries depend on certain strategic inputs that must be imported and cannot be produced internally unless, of course, we embark on a strategy of inefficiency on a still grander scale. The consequence of all this has been that instead of greater economic independence, our relationship with the world economy has retrogressed to the prenatal stage. Our most recent experience, the lack of foreign currency brought about by our temporary flirtation with exchange controls, has been of "mature" industries or firms halving production levels because of a lack of spare parts or production inputs of foreign origin.

A good indication of the results of trade policy in Mexico over the years is the change in the ratio of tradeables to GDP (table 10). Nontradeables maintained a stable share of approximately 53 percent of GDP from 1939 to 1955. From 1956 onwards, their share started increasing steadily, reaching an average of 60 percent during the 1970s.[15] However, not only did the share of non-

Table 10

Distribution of Tradeables and Nontradeables in GDP

	Total[a]	Nontradeables	Tradeables[b]	Exportables	Importables	Petroleum
1939	100.0	53.3	43.5	31.9	11.6	3.2
1940	100.0	53.6	43.3	31.7	11.6	3.1
1941–45	100.0	53.8	43.4	31.0	12.5	2.8
1946–50	100.0	54.2	42.9	30.1	12.8	2.9
1951–55	100.0	54.0	43.4	31.5	11.8	2.6
1956–60	100.0	56.7	40.4	29.8	11.6	2.9
1961–65	100.0	58.3	38.1	26.0	12.2	3.6
1966–70	100.0	59.8	37.2	22.6	14.6	3.0
1971–75	100.0	60.8	36.7	20.8	15.9	2.6
1976	100.0	60.7	36.6	20.5	16.1	2.7
1977	100.0	59.0	37.6	22.0	15.6	3.4
1978	100.0	58.1	38.4	21.3	17.1	3.5
1979	100.0	58.2	37.4	20.1	17.3	4.4

[a]Nontradeables plus tradeables plus petrolem. Figures are rounded.
[b]Exportables plus importables. Figures are rounded.
Source: Dirección General de Política de Ingresos, using data from Banco de México, and Nacional Financiera, S.A.

tradeables increase significantly, but also the share of exportables fell from 31.9 percent of GDP in 1939 to only 20.1 percent in 1979. The difference is made up partly by the rise in the share of importables from 11.4 percent of GDP to 17.1 percent. Thus the economy became less open to international trade. But at the same time it became more import-dependent, and had less capacity to export.

While some of the rise in nontradeables can be traced to the greater importance that services acquire in a growing economy, the change in composition in tradeables, which went from a share for exportables of 73.7 percent in 1939 to only 53.9 percent in 1979, is a reflection of a long-term trend resulting from embedded structural policies, and stems only partially from the "Dutch disease" that was a factor after 1976.

It is well known among economists, but little appreciated among policymakers, that import taxes are really a tax on exports. Following the Sjaastad methodology on "true" tariffs,[16] it was estimated for Mexico that 37 percent of the import tariff is, in fact, a tax on exports from the 1939–79 period.[17]

The entire trade story, however, is not told by import and export tariffs alone. Import and export permits play a part that is perhaps of greater importance, since often there is the feeling that because Mexico borders the U.S. market, tariffs may seem too high or alternatively turn out to be a weak instrument to protect a particular industry. In this context, one should make a distinction between transitory and permanent components of trade policy.

Appendix table A-7 shows how controlled imports went from 17.7 percent of import value in 1956 to a peak of 90.4 percent in 1976. The table also shows that since 1961 the share of controlled imports has never declined below 60 percent. The number of import categories controlled has had a greater variation, dropping as low as 24 percent in 1979; but this is a meaningless figure, though it is often used. A level of 60 percent or more of controlled import values must have some effect on the way importers regard production and export shortages, since they are at the mercy, or shall we say the whim, of trade bureaucrats.

After 1976 there was an apparent liberalization in import permits, both because the percentage of import value controlled was less and because permits were issued with relative ease and promptness. However, the liberalization must be interpreted in terms of the expectations of the public. If trade policy is perceived as permanently protective and the trend up to 1976 was unmistakable, decreases in that trend are of no significance to improved export performance. Less protection in these circumstances only triggers overstocking of inventories of imported goods, adding one more cost to the distortions imposed by protection.

Not only is there an additional implicit tariff imposed on imports through protection, with its negative effect on export potential, but exports are further discouraged through licensing. Whether because of sanitary limitations (perhaps because governments abroad do not take good care of their citizens' health), or to keep internal prices down, erratic policy changes on export permits have left many an exporter with broken commitments and diminished incentives to try again.

At a cost to the taxpayer, efforts have been made to smooth over these distortions through export subsidies, as the last column of table A-7 shows. The beneficial effects of these subsidies, however, are nil, because they are granted selectively, while the higher costs imposed on the economy by protection cut across the board. Also, the distinction between transitional and permanent policy traits is fundamental in this case. This means that subsidies are mostly seen as windfall profits, and are hardly ever a long-run determinant of investment and production decisions.

Despite the healthy long-term trend of gradually lowering import tariffs from an average close of 30 percent at the start of the 1930s to under 10 percent at the beginning of SD, we have had, under SD, the implementation of another structural policy conducive to inefficient resource allocation. This new policy meant raising again the average import tariff from 8.8 percent in 1954 to an average of 20 percent in the 1960s. Nominal import tariffs were again lowered in the 1970s but import and export licenses kept going up.

The long-run effects of trade policy were a greater and more vulnerable international dependency of the nation's economy, a maimed capacity to export, and an ingrained attitude among local industrialists and exporters that will be difficult to change. Incidentally, the lowering of the tariffs in the 1930s, together with a liberal import policy, coincided with the start of modern industrialization in Mexico. This trend was merely strengthened by the Second World War, rather than being initiated by it, as is commonly believed.

Human Capital: A Need for Investment

Unfortunately, modern Mexican history provides a laboratory on how two sets of policies can affect the economy. To many people, however, it has not been evident that structural policies that often apparently provide short-run benefits can have strongly negative long-run effects. Such policies were part of the economic strategy during both SD and the latter decade. They were the negative part of the legacy of SD, and their ill consequences for growth and well-being were only intensified by recent macroeconomic policies.

But perhaps the greatest omission in both periods has been the lack of investment in the most socially and economically productive capital: human beings.

Why has per capita growth not been higher? Why has the distribution of the ability to generate income not improved? Why has productivity remained low? All these questions may have an answer in the extraordinary information contained in table 11. From 1960 to 1975 the number of Mexicans with no schooling remained practically the same. The breakdown is not available for 1982, but it can be seen that as much as 74 percent of the population had had only six years of schooling or less in that year.

Table 11
Labor Force by Educational Group
(proportions)

Schooling in years	1960	1968	1970	1975	1982
No schooling	32.0	25.5	27.1	30.6	
1−6	57.8	60.8	59.9	53.4	74.2
7−9	5.4	6.5	5.6	8.3	
10−12	1.4	2.8	4.2	3.0	25.8
13 or more	3.4	4.4	3.2	4.7	

Source: Cardenas, "El Crecimiento Económico en México", Bachelor's thesis, Instituto Tecnólogico Autónomo de México, Mexico, 1977; E. Alducin, "Educación y Empleo 1982–1988", Unpublished paper, Mexico, 1982.

A bigger industrial plant, a sane trade policy, and a stable social and political environment for economic calculations should all contribute to better per capita growth. But how can industry, agriculture, and the other economic sectors successfully modernize if there is so vast an insufficiency of investment in human capital?

Appendix
Table A-1
Real Tax on Financial Interest

	Nominal interest[a]		Inflation[b]	Tax + inflation / Gross interest	Maximum personal income tax rate
	Gross	Net			
1950	9.00	8.10	9.65	117.22	30.00
1951			24.00	276.67	33.00
1952			2.23	24.78	40.00 →
1953			−1.88	−10.89	
1954			9.55	116.11	46.00 →
1955			13.37	158.56	
1956			5.13	67.00	
1957			3.90	53.33	
1958			4.69	62.11	
1959			0.90	20.00	
1960	10.00	9.00	4.89	58.90	50.00 →
1961			1.27	26.70	
1962			1.67	26.70	
1963			0.41	14.10	

Table A-1 (cont'd)
Real Tax on Financial Interest

	Nominal interest[a]		Inflation[b]	Tax + inflation Gross interest	Maximum personal income tax rate
	Gross	Net			
1965			1.96	29.60	35.00
1966			1.15	21.50	
1967			2.66	36.60	
1968			2.22	32.20	
1969	11.11	10.00	2.54	32.85	
1970	12.12	11.00	6.01	59.17	
1971	11.20	10.08	3.67	42.77	
1972	10.60	9.01	2.57	39.25	42.00
1973	11.72	9.51	15.99	155.29	
1974	13.73	11.53	22.43	179.39	50.00
1975	14.21	12.00	10.38	88.60	
1976	14.41	11.99	22.40	172.24	
1977	16.64	14.10	41.18	262.74	
1978	17.52	15.00	15.74	104.22	
1979	17.74	15.22	18.30	117.36	55.00
1980	24.58	22.06	24.43	109.64	
1981	34.80	31.78	24.52	79.14	

[a]One-year deposits.
[b]Wholesale price index.

Source: *Estadísticas Históricas de Precios*, Banco de México, Mexico, 1982; Oficina de Estudios Financieros, Banco de México; "Ley del Impuesto sobre la Renta," Ministry of Finance, various issues.

Table A-2

Indexes for Domestic Inflation and World Inflation, Nominal and Real Effective Exchange Rates, and Parity Index

| | Wholesale price indexes | | | | Effective exchange rate | | | | Parity Index | |
| | Mexico | | World | | Nominal | | Real | | 5=1/(2x3) | |
	1	a	2	a	3	a	4=2x3/1	a		a
1948	20.8	—	40.4	—	41.0	—	79.7	—	125.5	—
1949	22.8	9.6	38.6	−4.5	56.7	38.3	96.0	20.5	104.2	−17.0
1950	24.9	9.2	40.3	4.4	71.5	26.1	115.6	20.4	86.5	−17.0
1951	30.9	24.1	45.5	12.9	71.5	0.0	105.3	−8.9	95.0	9.8
1952	32.0	3.6	44.5	−2.2	71.6	0.1	99.5	−5.5	100.5	5.8
1953	31.4	−1.9	43.9	−1.3	71.6	0.0	100.0	0.5	100.0	−0.5
1954	34.4	9.6	43.9	0.0	92.9	29.7	118.5	18.5	84.4	−15.6
1955	39.1	13.4	44.1	0.5	103.5	11.4	116.7	−1.5	85.7	1.5
1956	40.9	4.6	45.6	3.4	103.4	−0.1	115.2	−1.3	86.8	1.3
1957	42.7	4.4	46.9	2.9	103.3	−0.1	113.5	−1.5	88.1	1.5
1958	44.6	4.4	47.6	1.5	101.9	−1.4	108.8	−4.1	91.9	4.3
1959	45.1	1.1	48.0	0.8	101.4	−0.5	107.9	−0.8	92.7	0.9
1960	47.3	4.9	48.2	0.4	101.2	−0.2	103.2	−4.4	96.9	4.5
1961	47.7	0.8	48.3	0.2	101.3	0.1	102.6	−0.6	97.5	0.6
1962	48.6	1.9	48.6	0.6	101.0	−0.3	101.0	−1.6	99.0	1.5
1963	48.8	0.4	48.9	0.6	101.0	−0.3	100.9	−0.1	99.1	0.1

Table A-2 (cont'd)

Indexes for Domestic Inflation and World Inflation, Nominal and Real Effective Exchange Rates, and Parity Index

| | Wholesale price indexes | | | | Effective exchange rate | | | | Parity Index | |
| | Mexico | | World | | Nominal | | Real | | | |
	1	a	2	a	3	a	4=2x3/1	a	5=1/(2x3)	a
1964	50.9	4.3	49.6	1.4	100.1	-0.6	97.5	-3.4	102.6	3.5
1965	51.9	2.0	50.9	2.6	99.5	-0.6	97.5	0.0	102.6	0.0
1966	52.5	1.2	52.8	3.7	98.9	-0.6	99.4	1.9	100.6	-1.9
1967	54.0	2.9	53.1	0.6	98.3	-0.6	96.7	-2.7	103.4	2.8
1968	55.1	2.0	54.4	2.4	97.3	-1.0	96.1	-0.6	104.1	0.7
1969	56.5	2.5	56.6	4.0	96.9	-0.4	97.0	0.9	103.1	-1.0
1970	59.8	5.8	58.9	4.1	97.0	0.1	95.6	-1.4	104.6	1.5
1971	62.1	3.8	61.2	3.9	97.4	0.4	96.1	0.5	104.1	-0.5
1972	63.8	2.7	64.5	5.4	98.8	1.4	99.8	3.9	100.2	-3.7
1973	73.9	15.8	73.4	13.8	100.6	1.8	100.0	0.2	100.0	-0.2
1974	90.5	22.5	88.9	21.1	99.1	-1.5	97.4	-2.6	102.7	2.7
1975	100.0	10.5	100.0	12.5	94.9	-4.2	94.9	-2.6	105.4	2.6
1976	122.3	22.3	108.6	8.6	112.9	19.0	100.3	5.7	99.7	-5.4
1977	172.6	41.1	118.7	9.3	161.1	42.7	110.7	10.4	90.3	-9.4
1978	199.8	15.8	128.5	8.3	165.4	2.7	106.4	-3.9	94.0	4.1
1979	236.4	18.3	146.1	13.7	164.9	-0.3	101.9	-4.2	98.1	4.4
1980	294.3	24.5	169.8	16.2	168.6	2.2	97.3	-4.5	102.8	4.8
1981	366.3	24.5	189.6	11.7	168.5	-0.1	87.1	-10.5	114.8	11.7
1982	571.7	56.1	204.2	7.7	330.2	95.9	117.8	35.2	84.9	-26.1

aPercent rate of growth: (1) Base 1975 = 100; (2) Divisia index of the wholesale price—indexes of the 21 countries that account for more than 95 percent of Mexico's trade (imports + exports, excluding petroleum). The shares of these countries in Mexico's trade were used as weights. The base is 1975 = 100; (3) Divisia index of the peso nominal exchange rates; (5) Base: median (1948–1981) = 100. The base was

Table A-3
Balance-of-Payments Deficit on Current Account
(as percentage of GDP)

Year	Usual compu-tation	Excluding inflation repayments of capital on public external debt	Year	Usual compu-tation	Excluding inflation repayments of capital on public external debt
1939	−3.6	−2.9	1961	2.7	2.6
1940	−0.7	−1.2	1962	1.9	1.8
1941	3.0	1.6	1963	1.6	1.4
1942	2.7	−0.6	1964	2.5	2.4
1943	−2.7	−4.3	1965	2.5	2.2
1944	−0.6	−0.9	1966	2.4	2.1
1945	−0.3	−0.6	1967	2.7	2.5
1946	3.9	2.9	1968	3.3	2.9
1947	3.9	2.4	1969	3.0	2.4
1948	1.9	0.9	1970	4.2	3.5
1949	−1.5	−1.7	1971	3.3	2.5
1950	−3.4	−3.6	1972	2.7	2.4
1951	4.3	3.4	1973	3.5	2.9
1952	3.4	3.2	1974	5.6	4.6
1953	3.7	3.1	1975	6.4	5.4
1954	3.7	3.7	1976	5.3	4.4
1955	−0.1	−0.03	1977	3.6	2.1
1956	2.5	2.4	1978	4.5	2.8
1957	4.3	4.0	1979	6.0	3.8
1958	4.1	3.9	1980	6.0	3.9
1959	2.3	2.2	1981	6.6	5.2
1960	3.6	3.5	1982	−1.6	−3.7

Source: *Estadísticas Históricas de Balanza de Pagos,* Banco de México, Mexico, 1981.

Table A-4
Public-Sector Revenue, Expenditure, and Deficit[a]
(as percentage of GDP)[b]

	Revenue			Expenditure			Deficit		
	Total	Internal	External	Total	Internal	External	Total	Internal	External
1965	18.5	16.8	1.7	19.5	18.1	1.4	1.0	1.3	0.3
1966	18.9	17.6	1.3	20.1	18.7	1.4	1.3	1.1	0.1
1967	19.2	17.7	1.5	21.4	19.5	1.9	2.2	1.8	0.4
1968	19.5	18.4	1.1	21.2	19.5	1.7	1.7	1.1	0.6
1969	19.9	18.8	1.1	21.5	19.9	1.6	1.6	1.1	0.5
1970	20.1	19.5	0.6	22.4	20.4	2.0	2.2	0.9	1.3
1971	19.5	18.8	0.7	21.2	19.7	1.5	1.8	0.9	0.8
1972	19.6	18.9	0.7	23.1	21.3	1.8	3.6	2.4	1.1
1973	21.2	20.6	0.6	26.1	23.4	2.7	4.9	2.8	2.1
1974	22.5	21.6	0.9	27.4	23.7	3.7	4.9	2.1	2.8
1975	24.3	23.3	1.0	32.3	28.7	3.6	8.0	5.4	2.6
1976	25.2	24.2	1.0	32.8	29.5	3.3	7.6	5.3	2.2
1977	26.5	24.7	1.8	31.4	27.8	3.6	5.0	3.1	1.8
1978	27.0	24.6	2.4	32.0	27.9	4.1	5.1	3.3	1.7
1979	27.7	24.2	3.5	33.2	28.8	4.4	5.5	4.5	0.9
1980	30.6	24.0	6.6	36.4	30.3	6.1	5.8	6.2	−0.5
1981	28.5	21.5	7.0	43.7	37.7	6.0	15.2	16.2	−0.9
1982	31.0	18.9	12.1	48.9	40.1	8.8	17.9	21.2	−3.3

[a]Figures for the public sector are necessary in addition to the federal government's because of the mixed character of the Mexican economy. Since the public-sector budget started consolidating government firms in 1965, data for the public sector are available from that year on to the present. Figures are rounded.

[b]See note for table 4.

Source: *Estadísticas de Finanzas Públicas*, Ministry of Finance, Mexico, 1981. Since 1980 the external figures come from balance-of-payments data of Banco de México. Total figures for 1981 came from the 1982 Report of the President

Table A-5
Adjusted Public-Sector Revenue, Expenditure,[a] and Deficit
(as percentage of GDP)[b]

	Revenue			Expenditure			Deficit		
	Total	Internal	External	Total	Internal	External	Total	Internal	External
1965	18.5	16.8	1.7	19.3	18.1	1.2	0.8	1.3	-0.5
1966	18.9	17.6	1.3	19.8	18.7	1.1	1.0	1.1	-0.2
1967	19.2	17.7	1.5	21.1	19.5	1.6	1.9	1.8	0.1
1968	19.5	18.4	1.1	20.7	19.5	1.2	1.2	1.1	0.1
1969	19.9	18.8	1.1	20.9	19.9	1.0	1.0	1.1	0.1
1970	20.1	19.5	0.6	21.7	20.4	1.3	1.6	0.9	0.6
1971	19.5	18.8	0.7	20.7	19.7	1.0	1.3	0.9	0.3
1972	19.6	18.9	0.7	22.8	21.3	1.5	3.2	2.4	0.8
1973	21.2	20.6	0.6	25.5	23.4	2.1	4.4	2.8	1.5
1974	22.5	21.6	0.9	26.4	23.7	2.7	3.9	2.1	1.7
1975	24.3	23.3	1.0	31.3	28.7	2.6	7.0	5.4	1.6
1976	25.2	24.2	1.0	31.9	29.5	2.4	6.6	5.3	1.3
1977	26.5	24.7	1.8	29.9	27.8	2.1	3.4	3.1	0.3
1978	27.0	24.6	2.4	30.3	27.9	2.4	3.1	3.1	-0.0
1979	27.7	24.2	3.5	31.0	28.8	2.2	3.3	4.5	-1.3
1980	30.6	24.0	6.6	34.3	30.3	4.0	8.7	6.2	2.5
1981	28.5	21.5	7.0	42.3	37.7	4.6	13.8	16.2	-2.4
1982	31.0	18.9	12.1	53.0	32.9	20.1	22.0	14.0	8.0

[a] Excludes inflation capital repayments on external public debt.
[b] See note for table 4.

Source: *Estadísticas de Finanzas Públicas*, Ministry of Finance, Mexico, 1981.

Table A-6
Public-Sector Deficit
Excluding Subsidies on Some Public-Sector Prices

	Implicit subsidies[a] a	Interest rate on external debt b	Imputed interest saving[b] c	Public-sector deficit d	Reduction in deficit e = a + c	Corrected deficit f = d − e	Ratios to GDP d	Ratios to GDP e	Ratios to GDP f
1965	11,627	4.35	506	2,503	12,133	−9,630	1.0	4.8	−3.8
1966	13,043	5.89	1,483	3,551	14,526	−10,975	1.3	5.2	−3.9
1967	12,260	6.10	2,374	6,740	14,634	−7,894	2.2	4.8	−2.6
1968	13,287	6.72	3,668	5,632	16,955	−11,323	1.7	5.0	−3.3
1969	13,722	6.62	4,764	5,982	18,486	−12,504	1.6	4.9	−3.3
1970	14,354	7.60	6,923	9,316	21,277	−11,961	2.2	5.1	−2.9
1971	16,794	7.18	8,243	8,086	25,037	−16,951	1.8	5.4	−3.7
1972	18,679	6.88	9,751	18,896	28,430	−9,534	3.6	5.3	−1.8
1973	21,439	9.16	15,839	32,227	37,278	−5,051	4.9	5.7	−0.8
1974	27,049	10.95	23,631	41,862	50,680	−8,818	4.9	6.0	−1.0
1975	25,830	11.00	29,179	83,373	55,009	28,364	8.0	5.3	2.7
1976	41,193	9.62	32,288	98,113	73,481	24,632	7.6	5.7	1.9
1977	71,174	8.18	35,918	86,373	107,092	−20,719	5.0	6.1	−1.2
1978	88,313	9.26	52,164	111,449	140,477	−29,028	5.1	6.4	−1.3
1979	129,713	11.82	88,084	158,340	217,797	−59,457	5.5	7.5	−2.1
1980	203,318	14.25	147,717	232,213	351,035	−118,822	5.8	8.7	−3.0

[a]The subsidy calculated results from the implicit loss in revenue to the public sector caused by not adjusting the prices of oil products to U.S. consumer levels and by not reflecting in the prices of electricity and railways their production costs.

[b]$c = b \cdot A$; where A is the additional debt incurred because of the subsidies. The number is calculated following a recursive series on time t=1965, 1966,...: $A_t = A_{t-1} + b_t + c_{t-1}$, beginning with $A_{1964} = c_{1964} = 0$.

Table A-7

Trade Policy Indicators

	No. of import categories			Percent of controlled import value	Ratio of import tax revenue to		Ratio of export tax revenue to total exports[a]	Ratio of export subsidies to private-sector exports
	Total a	Controlled b	Percent b/a		Total imports	Private-sector imports		
1956	4,129	1,376	33.3	17.7	9.2		14.6	
1957				35.1	8.1		14.8	
1958				42.5	11.5		13.0	
1959				43.2	13.3	15.2	12.8	
1960				37.8	12.7	15.4	11.8	
1961				53.8	12.4	15.5	10.8	
1962	5,204	2,313	44.4	52.5	12.4	15.7	10.3	
1963				63.5	13.6	16.9	9.4	
1964				65.5	14.0	17.2	8.7	
1965				60.0	17.9	21.4	8.5	
1966	11,000	6,600	60.0	62.0	18.2	22.1	8.4	

Table A-7 (cont'd)
Trade Policy Indicators

	No. of import categories			Percent of controlled import value	Ratio of import tax revenue to		Ratio of export tax revenue to total exports[a]	Ratio of export subsidies to private-sector exports
	Total a	Controlled b	Percent b/a		Total imports	Private-sector imports		
1967				65.2	22.0	28.7	7.2	
1968				64.4	19.9	25.0	8.5	
1969				65.1	21.0	26.5	7.0	
1970	12,900	8,400	65.1	68.3	21.9	28.8	6.3	
1971				67.7	20.6	25.8	5.7	0.8
1972				66.3	18.9	24.7	4.5	2.6
1973	16,000	12,800	80.0	69.6	13.0	18.9	4.9	4.9
1974				82.0	11.2	17.5	4.7	6.2
1975				68.4	12.5	20.3	3.8	6.8
1976				90.4	12.7	12.7	4.9	5.3
1977	7,340	5,859	79.8	67.7	8.3	13.3	5.0	2.0
1978				64.2	7.0	11.1	1.8	6.3
1979	7,776	1,866	24.0	60.0	10.3	15.0	1.1	6.3
1980					11.4	18.0	0.5	5.7
1981					8.3	12.8	0.0	9.2

[a]Since 1977 excludes tax revenue from oil.

Sources: "Documento de Discusión No. 1", Dirección General de Planeación Hacendaria; Bela Balassa, Trade Policy in Mexico, Conference on "Industrialización y Comercio Exterior", organized by the Colegio Nacional de Economistas, January 1983; Estadísticas de Finanzas Públicas, Ministry of Finance; Estadísticas Históricas de Balanza de Pagos, Banco de México; "Indicadores Económicos", Banco de México.

13

RÁMON DÍAZ

Uruguay's Erratic Growth

The Uruguayan economy experienced strong economic growth (5.2 percent average GDP growth per year) for nearly fifteen years through most of the 1940s and the early 1950s.[1] In 1955, for no apparent reason, economic growth in that country collapsed, and stagnation set in.[2] In the next thirteen years, from 1955 to 1967, GDP growth was only 0.4 percent per year—which, given a population increasing 1.3 percent per year—meant that per capita output *declined* in that period about one percent a year. Uruguay's economy recovered from the stagnation and experienced a period of healthy growth from 1974 through the end of the decade. But in the last several years, an explosion of public spending and other problems have depressed the economy once again, and the Uruguayan economy has struggled in the early 1980s.

Other economic indicators followed the fluctuation in GDP growth. The most unhealthy element of all was exports, which remained virtually motionless for the twenty-five year period up through 1967—a time when trade was booming in the rest of the world.[3] Exports then rose very rapidly—more than 7 percent a

year—in the following period, up through 1980. Inflation rose
from an annual rate of 8.1 percent per year between 1942 and
1954—somewhat high compared to the world rate, but not compared to other countries in the region—to 32 percent in the next
thirteen years, and actually exceeded 80 percent per year in the
growth years 1974 to 1979.

Uruguay's recent, erratic growth presents an excellent case
study in the relationship between economic performance and economic policy. The reason is that each of these turns in economic
fortune was the result of a marked change in policy. The moral of
Uruguay's experience is as simple as it is unsurprising. The moral
is that when a country pursues economic policies that encourage
growth, that will be the result. On the other hand, when economic
policy becomes irresponsible, the result will be stagnation and
even regression.

Some Historical Notes

A few outstanding facts and figures about Uruguay's history must
be given to sketch a portrait of Uruguay in its successful hour. Let
us place ourselves, to begin with, in 1866. The population was
about 300,000, one-third of which were immigrants—Spanish-,
Italian-, and French-born predominantly. That particular year
over 9,000 had arrived, of which 4,100, 1,600, and 1,000 respectively had come from the above-stated countries of origin. The
capital city and main port, which housed about 80,000 souls, was
growing fast. There were not many people to fill the rest of the
69,000-square-mile territory, but 4.5 million head of cattle and a
similar number of sheep grazed in the prairies, which were just
then being crisscrossed by wire fences. Exports—beef, cattle,
hides, mutton and lamb, wool, sheepskins—reached about 11
million gold dollars, roughly equivalent to ten times the figure in
1981 dollars, or $370 per inhabitant (incidentally about the same
figure as today, and one-third of present-day per capita exports
from the U.S.). Imports reached $15 million, the excess over ex-
ports being more than compensated for by the surplus in the
capital account. Gold, therefore, was flowing in.

To what use would the incoming metal be put? About half of it
would find its way to the coffers of the seven existing banks (all of

them banks of issue as well as commercial banks), which held about $5 million altogether, and the rest would go to the pockets and purses of consumers and to the tills of the 9,000 (nonfarm) business firms. Coins of many origins (American, French, Mexican, Chilean) circulated, but the English sovereign was predominant. They were used side by side with the bank notes issued by the seven banks.

The Uruguayan Republic never minted its own coins. In fact, it was only in 1862 that the national currency was defined in terms of gold by an act of Congress. Legislation on money had been hitherto limited to an 1842 act passed during a civil war, which, while granting the president extraordinary powers to secure revenue (including the power to tax by executive resolution), expressly forebade the printing of paper money.

Perhaps no other feature is so characteristic of the country during its first century as its strong attachment to monetary stability. Its only two neighbors, gigantic (from the Uruguayan perspective, at least) Argentina and Brazil, had both had paper currencies since their inception. As an Argentine province, during the war of independence against Spain, Uruguay had had a taste of galloping inflation. As a province of Brazil, which it later also was, the experience must have been renewed. The fact is that when it was made an independent state at the inspiration of British diplomacy in 1828 by an Argentine-Brazilian treaty as a means of stopping the two countries' three-year-long war, there emerged this implausible little country made of some 70,000 people, whose independence its English diplomatic sponsor refused to guarantee, so implausible did its viability appear. Lo and behold, this splinter state was, on monetary matters, a chip off neither of the old blocks; rather, it appeared puzzlingly devoted to the outlandish ideal of sound money. And to make things stranger, in the pursuit of this goal it resorted to, and perhaps hit upon, the only method that could safely lead to it—not to have its own money at all.

Well, to return to 1866, the Uruguayans had good reason, some years after independence, to be proud of themselves. National income was estimated that year at $48 million—about $1,600 per capita in 1981 dollars—by an expert brought from his native France to organize the Bureau of Statistics. The method employed was crude and the sum looked astonishingly high, but the ratios of

exports, tax revenue, and coins and currency in possession of the
nonbanking sector (three relatively safe variables to estimate) to
such national income figures were 22 percent, 8 percent, and 21
percent respectively, all of which sound credible. Furthermore, demand for labor was strong and wages high by international standards, as witnessed by the large immigration flow. Montevideo
harbored a university, an active stock exchange, an opera house
(with European singers every season), several theaters, several
daily papers, several periodicals edited in foreign languages (of
which altogether forty appeared during the nineteenth century),
and many well-stocked shops catering to the gourmet, to the ladies
and gentlemen of fashion, to the discriminating reader concerned
to be always à la page. The implicitly adopted growth strategy
(monetary stability; low government expenditure; and an economy wide open to trade, to finance, and, last but not least, to immigration) certainly seemed to work.

That was not, in effect, the conclusion that the people of
Uruguay and their leaders drew from the country's experience.
Beginning in the 1870s we witness a surprising story in which the
dominant note is dissatisfaction with the country as it then was,
and an urge to change some of its main features.

The avant-garde of this radical reform came with the wave of
protectionist legislation that was passed during the 1870s and
1880s. Until 1875 Uruguay had an across-the-board 20 percent
tariff, which supplied the Treasury with the bulk of its revenue.
That year an act was passed, to be supplemented and reinforced
later by further laws approved over a decade or so, that raised the
duties on the goods that were produced locally—or those the
authorities thought could be produced behind a tariff wall—and
lowered the duties on raw materials and capital goods.

One of the striking features of this reform was the rationale put
forward by its supporters. Agriculture, they held, particularly of
the livestock kind that predominated in Uruguay, did not afford
sufficient employment opportunities. Only manufacturing industry could create enough jobs. The irony of the situation was that
all along the country was receiving a substantial immigration
flow. The further irony is that from the 1890s on, the immigration
flow declined appreciably. Furthermore, the country's export performance became lackluster. This is as one would have expected,

since in economic theory the dampening effect of import duties on exports is well known.

The second innovation occurred in the field of money. In 1896 a State Bank was founded and invested with the exclusive privilege of issuing bank notes. The measure met with stiff opposition. In the press and in Congress, the advocates of sound money recalled that another state bank of issue in Latin America would mean another flood of inconvertible paper currency. Their prophesies took a long time to come to fulfillment. The peso remained linked to gold until 1914, while the State Bank showed exemplary restraint, then floated upward during World War I and downward later during the depression of the early 1920s; it then floated "dirtily" close to its gold parity until 1929.[4] Finally, during and after the Great Depression, the old monetary discipline began to give way. But the story of how Uruguay would become a high-inflation country will occupy us later.

The third area of reform concerned the role of government in the economy. Uruguay had been a remarkable case of laissez-faire economic policy, even for the nineteenth century, as exemplified strikingly by the fact that the government stayed out of the business of making money until 1896. Soon after the creation of the State Bank, all of that began to change fast. The government started operating power stations and railroads, set up its own insurance company, distilled alcohol, produced cement, refined petroleum, and nationalized telephones. Labor legislation became one of the country's specialties. The first forty-eight-hour labor week legislation in the world was passed in Uruguay in 1915. The notion that the country was "advanced," a pioneer in reform, became dominant. A social security system began developing at the turn of the century that by 1928 included the entire urban population. The idea that the existence of all of these benefits implied costs seems to have been only very dimly perceived by the country's leadership.

Uruguay Moves in Reverse

Let us get in the time machine again and return to the 1960s. In those days the case of Uruguay stood out, in international comparisons, like a statistical sore thumb.

Let us take a couple of examples. In the early 1970s the World Bank compiled an economic "atlas" that included data on per capita GDP growth rates for 122 countries during the 1960–69 period. The Popular Democratic Republic of Yemen came in last with −4.6 percent; second from the bottom was Cuba, with −3.2; then came Chad (−1.3), Haiti (−1.0), and Niger (−0.9). Uruguay tied for seventh worst place with Rwanda, scoring −0.8.[5]

A study by Paul Jonas of the University of New Mexico, "Selected Success Indicators for Developing Countries, 1960–69,"[6] is even more striking. The indicators of success or failure used by Jonas were GNP growth, growth of agricultural production, marginal savings rate, incremental capital-output ratio (ICOR), and inflation. The sample included between thirty-four and forty countries, depending on the indicator.

Uruguay came out last in the GNP growth contest, first in the inflation race—in both cases by quite a margin—and third to last in the agricultural growth indicator. But the result really worth looking into relates to the capital-output ratio. Jonas approached this idea quantitatively, applying the formula

$$\frac{I[60] + I[61] + \ldots + I[68]}{GNP[69] - GNP[60]}$$

where I represents gross investment and the numbers in brackets refer to the year when the investment or the GNP flows occurred. It is assumed that a firm produces (adds value to the inputs it buys from other firms) or a country produces (adds value to imports) by employing labor and capital services. If the firm or country wishes to produce more, it must employ more labor and more capital (unless it substitutes one factor of production for the other; the value of the ratio as an index of success is based on the idea that this substitution can be assumed away).

The idea that a country's low marginal capital-output ratio indicates success, then, is based on the assumption that by using capital very efficiently, the economy somehow relaxes the critical constraint on its economic growth. Jonas's study, for instance, shows South Korea to have had a marginal ratio of 1.7, implying that one extra dollar of output would call for a $1.70 investment. The median ratio for the thirty-six-country sample was three, implying that $3 of new capital was required for an additional $1 output. The second lowest ratio, Ghana's, was 6.6, showing that Ghana needed more than twice the capital that the median country required and almost four times that which Korea had to invest to produce the same output.

But at a level like 6.6 one begins to have problems interpreting results in light of the assumptions on which the whole study is based. There are three basic parameters at play, which are interconnected and therefore must be consistent with one another; namely, the marginal capital-output ratio, i.e., the increment of capital over the increment of output ($\frac{\Delta k}{\Delta q}$, which we shall call v); the rate of gross return on investment (which we shall call r, so that $r \cdot \Delta k$ is the incremental flow of gross income accruing to capital); and the marginal share of gross investment in incremental output ($\frac{r \cdot \Delta k}{\Delta q}$, which we shall call k). Obviously, we have defined k in a way that implies the equation

$$k = rv$$

Now we are told that for a certain period, Ghana showed a value for v of 6.6. Let us assume a relatively low (by international comparison) value for r of 0.1 (of which perhaps one-fifth will compensate capital consumption). This would lead to a level of 66 percent for k, implying labor's share to be only one-third of output, which is far lower than precedents would lead us to expect. If we start by assuming a fifty-fifty split between capital and labor, which only begins to be credible, we come out with a 7.6 rate of return on capital, which is quite low by international standards.

But we must not delay getting to the case of the last country in the sample, Uruguay, which showed a ratio of 24.5. First of all, the total disconnection of Uruguay's case from the rest is obvious. Second, and more substantially, it must be stressed that there is no way in which a ratio of 24.5 can be reconciled with normal levels for the other relevant parameters, even by stretching these to limit magnitudes. There must be some sense, therefore, in which the Uruguayan experience with investment and production departs from the assumptions that underlie Jonas's study and many other similar research pieces.

Capital and Output

The question underlying this freak statistic, which the author very carefully checked, could be expressed in the following terms: how could an economy enjoying a certain measure of capital accumulation remain totally stagnant over a period that encompassed several trade cycles (and was furthermore free from major cyclical disturbances)?

I believe a number of separate influences were at work, and different ones at different points of time. Basically, my proposed answer is made up of three elements:

- For part of the time *net* investment was very low, or even negative. The paradox of positive investment and no growth is, during this period, just an illusion.

- During the rest of the time, when net investment was significant, some of the investment was destined to substitute capital for labor.

- The rest of investment just resulted in unutilized capacity.

We shall now take up these three headings one by one.

Low investment. Table 1 shows that net investment during the years 1962–68 was less than 1 percent of net domestic product

Table 1
Average Growth Rates of Several Variables
by Selected Periods
(in percentages)

Period	Average ratio of net investment to net domestic product[a]	Average annual growth rate of net domestic product[a]	Average inflation rate
1956–59	4.6	−2.3	22.2
1960–61	5.8	5.0	22.6[b]
1962–68	0.6	0.1	57.3
1969–70	3.2	7.0	17.7
1971–73	3.5	−0.6	67.3
1974–79	7.6	4.0	82.7

[a]See text for basis of computation of net aggregates from the gross reported ones.
[b]1960 = 36.3; 1961 = 10.3

Sources: Central Bank of Uruguay, *Statistical Bulletin,* various issues.

(NDP)[7]. Therefore, the failure of the Uruguayan economy to grow in this period presents no mystery. The question naturally translates into why net investment was so low—negative, in fact, between 1964 and 1968—but we shall address that later.

Labor-saving investment. The standard literature about less-developed countries (LDCs) implicitly rules out this possibility, since LDCs are defined precisely as economies where capital is scarce and labor is overabundant. Uruguay's case goes a long way to show, however, that government's tampering with relative prices may result in prices' reflecting relative scarcities in reverse fashion.

Table 2 and figure 1 show that during 1942–54 the relative price of labor rose sharply. Originally a market-induced phenomenon, this development was subsequently institutionally enhanced by the establishment of a system of wage boards, where government representatives, as well as those of labor and management, sat to settle disputes over remunerations. The government-sponsored act that created the system, passed in 1943, set "fair" wages and "suitable" standards of living for workers' families as its goal, and

Table 2
Uruguayan Economy, 1942–80, by Thirteen-Year Periods
(annual rates of growth,[a] in percentages)

	1942–54	1955–67	1968–80
Real gross domestic product	5.2	0.4	3.1
Real exports	0.4[b,c]	0.3[c]	7.2
Real wages[d]	7.4	−0.2[c]	−6.6
Consumer price index[e]	8.1	32.0	60.7

[a]The reported rates have been obtained by fitting logarithmic trends to the variables.

[b]Corresponds to the period 1944–54. By using the 1942–54 sample a higher rate (2.0) is obtained, but it is still not statistically significant.

[c]Indicates that the figure is not significantly different from 0 at the 95 percent level of confidence.

[d]Original data resulted from pooling information from three different sources for different subperiods, and their homogeneity is doubtful. The author believes, however, that the general trajectory of the variable is adequately represented.

[e]CPI growth rates are "within-year" (or "December-to-December") rates.

Sources: Central Bank of Uruguay, *Statistical Bulletin,* various issues; Uruguay's Bureau of Statistics, several publications.

Figure 1

Uruguayan Economy, 1942–80

(one nominal and three real variables;
logarithmic vertical scales)

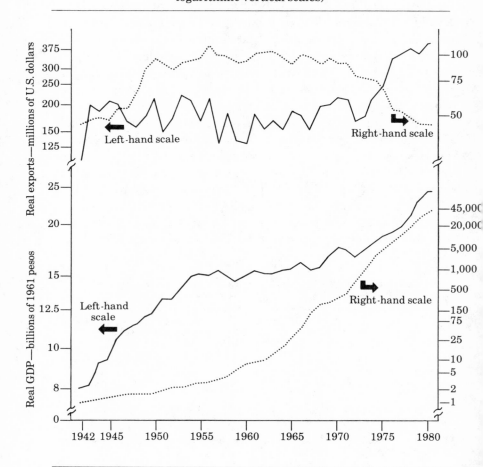

Source: Central Bank of Uruguay, *Statistical Bulletin,* various issues.

the government representatives on the boards accordingly sided with labor in most controversies. In itself, a policy geared to improve real wages by operating on nominal ones was bound to cause trouble. On top of that, employers were made to contribute heavily to the social security system based on the amount of their payrolls. But there was even more. All the while the rate of exchange was insulated from the surrounding inflation by a system of exchange controls, which since 1948 was coupled with a system of multiple exchange rates. The official policy of "industrialization" meant that imports of machinery and equipment enjoyed preferential treatment over tariffs and exchange rates. In effect, official policy implied the simultaneous subsidization of capital and taxing of labor. That firms should have employed more of the former and less of the latter is no wonder.

Misdirected investment. Another likely development might be described as an "overshooting" of investment in the local import-competing industries. The protectionist tendencies that we saw at work in the 1870s and 1880s were much enhanced by the Great Depression. Therefore, import control, a part of exchange control set up to fight the depreciation of the Uruguayan peso in 1931 for monetary reasons, had the real effects of a major raising of tariff walls. Discontinued during World War II, it was reinstated in 1948, this time to stop a loss of international reserves, but again with strong protectionist side effects. The result was that the manufacturing sector came to substitute foreign supplies, between 1949 and 1957, at an annual rate of 4.6 percent, whereas export-oriented agriculture showed zero growth in the meantime. The figures quoted in table 2, showing zero export growth and 5.2 overall output growth during 1942–54, point to the same process of an economy moving toward self-sufficiency. A part of our hypothesis is that the late 1940s and early 1950s were a stage of very high profits in the manufacturing, import-competing sector, which attracted further capital to that sector; but what the available data on investment show us from 1955 onwards is the tail end of this process, when all the best projects had already been implemented and a high proportion of the new ones had become financial flops. To the likely objection that this implies a very short period in which the import substitution process spent itself, the reply is that

388 RAMON DIAZ

in an economy with a domestic market of under 3 million people, the number of economically viable projects for substituting imports is not all that large.

Why Was Investment Low?

The general picture that we have presented may be seen in chronological perspective in table 1. First of all, we should abstract the periods corresponding to 1960–61 and 1969–70, which are atypical. They relate to two stabilization campaigns, which were prematurely abandoned but achieved a measure of success in temporarily decelerating inflation. It should be noted that the rate of investment rose in both periods. This leaves us with four other periods to consider:

- 1956–59, with high investment, negative growth, and an inflation rate which, although comparatively not high, implied very considerable acceleration (in the previous four years the inflation rate had remained at one digit);
- 1962–68, with low investment, low growth, and a tremendous acceleration of inflation. This is the central period in posing the problem of low investment;
- 1971–73, again with relatively high investment, negative growth, and tremendously accelerating inflation;
- 1974–79, with high inflation coexisting with high investment and growth.

We note that the two periods when the inflation rate moved up sharply (1962–68 and 1971–73) were poor growth periods, but the behavior of investment differed between them.

We further observe that in the last period (1974–79) very high inflation does not seem to have hindered growth and investment. This is a period in which economic policy may be characterized by the word *liberalization*. In 1974, exchange controls, which had been in effect since 1931 and uninterruptedly since 1963, were removed. Price controls were progressively relaxed. Interest-rate controls were abandoned in 1977. The conclusion seems to offer itself: it is not so much inflation as its repression by government controls that counts particularly in this context.

Beyond that, the following facts are to be taken into account:

- The net rate of return on capital during the lapse of low investment was also very low. Arnold Harberger and Daniel Wisecarver expressed their surprise at having found so low an average rate of return on total capital as 4.97 percent for the period 1967–71, which they compared to rates ranging between 8.5 and 12.5 percent estimated for Colombia, Canada, and the United States, and up to 15 percent found in Argentina, Brazil, and India. They report a somewhat better, but still low, rate of return on private capital (5.8 percent).[8] These authors, writing in 1976 or 1977, expressed their expectations that the rates would rise when the Uruguayan economy left stagnation behind. They did: for 1974–78, in the update by the Central Bank staff, the two rates averaged 6.6 and 7.8, and both seemed to be edging upwards.

- The ratio of net saving to NDP was very low, as table 3 indicates, particularly in the first four periods (fifteen years) when it averaged 0.5 percent.

- The remaining source of investment financing—external resources—fluctuated very intensely, and was negative in the critical period of 1962–68 (table 3).

Table 3
Net Saving, Net Investment, and Net
External Resources Received, by Selected Periods
(as percentages of net national product)

Period	Net saving[a]	Net receipt of external resources[b]	Net investment[c]
1956–59	−2.1	6.7	4.6
1960–61	1.6	4.2	5.8
1962–68	1.5	−0.9	0.6
1969–70	1.1	2.1	3.2
1971–73	3.0	0.5	3.5
1974–79	3.4	4.2	7.6
1956–79 average	1.5	2.5	4.0

[a]Deduction of net receipt of external resources from net investment.

[b]Imports minus exports.

[c]From table 1.

Source: Central Bank of Uruguay, *Statistical Bulletin,* various issues.

Low rates of return on capital again point to plenty of unused capacity. During an inflation, they further suggest an overvalued currency, price controls, and taxation rules that assumed stable money was also at play.[9]

A low savings rate has obvious explanatory power, but it calls in turn for an explanation. The early establishment of an unfunded social security system with comprehensive retirement benefits must have exercised a strong depressive influence on the level of savings.[10] The disruptive effect of interest-rate controls with high inflation on capital markets probably accounted for most of the rest.

Low saving meant that external resources became the dominant determinant of net investment variations, as table 3 indicates. The availability of these was undoubtedly hindered by monetary instability and exchange control.

Key to Stagnation

Most of the clues we have been pursuing point in the direction of one principal suspect—inflation, or more specifically, inflation under repressive conditions. Only intense protectionism, leading to major misallocation of capital resources, could be cited as a significant exception, but even that was largely a by-product of exchange control, an inflation-repressing instrument.

It is therefore of interest to look into the problem of why Uruguay should have become a high-inflation country, after having been a proud island of monetary stability in the Southern Cone of Latin America, and after having been furthermore rewarded for its hatred of unsound money by distinguished economic performance.

As might be feared, the trouble began in the field of ideas— ideas on money. The notion that had presided over Uruguay's stage of vigorous growth had been that an inconvertible paper currency was an unmitigated evil, to be avoided at all costs. State banks, the notion further went, holding the privilege to issue bank notes, even gold-backed and fully convertible bank notes, were dangerous institutions, because—as experience in the South American area had shown time and again—the road between convertibility and inconvertibility was short and easy. Towards the turn of the century, these thoughts had lost part of their strength, enough to allow the creation of a State Bank invested with the exclusive right to issue bank notes, but not enough to allow any possible penchant of the Bank governors towards monetary laxity to become manifest for several decades. Then came the Great Depression, and its unsettling power spread from the outer world of economic magnitudes to the inner realm of economic beliefs. By and large, however, the tradition of stern fiscal discipline that the gold standard had implanted held its ground for another quarter-century, keeping deficits at an average below 1 percent of GDP. Bank credit, on the other hand, was growing at a comparatively high rate all the while. If we refer to the 1956–59 period, which we saw in table 1 as a stage of negative real growth and relatively high inflation, we find fiscal deficits to average only 0.4 percent of GDP but credit expansion to reach 6.2 percent of GDP.

Credit was naturally flowing to the private sector. It went through the commercial banks, including a very large government-owned bank, which in their turn were credit-fed by the Central Bank. Until 1939 the Central Bank was constrained in its monetary expansion by its gold stock and a ceiling on the fiduciary issue. This constraint was then relaxed to allow the Central Bank to rediscount commercial bills maturing in no more than six months, provided they related to the sale of goods, without a ceiling. The theory was that since the demand for the goods preceded the creation of money, this could not have inflationary effects. It was no new idea, but rather the hard-dying "real bills doctrine" originated in England in the nineteenth century during the currency–versus–banking schools controversy, that has had a way of surfacing afterwards in different places at different times.[11]

Uruguay has provided one of its clearest factual refutations: the annual inflation rate in the twenty years prior to 1939, when the "real bills doctrine" was received by legislation, was 0 percent. In the ten subsequent years, it was 6 percent; in the next ten years (still before fiscal deficits grew beyond 1 percent of GDP) it was 12.5 percent. This was not yet the galloping inflation that would come when fiscal deficits added their share (in 1962 the budget deficit suddenly soared to 4.7 percent of GDP, and has fluctuated around 4 percent ever since), but this phase of mild, private credit–propelled inflation was essential in paving the road for what would follow.

Why did it happen? That is to say, why was the wrong monetary theory adopted? Why did the country allow itself to be lured away from the path of monetary stability, along which it had fared so well?

In necessarily compact form, we shall propose an answer to these questions. Before we do, however, there is an additional fact that I should like to bring up. It concerns the time path of the inflation rate, which up to the early 1930s and since the 1950s has been very clearly cyclical. The variable peaked five times in twenty-two years, so the cycle averaged three years and eight months. More significantly, of the six peaks, five corresponded to years immediately following the year an election was held (presidential, congressional, and local all together), always in November, with no other elections held. There was therefore an unmistakable electoral or political cycle associated with that of inflation. Only the 1963–67 electoral cycle was interrupted by a non-electoral-year inflation peak in 1965, which happened to be a year of record credit expansion. After Congress was dissolved by the president in conjunction with the armed forces in 1973, and no further elections were held, the path followed by inflation became quite irregular. Furthermore, all the monetary and fiscal variables that economic theory would associate with inflation follow the same pattern quite closely. Table 4 shows this very distinctly. Government expenditure, for instance, peaks in exactly every electoral year, hence one year before inflation, except when this falls out of step with the political cycle. The rediscount of commercial bills shows a peak one year before that of inflation, without exception, for as long as the system was in effect. The fiscal deficit has peaks either the year previous to that of inflation (four times) or simultaneously with inflation (twice) and only once does it precede inflation by two years. The last column bears the influence of the two previous ones, and the similarity of its pattern to the others is to be expected.

The overall pattern is clear-cut. On the approach of each election, the party in office invariably used its control over the country's monetary and fiscal systems in a way that, in its opinion, would improve its chances of electoral victory (which, by the way, favored the incumbent party five out of the seven times involved; how spending public money could have that effect is too obvious to

Table 4

The Political-Inflationary Cycle

(distance of peaks of several variables
to nearest inflation-rate peak)

Peak of inflation rate[a]	Peak of			
	Government expenditure	Commercial bills rediscounted	Fiscal deficit	Net domestic credit growth
1951	−1	−1	−1	−1
1955	−1	−1	−2	0
1959	−1	−1	−1	−1
1963	−1	−1	−1	−1
1965	−3	−1	0	0
1967	−1	−1	0	−2
1972	−1	—[b]	−1	−1

[a]All peak-inflation years immediately succeeded an election year, with the exception of 1965.

[b]The system of Central Bank rediscounting of commercial bills was discontinued between 1967 and 1972.

Source of basic data: Central Bank of Uruguay, *Statistical Bulletin*, various issues.

require comment). Let us just remark in passing how fortunate it was for the politicians that inflation would lag one year behind expenditure, and how unfortunate for the cause of monetary stability! But the aspect that we wish to emphasize is the connection between the electoral cycle and credit to the private sector.

Inflation works like a tax, and in the perception of many economists is in fact a kind of tax. Governments procure real resources by printing new money, thereby causing the public to cut down on their own expenditure in order to replenish the purchasing power of their cash balances. This much is clear. But what if the monetary authority injects credit into the system, thereby expanding the money supply and generating price inflation, while all along the government keeps a balanced budget? How does the conception of inflation as a tax stand under those circumstances?

Tax revenue is used by governments basically for two purposes: to purchase goods and services (public consumption and investment), and to make transfer payments. A tax and a subsidy may be so coupled that the money goes from the taxpayer's pocket to the subsidy recipient's purse only after a brief sojourn at the

Treasury's coffers. But even that swift passage through the exchequer is avoided if the tax resorted to is inflation.

The most likely beneficiaries of the subsidy when the inflation tax uses the channel of private-sector credit are the banks, and the next most likely beneficiaries are the bank's borrowers. The banks pay negative real interest rates for their deposits—the whole point of the policy is to depress interest rates—and their borrowers pay real interest rates that are also negative, but somewhat less so.

In support of the hypothesis that private banks were one of the subsidy beneficiaries, we shall merely refer to the number of banks on the Uruguayan money market. Between 1920 and 1944, their number fluctuated very slightly around a mean of nineteen. The commercial-bills rediscount program started, we pointed out earlier, in 1939, but took some time to get in full swing. By 1950 the number had risen by one-third to twenty-six; by 1955 the old average had more than doubled (41), and by 1965 it had almost trebled (56).

That was the peak. That year the banking system suffered a severe crisis. In the previous two or three years, the inflation rate had soared, having by then received additional momentum from high fiscal deficits. The public reacted by drastically reducing their demand for bank deposits of all kinds, time deposits in particular. With the high number of banks, the average real deposits per firm shrank to insignificance, and several crashes understandably followed. Three years later the number of banks had fallen by one-fourth, and the reduction continued for years.

We do not have so clear an indicator of the borrowers' sharing in the inflation subsidy, but for the relevant period for which we have data on banks' lending rates (1956–67)[12] we find that these were negative in real terms three-fourths of the time. By the author's reckoning, over that period two-thirds of the subsidy overflowed into the nonbanking private sector.

"The art of the possible" was Napoleon's definition of politics. An observer of the Uruguayan scene might prefer to say that it is *the fine art of stealthily transferring real resources from the general public to the ruler's political friends.* The thought ties in with John Stuart Mill's observation to the effect that capital accumulation will not occur unless "there is a preponderant probability that those who labour and spare will be permitted to enjoy."

The Recent Past

Uruguay managed to break loose from economic stagnation in the mid-1970s. Paradoxically, this resumption of growth closely followed the first oil shock. Totally dependent on imports for its petroleum consumption, not only did Uruguay have to face an oil bill blown up almost fourfold in 1974, but it also saw its export revenue cut down drastically, principally from beef prices plummeting to about one-fourth of their 1973 level. Throughout the 1970s Uruguay had to make do with worse terms of trade than at any other time since the Great Depression. Yet it was precisely as of 1974 that the economy got back on its feet and was again on the march (table 1, cols. 1 and 2).

Paradoxes are often illusory—upon more accurate perception they may vanish. The mystery surrounding Uruguay's recovery from economic stagnation in so unfavorable an international environment clears up as soon as it is realized that the oil shock brought the country from its mad dream of autarchy back into reality.

For a country the size of Uruguay, economic *reality* means trade; *realism* means opening up to trade and finance, accepting the consequent challenge, making the most of the upswings of the world economy, and adjusting promptly to the downswings. Uruguay had foolishly tried to ignore the law proclaiming that all successful small economies must be wide-open economies, like those of the Swiss and the Dutch, or those of Hong Kong and Singapore, and the gods had delivered upon it a terrible nemesis. In a certain sense, the oil shock was a blessing in disguise, unpleasantly imposing the right policies, a task not totally unlike that which Commodore Perry's fleet carried out for Japan in 1853.

After appointing an uncharacteristic minister of finance,[13] the Uruguayan government dismantled on one day in 1974 the exchange controls that for over four decades had submitted imports to a quota system, and for a shorter but considerable lapse had also severely restricted all other foreign exchange transactions. Henceforth the available foreign exchange would be allocated by the market rather than by the bureaucrat's rationing system. For the first time foreign investors found that they were free to remit interest and dividends home, indeed to repatriate all their capital if they so wished. Far from profiting from this newly gained liberty by sending capital out, they reacted to it by bringing more in. Since 1976 international reserves, after having dwindled for decades despite the obsessive official concern to preserve them, began to grow substantially.

There were other reforms adopted in the same spirit. Price controls were almost universally repealed. A tax reform that did away with hundreds of low-yielding taxes that were costly to administer, including the largely evaded personal income tax, made the value-added tax the mainstay of the system. By 1979 the Treasury accounts were back in the black for the first time in two decades. Finally, a gradual tariff reduction was announced, but for some reason the boldness that presided over external financial policy never extended over to commercial policy—the tariff reform never got very far.

In response to the breath of fresh air that the removal of controls allowed in, the economy reacted healthily. Exports, where stagnation had begun its sway over the Uruguayan economy, started growing at nearly 10 percent a year. Investment grew even faster. Total output set a growth trend exceeding 4 percent, which looked both sustainable and, given the low rate of population growth (about 1 percent), also satisfactory.

Lest we convey the impression that there is an unqualifiedly happy ending to the story of Uruguay's economic vicissitudes, in table 5 we have combined the data covering the resumption-of-growth stage with those covering the recession into which the economy began sliding in latter 1981 and fell freely in 1982.

Needless to say, a recession does not cancel out the gains shown over a long-run trend—all the more so when worldwide business conditions have played a major role in bringing it about and all countries in the area have been similarly hit, those following essentially *dirigiste* policy guidelines (like Brazil and Mexico) as well as those leaning toward a free-market orientation (like Chile and Uruguay). That the picture associating economic liberalization and success had been unfortunately dimmed in the popular perception is another story. However, with one aspect of the present Uruguayan recession, or rather of its domestically induced depth, we must become concerned; for it conveys a message that is relevant to the general scope of this volume. In a nutshell, the

Table 5
1974–81 Growth Period and 1982 Contraction
(trends of real variables and 1982 deviation from trend)[a]

	1974–81 trend	Deviation of 1982 levels from trend
Gross domestic product	4.1	−15.6
Gross domestic investment	15.8	−43.2
Private consumption	2.4	−7.0
Exports	9.2	−23.8
Imports	8.9	−23.8
Agricultural production	1.5	−4.7
Industrial production	4.5	−25.1
Output of construction industry	12.7	−35.3

[a]All variables are nominal flows corrected for price changes. Logarithmic trends were fitted to the 1974–81 period, then extrapolated one year to compare with the actual 1982 level.

Source: Trends and deviation from trends are the author's estimates from data in Central Bank of Uruguay, *Statistical Bulletin,* various issues.

message says two things: (a) there is more to rescuing an economy from the grips of mistaken policies than removing the wrong measures; the transition calls for specific lore and dexterity; (b) all this is particularly relevant over the monetary stabilization part of the transition.

As table 1 substantiates, the period 1974–79 recorded major achievements in the fields of capital formation and economic growth, but no progress at all with respect to curbing inflation. This became particularly regrettable when government deficit spending fell sharply in 1977 and 1978 to a mean of 1.2 percent of GDP, down from the 3.2 percent average of the previous decade, and was further transformed into a surplus in 1979–80. Inflation had existed to finance the substantial fiscal deficits in a country where the capital market offered the Treasury meager possibilities. Why should it proceed unabated now that it served no visible purpose?

In 1978 the country's authorities thought they had broken the secret of the inflationary plague. This was while they tried to sterilize the monetary effects of the foreign capital inflow. Under the current exchange rate system—a crawling peg—the Central

Bank was committed to buy whatever foreign currency the
market chose to proffer to it. As Central Bank officials tried to
offset the monetary consequences of their foreign exchange
purchases by selling Treasury bills on the open market, they saw
that the more Treasury bills they sold, the more money flowed in
from overseas that they were forced to buy. They realized the
money supply lay outside their control. Expectations themselves
were enough to keep prices rising. As prices rose, so did the
amount of money people wished to hold. Traditional theory said inflation could be fought under such circumstances by refusing to
print the new money demanded by the market. This, however, did
not seem to fit the facts of a small open economy with a fixed rate
of exchange, including the crawling-peg version, where private
transactors could "import" (externally borrow) the money they required, making inflation a self-fulfilling prophecy.[14]

On the strength of this realization, an alternative became apparent. Either the Uruguayan peso should be floated and allowed
to appreciate, thereby dampening inflation, or expectations should
be attacked directly. The authorities feared the effects of currency
appreciation on the levels of employment and chose the latter
course. Specifically, this choice meant that thenceforward the
Central Bank would announce the rates of exchange at which it
would be prepared to buy and sell U.S. dollars on each day for the
next six months or so. As one month went by, a new table with a
new batch of future quotations that were to rule six months later
would be posted. The devaluation rate would be made to decelerate, hopefully causing the rate of inflation to dampen in parallel
fashion.

Facts failed to conform to this smooth pattern. The main effect
of the new system was to attract even larger amounts of foreign
capital, now lured by the foreknowledge of the rate of exchange.
Investment was further boosted and domestic prices for a while
soared. A gap between the external purchasing power of the
peso—resulting from the foreposted decelerating exchange rates
—and its domestic purchasing power—run down by the accelerating inflation—opened up, then increasingly widened. Eventually
the overvalued peso began to tell on exporting industries and
those competing with imports. By 1980 it was clear that there
would have to be a painful adjustment. Inflation was finally losing

strength (as measured by the consumer price index, the within-year inflation rates for 1979, 1980, and 1981 were 83.1, 42.8, and 29.4 percent respectively)—but at the usual price of disinflation. Then two separate series of events combined to make things worse. First, in mid-1981 the American economy went into recession after barely twelve months' recovery, and most industrial countries followed suit. Commodity prices, already declining, then fell precipitously. (*The Economist*'s index records a disastrous 36 percent drop between October of 1980 and the same month in 1982.) Prices for beef, Uruguay's main export item, were among the hardest hit. This severe blow came at the worst possible time, adding its strength to the contraction forces already at play. Second, faced with the compounded effect of world recession and that which their own stabilization strategy had generated, the Uruguayan authorities tried a major reflationary stunt: in 1982 the overall deficit of the public sector jumped from its negligible levels in 1981 to a staggering 12 percent of GDP, and the state-owned mortgage bank made loans to a private sector amounting to approximately one-half of the fiscal deficit. The huge mass of money largely originated at the Central Bank's printing presses.[15] This was totally inconsistent with the foreign exchange policy, which the Uruguayan public promptly realized.

No sooner would money pour out of the Central Bank than it found its way back to the same institution, to be swapped for dollars at the preposted rates. Furthermore, the public understandably classified peso-denominated assets in the high-risk category, and were prepared to keep their deposits with the local banks only when interest rates rose to exorbitant levels.[16] The high interest rates, in their turn, inhibited private investment—table 5 shows that total investment and building industry output suffered worst of all—thereby making the government's "demand management" and "make work" programs actually counterproductive.

The system of preposted exchange rates was abandoned in November 1982 after the heavy reserve losses caused the Central Bank to close its dollar window and allow the peso to float down to less than half its previous external value in a few days, spreading insolvency to large sections of the business community.[17] It left behind the most negative of images: unjustifiedly so, in our view, for the system was ill-timed and inconsistently implemented, not

inherently bad. But the impression it left was so intensely negative, nevertheless, that the whole strategy of opening up the
Uruguayan economy to trade and finance has been called into
question by the bulk of public opinion.[18]

Conclusion

The economic history of Uruguay paints a picture in sharply contrasting colors. The bright hues abound, showing that the economy performed well. Over large sections, however, the greys and
blacks predominate. Why?

Here and there external forces account for some of the failings,
but most mirror the quality of economic policy. It is on this that
our concluding section will concentrate.

There is no sensible criterion by which to evaluate policy that is
not pragmatic. Bad policies are those that generate bad consequences. We have perceived the outstanding feature of Uruguay's
economic record since the 1950s—protracted stagnation—in association with a number of policy-induced characteristics. We
refer to insufficient opening to international trade and finance, insufficient incentives to save and invest, and misallocation of
capital resources. Much of this, furthermore, had to do with inflation. How does this glum area of the picture connect with policy activity?

Let us take policy sectors one by one.

- *Commercial policy.* It marks the oldest departure of Uruguay's
  strategy from the laissez-faire line along which it had done so
  well. In the late 1940s import quotas were manipulated to reinforce tariffs in a crash campaign of import substitution. We attribute top responsibility to commercial policy in the 1948–60
  period for resource misallocation.

- *Exchange rate policy.* The existence of import quotas and, over
  the years, several types of exchange controls, was interpreted
  by the authorities as implying a degree of freedom that they
  could use in fixing exchange rates with goals other than external balance in view, such as industrialization. It was another
  source of allocative inefficiency and export disincentive. This
  aspect had a spectacular change for the better in 1974, then an

ill-starred phase from October 1978 to November 1982, as pointed out in the last section.

The continuation and intensification of inflation made recurrent devaluations of the peso indispensable. Uncertainty in this respect combined with exchange controls in discouraging foreign investment, indeed in encouraging Uruguayan residents to brace the controllers and send their money out of the country.

- *Fiscal policy.* On the expenditure side there was by and large acceptable discipline until 1961. The next year—an election year—the discipline crumbled, and deficits financed with new money became the chief source of inflation. Inflation, in its turn, coupled with measures geared to repress it, intensified the negative effects of all other policies—real exchange rates became still lower, as did controlled interest rates; price controls blunted incentives still further, etc.

  On the revenue side an infinitely complex tax system evolved, and many of the taxes barely brought enough revenue to cover administration costs.

  Both aspects showed marked improvement from 1974; then the expenditure side had a major relapse in 1982.

- *Monetary policy.* The doctrine that says it is safe for the Central Bank to issue bank notes, provided it buys commercial IOUs with them—the "real bills" theory—accounted for the substantial inflation that occurred up to 1961. Later on the resulting practice was discontinued, but the Central Bank financing of fiscal deficits had already supplied a bigger and worse source of inflation.

  Topping interest rates in such a way that banks' borrowing rates were consistently negative, and lending rates frequently so, implied allocating available capital by other means than the market, thereby causing inefficiency as well as discouraging saving and promoting capital evasion. Interest-rate ceilings were discontinued in 1977.

- *Price controls.* Large areas of the economy were subject to price controls, which numbed business incentives and caused allocative inefficiency. Controls gradually have been removed since 1974.

- *Social security*. The broad coverage of benefits in all likelihood caused private savings to be much lower than was desirable to make a significant rate of growth sustainable.

There was no single cause of Uruguay's poor growth performance; there were many, each contributing its own share. Some of these made large contributions, others were not very important. In combination, however, they were formidable. The Uruguayan case reminds one of Gulliver's, when he woke up in Lilliput—each of the many strings that tied him to the ground were flimsy, yet he could not move.

14

ANNE O. KRUEGER

Problems of Liberalization

The experience of the past three decades has convinced almost all analysts that systems of direct controls and attempts to "thwart the market" are inefficient, if not ineffective, instruments to achieve virtually any objective of policy. The enormous success of Europe and Japan in expanding output and raising living standards during the postwar era has clearly been related to sustained liberalization of trade and capital flows. Among the developing countries progress has varied markedly, but notably the most successful developing countries have generally maintained liberalized trade and payments regimes, which in turn have been made feasible only by relatively liberal domestic economic policies.

   Still, despite the clear evidence on the subject, a large number of developing countries remain caught in a stifling web of controls over economic activity. In many cases, there is general agreement that the controls no longer serve the purposes for which they were imposed, even if they once did. Many countries have had periods in which efforts were made to alter the regime and reduce or eliminate direct controls on one or more aspects of economic activity.

Those efforts have sometimes met with failure, and have made others reluctant to attempt removal of controls. The question is why that should be so: what are the problems of liberalization? Why, given the evidence that the benefits are so great, is it so difficult to accomplish? Why are politicians (and often the entire community of informed citizens) so reluctant, if not downright unwilling, to liberalize their economies?

A simple answer might, of course, be that politicians are misinformed and, for one reason or another, oblivious to the benefits attainable by liberalization. While there are undoubtedly instances where this is so (or where vested political interests have enough stake in the existing system to render its maintenance rational from the viewpoint of those in power), that set of circumstances is disregarded here. Instead, our focus is on the difficulties that arise in the process of attempting to liberalize the system, and reasons—both political and economic—why a prime minister, even if convinced of the long-term benefits of liberalization, might be reluctant to attempt it; or attempting it, might fail to achieve his objectives.

At the outset, it is necessary to define what is meant by "liberalization." A narrow definition would be that a market is liberalized if there are no quantitative restrictions attempting to control either buyers or sellers—from which it would follow that liberalization is the act of removing quantitative controls. The difficulty with this definition is that there are a variety of economic policies that can have the effect of reducing the restrictiveness of quantitative controls, such as releasing more foreign exchange to permit imports under a licensing regime. Since a more "restrictive" set of controls is presumably one in which market participants would pay more to carry out the transactions that are not permitted, liberalization of controls, to be consistent, must imply a greater reduction in the scarcity value attached to restrictions. Hence for purposes of this chapter, liberalization is defined as any policy action that reduces the restrictiveness of controls— it may be their complete removal, or the replacement of a restrictive set of controls with a less restrictive one. Under this definition, it should be noted, an action such as devaluation in the context of an import-licensing regime "liberalizes" that regime.

A second initial question has to do with the range of markets to be analyzed. Of course, there are direct controls in almost every country—rent controls in New York City, underpricing of telephone and electrical services in many developing countries, and pricing of urban transport almost universally, to name just a few. While their removal can result in difficulties of the sort discussed here, it proves convenient to focus on a narrower set of markets, but a set that is interrelated and frequently subject to controls in developing countries. This includes the foreign exchange market (for both current and capital-account transactions), the financial market, the labor market, and the market for agricultural commodities. Controls on these markets have related to one another in ways that have had important macroeconomic effects, and have been a focal point of many liberalization efforts.[1]

As a starting point, it is convenient to sketch the conditions that prevail, or have prevailed, in many developing countries in which direct controls have been used. Thereafter, we will turn our attention to the macroeconomic and microeconomic issues of liberalization. This will set the stage for consideration of the issues of timing and sequencing of liberalization efforts, which seem to be the focus of most unresolved questions.

Finally we provide some conjectures as to factors increasing the likelihood of successful liberalization attempts.

The Prototypical Illiberal Economy

In many ways that are not well understood, there seems to be a logic to the evolution of direct controls on prices and quantities over time. Once intervention has occurred, e.g., in the foreign exchange market, the responses by private agents to the initial intervention often elicit modifications, and usually intensifications, of the control system. To illustrate, an initial move to import-licensing generally reduces incentives to export, evokes cries of "unfair" from many who attempt to persuade the authorities that the system should be altered to take into account their particular circumstances, and provides incentives to evade the regime via smuggling, under- or overinvoicing, or engaging in black market transactions. All of these responses tend to induce the authorities to restrict imports even further, to modify and usually complicate the allocation rules for those imports, and also to increase surveillance. These actions in turn are likely to evoke from agents a further response to the altered incentives. As the profitability of evading or avoiding regulations increases, the discrepancy between private and social profitability widens with mounting consequences over time.

Because of these "dynamic" tendencies, the typical economy in which liberalization is contemplated and would yield high returns is not one in which a single market is regulated; rather, it is usually an economy in which a variety of markets are subject to controls of varying degrees of severity and enforcement. Often these controls are accompanied by macroeconomic difficulties that may or may not stem from the same underlying factors.

Because multiple markets are subject to intervention, the very concept of liberalization itself can mean different things in different contexts, and an attempt to sort out liberalization problems conceptually must start with identification of the types of controls initially in effect, and must recognize the interaction between them. As a starting point, it is useful to consider the interaction between macroeconomic imbalances and intervention in individual markets.

Inflation and controls. Economists have long recognized that a perfectly anticipated inflation might have relatively low economic costs, largely because markets would adjust to inflationary expectations so that the real interest rate and other relative prices would not differ significantly from those that would obtain in the absence of inflation. In reality, however, price increases and altered inflation rates usually result from an effort on the part of the government to gain control over resources without offsetting tax increases. Sometimes this effort to obtain resources is part of planned increases in public-investment programs, although sometimes it is the immediate counterpart to direct controls (as, for example, when food prices to consumers are maintained at below-market levels through rationing while farmers are paid at higher prices).

Either way, once inflation starts, the usual response of governments is to attempt direct controls to offset some of its apparent effects. Maintaining a fixed nominal exchange rate, with reluctant adjustments that lag significantly behind inflation, is one of the most frequent responses. In many cases, governments have kept constant the prices of public-sector services, including utilities, transport, and outputs of public enterprises, in an effort to "control inflation." In the presence of an underlying inflationary process, of course, the budget deficit induced by financial losses from those activities tends to further intensify inflationary pressures, while simultaneously increasing the degree of distortion in the economy due to regulated prices. In some instances, governments have also attempted to impose price controls over private-sector economic activity. There have also been efforts to index wages and, even more frequently, to regulate nominal interest rates.

These markets—especially foreign exchange, credit, and labor—play key roles in the allocation of resources throughout the economy. When they are controlled, costs can be very high, and their liberalization is essential for markedly improved economic performance. Usually, however, liberalization measures are combined with policies aimed at least in part at reducing the rate of inflation, rather than at freeing the individual markets while permitting inflationary pressures to continue. Thus, it proves impossible to analyze direct controls and efforts to eliminate them without taking into account the macroeconomic setting in which those efforts are undertaken. While some countries have experienced inflation without direct controls, and a few countries (most notably India) have resorted to direct controls in the absence of inflation, the majority of direct controls either have been imposed in an effort to reduce inflation rates or have intensified their restrictiveness because of domestic inflation (as with a fixed nominal exchange rate).

Hence, there are strong and important interactions between the macroeconomic processes—the government budget and the determination of the money supply and domestic credit—and control conditions in individual markets. Moreover, when the nominal rate of interest and/or the exchange rate is fixed, reduction in the rate of inflation automatically permits some degree of liberalization, in the sense that the relevant price deviates less from the level that would obtain with prices that appropriately reflect opportunity cost than it would at a higher inflation rate.

Balance-of-payments difficulties. In principle, a country experiencing internal inflation could live within its budget constraint either by permitting its exchange rate to float (although there are interesting questions as to why domestic residents should continue to hold domestic money) or by strictly rationing available foreign exchange by one system or another. The latter technique would of course entail the distortion costs associated with disparities between the domestic marginal rate of transformation in production and the marginal rate of transformation through trade. However, either system would permit continuation of domestic inflationary policies without necessarily triggering balance-of-payment difficulties.

In practice, however, few governments that have experienced inflation have fully adopted either policy. Indeed, the same political and economic factors that lead to domestic inflation usually lead to balance-of-payments deficits. Even when exchange controls and import-licensing systems are in place, the nominal exchange rate is often adjusted too little and too late, and excess demand for goods is satisfied partially by imports financed by running down reserves or borrowing from abroad.

Often, the buildup of debt permits the continuation of trade and payments imbalances, and hence of expansionary macroeconomic policies, for a period of time. However, as debt and debt-service obligations increase while foreign exchange earnings stagnate or decline, lenders are increasingly reluctant to extend additional credit. Debt-servicing difficulties, or the inability to borrow sufficiently to finance existing import orders, are frequently the condition that triggers policy changes.

Serious debt-servicing obligations in themselves confound any process of adjustment. This is in part because such obligations must be met, and in part because the level of expenditure must be cut by at least the amount to which borrowing was previously excessive. However, difficulties are intensified largely because foreign debt has political connotations that make the perceived "foreign intervention" troublesome, and the "debt crisis" atmosphere is probably not conducive to systematic preparation of a liberalization plan and its political acceptance.

While a few genuine liberalizations have taken place where existing foreign debt or inability to sustain previous borrowing levels was neither a trigger nor a serious problem (e.g., South Korea in the early 1960s), such liberalizations have been the exception rather than the rule. And, as international financial markets have become increasingly integrated in recent years, debt-servicing difficulties have, if anything, assumed increasing importance as both an impetus to policy reform and as an additional problem to be resolved if those reforms are to be successful.

This complication is especially important in countries where earlier there had been substantial reliance on quantitative restrictions to restrain import levels. For in those cases, a necessary condition for liberalization is that the domestic price of importables must be permitted to fall relative to the domestic price of exportables, for when imports have been so restrained, both imports and exports are below the levels and shares of GNP that would prevail in the absence of the distortion. What is required, therefore, is an expansion of both imports and exports. The least inflationary means of achieving this would be to combine an increase in the nominal exchange rate with simultaneous import liberalization. This would bring down the domestic price of importables while raising that of exportables, which would in turn minimize inflationary consequences of liberalization. However, when import levels have been sustained by borrowing and when further credit is not possible, it becomes necessary to curtail imports. Such further curtailment is consistent with liberalization only if either the level of economic activity declines to shift import demand downward, or the nominal exchange rate is adjusted upward by a substantially larger amount than would be the case with an increased import flow.

The former choice—domestic recession—is politically painful and economically wasteful (economic activity would have to shift downward by the amount that imports must decline *times* the inverse of the marginal propensity to import). Especially if there are lags prior to an export response to increased incentives, the size of the required shift may be significantly greater than would be consistent with liberalization in the long run. The latter alternative— a larger devaluation—could in principle permit the removal of import-licensing mechanisms and the simultaneous adjustment of the demand and supply of foreign exchange. However, the larger size of the required devaluation would in itself give rise to a larger once-and-for-all jump in the price level, which would in turn contribute to the momentum of inflation and reduce the likelihood that the desired degree of real devaluation could be achieved.

While the observant skeptic may wonder whether a floating exchange rate might attain the desired result, it must be noted that such a solution would be consistent with liberalization only if the financial markets were also simultaneously liberalized and the rate of interest were permitted to be market-determined. For in the presence of controlled (and usually negative real) interest rates, full liberalization of the exchange regime for both current and capital account and a floating exchange rate would surely result in capital outflows and rapid depreciation of the currency in excess of the rate of inflation.

And, while full liberalization is clearly desirable, few governments (and perhaps even their economic advisers) are willing to take the complete plunge into full liberalization of financial and exchange markets simultaneously. There is insufficient experience with the "cold shower" approach to liberalization to provide confidence that its short-term costs can be contained within reasonable bounds. Indeed, if there were legitimate doubts in the early 1970s about the feasibility and desirability of complete instantaneous liberalization, the experiences of Argentina, Chile, and Uruguay have provided further support for the skeptics. Whether those experiences should be so interpreted is a topic deferred until later. At this juncture, the important point is that in the context of an initial debt-servicing crisis, attention is usually focused on the foreign exchange market; and the unpleasant choice, in the absence of additional lending from abroad, lies between greater inflationary pressures to restore equilibrium or domestic unemployment and deflation. Obviously, this highlights one of the important contributions international lending can make to a country when its leaders are genuinely committed to a full liberalization: it can permit higher levels of imports than would otherwise be feasible to bring about a quick adjustment of relative prices. Not only does this reduce the economic and political strains associated with liberalization, it also reduces business' uncertainty as to the likelihood that liberalization will persist.

Microeconomic aspects of liberalization. As has been seen, the same reluctance to maintain government expenditures in line with receipts that generates inflationary pressures in the first place also often results in government controls that—superficially at least—are intended to reduce the observed inflationary consequences. In many instances, these controls themselves introduce further macroeconomic distortions into the economy (as, for example, when price controls on output of public enterprises further fuel the government deficit), but they also distort important markets in the economy.

Inflationary pressures are not the only reason for sectoral distortions, however. Important markets are controlled for other motives as well: unwillingness to pass on increased energy prices; desires to "keep food prices down"; maintenance of below-market clearing rates of interest to "encourage capital formation in key sectors" or for other reasons; investment-licensing to "guide new investments into socially desirable channels"; and the raising of the real wage in the controlled part of the economy above its level elsewhere to "protect the worker."

These controls not only have significant economic costs in themselves, they also interact with other distortions. High labor costs combine with import restrictions to encourage development of very capital-intensive, import-competing activities. Exchange-rate overvaluation discourages the production of agricultural exports, and domestic controls on food prices further depress agricultural incomes, which in turn further stimulate out-migration to the cities. Moreover, some controls (such as domestic marketing boards for agricultural commodities) sever the link between domestic prices and international ones, thereby insulating the market in question from any automatic impact in the event of an exchange-rate change or other policy shift.

There are interesting and important questions concerning the payoff from various types of liberalization—in the presence of controlled markets elsewhere in the economy—to which economists do not as yet have satisfactory answers. What is clear is that the same liberalization measures may have very different impacts depending on the circumstances in other markets in the economy in question, and that an analysis of the effects of liberalization, one market at a time, may yield misleading results.

Difficulties of Liberalization

One of the major difficulties with liberalization is that it is usually undertaken in the midst of an exceedingly difficult situation, and often in a crisis atmosphere. Moreover, the fact that the prevailing distortions have induced uneconomic activities or techniques of production implies that a successful liberalization will necessarily penalize some of those who had earlier responded appropriately to the existing incentive structure.

These difficulties are in and of themselves serious enough. In practice, they are often confounded by the simultaneous effort to restore some degree of macroeconomic equilibrium and, in greater or lesser degree, to liberalize some key markets. That is, efforts to bring the government budget under control and to reduce the rate of inflation are often intertwined with policies designed to liberalize imports, to restore producers' incentives in agriculture and energy, and to eliminate price controls and licensing mechanisms.

In most developed countries, moreover, inflationary pressures usually have been permitted to be passed through into price increases; hence few direct controls have accompanied the inflationary process. As a consequence, anti-inflationary policies in developed countries have generally been undertaken under circumstances in which distortions in key markets are substantially smaller than those in some developing countries. Even for developed countries, however, efforts to reduce inflationary pressures have been at best partially successful and have required fairly determined political resolve for considerable intervals of time.

In developing countries in which inflation has been a substantial problem and direct controls have been an initial policy response, anti-inflationary programs are even more complex and fraught with difficulty than in developed countries because of the existence of so many controlled markets. A major difficulty with many liberalization efforts, and especially those focused on the trade sector of the economy, has been the presumption that an anti-inflationary program, simultaneously embarked upon, would succeed.[2]

It seems clear that, in practice, efforts to liberalize the trade sectors of developing countries have foundered more often upon the failure of the accompanying anti-inflationary program than

on any other single factor. Space limitations preclude a full analysis of the difficulties of combining an anti-inflation program with
efforts to liberalize other key markets. Only two fairly obvious
points need to be made. First, there are ways in which the dependence of trade liberalization on curbing inflation can be at least
reduced. Most notably, a crawling peg, rather than a higher fixed
nominal exchange rate, can assure some degree of independence
in the two reform efforts. Second, liberalization is more likely to be
achieved by anti-inflationary programs designed to assure that
governments will not resort to direct controls than by programs
aimed at attaining the lowest recorded rate of price increase over
the short term. For example, to remove controls on prices of essential government services will reduce the inflation rate more effectively in the long run than to set an initially realistic nominal
price that will erode again quickly unless inflation is contained.
Paradoxically, anti-inflationary programs structured to succeed
only if the inflation rate declines are less likely to bring down the
rate of inflation than are programs designed to liberalize markets
regardless of whether or not the anti-inflationary policies succeed.

With those comments as background, let us set aside the
difficult questions surrounding inflation control—and for that
matter the issue of whether there can be sustained liberalization
against the background of rising inflation rates—and focus
henceforth on actual liberalization of markets. Two general questions need to be addressed: (1) what reforms, undertaken in-
dividually, are likely to be welfare-improving even in the presence
of other controlled markets; and (2) which are the more important
markets to liberalize when one starts from a situation with multiple controls and distortions? Thereafter, our focus is directed on
each of the important markets, and the most frequently encountered problems of liberalization in each market are discussed in
turn. The difficult questions surrounding the timing and sequencing of reforms are deferred to the last section.

Welfare-improving liberalizations of individual markets.
The generalized theory of the "second best" tells us that whenever
there are significant links between markets, it is in general impossible to ascertain the direction in which welfare will change as
the result of a small reduction in the distortion operating in a

single market. Yet in most countries in which liberalization efforts are contemplated, total liberalization is generally infeasible; reforms, if undertaken at all, will be undertaken in some markets before they are undertaken in others.

The question arises, therefore, when a particular market can be freed in reasonable confidence that the net effect will be welfare-improving. In attempting to answer this question we will ignore considerations such as the degree of rent-seeking and the greater incentive effects of competition that may result from liberalization, which tend to lead to the presumption that freeing up any market may yield welfare benefits. Moreover, the analysis must of necessity be empirical rather than theoretical. As such, it must be recognized that situations could arise that would deviate sufficiently from the usual case so that the presumptions set forth here would be invalid.

Let us look at each of the major markets subject to controls in turn. Consider, first, agriculture. Here, the available evidence seems to suggest that producers base their production decisions on relative prices within their sector. For countries that are exporters of food crops, consequently, anything that moves relative prices of agricultural commodities closer to their international levels is probably on net potentially welfare-improving. (I ignore here the important short-run welfare losses of low-income persons paying higher prices for food, on the grounds that superior measures can be found to yield the same real income transfer.) Thus, freeing producer prices in agriculture to permit them to rise will improve welfare even if the exchange rate is overvalued: the relative prices of alternative agricultural crops will reflect their opportunity costs in the international market vis-à-vis each other, while the price of agricultural commodities relative to other goods and services will move in the appropriate direction.

A more difficult question arises in countries in which comparative advantage lies in export crops. These countries would, under efficient resource allocation, import food. In that circumstance, the decontrol of domestic producer prices under import-licensing may raise food prices relative to export crops. In the presence of an overvalued nominal exchange rate, resources may be further pulled from export crops to food, possibly with negative welfare implications. Hence, there is probably some question as to whether liberalization of domestic prices of agricultural commodities is necessarily welfare-improving unless it is accompanied by moves toward a more realistic exchange rate.

Likewise, it would appear that welfare could always be improved by liberalizing the financial market and permitting the real interest rate to become positive. Exchange-rate overvaluation and artificially low nominal interest rates tend to work in the same direction: they encourage the introduction of overly capital-intensive activities. Consequently, there is a presumption that moving either the exchange rate or the interest rate in an appropriate direction is likely to improve welfare.

Similar considerations would appear to apply to the labor market: even in the presence of exchange-rate overvaluation, the move to a freer market should be welfare-improving. Indeed, to the extent that there is exchange-rate overvaluation, reduction in the real wage will increase the profitability of activities in which a labor-abundant country has a comparative advantage.

Finally, there is the exchange rate and the market for traded goods. A first question is whether the move from a licensing system to a uniform tariff, holding the total level of imports constant, is welfare-improving. In theory, anything could happen as a result of such a move: resources previously allocated to exportables could be pulled into import-competing activities previously subject to less-than-average protection, possibly resulting in a further loss in welfare. In practice, however, it seems likely that, provided exporters are permitted to purchase their intermediate goods and raw materials at international prices,[3] a uniform rate of tariff is to be potentially welfare superior to import-licensing and associated dispersion of implicit tariff rates.

In addition, there is the question of the welfare effect of raising the nominal exchange rate in the presence of other controls. One can imagine a number of circumstances (e.g., the presence of domestic price controls) that would tend to reduce the impact of a change in the exchange rate, but it is difficult to imagine a situation in which increasing the nominal exchange rate would not be welfare-improving. Such a move necessarily reduces the bias of the trade regime toward import substitution. This follows because with import-licensing, the domestic price of exportables will increase. With the quantity of imports unaltered or increasing, the relative price of exportables must increase. As we have already seen, this will move agricultural relative prices in the appropriate direction, and simultaneously offset in part any distortion in factor markets arising from lower-than-average duties on imported capital equipment.

Another question arises with respect to the exchange rate— namely, whether it is advisable to liberalize capital flows in the presence of a highly restrictive set of controls on domestic financial flows. While there are some types of partial liberalization that may be welfare-improving in the presence of distorted domestic capital markets (e.g., easing of the restrictions on the inflow of private capital), it seems reasonably clear that the total liberalization of capital flows is infeasible in the presence of a controlled domestic interest rate: capital outflow would immediately result. A related problem pertains to liberalization of capital flows in the presence of a highly restrictive regime covering current-account transactions. This is a difficult and important question, and one on which analysis to date has not shed very much light. There is no strong presumption: one could legitimately argue that, since exchange of assets is exchange of the capitalized values of income streams, income streams generated by distorted prices are probably the inappropriate ones at which to trade. It would then follow that capital-account liberalization should not be undertaken unless both current account and domestic financial transactions are already liberalized. Whether further analysis can shed additional light on this important question remains to be seen. It would appear, therefore, that with the possible exception of liberalization of agricultural prices in the context of overvaluation in a country with comparative advantage in tree crops, and a liberalization of capital-account transaction in the presence of domestic financial controls or current-account controls, there is a presumption that liberalization of any of the other markets typically subject to controls is likely to be welfare-improving.

Which are the most important markets to liberalize? Whereas some theoretical presumptions permit inferences about the direction of welfare change resulting from liberalization of individual markets, it is much more difficult to provide a solid *a priori* basis for inferring the order of magnitude of costs associated with controls in different markets. Circumstances vary with both the nature of the controls in place and the structure of the domestic economy.

It might be, for example, that two countries had controls in both labor and capital markets. Country A might have had relatively little intervention in the labor market but high negative real rates of interest. Perhaps country B's labor legislation, by contrast, significantly raised the real cost of labor but its nominal interest rate was only slightly below that which would prevail in the absence of regulation. In some countries, controls may be relatively light in some markets and much more stringent in others, so that the welfare ranking would differ for that reason.

Differences in economic structure may also matter. For example, it is probably a reasonable conjecture that controls on producer prices in agriculture are more detrimental to welfare in some poor African countries than are overvalued nominal exchange rates—although the combination of the two is certainly more harmful than either one alone would be. The same distortions in South Korea would very likely be ranked in the opposite order in terms of their welfare effects: given the level of development of the economy and the diminished relative importance of the agricultural sector, exchange-rate overvaluation might clearly be more costly.

All that can be done, therefore, is to venture some tentative hypotheses about circumstances under which different controls might be more or less detrimental. Starting with the foreign trade market, it is likely that controls are more costly the smaller the size of the domestic market and the higher the per capita income of the country (because a larger fraction of economic activity is affected by the relative price of tradeables with economic growth). Certainly, for the countries now considered middle-income, it would appear that controls over foreign trade and overvalued exchange rates have been a major, if not the biggest single, source of distortion.

By much the same reasoning, controls over producer prices in agriculture have probably been more costly the lower the country's per capita income (because of the higher share of GNP originating in agriculture), the more the country's comparative advantage within agriculture lies in export crops, and the greater its overall comparative advantage in agriculture.

This leaves the labor and financial markets. Here, there is less evidence on which to base a judgment. There can be little doubt that subsidization of capital goods, either explicit or implicit, can become increasingly costly over time, as the South Korean and Israeli experiences have amply demonstrated. That this distortion is probably the major source of difficulty is a reasonable conjecture in both of these economies. The interesting questions, however, center more on the interaction between labor- and capital-market distortions on the one hand, and trade and exchange liberalization on the other.

In particular, a question of some importance is the extent to which the benefits of liberalization of the trade regime can be realized in the presence of highly restrictive wage legislation or of controlled financial and capital markets. It is of some interest that the highly successful Far Eastern exporters had relatively free labor markets as well as liberalized trade regimes, while regulation of financial markets and interest rates persisted. There is no instance that I know of, however, where a country's trade liberalization has been highly successful in the context of highly restrictive and enforced regulations surrounding the labor market.

Problems of liberalizing individual markets. It now seems fitting to examine the issues associated with liberalization in each of the key markets that affect overall resource allocation—the foreign exchange market, the labor market, the financial (and implicitly capital) market, and sectoral markets (most notably the agricultural market).

With regard first to foreign exchange, three issues are of particular importance. One—the interrelationship between anti-inflationary programs and the liberalization of the trade regime—has already been discussed. It bears repeating that more efforts at liberalizing the trade regime have foundered because a new nominal exchange rate was pegged and inflation did not abate, than for all other reasons combined. The second issue pertains to the elimination of quantitative restrictions, while the third relates to the difficulties surrounding the transition process.

Obviously, if it were possible to move to a completely open trade regime, questions concerning the dismantling of quantitative restrictions would arise only in connection with the pace of the program, a subject treated below. In most instances, however, the range of policy choices acceptable to politicians does not include an immediate move to free trade, but may include alterations of the existing machinery of controls. In some instances, quantitative restrictions have lost most if not all of their force through administrative devices, including the transference of items to a liberalized list for which licensing is not required, or abolishing licensing requirements altogether. (These actions were taken by Turkey in the devaluations of 1970 and the liberalization of 1980–81, respectively.) In other instances, administrative changes have significantly reduced the restrictiveness of the regime. These can include such measures as reducing the number of approvals required for a license, changing the import regulations from a negative list (in which all items not enumerated may not be imported), or simply granting licenses more readily to all comers. Finally, in a few instances, a country has dismantled quantitative restrictions with the intent of liberalizing but maintaining the degree of protection afforded to domestic producers. Two such cases were Israel and the Philippines.[4]

This latter attempt, while seemingly the most rational from an economist's viewpoint, is apparently the most difficult. While once-and-for-all administrative changes may have very different effects on the degree to which protection is reduced in different industries, experience suggests that reduction in protection afforded through quantitative restrictions in that way is feasible. By contrast, laborious efforts to replace quantitative restrictions with tariffs provide ample time for political pressures to be brought to bear; efforts of tribunals to find "fair" criteria for determining protection levels and then to apply them seem destined inevitably to slow down the entire process, if not to render it entirely ineffective.

One other troublesome aspect of import liberalization should be noted: in some countries, raw material and intermediate-goods imports have been liberalized first, on the plausible theory that all producers will be better able to compete when confronted with international prices for their inputs. While this argument is impeccable as far as producers of exportables are concerned, it is flawed for import-competing producers: if protection on inputs is reduced or removed before protection on output, effective protection to domestic producers in fact increases in the process of liberalization. This consideration brings clearly into focus the distinction between moving toward free trade and liberalizing the trade regime.

When it comes to the labor market, much less is known, and systematic study of liberalizations and how they have come about is urgently needed. One has the general impression that most successful liberalizations appear to have come about not by the removal or reduction of existing wage levels but rather by a failure to adjust wage levels fully with future inflation. Carvalho and Haddad, for example, have demonstrated how the Brazilian minimum wage gradually became ineffective as ever-higher percentages of the labor force were paid wage rates in excess of the minimum.[5]

Financial-market liberalization has been the focal point of considerable analysis,[6] although most of it was undertaken under the assumption that capital was relatively immobile internationally. This may have been an acceptable assumption in the 1960s, but with the greater willingness of developed countries' private financial institutions to lend to developing countries in the 1970s, a host of new issues have arisen, and there seem to be a large number of poorly understood problems. In the 1960s, some countries, notably Brazil and South Korea, seem to have been able partly to liberalize their financial markets without great difficulty. In more recent years, several efforts at financial liberalization have encountered financial difficulties of major magnitude: Argentina, Chile, and Turkey appear to be recent examples. Whether difficulties arose because of liberalization in the financial sector and the resulting competition between banks, or whether instead there was interaction between the liberalization of financial markets and that of the foreign exchange market, is a question requiring further analysis.

With regard finally to sectoral markets, the issues appear to be more political than economic. Whereas there are questions about the response of the banking sector to deregulation, the speed of response of the trade sector, and so on, there are fewer questions regarding economic behavior where sectoral markets are concerned. Instead, however, the difficulties become increasingly political, as questions of income distribution come to the fore. Resistance to reforms in the pricing of food, urban transport, energy, and other publicly provided goods and services is encountered largely because of consumer, rather than producer, interests.

Timing and Sequencing of Reforms

Our discussion up to this point has focused largely on what is known about liberalization and its problems. There remain two major issues on which much less is known, but that may be important if the probability of successful transition to a more liberalized economy is to be increased. These relate to the appropriate sequencing and timing of reforms.

The issue can best be posed by positing a set of initial conditions and then raising a series of interrelated questions. Take the case of an economy subject to exchange control, import-licensing, a negative real interest rate with credit rationing, indexed real wages with resulting open unemployment, and suppression of producer prices in agriculture. Assume further that the objective is to remove all of these distortions to the system, with a minimum present value of expected costs of the transition. A preliminary question is whether total and simultaneous removal of all controls is cost-minimizing. Unless the answer to that question is positive, questions arise as to the speed at which controls should be dismantled (the timing issue) and the chronological order (sequence) in which individual markets should be decontrolled.[7] A final question is whether, if a single distortion will remain in the system (e.g., domestic inflation due to a large government budget deficit), total and simultaneous removal of all other distortions is optimal.

The issues of sequencing and timing arise only if one believes that simultaneous and immediate removal of all controls is neither optimal nor feasible. There are some grounds for believing that the rapid removal of all controls may be the least painful way of proceeding: new signals in place will prevent resource misallocation in response to altered signals before the transition is complete; instantaneous adjustment may prevent political opposition to the move from diluting it; and, since there is considerable evidence that uncertainty about the likelihood that policy initiatives can be sustained causes delays in the responses to altered policy signals, an immediate transformation of the economic environment may reduce uncertainty. If these considerations are overriding, the issues of timing and sequencing do not arise except in a second-best context.

There are those, however, who believe that total and instantaneous dismantling of all controls may be nonoptimal. The difficulties associated with opening up capital-account transactions before the current account has been liberalized have already been discussed. A plausible argument can be made that optimal dismantling of controls might start with current-account transactions, agricultural pricing, and the domestic labor and capital markets, leaving capital-account transactions initially subject to controls. These controls would be removed (gradually? suddenly?) in a second stage of the liberalization once domestic resources had responded to altered policy signals.

Assuming that one could demonstrate that capital-account liberalization should be delayed, I know of no theory or set of conditions to provide any presumption as to the length of delay, nor for that matter whether the capital-account liberalization should then be gradual or instantaneous.

While the capital account would appear to be the best candidate for delayed liberalization, others have argued for gradual liberalization of current-account transactions or of domestic financial markets. The basis for the argument is largely judgmental, however, and it is difficult to present a systematic case. Clearly, further analysis of the liberalization efforts of the 1970s, especially in cases where domestic and international capital markets were important, is called for.

The major problem with liberalization, as with so many other economic policy problems, is that politicians, government officials, and the informed public can readily foresee those interests that are likely to be damaged in the short run by any liberalization effort; they cannot as readily see the economic activities that were harmed, and hence did not prosper, because of regulations. Moreover, even some who would in the long run benefit by liberalization (as for example the Korean businessmen who became exporters in the 1960s but were entrepreneurs in import-substitution industries in the 1950s) perceive the short-run harm that it would cause their interests and fail to recognize the new opportunities that would arise in the longer run.

That difficulty is political, and it pervades discussions of almost all changes in economic policy. But especially in the case of developing countries, the political resistance to liberalization is intensified by the enormous magnitude of the changes called for. It is almost unthinkable to citizens who have lived with exchange control, poor-quality domestic products, and domestic inflation, that their country's economy could behave far differently under a liberalized regime.

Add to this the genuine difficulties of transition—the necessary dislocations, the period of uncertainty that is likely to obtain until new signals have been maintained for a while, and the macroeconomic difficulties that in themselves present overriding problems—and it is small wonder that liberalizations are difficult to undertake and carry out. While it is clear that further research can increase our understanding of ways in which the costs of transition can be reduced, it also seems likely that determined leadership in individual countries is necessary if successful liberalization efforts are to be undertaken.

IV

Summary and Conclusion

15

ARNOLD C. HARBERGER

Economic Policy and Economic Growth

The overwhelming majority of participants in this conference—not only the authors of the principal papers, but also the formal discussants as well as the great bulk of attendees—have devoted a great part of their professional lives either to studying economic policy, consulting about it, or implementing it directly. In a very real sense, this was a conference of professionals talking to professionals, and its ambience and tone faithfully reflected that fact.

As in most fields, economic policy professionals come over time to share certain perceptions, attitudes, and concerns, even when their individual viewpoints on many specific matters may differ. The professionals in this field are certainly not naive—they do not need textbook lessons to convince them of the fearful complexity of the growth process. They *know* there is no magic formula—no combination of one or two or even ten or twelve policy buttons that, once pushed in the right order, will guarantee economic growth.

427

Economic policy professionals are also well accustomed to frustration. Proposals aimed at improving policy must run a veritable gauntlet of hazards and obstacles on their way to implementation. Most proposals do not survive, and of those that do, many emerge so mutilated or distorted that they no longer serve their intended purposes.

The frustrations of the policy process lead many professionals to become cynical after a time—to burn out, as it were. Some simply abandon their economic policy interests and turn to other things, usually in private life. Others just lose enthusiasm and "adapt to the system."

The conference group was not, however, made up of cynics and dropouts. They were members of a different clan—of dedicated people who somehow manage to bear frustration without losing hope or heart.

The foregoing paragraphs suggest the broad outlines of the professional's approach to the relationship between economic policy and growth. First is the broad recognition that policy can influence growth, either for good or ill, in many ways. The task is thus to try to exploit as many as possible of these avenues for the good. Second, it is clear that governments operate under political and social pressures from many different sources, and it would thus be foolhardy to expect those governments to march solely to the economist's drumbeat in formulating policy. Third, one must recognize that to the extent governments follow the beat of other drummers, they will probably sacrifice some amount of economic progress. And finally, successful economic policy consists in maintaining as high a batting average as possible in the countless policy decisions affecting the economy. When it must yield to other forces and pressures, successful policy will find ways to minimize the sacrifice or compromise of sound economic objectives, and will avoid critical errors of macroeconomic policy.

Some Lessons of Economic Policy

Following are some widely shared conclusions of policy professionals about the principal "lessons" associated with successful growth policy:

1. *Avoid false technicism in economic policymaking.* Too often,

and in too many countries, the task of economic planning has been conceived as that of making projections (predictions) of future economic progress. Sometimes these predictions have been elaborated in incredible detail, to the point of projecting the output of individual industries five or ten years into the future. Such exercises simply have not paid off. They have been a waste of good talent and money. They have distracted able people from the more important task of attacking real economic policy problems; and, to make things worse, they have generally been wide of the mark — often corrupted by commingling with political promises and propaganda.

2. *Keep budgets under adequate control.* Budgets need not be balanced, but there are severe limits to the budget deficits that can be incurred with relative impunity. Somewhere along the line, budgetary authorities must learn to say no to spending requests, and standing behind them, governments must learn to resist pressures to spend more. The time for governments and budgetary authorities to take their stand is clearly *before* budgetary discipline has broken down. Some bending and yielding there will (and probably must) always be, but once authorities have caved in too many times, it is as if a dam had broken, and they will be overwhelmed by a flood of requests from newly-hopeful solicitants.

3. *Keep inflationary pressures under reasonable control.* To encourage economic development in a small country, the optimal policy may be to live with the ongoing rate of inflation in the world economy. However, if, for whatever reason, a higher rate must be accepted, it should be kept both moderate and steady.

Most of the major inflations in the postwar period have had their roots in excessive fiscal deficits (see the previous point), which the governments could only finance by resort to the printing press. This was true in Argentina, Chile, and Indonesia in the 1960s, and in the recent eruptions of inflationary forces in Africa. But it is also possible to unleash very dramatic inflationary forces by printing money in order to grant credit to the private sector — as occurred in Uruguay for more than two decades, and in Brazil for about a decade beginning in the mid-1960s.[1]

Inflation undermines growth in two ways. First, it disturbs the most basic process whereby relative prices guide resources from lower-valued to higher-valued uses. In fact, the very essence of growth occurs as resource investments are made in situations featuring high relative output prices (benefits) and low input prices (costs). The key to the process is clear signals about relative prices. Inflation, on the other hand—especially when it is unsteady and thus unanticipated—disturbs those signals by obscuring the difference between *relative* and *absolute* price rises.

A second problem with inflation results from rewarding people for estimating the correct inflation rate—and thus making money from people who guess either too low or too high. Guessing the inflation rate does nothing to make the economy grow, and inflation thus diverts productive resources to non-productive purposes.

Finally, inflation tends, especially when it is unanticipated and unindexed, to generate capricious transfers of wealth among economic sectors and groups. This breaks the link between earnings and effort, and has been known to cause violent political upheavals sparked by the embittered losers.

4. *Take advantage of international trade.* It may be that most policy professionals, deep down, are free traders at heart. But this is not the way they speak in policy forums: on such a politically incandescent topic as protectionism, the professional's credibility with different groups depends on discretion. Thus, rather than openly celebrating free trade, modern policy professionals tend to emphasize the strategic choice between a relatively open versus a relatively closed economy.

The relatively open economy implies high imports and high exports relative to GDP. The relatively closed one implies the reverse: low imports (because of import restrictions) and low exports. Restrictions on imports act also as indirect restrictions on exports by causing changes in exchange rates, thus lowering the prices of exported goods. The underlying reason for this process is that imports must ultimately be paid for by exports; and if you limit one, you thus necessarily limit the other. Protecting imports thus *dis*-protects exports, distorting the most efficient allocation of resources as protection of relatively less efficient import-competing industries diverts resources (capital and labor) from more efficient export industries. In this volume, Taiwan presents the most vivid picture of advantages from liberalizing trade restrictions. With liberalization in the early 1950s, a veritable explosion of trade occurred over the next two and a half decades, increasing the dollar volume of Taiwan's exports 200 times between 1954 and 1980.

The policy professional's task at this stage is to moderate these distortions, to avoid reducing the volume of trade very seriously below its potential.

5. *Some types and patterns of trade restrictions are far worse than others.* Economists' understanding of restrictive processes took a giant step forward in the 1960s with the development of the concept of "effective protection." It was found, among other things, that the same tariff on a final product can imply incredibly different amounts of effective protection, depending on how important are imported inputs into the productive process and on how they are taxed.[2] The only sure way to guarantee against catastrophic variations in rates of effective protection—even with moderate-looking rates of nominal protection on final products— is to make the rate of nominal protection uniform across all products. This obviously means including raw materials and capital goods in the list of commodities subject to the uniform rate of protection. Even goods that are not produced in the country, and perhaps never can be, should still be subject to the uniform rate so as to keep "honest" the degree of effective protection granted to products in which they are inputs.[3] For only when all *nominal* rates of protection are equal are all *effective* rates equal to this same nominal rate. Only a given uniform rate of tariff can automatically avoid capricious and distorting variations in the effective rates of protection actually achieved. Modification of tariff schedules in the direction of greater equality is thus one of the most important reforms advocated by professionals.

6. *If import restrictions become excessive, and reducing them directly is politically impossible, mount an indirect attack on the problem by increasing incentives to export*—helping to compensate for the anti-export bias that comes with restrictions on imports. The most natural instrument for encouraging exports is to rebate at the border indirect taxes incurred during production. Such rebating is explicitly approved by the General Agreement on Tariffs and Trade (GATT) and has been implemented in whole or in part by many countries.

Other devices for encouraging exports include rebate of direct taxes and even (more drastic still) direct subsidies. (Although not approved by GATT, the latter have been used by some countries and are justified up to a point on purely economic grounds.) Obviously, when this neutralizing device has been fully implemented, further use of it ceases to be a corrective and becomes a new source of distortion.

7. *Make tax systems simple, easy to administer, and (as much as possible) neutral and non-distorting* with respect to resource allocation. The best tax for accomplishing all three of these purposes is the value-added tax. First introduced in France in the early 1950s, this tax has come to be the most important source of revenue in close to half the non-Communist world. Its neutrality, perhaps its most distinctive attribute, results from the fact that as goods pass through successive stages of production, they are taxed only on the value added at each successive stage. Thus, by the time they take shape as final products, each element or component of the final product has been taxed only once. This tax is a great improvement over the sales tax system it replaced in many countries—avoiding taxation of full value at each stage of the productive chain. This obviously ended up taxing the value added of the early stages several times, and also generated strong artificial incentives toward vertical integration of productive processes.

8. *Avoid excessive income tax rates.* There is little economic justification for rates exceeding 50 percent on any kind of income. Such rates distort behavior and create large disincentives to economic activity, while yielding little revenue. In general policy professionals favor careful and prudent design of tax systems, paying special attention to (a) allowing business firms a proper recovery of capital (for tax purposes over the economic life of an asset, and (b) preventing inflation from grossly distorting the calculation of income for tax purposes, and of the consequent tax liability.

9. *Avoid excessive use of tax incentives to achieve particular objectives.* Such incentives have been especially common in a number of Third World countries. The Brazilian law favoring investment in the northeast and in Amazonia is a good example. Under this law, a firm in another region that owes the government 1,000 in corporation income tax can take 500 of this and invest it in an approved project in the northeast, and end up paying only 500 in tax. In truth, the firm would be investing money that would otherwise belong to the government; but the firm would have claim to

the income produced. Note that the firm would be better off making the investment even if it ended up extracting only 200 or 300 in return—i.e., even if it made very bad, money-losing investments.

Another case was an investment tax credit at the incredible rate of 30 percent, which was in effect in Bolivia in the mid-1970s. Under this law, a firm could invest 1,000 yet have only 700 of "its" money involved. The remaining 300 would otherwise have gone to the government as taxes. Such a firm would probably be quite content if the investment produced a relatively quick return of 900 (viewed in light of "its" capital-at-risk of 700); yet the investment would be a disaster from an economic point of view (900 of return on a 1,000 investment). All investment tax credit schemes share this basic flaw. It was more obvious in the Bolivian case because of the very high 30 percent rate at which the tax credit was granted.

10. *Use price and wage controls sparingly, if at all.* They are rarely (if ever) justified on strictly economic grounds, so at the very least they represent a situation of non-economic objectives impinging on strictly economic goals, tending to frustrate achievement of the latter. Price and wage controls tend in particular to vitiate the crucial signaling role that prices are supposed to play— moving resources from lower-valued to higher-valued uses. High prices should reflect scarcity and attract resources to the activity in question; low prices should reflect abundance and help keep unwanted additional resources away. Most price controls reflect efforts to keep prices low in the face of scarcity, or—what often amounts to much the same thing—to perpetuate prices which used to prevail, in the face of drastically changed circumstances. The typical consequences of price controls in such situations are (a) production, responding to the signal of a low controlled price, fails to increase and may even decline in the face of scarcity; and (b) black markets emerge, frustrating for at least some buyers the efforts of government to keep prices low. Little good has ever come from government ventures into the swamp of price and wage controls.

11. *Quotas, licenses, and similar quantitative restrictions* on output, imports, exports and other economic variables are often found in tandem with efforts at price control of various types. Once again, only rarely can a cogent economic justification be found for such practices; for this reason policy professionals view them with

great suspicion. In general, such restrictions almost automatically indicate that resort is being had to some criterion other than price for rationing the limited supply among contending demanders. This gives easy scope for favoritism, which in practice can (and often does) readily degenerate into corruption. These evils are then added to the fact that such quantitative controls almost invariably reduce economic efficiency.

12. *Policy professionals tend to take a rather technical view of the problems associated with public-sector enterprises.* The professionals have typically seen too much of the world to take a dogmatically ideological position in connection with public enterprises. Some public enterprises, they know, have succeeded, while others have compiled records that no one will ever envy. The differences between the successes and the failures, it seems, can best be summarized by saying that public enterprises have succeeded on the whole when their governments allowed them to behave like enterprises. If the government is intent on using public-sector enterprises as vehicles to pursue other non-economic goals, then almost inevitably their success as economic entities is put in peril. The ways are countless in which governments have encroached on the economic functioning of their enterprises. They have artificially kept down the prices of the goods and services that public enterprises sell. This is dramatically true for electricity, gas, and telephone companies as well as other public utilities, often with the consequence that the companies, deprived of funds by low rates, were unable to maintain the quality of service. They have required the enterprises to pay above-market prices for inputs—most particularly for manual (blue-collar) workers, but also often for materials, via rules that preclude the enterprises from seeking least-cost sources on the international market. They have also set maximum salaries (usually related to those of high government officials) that were far below those prevailing in the private marketplace for major business executives. If under those circumstances public enterprises succeed in attracting managers comparable to those of similar private enterprises, it is only because some particularly dedicated people are willing to make major personal financial sacrifices. In addition, many public-sector enterprises are routinely precluded from taking the tough decisions that often make the difference between

viability and failure—to shut down a product line, to close a plant, to lay off workers when demand falls.

Policy professionals know that all of the above possibilities represent threats to the economic viability and success of public-sector enterprises. Thus they realize that public-sector enterprises are at an inherent disadvantage in the search for economic efficiency vis-à-vis private enterprises. Nevertheless, a number of public enterprises—in a goodly number of different countries—have somehow managed to surmount these obstacles and turn in good, at times even outstanding, economic performances. These successes have been achieved only through some sort of (at least tacit) understanding between the enterprise and the government, to the effect that the enterprise will not be forced or pressed to behave in an antieconomic fashion. Policy professionals hold up these cases as models for the rest.

13. *Finally, make the borderlines of public-sector and private-sector activity clear and well-defined. When the two compete in a given area, the same rules should govern their operations.* Arbitrary or capricious confiscations, without due compensation, tend to produce a typical and understandable reaction. In sectors that consider themselves threatened (even if confiscation has not yet occurred), private owners immediately tend to disinvest. Saving rates fall and capital tends to flow overseas, usually in a clandestine manner (via black markets in currency, underinvoicing of exports, overinvoicing of imports, and analogous maneuvers). Multiple examples exist of this counterproductive reaction. Rarely has a country ended up being the real gainer as the result of arbitrary and insufficiently compensated confiscation.

It would fly in the face of reality, however, to assert that a clear line can be drawn between public-sector and private-sector activities. The United States is one of the countries where the line is clearest—with electricity companies, transit systems, and other public utilities occupying much of the borderline. Most developing countries, however, have public-sector enterprises scattered widely, almost throughout the industrial complex. In these cases, the professionals' rule is clear: let the public and the private sector compete freely, under the same tax laws, the same regulations, the same rules. And, in the worst cases, if a public-sector enterprise cannot compete (a) let it go under, (b) bail it out by just

enough to keep it alive, but (c) never let it outcompete legitimate
private enterprises, simply by undercutting prices and making
losses that are then financed out of the public treasury.

The above vignettes should impart at least some insights into
the way of thinking of most policy professionals. It should be
clear from these examples that policy professionals believe they
can recognize instances where economic policy is "good" as well as
where it is irremediably bad. It should be clear, too, that some
cases are difficult to classify—complex mixtures of good and bad
elements, with the professional remaining confident of his
capacity to tell one from the other. Finally, it should be clear that
good policy, in these terms, does not carry with it any particularly
heavy ideological or political overtones. Certainly good policy
would appear to be feasible in the hands of European Social Democrats or Christian Democrats or Socialists, also in the hands of
British Conservatives or Labourites, or of American Democrats or
Republicans, or indeed of the great bulk of political groupings that
are likely to rise to governmental power (in the non-communist
parts of the world) in the foreseeable future.

The Professionals Read the Record

In this section, as editor of this volume, I will attempt to distill
some lessons from the contributions of the individual authors
represented in this volume. The exposition shifts to the first person here, so as to reflect the subjective nature of some of the judgments that had to be made in extracting from each contribution
just a page or two of observations and summary.

The industrial countries. Perhaps understandably, there was
more emphasis on macroeconomic stabilization policy in the
essays dealing with the industrial countries than was the case
with respect to the less developed countries. The stabilization
emphasis was strongest in the cases of the United Kingdom and
the United States; the essay on Japan occupied an intermediate
position; while those dealing with Germany and Sweden became
rather seriously involved in policies affecting the structure of the
economy.

The United Kingdom. Wilfred Beckerman emphasizes the fact that until recently there was not much difference between the policies actually implemented by the Labour and Conservative Parties in postwar Britain. It was the Conservatives who first instituted economic planning (via the National Economic Development Council) as a central government function. Also, when they replaced the Labour Party in the government, the Conservatives failed to undo any of the major changes (nationalization of industries and extensions of the welfare state) that Labour had implanted. Nor, one can add, did Conservative governments do much to impede or reverse the growth of government in the U.K. From 27 percent under the Conservatives in the late 1950s and early 1960s, the ratio of government expenditures to GDP rose to 31 percent under Labour in the late 1960s. In the early 1970s, it continued rising to 35 percent under the Conservatives; then to 38 percent under Labour in the late 1970s, and finally to 41 percent under Mrs. Thatcher between 1980 and 1982.[4]

In attempting to account for Britain's slow growth of GNP (at an average of 2.25 percent per year between 1953 and 1982), Professor Beckerman explores four hypotheses: (i) other European countries grew faster because they had more "catching up" to do (from wartime devastation); (ii) Britain was already a "mature" economy in the early postwar period and had little further to gain from transferring workers out of agriculture or exploiting industrial economies of scale; (iii) bad labor relations and class antagonisms operated as a severe brake on economic growth, especially as real wages kept rising in the face of economic stagnation and growing unemployment; and (iv) the British economy was hamstrung for some three decades, largely because it started the early 1950s suffering from a serious currency overvaluation—a malady which successive governments persistently refused to correct.

Professor Beckerman finds the last two hypotheses far more credible than the first two—a conclusion with which, on the basis of the evidence he presents, I am inclined to agree. I cannot help but feel, however, that the mounting weight of government, which grew virtually unchecked over a span of more than 30 years, probably also played a significant independent role.

The United States. Robert Gordon begins his essay with a diag-

nosis and ends with a series of prescriptions. The diagnosis notes
(i) that the growth rate of nominal GNP has been much more
volatile than that of money; (ii) that the rate of inflation has
moved relatively slowly over time, signifying that the instability of
nominal GNP is largely reflected in a volatile growth rate of real
GNP; (iii) that there is such a thing as a natural rate of unemployment, below which the inflation rate tends to accelerate and above
which inflation tends to subside; and (iv) supply shocks (such as
the oil price rises of the 1970s) tend to be reflected in sharp
changes in the inflation rate (the prices of non-shocked—e.g.,
non-oil products being sluggish to adapt). Efforts to blunt these
changes are likely to shift the burden of the shock onto real output.

   Based on these observations, Gordon recommends that the
monetary authority should take the growth rate of nominal GNP
to be its target in the short run, with the possibility of special *ad
hoc* adjustments of this target to accommodate sharp supply
shocks when they occur. He also observes that the velocity of cir-
culation of money has been relatively stable between cycles
(though not within them); hence the orthodox monetarist proposal
of a relatively stable rate of growth of the money supply meets
with his approval as a guidepost for the longer run.

   Gordon notes, though with somewhat less emphasis than I
would accord it, the phenomenal volatility of the "effective exchange rate" in recent years. He cites a rise of 26 percent in this
rate in the first three quarters of 1981 and another of 11 percent
up to the end of 1982. He notes that the decline in net exports during 1981–82 accounts for three quarters of the contemporaneous
decline in real GNP. He might have added that during 1978–80,
when the U.S. dollar was depreciating in unprecedented fashion,
the average price (unit value) of imports rose by nearly 50 percent, while that of exports (also to a substantial degree governed
by the exchange rate) rose by some 30 percent. The forces governing the exchange rate thus likely played an important role in
bringing about rises of 25 percent in consumer prices and of 19
percent in the GNP deflator in this earlier period.

   Gordon's principal policy recommendations are: (i) monetary
policy should be aggressively expansionary when the economy is
far below its normal growth path, but should put on the brakes as
that path is approached; (ii) temporary supply shocks should

clearly be accommodated by monetary policy, but relatively long-lasting shocks pose a dilemma in which one must choose between unwanted inflation on the one hand and unwanted shortfalls of output on the other; (iii) fiscal deficits, such as the recent and prospective ones in the U.S., are not greatly worrisome when the economy is far below its normal growth path; they became more of a problem as one nears that path; (iv) for the future the United States should pay more attention to "lessening institutional constraints" so as to "improve macroeconomic efficiency and place less of a burden on traditional policy tools." The institutional constraints to which he refers concern long-term wage contracts (which impose rigidities that impede short-run adjustment); interest rate ceilings (which raise the welfare cost of inflation); the lack of provisions in the tax law for adjusting interest payments and receipts, as well as capital gains, for inflation; the institutional barriers to countercyclical fiscal policy (both on the tax and the expenditure sides); and the absence of policies oriented toward reducing the natural rate of unemployment.

Japan. Yutaka Kosai begins with an analysis of Japan's most recent growth experience. He finds that the slowdown of Japan's growth rate from over 11 percent in 1965–70 to less than 5 percent in 1970–80 and to around 3 percent in 1980–82 can be explained by a few key factors: (i) gross fixed capital formation, which rose from 15 percent to over 20 percent of GNP during 1965–70, returned to 15 percent over the decade of the 1970s; (ii) a very sharp deterioration of the terms of trade occurred during the 1970s, linked in significant measure to the rise in energy prices; and (iii) technological progress slowed due (a) to the closing of the technological gap between the Japanese economy and those of what used to be more advanced economies and (b) to the growth in the relative share of services, which characteristically enjoy only modest technical advance.

Correctly diagnosing these forces as being substantially beyond the control of economic policy, Professor Kosai then inquires into the degree of success with which the Japanese economy met the challenges of the 1970s. He brings in a largely favorable verdict, the principal failure being an episode of stagflation in the mid-1970s. The inflation rate was in double digits for three years starting in 1973, and reached almost 25 percent in 1974. Meanwhile real GNP uncharacteristically (for Japan) fell between 1973 and 1974, and stood in 1975 only a percentage point above its 1973 level. Professor Kosai attributes this episode to an unwillingness of the Japanese authorities at the time to appreciate their currency; they responded to a higher influx of resources by nearly doubling the money supply between 1970 and 1973 and almost trebling it between 1970 and 1976. This was not typical of the behavior of the Bank of Japan during most of the postwar period. On the whole the authorities were quick to put on the brakes when balance-of-payments difficulties threatened. Moreover, one must also recognize that whatever inflation Japan has experienced during the postwar period has been compatible with a dramatic appreciation of her currency, from a fixed rate of 360 yen per dollar, which prevailed through the 1950s and up to 1970, to a rate that fluctuated between 200 and 250 yen per dollar during 1978–82.

One of the anomalies of the Japanese case is the degree to which the government was able to maintain a stable and successful economy in the face of persistently large budget deficits. Since 1978 the deficits have regularly exceeded 5 percent of GNP; more surprising still is the fact that financial institutions (including specialized credit institutions), increased their holdings of the obligations of government and of official entities by more than 5 percent of GNP in each year from 1975 to 1982.[5] There can be little doubt that the disruptive potential of these deficits, and particularly of the mode of financing them, was greatly assuaged by the high rate (oscillating around 20 percent since 1970) at which Japanese households saved out of their disposable income.

Germany. Frank Wolter documents in dramatic fashion the steady slide of the West Germany economy from the days of the "German miracle" in the 1950s to a state of virtual stagnation at the turn of the 1980s. In terms of a framework very similar to that set out in the introduction to this volume, he traces the decline of the growth rate emanating from non-residential private business. Some of his results are summarized in table 1. They show a steady deterioration of the rate of growth of private sector business output, an erosion that clearly derives from a steady fall in total factor productivity. When this in turn is broken down into its compo-

Table 1

Sources of Growth in the Federal Republic of Germany

(average rate of change in percent per annum)

	Non-Residential Private Business				
	1960–65	1965–70	1970–73	1973–79	1979–81
Real Gross Domestic Product per hour worked	6.0	5.8	5.3	4.5	1.8
Capital-Labor Substitution	1.1	1.4	1.6	1.7	1.4
Total Factor Productivity	4.9	4.4	3.7	2.8	0.4
Change in Labor Quality	1.1	0.4	0.3	0.3	0.4
Education	0.3	0	0.7	0.4	n.a.
Sex	0	0	0	0	0.1
Age	0.8	0.1	-0.4	-0.1	n.a.
Reallocation of Labor	0.7	0.7	0.4	0.4	n.a.
Reallocation of Capital	2.6	0.8	1.0	-0.1	n.a.
Volume Changes	0.4	0.6	0.1	0.1	-0.3
Economies of Scale	0.5	0.4	0.4	0.2	0.1
Capacity & Utilization	0.1	0.2	-0.3	-0.1	-0.4
Advances in Knowledge	0.1	1.9	1.9	2.1	n.a.

Source: This Volume, Chapter 5, tables 4 and A-2.

nents, it turns out that most of the principal components contributed to the decline—the change in labor quality, the reallocation of labor, the reallocation of capital, and changes in volume (both via economies of scale and via capacity utilization) all were weaker forces for growth during 1970–80 than they were in 1960–65. Only the forces of education and of advances in knowledge contributed more to growth in the recent past than they did in the early 1960s.

The decline of the German economy was, in Professor Wolter's words, "largely conditioned by a gradual erosion of market forces." In the early years policy was characterized by emphasis on the market mechanism, private control over resources, and reliance in competition and an open economy. The public sector, however, played an important role in monitoring the system, providing infrastructure, and helping overcome bottlenecks. Germany had inherited a strong aversion to inflation, which was kept within bounds by forceful and determined Bundesbank policy.

Growth slowed somewhat in the 1960s; as labor (particularly skilled labor) became progressively scarcer, reliance was placed on *Gastarbeiter* (guestworkers) from the Mediterranean countries. Real wages nonetheless rose, propelled in part by the growing scarcity of skilled labor.

The 1970s were marked by a shift of policy toward a welfare state philosophy. The immigration of foreign labor was largely halted, protection was accorded to labor intensive industries, mandatory employee benefits were expanded, and the firing of employees was made much more difficult. In addition, new transfer programs were enacted by the government, aiding

... the disabled, the unemployed and workers at large. Subsidies and benefits for education, retraining, child care, housing and savings were substantially increased, pensions were raised, . . . and subsidies for weak firms, weak industries . . . , and weak regions were piled up. In addition the public sector increased its supply of services and engaged in large-scale promotion of civil servants. As a result there was a massive expansion of public expenditures . . . and a shift from public investment to public consumption. (Wolter, p. 109)

Professor Wolter concludes with a succinct summary of the German case:

[There is a clear positive relationship between economic growth and capital formation and between the rate of capital formation and profit margins]. . . . Growth was rapid when government was small, and . . . slow when government became large. . . . Government . . . was strong when it was small, but became weak after it grew larger.

. . . Rapid economic development [occurred when] government largely confined itself to working the supply side, . . . by setting and monitoring the rules of the game and by supporting incentives to save and invest [and by deregulating] the economy—including the removal of barriers to . . . trade and factor movements. . . . Weak economic growth set in after a prolonged period of demand management. . . , sectoral and regional subsidies, [and the rise to prominence of] the relatively regulated tertiary sector.

Economic growth was high when wage policies were moderate and when the income distribution shifted in favor of capital; at the same time, real wages increased rapidly and full employment was achieved. . . . Growth became low [under] aggressive wage policies which pushed up the wage share in GNP; soon thereafter [the rate of] real wages increased slowly and mass unemployment emerged.

[Finally], economic growth was rapid when public transfers were moderate, but sharply declined [in the wake of] prolonged emphasis on redistribution.

Sweden. Ulf Jakobsson's account of Sweden's recent economic history parallels in many ways that of Germany. Sweden's growth rate of real GDP was over 4.5 percent per annum in the 1960s, dropped to less than 2 percent per year in the 1970s, and turned negative in the 1980s. Meanwhile her inflation rate rose from 4.4 percent per year in the 1960s to over 10 percent per year in the 1970s. Examination of the annual data reveals that it was around the middle of the 1970s that stagnation really set in. At about the same time the inflation rate hit double digits.

It is notable that Sweden's government deficit, which averaged less than 1 percent of GDP in the 1960s, and less than 2 percent of GDP in the first half of the 1970s, burgeoned to 5 percent by 1978, over 7 percent by 1979, over 8 percent by 1980, and over 9 percent by 1981. These deficits, moreover, were largely financed by the financial sector, whose credit to the government increased, between 1977 and 1978, by 5 percent of GDP—more than its entire accumulated growth between 1970 and 1975. Worse yet, between 1980 and 1981, financial sector credit to the government expanded by nearly 8 percent of 1980's GDP.[6]

Underlying the growing deficit was a dramatic rise in public sector expenditures. These grew as a fraction of GDP from around 50 percent in 1975 to around 70 percent in 1983,[7] while taxes and fees remained about constant. Jakobsson speaks of

the problems that were created by the rapid growth of public consumption and public expenditure in Sweden in the 1970s. There is reason to stress that the growth of public expenditure is part and parcel of a fundamental structural change in the Swedish economy, whereby the public sector has come to play an increasing part in every sector of the economy.

Dr. Jakobsson shows us, in his table 4, how the number of people in public-sector production plus those receiving income from public-sector programs grew from 44 percent of total employment in 1965 to 59 percent in 1970, 69 percent in 1975, and finally to 84 percent in 1980. He shows, too, how subsidies to food, to industry, to housing, and to other parts of the business sector grew from 3.7 percent of GDP in 1970 to 9.6 percent in 1980. In addition, regulations—particularly the designation of priority sectors to receive credits on particularly favorable terms—have discriminated against non-priority sectors (including industry), and placed them at a severe disadvantage.

The difficulties faced by Sweden in consequence of these multiple recent expansions of public-sector employment, expenditure, and activity are compounded by the fact that they came on top of a public sector that was, by international standards, already very large. Taxes were thus already extremely high before the great spurt of expenditure in the late 1970s. Jakobsson's table 5 reports that the full effective marginal rate of taxation was probably around 40 percent for the average blue-collar worker in 1955, but reached close to 70 percent by 1970—and apparently *could not* be increased significantly despite the great fiscal pressures of the late 1970s. Similarly, the full effective marginal rate of taxation for the average white collar worker would have been close to 45 percent in 1955, close to 70 percent in 1970, and close to 80 percent in 1980–82. Rates in that range are already too high by many criteria. To push them farther is likely to be counterproductive in terms of its effect on output, and may even lead to a fall in total tax receipts. Small wonder, then, that Sweden found it impossible to increase tax revenues to match the dramatic growth in expenditures in the late 1970s.

The less-developed countries. As distinct from the major industrial countries of the Western world, the LDCs, in part because of their number, in part because of the great variety of social and cultural backgrounds they represent, reveal great differences among their modes of social organization, the political philosophies of their respective governments, and, not least, the degrees to which and the effectiveness with which these governments have been able to exercise their authority. As the net result of the great variation among the countries in all these dimensions, we observe a whole spectrum of experiences, both good and bad. The notes that follow briefly summarize some of the main observations and insights perceived by the authors of the seven papers dealing with specific LDCs.

Jamaica. Gladstone Bonnick takes pains, in his paper, to disabuse us of simplistic and impressionistic interpretations of Jamaica's recent history. He objects to the frequent linkage of liberal, private-sector-oriented policies with good results and of centralizing, public-sector-oriented policies with bad results. From 1966 to 1972 the economy grew at over 6 percent per year, while from 1973 to 1980 it suffered an uninterrupted decline, which over the period totaled 18 percent. Meanwhile, inflation soared from an average of 7.5 percent per annum in 1966–73 to an average of 21.2 percent per year from 1973 through 1980. At the same time Jamaica's budget deficit rose from 2.5 percent of GDP in 1966 to 19 percent of GDP in 1978, and was still at 13.5 percent of GDP in 1981.

Professor Bonnick contends that the differences between the two main parties in Jamaica are mainly in rhetoric; he disputes, to a degree, the association of the Jamaica Labor Party (1962–72, and since November 1980) with free-market policies and that of the People's National Party (1972–80) with socializing and centralizing tendencies.

The thrust of Bonnick's argument is basically that the Jamaica Labor Party really did not have a liberal orientation. During 1962–72 it regularly implemented controls on prices and on foreign exchange, and intensified them after 1967. It was instrumental in imposing quantitative import restrictions to protect local manufacturing. It also implemented in the 1960s the

"Jamaicanization" of banks and insurance companies. Moreover, since returning to power in 1980, the JLP has nationalized the principal oil refinery of the country.

A counterpart of this argument is that many of the policy mistakes of the 1970s were the natural outgrowth or extension of policies initiated by the JLP in the 1960s. When the oil crisis of 1973 hit, when Jamaican's tourist flow slackened and withered, and when aluminum and banana exports started to decline, foreign exchange revenues were so sharply cut that they could barely cover the most urgent demands for basic foodstuffs and for material imports for industry. Bonnick's implication is that, were the JLP in power in the 1970s, it probably would have acted much as did the PNP.

But there can be no doubt that many of the PNP's actions flew in the face of sound technical economics. The government deficit, from 1972 to 1980, rose from around 4 percent to over 15 percent of GNP; the foreign debt multiplied by about 10 while total debt moved from less than 30 to nearly 80 percent of GNP; banking system holdings of public-sector obligations multiplied by 15. The failure of taxes to rise as a percentage of GDP, apart from a new bauxite levy (with very questionable incentive effects), is a dubious distinction in the light of the rise in government expenditures from around a quarter to over 40 percent of GNP. The size of the public administration doubled in relation to GDP between 1972 and 1979. Import controls, exchange controls, and price controls were greatly intensified. Banks and other industries were nationalized and lands acquired at a time when the budget was under unprecedented strain.

All these measures run counter to the mindset of the policy professional, as sketched above. To the extent that the two main parties coincide on such matters, the prospects of reversing the adverse trends that have characterized Jamaica's recent past remain dim indeed.

Ghana. Michael Roemer traces the tragic history of Ghana's economic policy and performance since 1950. It is a sad story because the best comes at the beginning, the worst at the end. In the early 1950s, Ghana was still under British rule; her economy was quite open; and she had one of the highest standards of living in Africa. By 1980 her living standard had fallen by almost a quarter, and her inflation rate had grown from virtually zero to the point where from 1976 to 1981, it oscillated between 50 and 120 percent.

The causes of this debacle are not obscure. Indeed, readers of this chapter can easily anticipate them, for in the period of economic decline, Ghana transgressed nearly every lesson of economic policy set forth above. With respect to false technicism, Professor Roemer reports:

The story of Ghana's debacle is partly the story of discredited theories of development, especially the "big push" and import substitution approaches. . . . In most important ways Ghana was a model of such development strategies, which include central planning of economic activity, and especially a strong commitment to industrial development protected by high trade barriers. Ghana, in many respects had turned out to be a model of how *not* to develop . . . a valuable case study from which to understand why some countries . . . have maintained strong economic growth rates over long periods, and why many others have not. (Roemer, p. 202).

Fiscal discipline prevailed in Ghana in the 1950s, but by the late 1960s fiscal deficits were ranging from 6 to 9 percent of GDP. After a brief dip in the early 1970s the deficits spurted again, this time to the range of 10–15 percent of GDP.

Clearly, inflation had gotten out of hand by the last half of the 1970s. In Ghana's case, the fiscal deficit was the overwhelmingly preponderant cause. In the 1950s Ghana's public sector actually was a net lender to the banking and monetary system; but in the early 1960s, government was already a substantial net borrower, taking about a third of bank credit. In the late 1960s and early 1970s this figure fluctuated between a third and one half. Then, as the great inflation broke out in the late 1970s, government (together with public enterprises) began to monopolize bank credit, with the private sector's share falling from about 20 percent in 1973–75 to less than 10 percent in 1980–82. All during this period each year's increase in the banking system's lending to the public sector was itself sufficient to make a major inflation of prices inevitable.

Professor Roemer has himself summarized how most of the other lessons of economic policy were violated:

448   ARNOLD C. HARBERGER

Thus, as export revenues stagnated, the government reduced the incentive either to diversify exports or to increase them . . .

The protective duties . . . were highly differentiated and import licensing—especially as corruption made the impact of quotas more unpredictable . . . [helped] to produce a [complex and] chaotic system. Effective rates of protection ranged from . . . negative effective protection for several export industries to over 200 percent for [many import-substituting] sectors. [Some industries even] used material inputs that, at world prices, were worth more than their outputs.

Policies toward factor prices exacerbated the adverse impact of Nkrumah's system of trade incentives. A combination of minimum wage legislation, controlled interest rates, an overvalued exchange rate, duty-free import of capital equipment, and tax-reducing investor incentives all conspired to make labor artificially expensive . . . , and thus to encourage capital-intensive choice of technology and industry. [In addition,] real interest rates ranged from −2 to −23 percent per year.

[These] policies pushed Ghana to virtual international bankruptcy with an overstimulated economy that could no longer be contained by import and price controls, an enlarged public sector that could not be managed effectively by . . . Ghanaian manpower, and economic structure unsuitable to Ghana's endowments, and a price structure that promised no solution to Ghana's . . . stagnation. (Roemer, p. 214).

Tanzania. The case of Tanzania is similar to that of Ghana in many respects, but the degree of the malady is somewhat lesser. Whereas Ghana's negative growth rate of per capita income increase began in the 1960s, Tanzania's dates from the 1970s. Ghana's slowdown started around 1960, Tanzania's after 1967. Ghana first moved into double-digit inflation in 1964, and Tanzania in 1967; and up through 1982 Tanzania had experienced only four years of inflation exceeding 20 percent, compared with Ghana's nine. Moreover, Ghana had two years of inflation of over 100 percent and six over 50 percent, while Tanzania's top recorded inflation rate was 30.3 percent.[8]

Tanzania's superior performance in comparison with Ghana was greatly influenced by the massive amounts of foreign aid it received (U.S. $2,700 million from 1971 to 1981), by the fact that most of its arable land was not under cultivation when the country achieved independence, and by the good fortune of having started with a widely diversified agricultural export base.

But within its own context, Tanzania's policy behavior was much like Ghana's. Although there was no significant trend in the terms of trade, export volumes fell by more than 50 percent over the 1970s. This was in considerable measure due to the deterioration of Tanzania's real exchange rate, which appreciated by nearly 50 percent between 1970 and 1981.

The appreciation of the real exchange rate, in turn, was due in part to the effects of an import-substituting industrial strategy, which increasingly squeezed out imports of manufactures and consumer goods in general, but which also drastically curbed imports of agricultural tractors and their replacement parts. At the same time internal inflationary finance pushed up local prices and costs far more than was occurring in the major world trading centers, and the nominal exchange rate was not adjusted to compensate for this difference. Indeed, over the decade of the 1970s, while the U.S. GDP deflator was doubling, that of Tanzania nearly trebled; yet the shilling was devalued, vis-à-vis the dollar, by only about 15 percent.

The internal inflation gave rise to an accentuation of price controls. Uma Lele reports that the number of commodities under price controls increased from 400 in 1974 to 3,000 in 1976. Black markets soon developed, in which prices reached up to six times the official peg.

Much of the thrust of Tanzania's policy was, like Ghana's, toward industrialization. And, as in Ghana, much of this development used public-sector enterprises as its vehicle. Similarly, a number of industrial projects emerged with negative value added, i.e., using more foreign exchange for buying imported inputs than they saved by producing the final product at home. Moreover, as in Ghana, artificial pricing (among other things) led to an artificially high level of capital intensiveness in industrial investments.

The emphasis on industry also diverted much-needed funds from the agricultural sector, which quite apparently harbored most of the products in which Tanzania had a significant comparative advantage. Moreover, government regulations of prices further confounded the agricultural scene. For nearly all controlled products, the official prices in real terms fell over the decade of the 1970s, and certainly from the mid-1970s to the end of the decade (Tanzania's worst crisis period). Part of the reason why the government pushed down real prices paid to producers was because the official marketing agencies were losing money.

On the other side, the government was reluctant to raise consumer prices—presumably for political reasons. The end result
was (i) large and growing subsidies to the public sector entities
that marketed food crops and (ii) still further borrowing by these
bodies from the banking system to cover their losses above and
beyond the subsidies they received. All of these problems associated with marketing came about after the government first supported agricultural marketing cooperatives in order to oust the
country's Asian minority from this sector (which Asians then
dominated), and later abolished these same cooperatives in favor
of public-sector enterprises.

In short, the net result of a great many of Tanzania's policy initiatives has been the proliferation of inefficiency throughout the
economy. Industry and agriculture have both been made more inefficient through decrees, regulations, and controls. The country
has lost much of the benefit that could be gained from foreign
trade. Its investments were often ill-chosen and ill-suited to their
purpose, proliferating inefficiency still more. And finally, in many
sectors a growing and highly inefficient public sector has sup-
planted what once was a thriving and economically effective private sector.

Mexico. Mexico presents an interesting contrast between two
major periods of its recent history. During 1955–73 she had virtually no petroleum exports, yet managed a compound annual real
growth rate of close to 7 percent and an average inflation rate
(GDP deflator) of only 5 percent per year. With the coming of the
petroleum boom (1973 to 1982) the real growth rate fell to less
than 6 percent while the rate of inflation averaged 26 percent, and
reached a maximum of 58 percent in 1982. Moreover, the country
suffered two grave balance-of-payments crises, in which the price
of the dollar leaped upward by 80 percent and 270 percent, respectively. The public-sector budget deficit, which in the earlier period
was largely kept below 2 percent of GDP, burgeoned to an average
of 8 percent in 1973–82, and reached a maximum (in 1982) of 19
percent of GDP.

Obviously, there was an incredible loss of fiscal restraint. It appears that when the authorities were really without significant
resources, they could with relative impunity deny funds to count-

less political claimants, but when Mexicans began to view their country as an oil-rich nation, the authorities simply caved in to demand after demand for public-sector funds. I believe that there is a great element of truth in this interpretation, but it must be tempered by a recognition that in the 1955–72 period economic policy was dominated by two giant figures—Antonio Ortiz Mena in the Ministry of Finance and Rodrigo Gomez in the Central Bank—whose force of will and character also played an important role in imposing monetary and fiscal discipline.

Professor Gil Díaz recognizes the great contrast between the pre-1973 and post-1972 period, particularly with respect to fiscal and monetary restraint. But he also take pains to point out that many of the policy mistakes that exacerbated Mexico's problems in the late 1970s and early 1980s were the fruit of seeds already planted in the earlier period. Many of these mistakes derived from a tendency to underprice utility services and other products of public-sector enterprises. Indeed, in a fascinating calculation presented in his table A-6, he estimates that, with "economic" pricing of the outputs of the public sector, its deficits from 1965 to 1980 would have been converted into surpluses except for two years, 1975 and 1976.

Some of the subsidies to public enterprise prices were an outgrowth of price control mechanisms; as controlled private-sector prices became (usually through inflation) more and more uneconomic, "the government first [supported] faltering firms with credit . . . and, eventually, [took] them over as they went under" (Gil Díaz, p. 342).

Trade policy is another area in which later mistakes were presaged by policies pursued during the 1955–72 period. The average import tariff was raised from 8.8 percent in 1954 to around 20 percent over the 1960s, but import licenses and similar controls were probably a more important source of trade restriction. In 1956 only 9 percent of import categories were subject to such controls; this figure reached 60 percent by 1966, 65 by 1970, and 80 percent by 1973.

In addition to these policy failings, Gil Díaz takes pains to point out a little-understood but profoundly important consequence of the world inflation for Mexico and many other LDCs—as world interest rates rose to reflect anticipated inflation, the payment of interest in effect came to represent a partial amortization of real debt (i.e., simply due to world inflation the real outstanding debt from any given loan goes down from period to period, and lenders are compensated for this loss by a higher, inflation-related interest rate). Close to 80 percent of Mexico's cumulative "external deficit" (i.e., its public sector borrowing from abroad) disappears when an adjustment (for U.S. inflation) is made to take this factor into account. (See Gil Díaz, appendix table A-2). Similarly, Mexico's perennial (since 1956) balance-of-payments deficits are reduced by about 20 percent when the component of interest payments reflecting the U.S. inflation rate is counted as amortization.

Mexico's troubles since the mid-1970s are thus viewed by Gil Díaz as being (i) partly the result of ill-advised pricing, trade and other policies, many of which had antecedents in the two preceding (and relatively calm) decades, (ii) partly the consequence of the way in which the international inflation interacted with the nation's international debt to exacerbate fiscal deficits and monetary expansion, and (iii) perhaps predominantly, a weakening of the will or capacity (or political courage) to bring under control a deficit that was growing increasingly out of hand.

Indonesia. Indonesia shares with Taiwan the distinction of being the countries which came out of the period under review in an ambience of virtually unalloyed success in economic policy. Her failures occurred earlier—specifically in the period of 1960–65; they were followed by a remarkably long and sustained recovery, which has carried up to the present. Indonesia also deserves special credit for being, from among the relatively populous oil-exporting nations, the one that apparently learned most about how to take advantage of oil booms.

On achieving independence, Indonesia inherited from the Dutch a tradition of conservative macroeconomic policies combined with substantial regulation and other intervention at the microeconomic level. During the decade of the 1950s, economic policy did not diverge greatly from its traditional path, though towards the end of the decade signs of a brewing inflation were felt, partly fueled by military expenditures. During the 1950s the country underwent postwar rebuilding, put down several secessionist rebellions, and engaged in armed confrontations against both the

Dutch and the Malaysians. It is surprising, under these circumstances , that per capita real income grew by as much as 1.2 percent per annum over the decade.

Indonesia's crisis period was clearly 1960—65, when per capita
income growth turned negative, and inflation soared, reaching
about 600 percent in 1965 and 1966. Official foreign exchange
reserves dwindled until they became negative; government
receipts were eroded from over 13 percent to around 4 percent of
GDP. Chaos reigned in the economy. The policy mistakes were the
familiar ones: massive government deficits financed by monetary
expansion, growing overvaluation of the currency, and a consequent stagnation of imports, which in Indonesia's case carried
with it a drastic fall in tax collections (as at that time taxes fell
mainly on traded goods); the fall of revenues, in turn, only exacerbated the deficit and the consequent monetary expansion.

Parallel to the scenario just described was a welter of controls
and restrictions. Many of them were not new, but were rendered
much more burdensome by the growing shortages of traded goods
and by the exploding inflation. Also, owing to its fiscal strains, the
government was unable to accomplish even rudimentary maintenance of the nation's infrastructure; after the close of this chaotic
episode, it took nearly a decade to restore public utilities, and
transport and irrigation services.

Indonesia's new government under General Suharto has
followed a quite consistent set of economic policies from 1966 to
the present. Its key precepts have been macroeconomic: avoiding
inflationary excesses in the budget, and steering clear of any kind
of exchange control. In early actions, the Suharto government
doubled real tax collections, and sharply raised the prices charged
by public enterprises. It also implemented several financial
reforms, and replaced a set of sharply negative real interest rates
with a pattern of decidedly positive ones. The revenues, together
with foreign aid averaging about 3 percent of GDP, set the stage
for one of the most remarkable stabilization experiences ever
recorded. From around 600 percent in 1965 and 1966 the rate of
inflation dropped to 111 percent in 1967, to 84 percent in 1968,
and to 10 and 9 percent, respectively, in 1970 and 1971 (see Gillis,
table 3). Meanwhile, GDP grew by 2.3 percent in 1966 and 1967,
by 11.1 percent in 1968, 9.2 percent in 1969, and 6.5 and 4.9 per-

cent, respectively, in 1970 and 1971. Over the whole stabilization episode, the average compound rate of growth of GDP was an impressive 4.5 percent per annum (1.9 percent in per capita terms).

Indonesia's record on handling an oil boom reveals a very distinct learning process. During the spurt in oil prices of 1974 and after, Indonesia's exports of petroleum and its products rose from U.S. $1.5 billion in 1973 to $4.9 billion in 1975 and $5.6 billion in 1976. Meanwhile the foreign assets of the monetary system, which started at U.S. $710 million in 1973, peaked at $1.6 billion in 1974 and turned negative in 1975 and 1976. This was largely a reflection of the squandering of foreign exchange resources by PERTAMINA (the state-owned oil company) in the debacle referred to by Professor Gillis (chapter 9, p. 247). However, Indonesia was much more prudent in handling the second oil boom, which started in 1979. In this case oil exports rose from U.S. $7.4 billion in 1978 to $8.9 billion in 1979 and $12.9 billion in 1980. Over the same lapse of time, the foreign assets of the monetary system grew from U.S. $1.7 billion in 1978 to $4.7 billion in 1979 and $9.6 billion in 1980. The wealth taken from the ground was largely being "parked" in the capital markets of the world until good uses could be found for it. No other populous oil country has managed an oil boom this well.

Professor Gillis notes other achievements of Indonesian economic policy—successful maintenance (through timely devaluations) of non-oil exports in the face of both petroleum booms, steady reduction of customs duties, elimination of excessive rates of income tax, etc. Yet he notes ample flaws as well: a long-standing policy (just recently corrected) of massive subsidies to the local users of petroleum products, a maze of unjustified fiscal incentives and "unadministerable taxes," "the persistence of strong protectionist policies [particularly through quantitative restrictions] and the ponderous and restrictive system of licensing and regulation." (Gillis, p. 258). It often takes two or more years to process an investment license, and reductions in customs duties by the Department of Finance have been countered by "import quotas, bans, and other quantitative restrictions [imposed by the Departments] of Industry, . . . of Agriculture, . . . and of Trade." Rates of effective protection still range from negative to as high as 4000 percent (for tires). Protection of textile and footwear industries imposes nearly $500 million a year of costs on Indonesian consumers.

Indonesia's successful development is thus an example of how a preponderance of good policies in critical areas can be sufficient (perhaps with a little luck on the side) to generate an enviable rate of economic growth, in spite of the presence on the country's policy record of obvious and important blemishes and failings.

Taiwan. Taiwan is clearly the exemplar among the countries treated in this volume. Not only were its achievements more dramatic even than Indonesia's, its errors and failings of policy also seem to have been minimal, once its growth process got on track. Initially (1950–54) Taiwan followed what were then modish policies of high barriers of trade, low interest rates. In addition, from 1950 through 1953, inflation ran at the rate of over 5 percent per quarter more than two thirds of the time, and over 10 percent per quarter more than a third of the time. Exports measured in U.S. dollars were only $96 million in 1954 compared with $93 million in 1950, and meanwhile the U.S. dollar had suffered a 15 percent inflation. Imports exceeded exports by more than 50 percent from 1951 through 1954, and were more than double 1954's exports. Domestic saving languished at around 5 percent of national income. How this panorama changed over subsequent years is shown in table 2. By 1980, real national income had experienced an eightfold increase, and per capita income had more than quadrupled. Exports had multiplied by 200, and imports by more than

Table 2
Basic Economic Data of Taiwan

	1955	1960	1970	1980
National Income (1967 NT$)				
Total (Billion NT$)	112.8	151.7	38.72	879.1
Per Capita (NT$)	11,895	13,601	26,582	49,832
Domestic Savings as Percent of National Income	4.9	7.6	23.8	32.9
Exports (Million US$)	127	164	1,469	19,575
Imports (Million US$)	185	287	1,363	19,428

Source: S. C. Tsiang, This Volume, Chapter 11.

100, measured in U.S. dollars. Professor Tsiang's table 1 indicates that, in terms of quantities, exports multiplied by 50 and imports by 20.

Tsiang emphasizes the extent to which the Taiwan miracle involved implementing the basic policy guidelines that one can derive from economic science (and, in general, from common sense as well). He deals in turn (i) with the necessity for the nation to exploit the opportunities afforded by international trade and international investment, and (ii) with the importance of maintaining realistic (and positive) real interest rates, both as an incentive to save and as a means of ensuring that available investible funds are allocated to the most productive investments.

Under the first heading he details how the Taiwanese government jettisoned a whole set of protectionist trade policies—high protective tariffs, import licenses and quotas, multiple exchange rates. This liberalization of the economy so boosted the real exchange rate facing exporters that many new exports were stimulated. Exports doubled from 1954 to 1961, doubled again from 1961 to 1964, and again from 1964 to 1968–69. From 1968–69 to 1971 they doubled again. By 1980 exports were nearly twenty times those of 1969, 100 times that of 1961, and 200 times those of 1954.

This export expansion involved hard work as well as policy liberalization. As new commodities entered the list of exports, many of them enjoyed tremendous booms. But, for many new exports, and particularly for those that grew the most, import quotas, "voluntary restraints," and other barriers tended to rise to put a cap on the boom. Taiwan's response was to remain undaunted, to accept the limits that emerged, and to obtain a policy environment in which yet other new exports could develop and prosper.

Taiwan's second major policy thrust concerned the capital market. One major key here was maintaining positive real interest rates. In the first experiment in this direction, Taiwan's ongoing inflation was quickly brought down to less than .5 percent per month in the second quarter of 1950, only to spurt again when the policy of high interest rates was relaxed in the third quarter. But the Taiwanese authorities learned the lesson well; average real interest rates on one-year time deposits were significantly positive in each of the subsequent twenty-two years, and the lapse from policy discipline in this regard (in 1973) was mercifully brief.

Uruguay. It is perhaps fitting that this review should end with Uruguay following Taiwan. No case treated in this volume is more pervasively successful than that of Taiwan, and none is more classically tragic than that of Uruguay. Uruguay not only possessed all the ingredients for dramatic economic success; she already had attained it more than 100 years ago; and, to a degree at least, had maintained it during much of the first half of this century. She then failed ignominiously in the late 1950s and the 1960s, but recovered sharply starting in 1974, only to stumble once again in the early 1980s.

The ingredients of the Uruguayan drama are by now familiar. The biggest secret of her success up to the 1950s was fiscal discipline and monetary restraint. Indeed, for the first thirty-five years (1828–62) of her existence as a nation—years, by the way, characterized by great prosperity—Uruguay had no money of her own at all. The level of per capita income estimated for 1866 (1600 U.S. dollars of 1981 purchasing power) was so high that it is hard to imagine that much growth could have occurred in subsequent decades. At the very least retrogression did not set in, and the Uruguayan standard of living must have compared well with those of Western Europe and North America.

Many things happened in the years after 1866. In 1875 a low uniform tariff was replaced by a highly protective, differentiated system, with a consequent loss of dynamism on the export front. In 1896 a State Bank was formed, which later was to become an important engine of inflation; it was soon joined by other public sector companies in a variety of industries. Still later the country gravitated in the direction of the modern welfare state, installing an expensive social security system during the first quarter of the twentieth century and enacting a 48-hour work week as early as 1915.

Professor Rámon Díaz sees several underlying weaknesses of Uruguayan policy, some of them significantly antedating the country's economic retrogression of 1955–68. These weaknesses included a highly protectionist commercial policy; an exchange rate that was overvalued most of the time, in part because of import restrictions, in part because internal inflation tended to produce a growing overvaluation any time the effort was made to maintain a given exchange rate or to blunt the size of a required devaluation; and a fiscal policy which, though historically quite conservative, ran significantly to deficits in the 1960s and terribly so in the early 1980s. Besides these problems, the tax system was far too complex for a country of Uruguay's size, and it produced serious inefficiencies. The country also pursued a monetary policy that, especially in the period after 1955, produced inflation (through private credit expansion) even when policymakers were containing fiscal deficits; and its controls over prices and interest rates, which would have produced harmful effects even without inflation, produced grossly distorted resource allocation when combined with one of the world's most rapid inflations. As if these problems were not enough, the country also had a social security system that greatly inhibited private incentives to save without making any significant contributions of its own to national capital formation.

Professor Díaz emphasizes that most of these specific failings of policy either helped to produce Uruguay's great inflation or were themselves grossly exacerbated by it. In this light it is ironic that the nation's finest economic performance of recent times (1974–81) was characterized by a significant improvement on nearly all of the listed policy fronts, but not in the control of inflation, which averaged some 60 percent per year throughout this period and remained this high even in 1979 and 1980. Though inflation dropped in 1981 and 1982, the money supply (including quasi money) grew by 50 percent and 77 percent in these two years. The stage was set for another crisis, which indeed can be said to have occurred in 1982, when GDP, investment, exports, imports, and industrial production all fell drastically. The stage may now be set for another period of recovery—Alejandro Vegh Villegas, who guided the nascent boom of 1974–75, returned as Finance Minister in late 1983 to try to duplicate his earlier feat.

Some Observations and Reflections

To me at least, the experiences recorded in this volume confirm and reinforce the wisdom of the policy professionals. Without a doubt, the more successful economies have come closer to implementing the tenets of policy design that these professionals would set than have those economies that have foundered or stagnated.

The less-developed countries. In Ghana, by far the worst-performing country represented here, we have what can only be called a wholesale violation of these tenets; in Tanzania the violation is probably less extreme, and it has been moderated by the inflow of huge amounts of foreign aid. Jamaica experienced a debacle much like that of Ghana, also grossly violating policy norms in the process; the recent stemming of the decline in her real GDP also seems to be due more to massive doses of foreign aid than to any major turnaround in policy.

On the plus side, Taiwan is quite clearly the country that came closest to putting into effect a very wide range of policies of the types that professionals recommend. Indeed, Professors T. C. Liu and S. C. Tsiang were important participants in the formulation of economic policy there for most of the period from 1955 onward, and had a direct influence on the process. Among the less-developed countries surveyed, Indonesia probably gets, after Taiwan, the best overall marks for the great bulk of the period studied. Here we see a pattern that is repeated in a number of LDC's (specifically in Mexico during the 1955–73 period), of quite successful macroeconomic policy combined with a rather mediocre performance on the microeconomic front.

The distinction between micro and macroeconomic policies can easily be blurred, particularly when one considers the general "opening up" of an economy to international trade to be a distinctly macroeconomic action. At the extremes it is clear that the implementation of a particular investment project or the reduction of a small group of tariffs belongs on the micro side; while a generalized expansion or contraction of credit, or an across-the-board reduction in trade restrictions belongs on the macro side. The problems lie with the murky area in between, and here the greatest difficulty concerns policy with respect to international trade.

I have come to consider a trade policy to be liberalizing in a macroeconomic sense when it stimulates the expansion of non-traditional exports.[9] Taiwan from 1955 onward has passed this test brilliantly, and Mexico from 1955 to 1973 (with the dollar value of non-oil exports trebling while U.S. prices increased by only two thirds) did more than moderately well. By way of contrast, from 1973 to 1981 Mexico's non-oil exports increased only about 10 percent in dollar terms while U.S. prices nearly doubled.

Mexico thus gets quite good marks for macroeconomic policy in the earlier period (when, one should recall, the budget was kept under control, inflation held in check, and the exchange rate successfully maintained), despite many policy flaws at the microeconomic level. But in the later period Mexico fails all the macroeconomic tests (budget, inflation, openness to trade) and certainly does no better than before on microeconomic policy matters. Indonesia, also with a less than ideal set of microeconomic policies, carried out an exemplary stabilization program in the late 1960s, and subsequently maintained budgetary discipline while non-oil exports rose from U.S. $700 million in 1970 to U.S. $9 billion in 1980.

Jamaica is another country where policy was substantially flawed, from a technical point of view, even when it was at its best. But there is no doubt that this policy was technically much sounder before 1972 than it has been subsequently. Jamaica's policy fails on macroeconomic grounds (budget, inflation, and trade and exchange restrictions) in the later period, at the same time as some of its microeconomic blemishes were being transformed into festering sores. Jamaica's record is one of acceptable growth in the earlier and disastrous retrogression in the later period. Incidentally, Jamaica's nontraditional exports (total exports minus those of aluminum, bauxite, and sugar) grew during the "better" policy phase (1962–72) from 132 million to 166 million U.S. dollars of 1980 purchasing power, only to stagnate and then decline during the subsequent period of failing technical policies. The decline in the real value of non-traditional exports continued after 1980, thus tending to support Professor Bonnick's contention that major structural reforms have not been undertaken by Jamaica's new government.

In Tanzania, many policies have been pursued that run counter to the professionals' best judgment, but massive inflows of foreign aid have helped to counterbalance their effect. Tanzania's experience looks very good in comparison to Ghana's, and quite bad compared with Indonesia's. Her failings of macroeconomic policy tended to grow through time, the budget deficit on the whole staying under 5 percent of GDP up to 1973, and ranging from 5 to 10 percent of the GDP thereafter. The inflation rate also rose through time. Prices (GDP deflator) took about ten years to double after 1965, they doubled in six years from 1974 to 1980, and consumer prices trebled in the six years leading up to 1982. On the trade side, Tanzania's exports of products other than coffee, cotton, and sisal multiplied by 2.5 (in dollars of 1980 purchasing power) in the decade following 1955, then increased by only a quarter in the subsequent decade, and finally fell by about 10 percent between 1975 and 1980. This confirms Uma Lele's perception that Tanzanian policy was operating to place ever tighter restrictions on trade as time went on.

Uruguay contrasts with Indonesia and Mexico in that the major differences between its policies in its "good" and "bad" periods were more on the microeconomic than on the macroeconomic side. A general liberalization from controls (most dramatic in the case of exchange controls) and a major tax reform were the dominant characteristics of the reform period that started in 1974. Budgetary restraint prevailed most of the time prior to 1974, and very distinctly from 1974 through 1980, but it was gross budgetary laxity starting in 1981 that helped cause the crisis of 1982–83. Yet even while the budget was being kept under control the inflation problem persisted; at no point in Uruguay's post-1974 boom could one say that this particular macroeconomic challenge had been surmounted.

Uruguay took steps to liberalize its trade policy in the mid- and late-1970s, but she certainly did not go as far in this direction as the professionals' policy tenets would have dictated. Nonetheless, at least when one gauges the success of Uruguay's trade liberalization efforts by the performance of her nontraditional exports, the record is quite good. When policies were at their worst (1955–65), Uruguay's exports (other than wool, meat, and hides) dropped from 165 million U.S. dollars (of 1980 purchasing power) to $58 million. As policies improved somewhat starting in 1966, this figure grew to $131 million in 1973. Then under the major policy reforms that started in 1974, nontraditional exports grew to reach, in 1981, the total of 450 million 1980 dollars. Notably, as the coherency of Uruguay's policy fabric began to break down (in the 1982–83 crisis period), nontraditional exports once again stagnated.

Thus, as far as the LDCs are concerned, it is probably fair to say that at least a crude sort of "justice" prevails in the economic policy realm. Countries that have run their economies following the policy tenets of the professionals have on the whole reaped good fruit from the effort; likewise, those that have flown in the face of these tenets have had to pay the price.

It seems, too, that this crude justice also entails punishments that, to a fair degree, fit the crime. Microeconomic policy comprises the thousands, maybe even tens and hundreds of thousands of ways in which the public sector impinges on the economic life of a country. No single point of contact is likely to be so important that a major flaw or even outright failure would be fatal; each transgression carries a small price, but the penality adds up if the transgressions are many. It is the overall "batting average" that counts—in microeconomic policy. If there is a single mortal failure in microeconomic policy, it is that of approaching such policy with an attitude that ignores, fails to respect, or even disdains the findings of economic science and the judgments of policy professionals. Many countries have adopted such attitudes, and it is for them that the cost of their failings of microeconomic policy has been highest.

Macroeconomic policy is quite another matter. Here a single major error can carry large costs, and the interaction of two or three big mistakes can carry a country to the brink of disaster. Inflation is a bad mistake to begin with; when combined with an exchange rate that fails to adjust to reflect an ongoing inflationary process it becomes much, much worse; add to this a pervasive attempt to keep down prices by fiat and the mixture becomes downright explosive.[10]

In general, the record also shows that stability of economic policy, of the type that engenders confidence on the part of the public, is a tremendous asset. This is particularly true where macroeconomic policy is concerned, because of the high significance of the public's perceptions and expectations in this area. The Mexican and Indonesian cases are especially good examples, for in each of them the "good" period of economic policy was characterized by a stable leadership that tried to stay close to the macroeconomic "rules of the game." Even though both these countries pursued microeconomic policies with many flaws, the stability of their macropolicies along with the continuity of their economic leadership seem together to have pointed a good path to progress. Uruguay experienced its greatest growth during 1974–81; here again there was a great stability of economic leadership. Ghana's success in the early years of independence likewise reflects a continuity of policy from the past, followed by failure when the continuity was broken. And, needless to add, Taiwan represents a sterling example of what a stable and well-oriented policy environment can do.

It is perhaps worth noting that among industrial countries also, erratic policies seem inimical to growth. Within countries long expansions have tended to be characterized by stable policies, and among countries those with the best histories seem also to have had greater policy stability. The world champions in this respect are without doubt Switzerland and Japan.

The industrial countries. I believe that the most profound lesson that emerges from the reviews in this volume of the experience of the more advanced countries is simply that, viewed from the standpoint of economic criteria, governments can grow too big. The country with the most favorable recent growth experience—Japan—is the one with the smallest public sector; those with the least favorable growth—Sweden and the United Kingdom—have the largest public sectors relative to the size of their economies. More direct evidence is provided by the studies of Sweden and Germany; in both case the authors attribute the progressive decline in the rate of economic growth to the increasing size of government and the growing pervasiveness with which it impinges on the private sector.

I do not want the above statement to be taken as a value judgment. It is arguable—and to a degree both authors can be interpreted as conceding—that the additional functions that the German and Swedish public sectors have taken on reflect the wishes of their respective populations—welfare-state programs usually have a sizable cliente'e, often a majority. The message that I derive from the studies in question is not that large and pervasive government should necessarily be avoided, but rather that large and pervasive government carries with it a significant economic cost, in terms both of the efficiency with which the economy functions and of the rate at which it is likely to grow.

The Human Side of Economic Development

This is an area in which, by the very nature of the case, there will be less than total consensus, even among policy professionals. Yet there are many points on which, I believe, substantial agreement can be attained.

First, most of us would agree with the late Harry G. Johnson in considering it more appropriate, when it comes to the human side, to think of poor people, not poor countries. Far too often financial or other aid that was motivated by humanitarian values has ended up being creamed off by governmental elites or other power groups whose living standards were not much different from those of legislators and bureaucrats in the industrialized (developed) countries. Humanitarian aid, when given, should find its way to those groups and classes in society by whose position or plight it was motivated.

Second, most of us realize that the life of the upper and middle classes in a great many developing countries is certainly not much worse, and sometimes a good deal better than our own. The social problem of such societies lies not in the standard of living of these classes, but in the presence, side by side with them, of a huge group (usually a substantial majority) of disadvantaged people, living in poverty.

Third, one cannot legislate poverty out of existence in such a country. The state of underdevelopment for an economy stems from the low productivity of the great mass of the people. The only tried and true way out of that state is to fundamentally improve their productivity. For this, the most obvious route is investment in human capital. The second clear route is the accumulation of physical capital, which raises what economists call the marginal productivity of labor. On the whole, it has been found that where adequate investment in human capital has been made, where the society has a labor force that is capable of using modern technology, and where the government provides an environment conducive to the accumulation of capital at home and possibly for its import from abroad, the capital stock grows so as to permit the real wages of labor to increase substantially. The "miracles" of Taiwan, Korea, Singapore and Hong Kong all attest to this. So, too, do the "miracles" of Japan, Italy, Spain, Greece, Brazil, and Mexico.

Fourth, the funding of efforts to improve human capital need not all come from the State. I believe most professionals feel that too much of such public funds have typically been allocated, in many LDCs, to the children of the middle and upper classes, too little to the children of the very poor.

Fifth, when thinking about human progress, one must think in realistic, plausible, sensible terms, not utopian ones. Thinking in utopian terms is one of the important sources of the ill-advised economic policies with which much of this volume has been concerned. One must realize that for the great bulk of human history, each succeeding generation lived almost exactly like its forebears. It is only during the last few centuries that this pattern has been broken, and it still prevails for many people in many parts of the world.

But, sixth and finally, the world's recent economic history contains much to be proud of. It is probably true that for the poor people of the world the quarter century between 1950 and 1975 was the best quarter century in history. We should not forget this basic fact. While we inquire as to what mistakes were made, and as to where we went wrong, we should also ask ourselves what we did right.

Consider, then, the record of the recent past. The World Bank reports that the low income countries averaged 2.9 percent per year in per capita income growth in the period 1960–81; the middle-income countries 3.7 percent, and the industrialized countries 3.4 percent per year. This is a truly astounding performance. The historic rate of growth of per capita income in the United States, say from 1900 to 1950, was not much more than 1.5 percent per year. And this was a period during which the U.S. was genuinely pulling ahead of most of the world. Now, since 1960, we have the poorest of countries doing as well as the U.S. did while it was on its way to reaching its apogee as the dominant economy in the world (a spot from which it has been clearly receding since 1950).

Moreover, the improvement in *welfare* as distinct from income has been even more dramatic. The crude death rate of the low-income countries today is approximately equal to that of the middle-income countries in 1960; the crude death rate of the middle-income countries today, in turn, is approximately equal to that of the industrialized countries in 1960 (and, indeed, even now, for the latter figure hasn't changed much). The story with respect to life expectancy is also impressive. In the low-income countries it went from 41 years in 1960 to 58 years in 1981, in the middle-income countries it went from 50 years to 60 years, in the industrialized countries it went from 70 years to 75 years. So we can probably say that life expectancy in the low-income countries is today higher than it was, on the average, in the middle-income countries during the decade of the 1950s.

Many factors influenced these dramatic achievements, but surely those related to public health measures and innovations were of great significance. As far as general economic growth performance was concerned I would again emphasize the human capital aspect. In the low-income countries other than India and China the proportion of the relevant age group attending primary school went from 50 to 83 percent for males, and from 24 to 55 percent for females; secondary school attendance in these same countries went from 6 to 19 percent of the age cohort; those in higher education doubled, from 1 to 2 percent of their cohort. Interestingly, the low-income countries as a whole (including India and China) have now reached, in these respects also, levels that exceed those of the middle-income countries in 1960. It is my hope that by learning from our successes and our failures, and by increasing diligence in improving the understanding of economic forces and processes that we get from economic science, we can help ensure that this transformation of the economic lot of the poor of the world will continue for a long time to come.

Notes
Contributors
Index

NOTES

1. Arnold Harberger: "Introduction"

1. This set of developments is the fruit of work done by Solow, Kendrick, Schultz, Abramovitz, Dennison, and more recently Griliches, Jorgenson, and many others.

2. A particular policy, say, for instance, subsidizing investment in the chemical industry, may simultaneously add to the overall stock of capital (thus tending to promote growth) and distort the allocation of the capital stock among industries (thus tending to deter growth).

3. The figures cited in the foregoing resumes of LDC experience, (with the exception of Taiwan), were taken from the International Monetary Fund, *International Financial Statistics Yearbook* (Washington, D.C.: 1983).

2. Wilfred Beckerman: "Economic Policy and Performance in Britain since World War II"

1. From Michael Surrey's chapter on the United Kingdom in *The European Economy: Growth and Crisis*, ed. A. Boltho (Oxford: University Press, 1982), ch. 18, p. 528.

2. As regards the extent to which the two parties differed in any other objectives, see my chapter in *The Labour Government's Economic Record, 1964–70*, ed. W. Beckerman (London: Duckworth's, 1972), especially pp. 30–37. For estimates of the degree to which the distribution of income after taxes and benefits has changed, see J. L. Nicholson's chapter in *Poverty, Inequality and Class Structure*, ed. Dorothy Wedderburn (Cambridge: University Press, 1974).

3. Surveys are available in W. Beckerman et al., *The British Economy in 1975* (Cambridge: 1965); W. Beckerman, "Britain's Post-War Economic Performance and Prospects," in the *Proceedings of the International Symposium on the Path for Revitalizing World Economy* (Tokyo: Japan Economic Research Center, 1982); Boltho, ed., especially chs. 1 and 18; and the chapters by Christopher Allsopp in *The Economic System in the UK*, ed. D. Morris (Oxford: University Press, 1979) and in *Slow Growth in Britain: Causes and Consequences*, ed. W. Beckerman (Oxford: University Press, 1979).

4. R. Caves et al., *Britain's Economic Prospects* (Washington, D.C.: Brookings, 1968), and *Britain's Economic Performance*, ed. R. Caves and L. B. Krause (Washington, D.C.: Brookings, 1980).

5. Many studies of the differences in productivity between British plants owned and run by overseas companies and technically identical plants under British management tend, on the whole, to support this view. But a recent, very interesting addition to the evidence concerning the special role of class distinctions has been the impressive results obtained by the Toshiba Plymouth factory producing TV sets and the Sanyo Lowestoft factory producing video cassette recorders. In both of these factories, all of the usual class distinctions in British factories (and, to some extent, those in other countries) have been abolished. For example, all personnel share

the same eating facilities and even wear the same overalls, so there is simply no way that senior management can show their old school ties. In addition, management is conducted on a very open basis and the work force is taken fully into management's confidence on all matters concerning operations and financial performance. It would be foolish to expect the group-loyalty traditions of Japanese society to be transplanted easily or successfully to a completely different cultural environment; however, it does seem that, insofar as pressures in this direction break down class distinctions within productive groupings, the effects are highly beneficial.

6. Jacques Mazier, "Growth and Crisis—A Marxist Interpretation," in Boltho, ed. p. 38−71. A leading British Marxist economist, Andrew Glyn, also implicitly subscribes to a similar view. He has recently argued, in accordance with a part of Marxist theory, that production has to be seen as a social as well as a technical process, so that, for example, differences in the relative power of workers and employers will be reflected in differences in the intensity of the work effort. He refers to this mainly to explain how the sharp rise in unemployment over the last few years has increased the relative power of employers and enabled them to extract a greater work intensity from their labor forces, so that productivity has increased. But this view also implies, presumably, that in the earlier years—i.e., until the mid-1970s—the very low levels of unemployment (especially in Britain) had moved the balance of power in favor of the labor unions so that they would have been more able to resist any increases in work intensity or any innovations that might have made them redundant. Indeed, some of the quotations from interviews with various workers given by Glyn referring to how things used to be run before the current recession say precisely this. See Andrew Glyn, "The Productivity Slow-Down: A Marxist View," in *Slower Growth in the Western World,* ed. R. C. O. Matthews (London: 1982).

7. See, in particular, Mancur Olson's latest book, *The Rise and Decline of Nations* (New Haven, Conn. and London: 1982).

8. It is true that there was a problem—basically technical—arising from the large overseas holdings of sterling balances.

9. *The Financial Times* (London), January 5, 1983, p. 15.

10. A succinct and very recent survey is contained in Andrea Boltho, "Growth," in Boltho, ed., especially pp. 26 and 27. See also the introduction by R. C. O. Matthews in Mathews, ed.

11. *Brookings Papers on Economic Activity,* 1981, no. 2, p. 378. The comment is recorded in the summary of the general discussion by Willem Buiter and Marcus Miller in "The Thatcher Experiment: The First Two Years," pp. 315−67, from which several points in the following few pages have been drawn.

12. The Buiter and Miller analysis is by no means a minority view and is widely echoed by economists closely linked to the City, such as David Lomax, writing in the *National Westminster Bank Quarterly Review* (August 1982): 12; or Geoffrey Maynard of the Chase Manhattan Bank, writing in the *Lloyds Bank Review* (July 1982), especially p. 12. There are, of course, alternative explanations of exchange rate "overshooting." See Anne Krueger, *Exchange-Rate Determination* (Cambridge: University Press, 1983), pp. 56ff, for a particularly clear and succinct discussion.

13. The terms of trade of the economy as a whole may well improve as a result of appreciation of the exchange rate, but the terms of trade of manufacturing will tend to worsen. Manufacturing is a highly tradeable goods sector whose prices are unable to move far out of line with world prices. The overall improvement of the terms of trade means that workers receive a bonus, cet. par. in terms of real income.

14. For an explanation of some of the reasons for this phenomenon, see Rudiger Dornbusch et al., *Macroeconomic Prospects and Policies for the European Community* (Brussels: Centre for European Policy Studies, April 1983), especially ch. 11 and Appendix 2. This analysis is, moreover, confined to static equilibrium models; in a dynamic setting, in which technical

change takes place, changes in the shares of wages in national income—which is the same as a deviation of real wage changes from the "warranted" change—do not imply anything about whether the change in real wages is excessive or deficient.

15. A recent article on "The Economic Effects of North Sea Oil" by F. J. Atkinson et al. in the *National Institute Economic Review* (May 1983) reaches a very different conclusion concerning the impact of North Sea oil on the level of activity and employment. This is because the model it uses implies that a lower exchange rate in the absence of oil leads to higher inflation, and that this reduces consumption demand more than it adds to net (nonoil) exports. The reduction of consumption demand in this model is apparently the result of an assumed failure of money wages to keep up with the higher inflation, plus, perhaps, real balance effects. The implication here—namely that devaluation would always solve balance-of-payments deficits since there would be no absorption problem given the flexibility of real wages—is not one that would be universally accepted by other economists.

16. An excellent discussion of the statistical problems of international comparability of tax rates and some careful comparisons are in the O.E.C.D. *Income Tax Schedules: Distribution of Taxpayers and Revenues* (Paris: O.E.C.D., 1981). See also A. Prest's chapter in *The State of Taxation* (London: Institute for Economic Affairs, 1977), and B. Bracewell-Milnes, *The Camel's Back* (London: Centre for Policy Studies, 1976).

17. For a survey of the evidence see J. Pechman, "Taxation," in Caves and Krause, eds.

18. Ibid.

19. C. N. Morris and A. W. Dilnot, "The Tax System and Distribution, 1979–82," in *The 1982 Budget* (London: Institute for Fiscal Studies, 1983).

20. See evidence for this view both in G. C. Wenban-Smith's article "Factors Influencing Recent Productivity Growth—Report on a Survey of Companies," *National Institute Economic Review* (August 1982), pp. 57ff, and table 2 in "Manufacturing Decline," *Lloyd's Bank Economic Bulletin* (March 1983).

21. After all, even the most dedicated believer in the operation of market forces is not obliged to believe that the "natural rate of unemployment" is low. Indeed, some estimates in Britain put it at over 10 percent recently, and it will no doubt continue to rise in line with actual unemployment.

3. Yutaka Kosai: "Japan's Growth Problems"

1. The debate was sparked by an essay by Hitosubashi University Professor Fujino Shozaburo, "Teika shita Nihon no Senzai Seicho ritsu" ("Japan's Potential Growth Rate has Declined"), in *Nihon Keizai Shimbun*, May 10, 1982.

2. For more detail see Kosai Yutaka, "Dissecting Japan's Strong Economic Performance", *Economic Eye*, Keizai Koho Center, Sept. 1981.

4. Ulf Jakobsson: "Economic Growth in Sweden"

1. The author wishes to thank discussant Eli Schwartz and the other participants for useful comments.

2. Y. Aberg, "Producktivitetsutvecklingen i industrin i olika OECD-lander 1953–1980," unpublished manuscript, 1982.

3. See P. Wissén, *Wages and Growth in an Open Economy,* (Ph.D. diss., Stockholm School of Economics, 1982), and E. Lundberg, "Productivity and Structural Change—A Policy Issue in Sweden," *The Economic Journal* 82 (1972): 465–485. For a quantitative study of the contribution of structural change to productivity, see B. Carlsson, "Den tekniska utvecklingens innehall och betydelse för den ekonomiska tillväxten," in *Företagen i Marknadsekonomin* (Stockholm: Industriens Utredningsinstitut, 1979).

4. For a discussion of this model, see D. Robinson, *Solidaristic Wage Policy in Sweden* (Paris: OECD, 1974). K–O. Faxén, "Incomes Policy and Centralized Wage Formation," in *The European Economy*, ed. A. Boltho (London: Oxford University Press, 1982) gives an account of wage dispersion in some European countries, including Sweden.

5. G. Edgren, K–O. Faxén, and C–E. Odhner, *Wage Formation and the Economy* (London: Allen & Unwin, 1973).

6. An analysis of Swedish wage formation in a macroeconomic context is given in Lundberg.

7. OECD, *OECD Economic Surveys* (Paris: OECD, 1981).

8. The discussion in this section follows quite closely the Government Medium-Term Survey 1982, *Growth or Stagnation* (Stockholm: Ministry of Economic Affairs, 1982).

9. Since this discussion deals mainly with structural problems in the Swedish economy, stabilization policy is not treated. It is, however, obvious that stabilization policy in the 1970s has been significantly less well-adapted to the economic environment than in the preceding postwar decades. Probably this is part of the explanation for the deterioration of performance in the Swedish economy in the 1970s. For a review of Swedish stabilization policy in the early postwar period, see A. Lindbeck, *Swedish Economic Policy* (Berkeley: University of California Press, 1974). In *Trouble in Eden: A Comparison of the British and Swedish Economies* (New York: Praeger, 1980), E. Schwartz covers postwar structural developments as well as some of the problems of stabilization policy in the 1970s. A brief review of Swedish stabilization policy in the 1970s is given in U. Jakobsson and J. Herin, "Stabilization Policy during the 1970s," *Skandinaviska Enskilda Banken Quarterly Review* 3–4 (1981): 42–53. J. Myhrman and H. Tson Söderström, in "Svensk stabiliseringspolitik: Erfarenheter och nya villkor," *Svensk Ekonomi*, ed. B. Sodersten (Stockholm: Rabén & Sjögren, 1982), give a fairly detailed discussion of postwar stabilization policy in Sweden.

10. See, for example, L. A. Sjaastad and K. W. Clements, "The Incidence of Protection: Theory and Measurement," in *The Free Trade Movement in Latin America* (London: MacMillan, 1981).

11. For documentation of this diagram, see note 8.

12. The area of industrial subsidies has recently been studied rather extensively by different authors. See C. Hamilton, "Public Subsidies to Industry: The Case of Sweden and its Shipbuilding Industry," in *Europe's Manufactured Import from the South—A Political Economy View*, ed. H. Hughes and J. Waelbroek (London: MacMillan, 1983), and N. Lundgren and I. Stahl, *Industripolitikens Spelregler*, Industriforbundets Forlag, 1981. An overview of Swedish industrial subsidies in the 1970s is given in the Government Commission Industristodsutredningen, 1981.

13. This estimate is given in Hamilton et al., *Fördelning, Stabilitete, Tillväxt* (Stockholm: SNS, 1981).

14. C. E. Stuart, "Swedish Tax Rates, Labour Supply and Tax Revenues," *Journal of Political Economy* 81 (1981).

15. E. L. Feige and R. T. McGee, "Sweden's Laffer Curve: Taxation and the Unobserved Economy," *The Scandanavian Journal of Economics* (1983): 499–519.

16. I. Hansson and C. E. Stuart, "Laffer Curves and Marginal Cost of Public Funds in Sweden," unpublished manuscript, 1983.

17. U. Jakobsson and G. Normann, "Welfare Effects of Changes in Income Tax Progression in Sweden," *Studies in Labor Market Behaviour: Sweden and the United States*, Stockholm, 1981.

18. I. Hansson, "Skattereformen och de totala marginaleffekterna," *Ekonomisk Debatt* 1 (1983).

5. Frank Wolter: "From Economic Miracle to Stagnation: On the German Disease"

1. The figure for the OECD countries excludes Germany and was calculated from the OECD National Accounts Statistics and Main Economic Indicators. The long-term estimate for Germany refers to real net national product, 1852–1982, and was calculated from Hans H. Glismann, Horst Rodemer, and Frank Wolter, "Lange Wellen wirtschaftlichen Wachstums: Replik und Weiterfuhrung," *Kiel Discussion Papers,* no. 74 (Kiel, West Germany: Institut für Weltwirtschaft, December 1980).

2. Egon Sohmen, "Competition and Growth: The Lesson of West Germany," *The American Economic Review* 49, no. 5 (1959): 986–1003. The reestablishment of free markets was endorsed by the Allied Forces and was brought about in successive steps. It started with a currency reform in 1948 and was completed with the announcement of full convertibility of the deutsche mark ten years later. In the context of the currency reform, most markets for manufactures were deregulated (which meant the end of a twelve-year period of more or less frozen relative prices); wage controls were removed; and about 60 percent of the import volume from OEEC countries was liberalized. For details, see Henry C. Wallich, *Mainsprings of the German Revival* (New Haven, Conn.: Yale University Press, 1955); Karl Roskamp, *Capital Formation in West Germany* (Detroit: Wayne State University Press, 1965); and Wolfgang F. Stolper and Karl Roskamp, "Planning a Free Economy: Germany, 1945–1960," *Zeitschrift für die gesamte Staatswissenschaft* 3 (1979): 374–404.

3. Walter Eucken, "Die Wettbewerbsordnung und ihre Verwirklichung," *Ordo-Jahrbuch für die Ordnung von Wirtschaft und Gesellschaft* 2 (1949): 1–99.

4. The rationale for substituting the invisible for the visible hand was that, in view of the structural shortages in food, basic industrial material, and housing, deregulation could have led to price explosions in the bottleneck areas that were likely to creep through the economy, thereby paralyzing the efforts to restore confidence in the (new) currency. Also, social considerations were put forward to keep rents and prices for basic foodstuffs at too low a level to boost supply through profits.

5. Soft loans were granted to cushion the negative impact of high interest rates upon investment. The loans were largely made available from government and social security funds and allocated by a special capital market committee. High priority was given to the bottleneck sectors mentioned above. The measures to prop up these key sectors included also an enforced loan of one billion deutsch marks from the business community at large to these industries in 1952.

6. Mancur Olson, *The Rise and Decline of Nations: Economic Growth, Stagflation, and Social Rigidities* (New Haven, Conn., and London: Yale University Press, 1982).

7. Besides, threats to strike lacked credibility because the wealth of the unions had become a sacrifice of the currency reform.

8. Throughout the 1950s, private households contributed less to savings than either the business sector or the government. Given the low income level, most households had a very low propensity to save even though interest rates were high and tax incentives were granted. However, there were substantial enforced savings by prices and profits in the goods markets and by tax receipts. Despite huge welfare payments (war victims), the government proved capable of holding expenditures well below receipts, in part because of low debt, defense, and occupation burdens. In fact, substantial government savings were built up in expectation of future defense expenditures ("Juliusturm"). See Roskamp, pp. 82ff.

9. Except for 1950, when the massive import liberalization led to a balance-of-payments crisis, Germany's current account was well in surplus throughout the 1950s.

10. In the 1950s, for a prolonged period of time the inflow of foreign exchange was partly sterilized by government savings for future defense expenditures, the above-mentioned "Juliusturm."

11. See Hans H. Glismann, Horst Rodemer, and Frank Wolter, "Zur Natur der Wachstums-schwache in der Bundesrepublik Deutschland—Eine empirische Analyse langer Zyklen wirt-schaftlicher Entwicklung," *Kiel Discussion Papers*, no. 55 (Kiel, West Germany: Institut für Weltwirtschaft, June 1978).

12. The share of investment in gross national product, on an annual basis, ranged between 21.4 and 26.3 percent in the 1950s and between 23.0 and 28.5 percent in the 1960s (all figures based upon data in current prices).

13. This was underlined by the "Godesberger Programm" of 1959, in which the Social Democratic Party accepted the market economy based upon private ownership of the German economy, ending its prior pleas for central planning, nationalization of industries, and central investment control.

14. Trade liberalization was not continuous over time or even across industries. In the German case, tariff protection vis à vis suppliers of member countries of the European community was virtually abolished in 1964. On the other hand, the effective rate of protection of German industry in trade with third countries increased between 1958 and 1964 because of the EC tariff harmonization, and decreased only thereafter (it was lower in 1972 than in 1958). Agriculture was exempted from the GATT rounds. Further, because of relatively high tariff reductions for inputs and relatively low tariff reductions for outputs, the maintenance of import quotas, and/or a substitution of trade for nontariff barriers (fiscal protection, voluntary export restraint agreements, long-term agreement on cotton textiles; later, multifiber agreement, orderly marketing agreements, etc.), many industries remained highly protected. These included mining, steel, nonferrous metals, pulp and paper, textiles, clothing, and fine ceramics. The successful resistance of specific industries to trade liberalization is one indication of the rising power of special-interest groups. For detailed analyses of protection and adjustment policies for German industry, see Juergen B. Donges, Gerhard Fels, Axel D. Neu, and others, "Protektion und Branchenstruktur der westdeutschen Wirtschaft," *Kieler Studien*, no. 123 (Tübingen: J. C. B. Mohr, 1973).

15. The estimates presented in tables 3, 4 and appendix table A-2 are derived from a growth accounting exercise. This method is due to the pioneering work of Edward F. Denison, *Why Growth Rates Differ* (Washington, D.C.: Brookings, 1967). It has been used in subsequent studies to delineate the sources of productivity change in the United States and other advanced countries. Edward F. Denison, *Accounting for Slower Economic Growth: The United States in the 1970s* (Washington, D.C.: Brookings, 1979) and John W. Kendrick, "International Comparisons of Recent Productivity Trends," *Essays in Contemporary Economic Problems: Demand, Productivity, and Population* (Washington, D.C., and London: American Enterprise Institute, 1981), pp. 125–70 count among the most recent investigations. The methodology has a number of serious shortcomings (Richard R. Nelson, "Research on Productivity Growth and Productivity Differences: Dead Ends and New Departures," *Journal of Economic Literature* 19[1981]: 1029–64); but "it is the only theoretically defensible technique that allows a quantitative decomposition of . . . growth" (William D. Nordhaus, Economic Policy in the Face of Declining Productivity Growth," *Cowles Foundation Discussion Papers*, no. 604 [New Haven, Conn.: Yale University Press, September 1982], p. 8). Details of the estimates presented here are available from the author upon request.

16. Between 1960 and 1970, the (nominal) yearly work-time per employee decreased by 10.6 percent.

17. Between 1960 and 1970, the number of foreign workers increased from 279,000 to 1.8 million persons.

18. In particular, foreign labor had a positive impact on intra- and interregional labor mobility.

19. Herbert Giersch, *Growth, Cycles, and Exchange Rates—The Experience of West Germany*, Wicksell Lectures 1970 (Stockholm: Almquist and Wicksell, 1970), p. 11.

20. The prominent role of the reallocations of capital is particularly marked in the case of the nonresidential private business sector.

21. The residual identified in Table 4 nets out all effects acting upon productivity growth other than those explicitly mentioned, including possible accounting errors. Hence there is a measure of uncertainty with regard to this observation. On the other hand, in the early 1960s research and development activities in the German economy were only starting to resume historical levels; a significant lag between effort and return constitutes a typical feature of research and development activity.

22. The funds devoted to research and development expanded more or less steadily from 1.36 percent of gross national product in 1962 (the first year of observation) to 2.37 percent in 1970 (estimates of the Institut fur Weltwirtschaft based upon surveys of the Stifterverband für die Deutsche Wissenschaft).

23. As mentioned above, the early 1950s were governed by exceptional circumstances and do not provide a reasonable reference.

24. According to estimates by Lauritz R. Christensen, D. Cummings, and Dale W. Jorgenson, "Relative Productivity Levels, 1947–1973: An International Comparison," Discussion Paper no. 773 (Cambridge, Mass.: Harvard Institute for Economic Policy Research, 1980), pp. 39ff., between 1960 and 1970 Germany's level of total factor productivity increased from 74 to 91 percent relative to that of the United States.

25. Gerhard Fels, "Der internationale Preiszusammenhang. Eine Studie uber den Inflationsimport in der Bundesrepublik," *Schriftenreihe Annales Universitatis Saraviensis*, vol. 46 (Koln, Berlin, Bonn, and München: C. Heymanns, 1969).

26. Throughout the 1960s, fiscal and monetary policy proved incapable of keeping the economy on a steady growth path. Efforts to stabilize the economy through fiscal policy failed because (1) the progressive income tax was paid only with a long lag and (2) the built-in anticyclical expenditures (primarily unemployment insurance) of the federal government were paralyzed by procyclical expenditure behavior of the Länder and the local communities (primarily through public investment). On the other hand, given full convertibility and a fixed exchange rate, the scope for monetary policy was severely circumscribed, even ignoring the lags involved in discretionary action. Hence, economic growth was accompanied and conditioned by distinct fluctuations in the rate of realization of potential output, with peaks in the years 1960, 1965, and 1970 and troughs in the years 1963 and 1967. As in the 1950s, the cyclical pattern in Germany followed that of the United States with a certain lag, except for the recession of 1966 and 1967. The fixed exchange rate provided for a rapid and direct transmission of the rhythm of economic activity abroad. See Herbert Giersch, "Growth, Cycles, and Exchange Rates—the Experience of West Germany," *Wicksell Lectures 1970* (Stockholm: Almquist and Wicksell, 1970).

27. Giersch, p. 28.

28. Gerhard Fels, Klaus-Werner Schatz, and Frank Wolter, "Der Zusammenhang zwischen Produktionsstruktur und Entwicklungsniveau—Versuch einer Strukturprognose für die westdeutsche Wirtschaft," *Weltwirtschaftliches Archiv* 106(1971): 240–78.

29. Klaus-Werner Schatz, "Wachstum und Strukturwandel der westdeutschen Wirtschaft im internationalen Vergleich," *Kieler Studien* (Tübingen: J. C. B. Mohr, 1974), pp. 202–17.

30. "Gesetz zur Förderung der Stablilitat und des Wachstums der Wirtschaft," *Bundesgesetzblatt*, pt. I, June 1967, pp. 582–89.

31. The preliminary or expected rates of change of gross domestic product over the previous year are −1.1 percent for 1982 and 0.5 percent for 1983. There are indications, however, that the statistical picture overestimates the extent of the economic malaise. As recent empirical investigations suggest, the German underground economy has grown faster than the official economy, in particular over the last decade. But these investigations are still too preliminary

to allow any firm conclusions. See Bruno S. Frey, Hannelore Weck, and Werner Pommerenke, "Has the Shadow Economy Grown in Germany? An Exploratory Study," unpublished paper, 1982, and Enno Langfeldt, "The Unobserved Economy in the Federal Republic of Germany: A Preliminary Assessment," *International Conference on the Unobserved Sector* (Wassenaar: Institute for Advanced Studies, June 1982).

32. Between 1962 and 1981, expenditures for research and development increased from 1.36 to 2.68 percent of gross national product (estimate of the Institut für Weltwirtschaft based on a survey of the Stifterverband für die Deutsche Wissenschaft, 1981, an original survey figure).

33. In 1970 and 1971, efforts to pursue a restrictive monetary policy were largely undermined by capital imports.

34. See Frank Wolter, "Restructuring for Import Competition from Developing Countries: The Case of the Federal Republic of Germany," *Journal of Policy Modeling* 2 (1980): 185–204.

35. Available information did not permit a quantitative assessment of the effects of these regulations; the impact is subsumed under factors not classified elsewhere. See Klaus-Werner Schatz, "Neue Wege im Umweltschutz," in *Agenda für die deutsche Wirtschaftspolitik*, ed. Herbert Giersch, forthcoming.

36. There is no need to demonstrate the positive impact of social peace, improved health and education, and labor mobility on economic growth. Yet the changes in the transfer system are likely to have been too comprehensive, too generous, and too rapid not to affect negatively Germany's growth performance because of increased moral hazard, increased tax and social security burdens, and increased rigidities imposed by the new regulations on the labor market. Social levies in percent of gross wages and salaries (including employers' social security contributions) increased from 21.9 percent in 1960 to 23.8 percent in 1970 to 29.7 percent in 1981. And while the share of taxes in gross national product hardly changed over the last twenty years, the average and marginal tax rates on earned income increased significantly: the tax burden was shifted from the expenditure side to the income side, thus impairing incentives for further growth. For a brief survey of social security legislation in the 1970s, see Horst Dohm, "Chronologie des Versorgungsstaates," *Frankfurter Allgemeine Zeitung*, September 25, 1982, p. 15.

37. Inflation undermined the incentives to invest and to achieve through a variety of channels. Notably, apart from raising the level of uncertainty, it imposed a higher tax burden through the progressive income tax; it led to the taxation of phantom profits; and it biased investment towards real estate and other assets whose nominal increase in value remained untaxed. Inflation also quasi-automatically diverted resources from private to public uses. Presumably, this implied waste because allocative decisions of the public sector are remote from the penalties and the rewards of market forces.

38. The productivity slow-down was less significant in Germany than in other advanced countries, the United States in particular. Presumably, this is due to stronger real wage rigidities: the deterioration of the terms of trade of labor vis à vis energy, raw materials, and the environment translated itself into classical unemployment rather than a decline of productivity at a lower level of real wages and a higher level of employment. See Herbert Giersch and Frank Wolter, "Towards an Explanation of the Productivity Slowdown: An Acceleration-Deceleration Hypothesis," *The Economic Journal* 93 (1983): 35–55.

39. With the removal of the undervaluation, wage leadership passed from the export sector (manufacturing) to the public sector.

40. Moreover, the structure of unemployment mirrored the relative wage increases and the relative increases in job protection for the various segments of the labor force: unemployment rates became particularly high for the young, the unskilled, the old, the disabled, and female labor. See also Gerhard Fels and Frank Weiss, "Structural Change and Employment: The Lesson of West Germany," in *Capital Shortage and Unemployment in the World Economy*, ed.

Herbert Giersch (Tübingen: J. C. B. Mohr, 1978), pp. 31–53, and Karl Breithaupt and Rüdiger Soltwedel, "Nivellierungs und Differenzierungstendenzen der inter-und intrasektoralen Lohnstruktur," *Die Weltwirtschaft* (Tübingen: J. C. B. Mohr, 1980), pp. 61–78.

41. This approach was designed by the German Council of Economic Experts (Sachverständigenrat) in 1976 and gradually, though neither fully nor purely, applied by the federal government thereafter. See Sachverstandigenrat zur Begutachtung der Gesamtwirtschaftlichen Entwicklung, *Jahresgutachten* (Stuttgart and Mainz: Kohlhammer, 1976 [pp. 731–78] and 1981 [pp. 140–50]).

6. Robert J. Gordon: "U.S. Stabilization Policy: Lessons from the Past Decade"

1. Specialists in international economics, of course, deal with such concerns all the time. In my experience, questions involving the open economy arise in U.S. domestic policy discussions mainly in connection with three issues: (1) the role of the exchange rate and OPEC in accounting for the rapid deceleration of U.S. inflation in 1981–83 (unexpected by many forecasters who ignored these phenomena); (2) the role of the appreciation of the dollar in accounting for the collapse of the U.S. real trade balance, which accounts for between one-half and two-thirds of the decline in real GNP in the 1981–82 recession (depending on the exact dates chosen as the beginning and end points); and (3) the possible failure of large U.S. banks heavily involved in loans to foreign nations that exhibit signs of default risk.

2. Robert Lucas and Thomas J. Sargent, "After Keynesian Macroeconomics," in *After the Phillips Curve*, Federal Reserve Bank of Boston Conference Series 19, 1978, pp. 49–72.

3. The estimates of the natural unemployment rate and corresponding natural level of real GNP are developed in Robert J. Gordon, "Inflation, Flexible Exchange Rates, and the Natural Rate of Unemployment," in *Workers, Jobs and Inflation*, ed. M. N. Baily (Washington, D.C.: Brookings, 1982), pp. 88–157.

4. Friedman's seminal articles on economic policy (1948, 1953) recognized that there was an irreducible error term that guaranteed continuing fluctuations. The most complete statement of the case for a CGMR is contained in Milton Friedman, *A Program for Monetary Stability* (New York: Fordham University Press, 1960).

5. The output ratio measure in column (8) of table 1 exceeds 100 percent in 38 of the 43 quarters between 1963:Q4 and 1974:Q2.

6. This empirical interpretation of inflation in the 1973–75 period was introduced in Robert J. Gordon, "The Impact of Aggregate Demand on Prices," *Brookings Papers on Economic Activity* 6, no. 3 (1975): 613–62. It was confirmed later in Alan S. Blinder, *Economic Policy and the Great Stagflation* (New York: Academic Press, 1979); Alan S. Blinder, "The Anatomy of Double-Digit Inflation in the 1970s," in *Inflation: Causes and Consequences*, ed. R. E. Hall (Chicago: University of Chicago Press for the National Bureau of Economic Research, 1982), pp. 261–82; and Otto Eckstein, *Core Inflation* (Englewood Cliffs, N.J.: Prentice-Hall, 1980). A simple theoretical analysis showing the conditions necessary for a supply shock to create a recession in the rest of the economy is developed in Robert J. Gordon, "Alternative Responses of Policy to External Supply Shocks," *Brookings Papers on Economic Activity* 6, no. 1: 183–206, and Edmund S. Phelps, "Commodity-Supply Shock and Full-Employment Monetary Policy," *Journal of Money, Credit, and Banking* 10 (May 1978): 206–21.

7. On the CPI measurement error see Robert J. Gordon, "The Consumer Price Index: Measuring Inflation and Causing It," *The Public Interest*, no. 63 (Spring 1981): 112–34.

8. The sudden drop of the inflation rate in early 1986 along the "full rebound" and "half rebound" paths occurs because the rebound of the supply shock variables is assumed to extend only over the three years of the recovery, 1983 through the end of 1985.

9. Arnold C. Harberger, in a recent conversation evaluating general lessons of Latin Amer-

ican inflation, reports that the public used to act as if inflation were costly at a 100 percent rate, but further institutional adjustments have raised this threshold of pain to a 400 percent rate.

7. Uma Lele: "Tanzania: Phoenix or Icarus?"

1. This paper has benefitted from the work of a number of colleagues at the World Bank and the International Monetary Fund, and from many Tanzanian nationals. Their comments on an earlier draft were especially useful. However, I alone am responsible for the views expressed here. This paper does not necessarily represent the positions of the institutions or individuals who have provided data or analytical support. I am grateful to Ton T. T. Long for his assistance in the preparation of background material.

2. The Arusha Declaration of 1967, adopted by the Tanganyika African National Union (TANU), committed Tanzania to the creation of a socialist state and a socialist strategy of development. This was amplified by a series of writings by President Nyerere, the two main themes of which were egalitarianism and self-reliance. See J. K. Nyerere, *Freedom and Socialism. A Selection from Writings and Speeches, 1965–1967* (Dar es Salaam and London: Oxford University Press, 1968).

3. See Goran Hyden, *Beyond Ujamaa in Tanzania: Underdevelopment and an Uncaptured Peasantry* (Berkeley: University of California Press, 1980); also Andrew Coulson, *Tanzania: A Political Economy* (Oxford: Clarendon Press, 1982).

4. *The National Economic Survival Programme,* prepared by the Ministry of Planning and Economic Affairs, Dar es Salaam, Jan. 1982, pp. 1–2. The country's economic problems are attributed to four factors outside its control: petroleum price increases, capital goods import price increases, stagnant or declining export prices, and unfavorable weather.

5. The cost can be broken down in millions of U.S. dollars (1978) as follows: terms-of-trade loss for 1973 to 1982, including all net terms of trade annually since 1973 (1978 = 100): $630 million; total value of food imports, both commercial and financial, for 1973 to 1981: $413 million (this overstates the cost of poor weather since it includes all food imports over the period and thus does not distinguish policy-induced from weather-induced shortfalls); Uganda war costs: $500 million; breakup of the East African Community: $200 million. Total: $1 billion, 743 million. Data from World Bank, *Tanzania Agricultural Sector Report*—hereafter *Tanzania Report*—August 1982, p. 2.

6. See for instance, J. K. Nyerere, *The Arusha Declaration Ten Years After* (Dar es Salaam: Government Printer, 1977). In recent speeches, Nyerere also repeatedly referred to various symptoms of the national malaise, including the poor performance of agriculture, the "corruption growing like cancer," and vested bureaucratic interests looking after themselves in a situation of dire shortages.

7. The per capita amount of net official development assistance to Tanzania in 1979 was U.S. $32, compared to $23 for Kenya, $24 for Malawi, $15 for Zaire, and $31 for Sudan. See *Accelerated Development in Sub-Saharan Africa: An Agenda for Action* (World Bank, 1981), p. 164.

8. *Tanzania Report,* p. 2.

9. According to World Bank classification, Tanzania belongs to the group of poorest countries, with a per capita income of U.S. $330 or less in 1981.

10. Ellen Hanak, "The Commercialization of Tanzanian Agriculture, 1945–1970," unpublished World Bank study, 1982.

11. For 1980, of about $400 million total aid, roughly U.S. $100 million (25 percent) was program aid. In 1981, the proportion was about 40 percent (International Monetary Fund data).

12. Tanzania has been successful in securing a large volume of external aid and loans on very concessionary terms. Consequently, according to the IMF, total debt-service payments in

1981 was U.S. $39 million or 5.9 percent of export earnings, excluding short-term debt services and IMF fund purchases (IMF data).

13. *Tanzania Report,* pp. 22—26.

14. This discussion is based on *Tanzania Report,* pp. 32—36.

15. Ibid., p. 7.

16. World Bank sources.

17. Had foreign exchange been available, food imports could have been higher given the shortages being experienced in all major urban and many rural areas.

18. This section is based on Hanak.

19. The following data are from the World Bank, "Economic Memorandum on Tanzania," January 1981, p. 1, and the World Bank, *World Development Report, 1982* (New York: Oxford University Press, 1982).

20. The percentage of students attending secondary school in 1979 was 18 percent for Kenya, 9 percent for Mali, 19 percent for Zaire, 16 percent for Sudan, 36 percent for Ghana, 10 percent for Senegal, 17 percent for Zambia, 15 percent for Zimbabwe and 15 percent for the Ivory Coast (*World Development Report, 1982,* p. 154).

21. *Manpower Development Plan (1975 – 1980)* (Dar es Salaam: Government Printer, 1979). See also R. Sabot, "A Preliminary Overview of Educational Policy, Inequality and Productivity: An East African Comparison," unpublished World Bank study, 1981.

22. The statistics in this section are from *Tanzania Report,* pp. 151—152.

23. The statistics in this section are from the World Bank "Economic Memorandum on Tanzania" and *World Development Report, 1982.*

24. IMF data.

25. "Economic Memorandum on Tanzania," p. 17.

26. IMF estimates.

27. The following discussion is based on IMF data and estimates.

28. *Tanzania Report,* pp. 16—19.

29. The estimates are from the IMF.

30. See World Bank, *The Economic Development of Tanganyika* (Baltimore: Johns Hopkins University Press, 1961), and also Hyden.

31. See Coulson, pp. 165—66, and pp. 218—19.

32. Hanak, p. 17.

33. The average share of the transport sector in capital budget allocations is about 22 to 25 percent in Kenya, 25 percent in Zambia, and about 31 percent in Malawi, according to World Bank estimates.

34. Even within the agricultural sector, however, there have been major imbalances in past investments that need to be corrected. These include neglect of agricultural research in favor of substantial investment in capital-intensive agro-processing facilities in the case of crops such as tobacco or cashews. Substantial investment in production programs has taken place without attention to processing for other products such as cotton, and there have been few investments either in production or processing in sisal. Investment in the development of the necessary high-level manpower has also been neglected, while there has been a substantial expansion of the established posts for field services. Transportation routes critical for agriculture have similarly received few resources. Substantial improvement in allocations would thus be needed both within agriculture and its supporting sectors over a considerable period of time for Tanzania to be able to return to a long-term growth path.

35. *Tanzania Report,* p. 50.

36. Ibid., p. 52.

37. Ibid., p. 72.

38. Ibid., p. 156.

39. For example, in post-independence peak years, the government's purchases of food crops were 109,800 tons from Arusha, 41,000 tons from Kilimanjaro and 43,000 tons from Iringa. In the 1980–81 season, food crop purchases were 41,000 tons, 300 tons and 24,000 tons for the three regions respectively. Export crops from these three regions showed the same picture of declining government purchases, with peak year figures of 11,200 tons for Arusha, 34,400 tons for Kilimanjaro and 14,500 for Iringa, while the figures are 8,256 tons, 25,874 tons and 10,105 tons for the three regions respectively during the 1980–81 season (data from the Tanzanian Ministry of Agriculture).

40. See Coulson, Chapters 22 and 23, for a detailed description and analysis of these institutional changes.

41. Coulson, pp. 150–52.

42. *Tanzania Report,* p. 70.

43. World Bank estimates.

8. Michael Roemer: "Ghana, 1950–1980: Missed Opportunities"

1. I would like to thank Tony Killick, Linda Roemer, and Joseph Stern for their comments on an earlier draft.

2. Unless otherwise noted, economic data are from the World Bank, *World Tables, 2nd ed.* (Washington, D.C.: World Bank, 1980), pp. 86–87; World Bank, *World Development Report 1982* (Washington, D.C.: World Bank, 1982), pp. 110–52; and the International Monetary Fund, *International Financial Statistics Yearbook 1982* (Washington, D.C.: IMF, 1982), pp. 206–7.

3. Data on trade unit values are from the Internationational Monetary Fund, *International Financial Statistics Yearbook 1982.*

4. John C. de Wilde, "Case Studies: Kenya, Tanzania and Ghana," in *Agricultural Development in Africa,* ed. R. H. Bates and M. F. Lofchic (New York: Praeger, 1980), p. 57.

5. Tony Killick, *Development Economics in Action: A Study of Economic Policies in Ghana* (London: Heinemann, 1978), p. 4. Killick's book is by far the best, most comprehensive and balanced general account of Ghana's development up to the early 1970s.

6. World Bank, *World Development Report 1982,* pp. 150–53.

7. J. Clark Leith, *Foreign Trade Regimes and Economic Development: Ghana* (New York: Columbia University Press for the National Bureau of Economic Research, 1974), p. 5. This paper owes much to Leith's analysis of Ghana's shifting trade regimes.

8. Ibid., pp. 11–13.

9. International Monetary Fund, *Surveys of African Economies* vol. 6 (Washington, D.C.: IMF, 1975) pp. 98–99.

10. The International Monetary Fund, *International Financial Statistics Yearbook, 1982,* pp. 206–9.

11. Robert Szereszewski, "Capital," in *A Study of Contemporary Ghana, Volume I: The Economy of Ghana* (Evanston, Ill.: Northwestern University Press, 1966).

12. Calculated from Ibid., p. 206.

13. Killick, p. 34.

14. Ibid., chs. 2 and 3.

15. Ibid., p. 53.

16. Ibid., pp. 217, 326–80.

17. Calculated from Ibid., pp. 87 and 102. Other data are from the World Bank, *World Tables,* 2nd ed., pp. 86–87, and the International Monetary Fund, *International Financial Statistics Yearbook, 1982,* pp. 652–53.

18. Reported by Killick, pp. 147 and 150.

19. Ibid., pp. 228–33.

20. Ibid., pp. 228–33.

21. Leith, p. 84.

22. Killick, p. 219.

23. Ibid., pp. 223–25.

24. Ibid., p. 193.

25. Leith, p. 11.

26. Ibid., p. 176.

27. Ibid., p. 42. The price-deflated effective exchange rate is defined as

$$EER_m = (1 + t_m)r_o/P_d$$

for imports and

$$EER_x = (1 - t_x)\, r_o/P_d$$

for exports where t_m and t_x are taxes of all kinds net of subsidies on imports and exports, respectively; r_o is the official exchange rate; and P_d is an index of domestic prices, the implicit GDP deflator in Leith's measures.

28. Ibid., pp. 68–77.

29. An unpublished study by the author and Joseph Stern, conducted through interviews with plant managers in 1970, gave similar results.

30. Michael Roemer, "Relative Factor Prices in Ghanaian Manufacturing, 1960–1970," *Economic Bulletin of Ghana* 1 (1972): 3–27.

31. Michael Roemer, "The Neoclassical Employment Model Applied to Ghanaian Manufacturing," *Journal of Development Studies* 11 (January 1975): 75–92.

32. Killick, p. 92

33. Leith, pp. 11, 13, and 42.

34. Ibid., p. 139.

35. Ibid., p. 7.

36. Killick, pp. 56–57.

37. Ibid.

38. David Denoon, "Aid: High Politics, Technocracy or Farce?" (Unpublished Ph.D. diss., Massachusetts Institute of Technology, 1975), p. 274.

39. Killick, pp. 80–83 and 94.

40. Ibid., pp. 54–58.

41. This account is based largely on an unpublished paper, first written in 1972 and revised in 1977, by Tony Killick, Michael Roemer, and Joseph Stern, "The Political Economy of Devaluation: Ghana, 1971." All three writers participated in the analysis leading to the 1971 devaluation. For an account (and a useful chronology) by a neutral observer, see Denoon.

42. This forecast, based on an elaborate model of the world cocoa market by Merrill Bateman (financed by the World Bank) was quite influential—and may have been pivotal—in the devaluation decision. This is an exception to Harberger's observation that "most important policy decisions are fundamentally independent of specific quantitative projections." See Arnold Harberger, "Economic Science and Economic Policy,"in *Applied Economics: Private and Public Decisions,* ed. Sisay Asefa (Ames, Iowa: Iowa State University Press, forthcoming 1985).

43. Denoon, pp. 280 and 284.

44. Keith Hart, *The Development of Commercial Agriculture in West Africa* (New York: Cambridge, 1982); Poly Hill, *The Migrant Cocoa Farmers of Southern Ghana: A Study in Rural Capitalism* (Cambridge, England: Cambridge University Press, 1963); William O. Jones, "Agricultural Trade within Tropical Africa: Historical Background" in *Agricultural Development in Africa,* ed. R. H. Bates and M. F. Lofchic (New York: Praeger, 1980), pp. 10–44; Carl K. Eicher and Doyle C. Baker, "Research on Agricultural Development in Sub-Saharan Africa," in *A Survey of Agricultural Economics Literature,* vol. 4, ed. L. R. Martin (St. Paul, Minn.:

University of Minnesota Press, 1981); and Helge Kjekshus, *Ecology Control and Economic Development in East African History* (Berkeley, Calif.: University of California Press, 1977).

45. De Wilde, p. 156, suggests that 5 to 7 percent of annual production may be smuggled into Togo and the Ivory Coast.

46. Michael Roemer, "Economic Development in Africa: Performance since Independence and a Strategy for the Future," *Daedalus* (Spring 1982): 125–48, and World Bank, *Accelerated Development for Sub-Saharan Africa* (Washington, D.C.: World Bank, 1981).

9. Malcolm Gillis: "Episodes in Indonesian Economic Growth"

1. The World Bank, *Indonesia: Financial Resources and Human Development in the Eighties* (Washington, D.C.: The World Bank, May 1982), p. 1.

2. Malcolm Gillis, "Taxes, Risk and Returns in Developing Country Petroleum Contracts," Harvard Institute for International Development, Discussion Paper no. 144, p. 4.

3. The World Bank, *World Development Report 1982* (Washington, D.C.: World Bank, August 1982), Appendix table 2.

4. See especially J. A. C. Mackie, *Problems of the Indonesian Inflation* (Ithaca, N.Y.: Cornell University, 1967); Herbert Feith, "The Dynamics of Guided Democracy," in *Indonesia*, ed. Ruth McVey (New Haven: HRAF Press, 1963); and Ruth McVey, *Indonesia* (New Haven: HRAF Press, 1963).

5. Bruce Glassburner, "Economic Policy-Making in Indonesia, 1950–1957," in *The Economy of Indonesia*, ed. Bruce Glassburner (Ithaca, N.Y.: Cornell University Press, 1970), pp. 83–86.

6. C. Peter Timmer, "The Political Economy of Rice in Asia," *Food Research Institute Studies* 14(1975): 218–20, provides a cogent discussion of the Dutch rationale for controls in colonial Indonesia. For a discussion of the regulatory infrastructure in place at the time of independence, see Benjamin Higgins, *Economic Development: Problems, Principles and Politics* (New York: Norton, 1963), p. 63, and Anne Booth and Peter McCawley, "The Indonesian Economy since the Mid-Sixties," in *The Indonesian Economy During the Suharto Era*, ed. Anne Booth and Peter McCawley (Kuala Lumpur, Malaysia: Oxford University Press, 1981), pp. 1–22.

7. Ali Wardhana, "The Indonesian Banking System: The Central Bank," in Glassburner, pp. 338–59.

8. See Mackie, pp. 20–25.

9. Glassburner, pp. 81–95.

10. The 1963 deficit was 4.1 percent of estimated NNP, as well as can be ascertained. The money supply doubled.

11. Mackie, p. 62.

12. Data provided by the Bureau of Planning, Ministry of Finance, Republic of Indonesia.

13. See Ronald I. McKinnon, *Money and Capital in Economic Development* (Washington, D.C.: Brookings, 1973), p. 31.

14. For most of the period between 1967 and 1982, the principal gauges of success or failure applied to government policy (both by the public and the government) were annual increases in rice production and the retail price of rice, particularly on the densely populated island of Java (58 percent of total population). There were good reasons for the extreme sensitivity to rice prices. Rice furnished 53 percent of caloric consumption in both 1971 and 1976, and it had a weight of 17 percent in the general cost of living index. For a detailed treatment of the pivotal nature of rice in Indonesia, see Leon A. Mears, *The New Rice Economy of Indonesia* (Yogyakarta: Gadjah Mada Press, 1981). Percentages on caloric intake are found on p. 57; information on production and prices are in chs. 2 and 7.

15. For reasons, see Malcolm Gillis, "Economic Growth in Indonesia: 1950–1980," Harvard Institute for International Development, Discussion Paper no. 147, 1983.

16. For 1971, total liquidity grew by 37 percent, while inflation was only 4 percent. This rate of growth in liquidity was consistent with price-level stability, since people were still attempting to rebuild real money balances after the hyperinflation. Growth in liquidity jumped to 60 percent in 1972 and was 43 percent in 1973 and 1974. For the second oil boom of 1979 through 1981, liquidity had been growing only at about 19 percent per year in the previous two years. Even though liquidity growth was allowed to reach 37 percent in 1979, after the November 1978 devaluation, inflation was only 22 percent in that year; it declined to 7 percent by 1981. For the budget, government consumption was allowed to grow rapidly in 1974 and 1975 but, more importantly, the state oil enterprise failed to forward to the Treasury over 600 million U.S. dollars in tax revenues collected from oil companies, so that there was an unexpected shortfall in revenues; this put the budget in deficit. In the second oil boom, government consumption growth was restricted and the state oil enterprise met its tax obligations, resulting in large budgetary surpluses.

17. For details on the PERTAMINA disaster, see Seth Lipsky, *The Billion Dollar Bubble* (Hong Kong: Dow Jones, 1978).

18. The World Bank, *Indonesia, Financial Resources,* Annex II, table 3.2.

19. One set of calculations by The World Bank indicated that, by mid-1978, the competitiveness both of Indonesia's import substituting industry and of manufactured exports decreased by about 38 percent (The World Bank, *Indonesia: Long-Run Development and Short-Run Adjustment* [Washington, D.C.: The World Bank, February 1980], pp. 7–10).

20. Some World Bank estimates indicate that the capital intensity of production in the importables sector in 1976 was about four times that of the exportables sector.

21. Figures on increases in categories of manufactured exports are from an unpublished document of The World Bank.

22. Stephen Grenville, "Monetary Policy and the Formal Financial Sector," in Booth and McCawley, p. 121.

23. Much of the discussion of energy pricing in this section is based upon Malcolm Gillis, "Energy Demand in Indonesia: Projections and Policies," Harvard Institute for International Development, Discussion Paper no. 92, 1980. Very compatible conclusions on the implications of heavy oil subsidies on equity and the environment are presented in Howard Dick, "The Oil Price Subsidy, Deforestation and Equity," *Bulletin of Indonesian Economic Studies* 16 (1980): 32–60.

24. The World Bank, *Indonesia, Financial Resources,* p. 45.

25. Gillis, "Energy Demand in Indonesia: Projections and Policies," pp. 53–60.

26. See Mears, pp. 424–25.

27. Effective protection figures from The World Bank, *Indonesia's Development Prospects and Policy Options* (Washington, D.C.: The World Bank, April 1982), p. 18.

28. The researchers (including the author) estimated that, of the $435 million in extra cost to consumers of protected textiles, only about $50 million was collected by the government in taxes. Another $115 million represented economic waste in inefficient production, and the remainder ($270 million) a gain to capitalists in the textile and footwear industry.

29. See Anne Booth and R. M. Sundrum, "Income Distribution," in Booth and McCawley, pp. 200–217, and David Dapice, "Income Distribution in Indonesia," *The Indonesian Economy* (New York: Praeger, 1980), ch. 2.

30. David Dapice, "A Review of Recent Trends of Consumption in SUSENAS," unpublished.

31. W. R. Collier, "Rural Development in Java," *Bulletin of Indonesian Economic Studies* 16(1982): 84–100.

32. Thanks are due to David Dapice for compiling and interpreting these data.

33. Data on social indicators were compiled by David Dapice from a variety of official Indonesian sources, World Bank Health and Education surveys, and his own considerable files on Indonesia.

10. Michael Connolly: "Comments" on "Jamaica: Liberalization to Centralization, and Back?"

1. These calculations are from the *International Financial Statistics 1982 Yearbook* for the period 1972 to 1981.
2. From Lloyd Best and Alister McIntyre, "A First Appraisal of Monetary Management in Jamaica," *Social and Economic Studies* 10(1961): 354.
3. Abba Lerner, "The Symmetry between Import and Export Taxes," *Economica* (August, 1936).
4. Harry Johnson, "Optimal Intervention in the Presence of Domestic Distortions," in Robert Baldwin, et al., *Essays in Honor of Gottfried Haberler* (New York: Rand McNally, 1970).

11. S. C. Tsiang: "Taiwan's Economic Miracle: Lessons in Economic Development"

1. W. A. Lewis, *The Theory of Economic Growth* (Homewood, Ill.: Irwin, 1955), pp. 225–26.
2. These were the old wholesale price indices published by the Directorate-General of Budget, Accounting and Statistics. Their new revised wholesale price indices would give an increase of only 4.5 percent in 1972 and 22.9 percent in 1973, followed by a major increase of 40.6 percent in 1974.
3. Lewis.
4. S. C. Tsiang, "A Model of Economic Growth in Rostovian Stages," *Econometrica* 32 (1964): 619–48.
5. This requirement can be expressed as $S > (\frac{K}{L})L$, where S is total annual domestic savings, L is total population (labor force), K the total productive capital in existence, and $\dot{L}$ the annual increase of population (labor force). By dividing both sides of the inequality with the aggregate annual real income Y, this inequality can be transformed into a more familiar form, viz., $\frac{S}{Y} > (\frac{K}{Y})(\frac{\dot{L}}{L})$.
6. See for example Simon Kuznets, "Economic Growth and Income Inequality," *American Economic Review* 45 (1955): 1–28; Idem, "Quantitative Aspects of the Economic Growth of Nations: VII, Distribution of Income by Size," *Economic Development and Cultural Change* 11 (1963): 1–80; Felix Paukert, "Income Distribution at Different Levels of Development: A Survey of Evidence," *International Labor Review* 108 (August/September, 1973): 97–124; Irma Adelman and Cynthia Taft Morris, *Economic Growth and Social Equity in Developing Countries* (Stanford: Stanford University Press, 1973). For discussion of how Taiwan achieved both growth and equitable income distribution, see G. Ranis, J. C. H. Fei and S. W. Y. Kuo, *Growth with Equity: The Taiwan Case* (London: Oxford University Press, 1979) and S. W. Y. Kuo, G. Ranis, and J. C. H. Fei, *The Taiwan Success Story: Rapid Growth with Improved Distribution in the Republic of China, 1952–1979* (Boulder, Colo.: Westview Press, 1981).

12. Francisco Gil Díaz: "Mexico's Path from Stability to Inflation"

1. My appreciation to Juan Manuel Perez Porrua, whose painstaking table-building made this work possible.
2. J. Bergsman, "La Distribución del Ingreso y la Pobreza en México," in *Distribución del Ingreso en México* (Mexico: Banco de México, 1982), vol. 1.

3. A. Ortiz Mena, "Una Década de Estrategia Económica en México," in *El Mercado de Valores* (Mexico: Nacional Financiera, S.A., November 1969), no. 44.

4. International Monetary Fund, *Government Finance Statistics*, Washington, D.C., 1977, vol. 1; *International Financial Statistics*, Washington, D.C., 1982 Yearbook.

5. L. Solís, *Economic Policy in Mexico: A Case Study for Developing Countries* (New York: Pergamon, 1981).

6. E. Cárdenas, "Mexico's Industrialization during the Great Depression" (Ph.d. diss., Yale University, 1982.)

7. Ibid., p. 69.

8. A note describing how the real exchange rate was calculated can be found at the bottom of table A-2. For more details, see F. Gil Díaz, "Covered Interest Arbitrage and the Purchasing Power Parity Theorem," paper presented at the Third Latin American Econometric Society Congress, Mexico, 1982.

9. The well-known expression for interest rates is $i = r + p + rp$ (derived from Irving Fisher) where the nominal interest rate is equal to the real interest rate, plus expected inflation, plus another term involving it and the real interest rate. The problem with this definition is that the nominal interest rate ought to be defined strictly as $r(l + p)$, leaving out the term p, which should be handled separately, labeling it as a reimbursement for the erosion of principal due to inflation. Once this distinction is recognized, it becomes clear why standard balance-of-payments accounting is wrong and may provide a distorted view of what is going on. A correct classification ought to take p (U.S. inflation) times the foreign debt out of the current account, thereby reducing the current account deficit, and put it into the capital account, thus reducing the capital account surplus by the same amount.

10. The reserve should have equaled the difference between the peso loan rate and the dollar loan rate, multiplied by the amount of their debt.

11. At a much higher cost than the one charged by the Banco de México, there was a futures dollar market available in the U.S.

12. This figure is preliminary. The final figure may be much higher.

13. This argument is well developed by Manuel Fernández in "Análisis del Comportamiento de la Administración Pública," bachelor's thesis, Instituto Technológica Autónomo de México, 1982.

14. A real interest rate of 5 percent and a mortgage twice the annual salary of an individual are assumed.

15. Seventy-two branches of economic activity were classified. An activity was considered an exportable if it had a favorable trade balance; as importable, when its trade balance was negative; and as nontradeable when its foreign trade was negligible (less than 2 percent of final sales). Tourism was included as an exportable.

16. L. Sjaastad, *Commercial Policy Reform in Argentina, Implications and Consequences* (Argentina: CEMA, 1980).

167 Margarita Favela Gil, "Aranceles y Protección Efectiva Verdaderos para la Economia Mexicana" (Bachelor's thesis, Universidad Autonoma Metropolitana, Mexico, 1982).

13. Rámon Díaz: "Uruguay's Growth Performance: A Failure Story"

1. The few annual data that exist on global output, prior to 1942 seem to have been too strongly influenced by the world trade cycle to warrant extending the trend beyond the selected starting point.

2. The word *major* should be emphasized here. The 1955–62 period showed a sustained fall in commodity prices that hurt Uruguay's exports. When prices picked up in 1963 through 1965, however, the Uruguayan economy failed to react, and the same thing happened with subsequent international price stimuli.

Notes

3. That is, from the early postwar period onward. Between 1948 and 1960, world exports grew at a rate of 7.3 percent in nominal terms, compared with Uruguay's −3.3 percent. Between 1960 and 1970, the world rate was 9.3 percent to Uruguay's 4.5 percent. Only in the 1970s did Uruguay's 17.4 percent approximate the world rate of 20.3 percent. International data from the General Agreement on Tariffs and Trade (GATT), quoted by Lord McFadzean of Kelvinside in his (ed.): *Global Strategy for Growth: A Report on North-South Issues* (London: Trade Policy Research Center, 1981) p. 38..

4. That is, the State Bank intervened actively in the foreign-exchange market.

5. The World Bank, *Finanzas y Desarrollo*, n.d.

6. Mimeographed report commissioned by the USAID India Mission, undated.

7. The depreciation charges required for the conversion of gross investment and domestic product were obtained from a study by Arnold Harberger and Daniel Wisecarver, *Tasas de Retorno al Capital en los Ambitos Privado y Social en el Uruguay* (Montevideo: Central Bank of Uruguay, 1977); see also Arnold Harberger, *Estudios Preparados por el Profesor Harberger para el Uruguay* (Montevideo: Central Bank of Uruguay, 1978). This research was subsequently updated by the Central Bank's staff in 1980; this author has allowed one year's extrapolation at each end of the series.

8. Harberger and Wisecarver, pp. 31−41.

9. Uruguay had a particularly obnoxious tax, from this viewpoint, between 1943 and 1960. Called an "excess profits tax," it taxed profits in excess of 12 percent of net assets. Since the flow of business income was measured at current-value units and the stock of capital was implicitly measured at an average of past units—depending on the asset structure of each firm— the tax was guilty of logical inconsistency in the first degree. In addition, there was flagrant discrimination against the use of capital, particularly of long-life assets. After 1960, Uruguay's taxation was just one of many offenders against the adequate representation of net income for tax purposes, gradually accepting correction for inflation-generated distortions, but always too little and too late.

10. Although the effects of social insurance on savings have been the subject of controversy, the bulk of evidence points to a significant negative influence. This has been shown by Martin Feldstein in "The Effect of Social Security on Saving," *The Geneva Papers on Risk and Insurance*, 15 (February 1980).

11. Arnold Harberger has drawn attention to the role played by this theory in the private-sector inflations in Latin America in "A Primer on Inflation," *Journal of Money, Credit and Banking* (1978):513−14. He shows that the error in this theory stems from neglecting the difference in magnitude of money stock and real capital. An attempt to finance an inventory accumulation on the order of 1 percent of total capital would mean increasing the money supply probably as much as 25 percent—far more than the public would be prepared to increase the cash balance under conditions of stable prices and normal growth.

12. Banda, A. and Mugica, L., *Politica Monetaria y Rentabilidad Bancaria.* Central Bank of Uruguay, mimeo.

13. Economist Alejandro Vegh, a Harvard graduate, was appointed in June of 1974. He served until 1976, and is currently Uruguay's ambassador to Washington.

14. In fact, economic theory did not lack an account of that situation; at least, not since the monetary approach to the balance of payments was developed in the 1960s by Robert Mundell and Harry Johnson, among others.

15. The rest came from the international commercial banks, from whom the government agencies borrowed recklessly, using Uruguay's theretofore excellent credit rating. Subsequently, the Uruguayan government applied for and secured an International Monetary Fund (IMF) standby facility and a restructuring of its foreign debt with the international banks.

16. The borrowing rate of banks reached the 60 to 70 percent range, while domestic inflation was running just over 10 percent.

17. The cost of hedging foreign exchange risks had become prohibitive.

18. At this writing, the Uruguayan economy lies flat on its back, neither contracting further nor showing any signs of recovery.

14. Anne O. Krueger: "Problems of Liberalization"

1. In the 1970s, the energy market was subject to controls very similar to those of agriculture in many countries. Most of the analysis of agriculture that follows also applies to energy.

2. See William R. Cline and Sidney Weintraub, eds., *Economic Stabilization in Developing Countries* (Washington, D.C.: Brookings Institution, 1981) for a series of analyses of these issues in individual countries. See also the paper by Krueger "Interactions Between Inflation and Trade-Regime Objectives in Stabilization Programs," in that volume for further analysis of the interrelationship between inflation and liberalization.

3. This qualification is made because most licensing systems implicitly or otherwise permit imports of intermediate goods and raw materials at lower-than-average rates of duty. To increase duties on these goods without permitting exporters to purchase at international prices would lower effective protection rates—presumably already negative—to them.

4. For a description of these efforts, see Robert E. Baldwin, *Foreign Trade Regimes and Economic Development: The Philippines* (New York: Columbia University Press, 1975), ch. 3, and Michael Michaely, *Foreign Trade Regimes and Economic Development: Israel* (New York: Columbia University Press, 1975), ch. 2.

5. Jose Carvalho and Claudio Haddad, "Foreign Trade Strategies and Employment in Brazil," in *Trade and Employment in Developing Countries, Vol. 1. Individual Studies*, ed. Anne O. Krueger, Hal B. Lary, Terry Monson, and Narongchai Akrasanee (Chicago: University of Chicago Press, 1981).

6. See Ronald McKinnon, *Money and Capital in Economic Development* (Washington, D.C.: Brookings Institution, 1973) for an analysis of the importance of developing financial markets.

7. There is another reason why instantaneous abandonment of the entire control regime might be infeasible: when liberalization starts from a situation in which there is a large government deficit, it inherently requires time to reduce government spending and to raise taxes. In that circumstance, one might question whether total decontrol of all other markets should precede macroeconomic stabilization. I have not seen any analyses of this circumstance; hence I subsume it under other reasons for objecting to instantaneous decontrol.

15. Arnold C. Harberger: "Economic Policy and Economic Growth"

1. During the last few years, inflation in Uruguay seems to have been of fiscal origin, but before that—for more than two decades—it was due principally to excessive credit extended to the private sector. In both Uruguay and Brazil, the excessive credit expansion was mainly centered in a state bank (the Banco de la Republica in Uruguay and the Banco do Brasil in Brazil), which was not under the effective regulatory control of the central bank and which acted with an almost imperious autonomy.

2. If a final product costing 100 in world markets is granted a tariff of 20 percent, and if the local substitute uses 60 of imported inputs, which enter duty free, the production of the local substitute saves only 40 (= 100 − 60) of foreign exchange. But since the internal price can now rise to 120 (= 100 + 20%), the local firm will make money so long as its costs do not exceed 60 (= 120 − 60). Its costs can be as high as 60 in order to save 40 of foreign exchange; its "effective protection" is therefore 50 percent [= 60/40) − 1]. Let the product in question be a woolen sweater, and the imported input be woolen yarn. Suppose, too, that some firms in the country make cashmere sweaters, which sell for 200 in the marketplace and use 160 of imported cashmere yarn, which also enters free of duty. Now the degree of effective protection is much

higher. A 20 percent tariff on a world price of 200 means that the internal price can rise as high as 240. The imported input (cashmere yarn) costs 160. Hence domestic costs of up to 80 can be incurred (behind the 20% tariff barrier) with the operation still yielding a profit. Since only 40 (= 200 − 160) of foreign exchange is saved, and since up to 80 of domestic costs can be incurred in order to do so, the effective protection in this case is 100% [= (80/40 − 1].

3. If the yarn used to make woolen sweaters (in the example of the preceding footnote) were subject to a 20 percent duty, the cost of imported inputs would have been 72 (= 60 plus 20%). The margin for profitable use of domestic resources would have been 48 (= 120 − 721), which, taken together with a foreign exchange saving of 40 (= 100 − 60) implies effective protection of 20 percent [= (48/40) − 1]. If the cashmere yarn had been subject to 20 percent duty, its cost per cashmere sweater produced would have been 192 (=160 plus 20%). The final product, with a 20 percent duty, could sell for up to 240 (=200 plus 20%). Domestic costs of up to 48 (= 240 − 192) can therefore be incurred in order to save 40 of foreign exchange. Effective protection is thus once again 20 percent [=48/40) − 1].

The general formula for the rate t_{ej} of effective protection of activity j is

$$t_{ej} \;=\; \frac{t_{nj} - \sum_i \alpha_{ij}\, t_{ni}}{1 - \sum_i \alpha_{ij}}\,,$$

where t_{ni} is the nominal rate of protection accorded to imported input i and α_{ij} is equal to the fraction of j's total costs (measured at world prices) that are accounted for by imported input i. It is easy to see that when $t_{nj} = t_{ni} = t^*$, i.e., when a uniform tariff of t^* prevails,

$$t_{ej} \;=\; \frac{t^* - \sum_i \alpha_{ij}\, t^*}{1 - \sum_i \alpha_{ij}} \;=\; \frac{t^*\,(1 - \sum_i \alpha_{ij})}{(1 - \sum_i \alpha_{ij})} \;=\; t^*.$$

That is, all effective rates of protection are equal to t^* when that is the nominal rate applying to all imports.

4. International Monetary Fund, *International Financial Statistics Yearbook, 1983.*

5. Ibid., pp. 309−311.

6. Ibid., pp. 478−481.

7. See Ulf Jakobsson, this volume, Chapter 4, Diagram 8.

8. Data from International Monetary Fund, op cit.

9. Readers should note that the expansion of nontraditional exports is a rough indicator whose movements should be interpreted with caution and common sense. Nontraditional exports of a country might boom because of a great mineral discovery or because of a dramatic rise in their international prices; this would not be a reflection of a liberalizing policy. Likewise, movements of their international prices might cause them to fall, or they may be squeezed out by the effects on the real exchange rate of a price boom in the traditional exports or a huge inflow of capital. But on the whole it should be noted that, while usually, for LDCs at least, traditional exports tend to be small in number, each accounting for large export receipts, nontraditional exports (actual and potential) tend to be much more numerous, and the balance of payments is much less vulnerable to movements in the world price of any one of them. Moreover, where trade is initially highly restricted, a government has a simple way of itself giving a strong positive stimulus to all exports—namely by liberalizing import restrictions. Historically, strong liberalizing policies have in fact tended to generate palpable stimuuli to nontraditional exports taken as a group.

10. Professor Anne Krueger has an excellent description of the way in which the costs of policy errors magnify when these errors interact in a section entitled "The Prototypical Il-liberal Economy." See Anne O. Krueger, this volume, Chapter 14.

CONTRIBUTORS

YAW ANSU is an economist at the World Bank.

WILFRED BECKERMAN is a fellow at Balloil College, Oxford, and a university reader in economics. He has previously been professor of political economy at the University of London and head of the department of political economy at University College, London. He was economic advisor to the Board of Trade, and has been consultant to the OECD, the World Bank, and other organizations. He has published several books and articles in academic journals.

GLADSTONE G. BONNICK is mission chief of the Inter-Agency Resident Mission in St. John's, Antigua. The mission was set up by the Caribbean Group for Cooperation in Economic Development and is a project of the United Nations Development Program being executed by the World Bank. Mr. Bonnick, a staff member of the World Bank, has been an economist and senior economist in the Latin American and Caribbean programs department. Before joining the World Bank he was deputy governor of the Bank of Jamaica, chief technical director of the National Planning Agency, Jamaica, and director of the Central Planning Unit, Jamaica.

MICHAEL J. BOSKIN is a professor of economics, chairman of the Center for Economic Policy Research, and senior fellow (by courtesy) at the Hoover Institution, Stanford University.

MICHAEL CONNOLLY is professor of economics at the University of South Carolina.

RAMON DÍAZ teaches international law and political economy at the University of Montevideo. He is editor and a founder of Búsqueda, a weekly periodical for the lay public and specializing in economic affairs. He has also held political office, as assistant-secretary for industry and trade, and secretary of budget and planning. He is the author of *The Long-Run Terms of Trade of Primary-Producing Countries*, IIER London, 1973; *The Monetary Approach to the Balance of Payments* (in Spanish), BCU Montevideo, 1981; and numerous articles.

489

FRANCISCO GIL DÍAZ is deputy director in charge of economic research at Banco de México. Formerly director of tax policy at the Department of Treasury, he has also been professor of economics and in charge of the economics department at the Instituto Tecnológico Autónomo de México (ITAM). He has contributed chapters to several books and published articles in various journals.

MALCOLM GILLIS is institute fellow, Harvard Institute for International Development and lecturer in economics, department of economics, Harvard University. He formerly taught at Duke University and has carried out research and advisory work in several countries including Ghana and Zambia in Africa, Colombia and Ecuador in Latin America, and Indonesia and Philippines in Southeast Asia. He has written over 30 articles and 6 books on fiscal, natural resource, trade, and development issues, and has recently completed a textbook with other Harvard co-authors, *Economics of Development*. Concurrent with his teaching and research duties at Harvard, he organized and directed a large tax reform study for the Government of Indonesia, finished several months after his article for this volume was prepared.

ROBERT J. GORDON is professor of economics at Northwestern University and research associate at the National Bureau of Economic Research. He is fellow and treasurer of the Econometric Society and organizer of the annual International Seminar on Macroeconomics. A former consultant to the U.S. Treasury, and Department of Commerce, he was also co-editor of the *Journal of Political Economy* from 1970–73 and member of the editorial board of the *American Economic Review*, 1975–77. His latest books include *Challenges to Interdependent Economics: The Industrial West in the Coming Decade* (with Jacques Pelkmans, 1979), *Macroeconomics* (1984), and *The Measurement of Durable Goods Prices* (forthcoming).

ARNOLD C. HARBERGER is Gustavus F. and Ann M. Swift Distinguished Service Professor at the University of Chicago, as well as professor of economics at UCLA. He has been a consultant to central banks, finance ministries, and planning agencies in more than a dozen developing countries, as well as serving in a similar role for the World Bank, the International Monetary Fund, several regional development banks, and the foreign aid agencies (as well as others) of the United States and Canada. He is the author of *Project Evaluation* (1972), *Taxation and Welfare* (1974), and the editor of *Key Problems of Economic Policy in Latin America* (1970).

ULF JAKOBSSON is economic advisor at the Swedish Employers' Confederation. He has been research economist at the Industrial Institute of Social and Economic Research in Stockholm and head of planning at the ministry of economic affairs, where the government medium-term surveys were among his responsibilities. He has written books and articles on economic policy, planning and forecasting, taxation, and income distribution.

YUTAKA KOSAI is professor of economics at Tokyo Institute of Technology. He has also served as an economist with the economic planning agency of the Japanese government where he held a number of positions including head of the office for the system of national accounts and general senior research officer of the Economic Research Institute. He has been a member of several advisory committees, and is the author of numerous books on economics and financial systems.

ANNE O. KRUEGER is vice president, economics and research, the World Bank. She has been professor of economics at the University of Minnesota and held numerous international visiting professorships. She has also been research associate of the National Bureau of Economic Research, vice president of the American Economics Association, and is a fellow of the Econometric Society and the American Academy of Arts and Sciences. She has authored many books and articles and served on the editorial boards of numerous journals. Among her most recent publications are *Exchange-Rate Determination* (1983) and *Trade and Employment in Developing Countries, 3: Synthesis and Conclusions* (1983).

DAVID LAIDLER is professor of economics at the University of Western Ontario, London, Ontario.

LAWRENCE J. LAU is professor of economics at Stanford University.

UMA LELE is chief, development strategy division, development research department, economic and research staff, the World Bank. She has also served as senior economist and deputy chief for the East Asia and Pacific region and the East Africa region, the World Bank. She is the author of *The Design of Rural Development: Lessons from Africa* (1975 and 1979) and *Food Grain Marketing in India* (1971) as well as many scholarly articles on development.

MICHAEL ROEMER is executive director and institute fellow of the Harvard Institute for International Development, and senior lecturer in the department of economics, Harvard University. He has lived and worked as an economic adviser in Ghana, Kenya, and Tanzania, and has had short-term assignments in several countries in Asia and Latin America. Much of his writing has focussed on issues of trade, industrialization, development, and project analysis. He is the author or co-author of several books on development, including *Economics of Development* (1983, with M. Gillis, D. Perkins and D. Snodgrass), *Cases in Economic Development* (1981, with J. Stern), and *The Republic of Korea, 1945–1975: Growth and Structural Transformation* (1979, with K. S. Kim).

KNUD ERIC SVENDSEN is director of the Center for Development Research in Copenhagen.

S. C. TSIANG is professor of economics at Cornell University and concurrently president of Chung-Hua Institution for Economic Research in Taiwan. He has been an economist for the research and statistics department at the International Monetary Fund, professor of economics at the University of Rochester, and consultant to the United Nations. He has been editor of the *American Economic Review* and is the prolific author of articles on economics, foreign exchange, and monetary theory.

FRANK WOLTER, formerly of the Kiel Institute of World Economics (Germany) where he headed a research team on long-term analysis of economic development, is presently a counselor in the research and analysis unit of the General Agreement on Tariff and Trade (GATT) in Geneva. A prolific writer, his main fields of research and publication include the international division of labor, economic growth, and structural change in advanced economic and sector-specific adjustment problems. He is the author of *Strukturelle Anpossungsprobleme der Westdeutschen Stahlindustrie* (1974) and co-author of *Industrial Development Policies for Indonesia* (1984) and the forthcoming *International Trade, Employment and Structural Adjustment: The Case of the Federal Republic of Germany.*

INDEX